CATALINA SAGA

An Historical Cruise Around Santa Catalina Island . . .

For Angelia + Peter —
Happy Anniversary!
Enjoy Catalina —

Tom Andrews
and your friends
at HSSC

July 14, 2003

Avalon in 1904

SS *Cabrillo* arrives at Avalon

A five-ton catch in Catalina waters, 1902

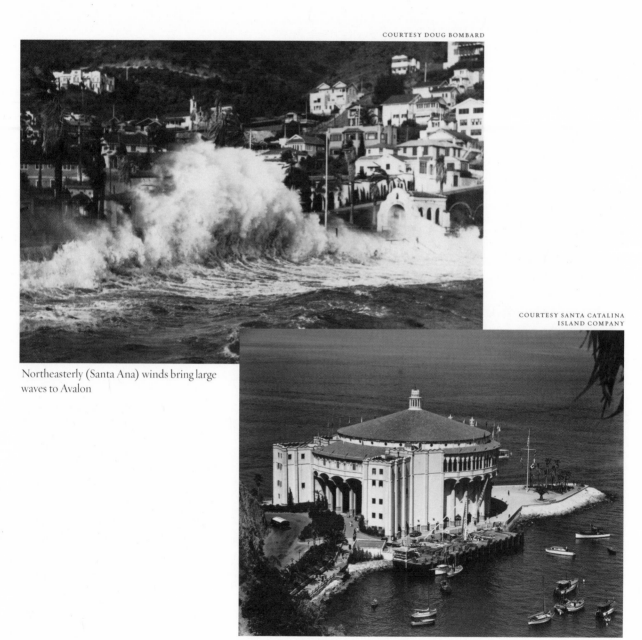

Northeasterly (Santa Ana) winds bring large
waves to Avalon

The Casino prior to 1967

Avalon from Sugar Loaf Rock before mooring buoys

Two Harbors and Bird Rock in 1990

Isthmus Bay and Catalina Harbor during Banning ownership

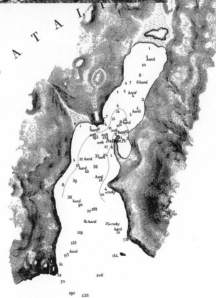

Tourist coach at Indian Head on the island's back side, circa 1900

The desolate West End

SANTA CATALINA TIMELINE

500 B.C.
The most recent Indian culture on Catalina begins and extends into the 19th century when all offshore island Indians are removed to the mainland.

1542
Juan Rodriguez Cabrillo arrives at the island on October 7 and names it San Salvador, after his flagship. Cabrillo dies January 3, 1543, on one of the islands after wintering at Catalina Harbor.

1602
Explorer Sebastian Viscaino anchors at San Salvador on November 27, the feast day of Saint Catherine, and renames it Santa Catalina.

Viscaino's onboard cosmologist, Geronimo Martin Palacios, prepares the first chart of Catalina.

1769
Gaspar de Portola and Father Junipero Serra explore on land and occupy California to establish missions and pueblos. Offshore islands are largely ignored by the Spanish.

1784
The Spanish government enters the California sea otter trade, which continues into the 1840s.

1796
The first "Boston vessel" arrives on the California coast to trade. Yankee seamen dominate California trade, legal and (mostly) otherwise, for the next 50 years.

1805
The first Yankee ship to come ashore on Catalina, the 175-ton *Lelia Byrd*, is careened for repairs at Port Roussillon, now the Isthmus.

1823
Thomas Robbins, Yankee trader, arrives in California aboard the schooner *Rover* out of Boston.

1846
Thomas Robbins, a naturalized Mexican citizen since 1830, becomes the first private owner of Catalina owing to a grant by the last Mexican governor, Pio Pico.

1853
The last native Channel Island Indian is removed from San Nicolas Island.

1860s
Estimates of the livestock population on leased pasture land on Catalina run as high as 22,000 sheep, 4,220 cattle, and 15,000 goats.

1863
Gold mining begins on the island, resulting in a minor gold rush.

1864
Union military take possession of Catalina to forestall a feared Confederate seizure and establishment of a privateer base.

Civil War barracks are built on Isthmus to house Union troops. The barracks are still used.

Early 1880s
Phineas Banning, with his sons, and Augustus W. Timms begin to transport tourists to the island.

1887
Avalon is named; however, its Dakin Cove name survives until the 1934 *Coast Pilot* is published. It is called Avalon Bay starting in 1937.

George R. Shatto becomes new owner of Catalina. His Hotel Metropole is completed. Avalon is promoted as a resort and real estate venture.

1889
The first detailed chart of Dakin Cove (Avalon Bay) and the Isthmus is published.

1890
The first chart showing all of Catalina in relation to the mainland is issued, nearly a half century before the first detailed chart of the entire island is published in 1936.

1891
Brothers William, J.B., and Hancock Banning buy the island, becoming its 11th owners.

1893
The Bannings establish Catalina Country Club, a three-hole golf course, soon expanded to nine holes. Equestrian stables are added later.

1894
Banning brothers found the Santa Catalina Island Company.

Walter L. Vail, of Arizona's Empire Ranch, and partner Carroll W. Gates obtain a lease from the Bannings to range cattle over most of the island.

Construction begins on the first segment of the coach road from the Isthmus to Little Harbor, later connecting to Avalon in 1903. Stage coaching becomes a thrilling experience for tourists.

1896
The Vail-Gates lease terminates. In 1901 the Vail family buys Santa Rosa Island, moving their cattle operations from the mainland.

1898
The Tuna Club is founded by Dr. Charles Frederick Holder. The clubhouse opens in 1908.

1900
Banning brothers attempt to establish the resort community of Cabrillo at the Isthmus. The effort is abandoned after several years.

1901
First electric light plant is installed.

1902
Hancock Banning establishes a serpentine marble quarry in the Valley of Ollas, inland from Empire Landing. The quarry closes in 1919.

1911
Catalina is the backdrop for more than 200 films over the next 76 years: one of them, *Terror Island,* with Harry Houdini, 1920.

1912
First flight over channel in aviation history from Balboa to Avalon and return is made by Glenn C. Martin.

1913
Avalon is incorporated as a city.

1915
A November 15 fire destroys approximately half of Avalon.

1919
William Wrigley Jr. becomes the owner of Catalina, buying all of the Banning assets, including the Wilmington Transportation Co.

1920s
San Clemente sea monster is sighted by several fishing parties.

1921
Philip K. Wrigley organizes Wilmington–Catalina Air Line Ltd. and builds an amphibian airport at Hamilton Beach. William Wrigley Jr.'s Chicago Cubs establish their spring-training camp at Catalina; they stay for 26 years.

1924
The SS *Catalina,* the big white steamship, makes her maiden voyage to Avalon. She transports 391,190 passengers her first year and is on the Wilmington–Avalon run until 1976.

Mining for galena, lead, and zinc begins on Black Jack Mountain. The mine and mill are closed in the '30s.

Bison are brought to the island as movie extras. More are added in the 1930s, then in 1969 and 1971.

1927
The Bird Park opens on eight acres in Avalon Canyon. Girders for the giant aviary come from the demolished Sugarloaf Casino.

1929
The new Casino is completed.

1932
William Wrigley Jr. dies at age 77. His son Philip K. Wrigley is elected president of the Santa Catalina Island Co.

1940
Construction of the Airport-in-the-Sky begins. United Airlines starts service to Catalina in 1946.

1941
Japanese surprise attack December 7 on U.S. forces at Pearl Harbor, Hawaii, begins the war in the Pacific.

1942
Civil War barracks at the Isthmus are used by U.S. Coast Guard to house trainees. Various areas of the island are used by other branches of the military.

1965
The first gift of 5.3 acres from Philip K. Wrigley family establishes the USC Catalina Marine Science Center at Big Fisherman Cove.

1975
The Wrigley family deeds 86 percent (42,139 acres) of Catalina to the Santa Catalina Island Conservancy.

1977
Philip K. Wrigley dies at age 82. He is succeeded as president of the Santa Catalina Island Co. by Paxson Offield.

1991
A 132,000-gallon-per-day desalinization plant becomes operational on July 1. It is intended primarily for drought years.

1998
Santa Catalina Island Co. sells Wilmington Transportation Co. to Foss Maritime.

2000
Some 400 native California plant species are on Catalina.

WEST END

PARSON'S LANDING

EAGLE ROCK

EMERALD BAY

INDIAN ROCK

JOHNSON'S LDG.

EAGLE REEF

SHIP ROCK

BIG & LITTLE GEIGER

HOWLAND'S LDG.

BIRD R

IRON BOUND COVE

RIBBON ROCK

BALLAST POINT

CATALINA HARBOR

LITTLE HARBOR

INDIAN HEAD ROCK

MILLS LANDIN

BEN WESTON PT.

CHINA PT.

Map by Sanford Smith

SANTA CATALINA ISLAND

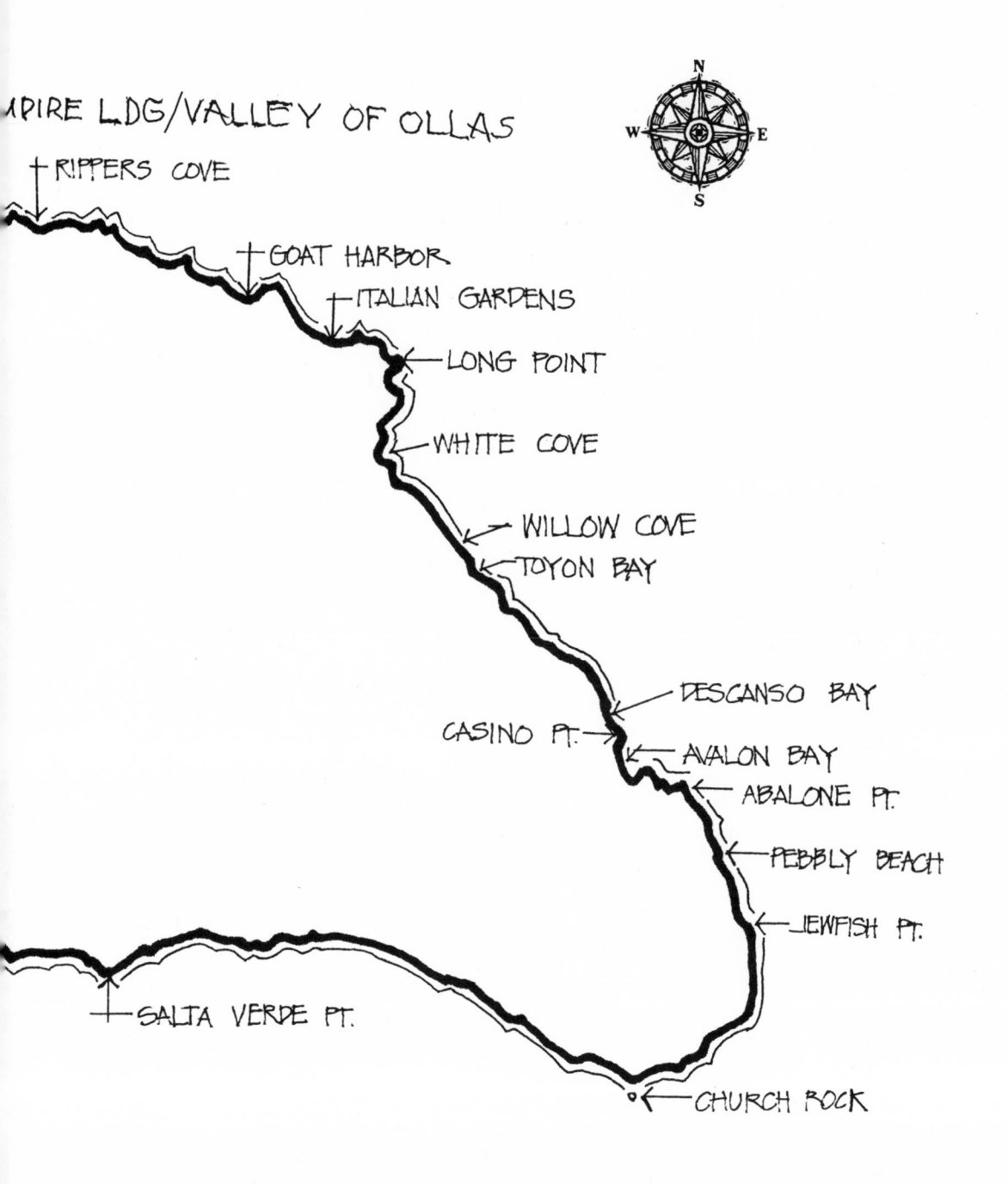

MPIRE LDG/VALLEY OF OLLAS

RIPPERS COVE

GOAT HARBOR

ITALIAN GARDENS

LONG POINT

WHITE COVE

WILLOW COVE

TOYON BAY

DESCANSO BAY

CASINO PT.

AVALON BAY

ABALONE PT.

PEBBLY BEACH

JEWFISH PT.

SALTA VERDE PT.

CHURCH ROCK

An Historical Cruise Around
Santa Catalina Island

CATALINA SAGA

RICHARD & MARJORIE BUFFUM

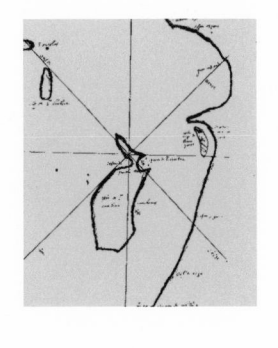

ABRACADABRA PRESS 2003
BALBOA ISLAND, CALIFORNIA

Library of Congress Control Number: 2003101081

International Standard Book Number 0-934542-02-3

First Edition

RICHARD AND MARJORIE BUFFUM
Post Office Box 334
Balboa Island, California 92662

Printed in the United States of America

This history is dedicated to

the late DR. JOHN HASKELL KEMBLE, emeritus professor of history at Pomona College, Claremont, California, and distinguished nautical historian, and to

DR. WILLIAM O. HENDRICKS, historian and director of the Sherman Library, Corona del Mar, California,

both of whom encouraged us and guided us to valuable sources of historic information relating to Santa Catalina Island.

Contents

Illustrations

CATALINA SAGA

Introduction

Our little *Herald Bird* is a Marconi-rigged, twenty-seven-foot-long sloop that is blessed with the classical grace of line that was the hallmark of her designer, the late L. Francis Herreshoff of Marblehead, Massachusetts. Herreshoff created the Offshore 27 that is our *Herald Bird* (also called the *Bird*) for Cheoy Lee Shipyard in Hong Kong. Her low freeboard makes her enough of a sea snuggler to be rather wet in rough weather. Yet she drives her three and one-half tons with a full-ballasted keel through it all in a sea-kindly manner, and does not begin to labor excessively at the helm (she steers by tiller) until the wind velocity approaches twenty knots. Then it is prudent to reef her mainsail down to the first batten cranking a handle at the foot of the boom. This wraps the sail around the boom, much like a manual window shade roller.

I prefer not to work hard at sailing, or press the vessel hard, heeding the splendid advice of Hilaire Belloc, stalwart British yachtsman and author who sailed the English coast in his beloved sloop *Nona* in the 1920s. "Cruising is not racing," Belloc said. He claimed that sailing renewed in us all the past in our blood, but he felt the same past was corrupted by racing. He regarded his boat not as an expensive machine but rather as "a home and a companion ... a genius that takes you from place to place and, what is more, a good angel, revealing unexpected things, and a comforter and introducer to the Infinite Verities."

Our *Bird* is certainly not a racer, as evidenced by the fact that she carries only one suit of working sails, consisting of 303 square feet of mainsail and 223 square feet of jib. What's more, she is too heavily laden with gear and comforts to race. She is, however, companionable, a cozy home to hole up in after a cold, wet passage.

When the wind deserts us or we become impatient, the *Bird* is driven by a two-cylinder, ten-horsepower Volvo Penta diesel marine engine. At best, this pushes her along at six knots. Her hull and cabin trunk are made of sturdy hand-laid fiberglass and her deck is planked with teak laid over a thick sandwich of mahogany. Her greatest breadth is seven feet, eight and one-half inches. She draws four feet, four inches of water. So much for the vital statistics, except to note that Herreshoff, according to Muriel Vaughn, his longtime secretary and companion, was displeased with the builders because they raised the cabin trunk to what he felt was an unaesthetic height. This created an ample six feet of headroom within the main portion of the cabin, which pleases me, for I am six-foot-one and can stand inside with only a slight stoop. I acquired the *Herald Bird* in June of 1972, the year she was built. She

had come from China on the deck of a freighter, and when I discovered her on a cradle beside a yacht broker's office in Marina del Rey, it was love at first sight. That very same year, in December, Herreshoff died at the age of eighty-two.

As for her name, a herald bird exists, but not in an ornithological book. It was discovered by my first wife, Hazel Sorensen Buffum, as she was approaching the end of a decade's battle with cancer. During her last days at home, when she had trouble sleeping, she learned that at dawn's first glimmering a lone bird sang an announcement that day had begun. Its purpose, she believed, was to awaken all the other birds. Soon the entire feathered neighborhood was singing, at first a few sleepy voices, then all joining in a joyful obbligato heralding the new day. Listen and you, too, shall hear the herald bird proclaiming a message of renewal that rides in on the wings of morning from a place of limitless horizons where future dawns are kept.

In 1973, when my boat *Herald Bird* was new and after Hazel was gone, I married Marjorie Meyer Smith Driscoll, a journalist on the Orange County edition of the *Los Angeles Times,* for which I was a general columnist. For nearly thirty years Marjie and I sailed in and out of Catalina's coves together and rummaged among many books and papers, seeking information about Catalina. It is this material we want to share with you, in the hope that you will join us on a cove-by-cove circumnavigation of this endlessly fascinating island.

The theme of this book can be easily grasped if you slightly alter John Donne's statement that no man is an island. Simply substitute "island" for "man." "No island is an island, entire of itself; every island is a piece of the continent, a part of the main." Here we will attempt to show that Santa Catalina Island is a microcosm in the sea that reflects mainland California. Use of the first person throughout the text refers to Richard Buffum.

Our saga begins in the once forebodingly barren San Pedro Harbor, about twenty miles south of what was tiny el Pueblo de Los Angeles, during the era when Richard Henry Dana Jr. was hustling hides on the brig *Pilgrim*. A "rascally hole," Dana called the old harbor, unsafe in most weather, particularly during southeasters. However, it was a violent northeaster (Santa Ana wind) that sent the brig *Pilgrim* at San Pedro "off with flowing sheet, and hove-to under the lee of Catalina Island, where we lay three days, and then returned to our anchorage," Dana wrote in his two-volume set of *Two Years Before the Mast,* with notes by John Haskell Kemble (Ward Ritchie Press, 1964). That was during February of 1836. An earlier vessel here was not as fortunate.

We start with a significant shipwreck.

1 Wreck of the *Danube*

This anchorage is good during the summer months. In the winter season, South East gales prevail, and vessels should so anchor as to bring Pt. Fermin to bear W.S.W. and Dead Man's Island North, being ready to slip as soon as a gale commences. If compelled by stress of weather to get under way it is best (if the wind admits) to cast to port and stand over to the North shore, then to tack when Pt. Fermin will be easily weathered.

Sailing directions for San Pedro Harbor on the U.S
Coast Survey's 1852 Chart J, No. 5 (initial U.S. survey)

The wind did not admit the 274-ton American brig *Danube* out of New York under Samuel Cook, master, to stand over to the north shore and tack in order to safely avoid Point Fermin. A vicious southeaster had sprung up. Before her anchors could be weighed completely and her sails set, the *Danube* was aground. It happened on Christmas Eve of 1828. Perhaps her twenty-eight-man complement had been lulled into the convivial complacency of the Yuletide. At any rate, the captain and crew made it ashore without serious mishap and began the twenty-mile hike toward the pueblo of Los Angeles, largest settlement in the state at the time with about 400 residents. The pueblo was founded September 4, 1781.

Word of the disaster must have spread quickly for, while the *Danube*'s sailors were hiking up the great alluvial plain with its widely scattered haciendas and cattle ranches, they were offered rides on three heavy wooden carts pulled by oxen. It was axiomatic among the hospitable Spaniards that sailors could not ride horses, so the carts had been sent to transport them to a Christmas party in the pueblo. The sailors were welcomed at the home of Antonio Rocha, a Portuguese who had helped build San Luis Rey Mission, later marrying and settling in Los Angeles. At one time Rocha owned the La Brea Rancho. The preceding August, Rocha, a hospitable man, had opened his home to four American fur trappers: Nathaniel Pryor, Richard Laughlin, Jesse Ferguson, and James Ohio Pattie (Paty), who had been detained in San Diego for lack of California passports. They were eventually released through the intervention of Father Antonio Peyri, founder of San Luis Rey Mission. Pattie then departed, but the others remained at Rocha's adobe. When the *Danube*'s crew arrived at Rocha's home on Spring Street, they were "soon seated at an abundant repast. And never was there a happier Christmas party in Los Angeles than that, where trappers and sailors drank [to] their entertainer's health in bumpers of old Lugo's wine," reminisced pioneer Stephen C. Foster in an 1887 publication of the Historical Society of Southern California.

"Old Lugo" was Antonio Maria Lugo, a wealthy rancher with a townhouse on the road to San Pedro. Rocha and Lugo had vied over who should host the party. Rocha won the contest, so Lugo furnished the wine. Of the crew of the *Danube,* two eventually remained in southern California: Johann Groningen, a native of Hanover, the first German settler in Los Angeles, and Samuel Prentice (or Prentiss), a native of Connecticut, who became one of Catalina Island's legendary characters, settling eventually near the Isthmus.

The Catalina connection doesn't end with the wreck of the *Danube.* Salvaged materials from the brig were used to construct part of several locally built small schooners: the *Santa Barbara,* the *Guadalupe,* and the *Refugio,* which carried sea otter hunter George C. Yount to Catalina, where he reportedly discovered a gold-bearing ledge, a story that later stimulated a gold rush on the island. The *Santa Barbara,* first Mexican schooner that was completely built in California, had as her original captain Thomas M. Robbins, later to become the first private owner of Santa Catalina Island.

All these vessels were small coastal schooners in the neighborhood of forty to eighty feet. There was adequate salvageable material from the ninety- to one-hundred-foot *Danube* when new lumber was added to build several smaller vessels. Constructed of white oak, pine, and locust, her bottom sheathed in copper, the *Danube* carried two iron-chain cables. She was surveyed in New York in May 1828, then sailed from New York loaded with cargo for trade by her owners, Wood & Co. The *Danube* made it around Cape Horn, only to have Point Fermin claim her on Christmas Eve (Lloyd's Registry of Shipping, 1927–28).

One of the men who supervised the building of the *Santa Barbara,* of thirty-three to thirty-five tons, was Michael C. White, an Englishman known to the Californians as Miguel Blanco. Michael White discussed the construction of the schooner *Santa Barbara* in a narrative dictated in 1877 to Thomas Savage, one of historian Hubert Howe Bancroft's staff (*California All the Way Back to 1828*).

White said that in 1828 he was superintending a group of eighteen men who were building a schooner "at a place called Mescalitan," which "was afterwards called La Goleta in consequence of the building of the schooner for De la Guerra." *La goleta* means schooner in Spanish.

This area, now known as the Goleta Slough, is at Isla Vista, adjacent to the University of California, Santa Barbara. The area was a good refuge in the early days and potentially a fine harbor, better than the Santa Barbara bight, which verged on being an open roadstead. But in the winter of 1861–62, La Goleta silted up. That year's unusually heavy rains caused floodwaters from nearby creeks to deposit fourteen feet of rich silt in the Goleta Valley, destroying forever its navigable waterways.

It is possible that the schooner *Santa Barbara* was originally named *La Fama,* said to have been built at the Goleta estuary in 1828 by shipwrights Michael White and his cousin, Henry Paine, for William Goodwin Dana, captain of the port of Santa Barbara, and Carlos Carrillo, Dana's father-in-law, later a governor of California. William Benjamin Foxen, known as "Don Julian" to the Californians, was originally commissioned by Dana to build and launch the schooner, and White's narrative notes that the building of the schooner was discontinued when the *Danube* was wrecked. Paine was sent to San Pedro by Jose De la Guerra y Noriega to survey the wreck, "a splendid vessel," and "get her off, and put such repairs on her as might be necessary."

But on New Year's Eve, before the *Danube* could be rescued, a gale blew up, White said, leaving the *Danube* "high and dry" and "knocked all to pieces . . . We saved all the materials and built a schooner out of them. She was named the *Santa Barbara,* and was the first vessel ever built in California."

Historian Bancroft noted that De la Guerra and William Goodwin Dana, with a eye toward profit, bought the *Danube's* cargo for $3,316 and her hull for $1,716, a considerable sum. De la Guerra, *comandante* of the Santa Barbara presidio, and Dana, captain of the port of Santa Barbara and a relative of author Richard Henry Dana, were among the most prominent men in California at the time. Dana owned a store in Santa Barbara and wanted the schooner for coastal trading. He was not averse to a little sea otter hunting as well, having acquired a coveted license for the hunt from the Mexican government. Dana was married to Josefa Carrillo, a daughter of Don Carlos Carrillo, another leading Santa Barbaran.

The completed *Santa Barbara* was launched in 1830 and put under the command of twenty-nine-year-old Thomas Robbins, originally a Nantucket man. She traded as far south as San Blas and Mazatlan. Robbins had arrived in Santa Barbara in 1823 aboard the brig *Rover,* a hide and tallow ship out of Boston. By the age of twenty-six, he had already served as master of the 142-ton Hawaiian brig *Waverly* and the 121-ton American schooner *Guibale.* A few years later he became a Catholic and naturalized Mexican citizen so he could marry Encarnacion Carrillo. With the marriage, Robbins became Dana's brother-in-law.

During Captain Robbins' voyages he may have cast covetous eyes on Catalina, claimed by Mexico since 1821 after Mexico's successful revolt against Spain. He was certainly familiar with the island's anchorages, frequently used by many early ships. Finally, in 1839, Robbins petitioned the governor, Juan Bautista Alvarado, for "the concession of the Island called Santa Catalina, in order that I may devote myself to the branch of agriculture and breeding of cattle." At the time Robbins was in the employ of the Departmental Government of California and in command of the 100-ton government schooner, *California,* out of Monterey. The *California* carried dispatches between Monterey, Mazatlan, and San Blas, delivering messages between the Department of California and the supreme government in Mexico (Davis, p. 76). She was also the nucleus of a west coast navy to enforce, if needed, California's autonomy as a Department of Mexico.

Aboard the original brig *Pilgrim,* under ship's master Francis A. Thompson, Richard Henry Dana Jr. spent two years before the mast, 1834-36, much of it in southern California waters. This replica is a classroom operated by the Orange County Marine Institute, Dana Point, California. Her length on deck is 98 feet, sparred length 130 feet, and beam 24 feet, 6 inches.

Alvarado seems to have ignored Robbins' petition, but seven years later, on July 4, 1846, Alvarado's successor, Pio Pico, granted Catalina to Robbins. It was one of the last acts of the last Mexican governor of California. Robbins had an adobe and wood house constructed on the northwestern part of the island, near the Isthmus, and established two men there to tend his cattle and cultivate some land (W.W. Robinson 1948, p. 18).

2   The Schooner Tradition

There is a difference between tonnage figures of American vessels built before 1865 and those built later. Until 1865, a mathematical formula based on beam, depth, and length was used. After that date, tonnage was expressed in units of 100 cubic feet of the actual internal capacity of a vessel. RICHARD BUFFUM

San Pedro's rocky shore, with Deadman's Island situated in the bay to the east, was the site of a gala affair in 1831. People were invited from miles around to witness and help celebrate the launching of the second California-built schooner, the *Guadalupe*.

Nearly every piece of her timber had been hewn and fitted, i.e., prefabricated, at San Gabriel Mission near the foothills, then hauled thirty miles to the beach on ox carts. There is evidence that parts of the *Danube* were used in her construction. The *Guadalupe* was assembled on shore near the hide house, a one-story adobe building used to store hides, horns, and merchandise destined for trade. The adobe had been built by Indian laborers in 1823 for Hugh McCulloch and William Hartnell, Englishmen and partners in John Begg and Company, a trading firm based in Lima. The building was later owned by the San Gabriel Mission.

Michael White claimed in his 1877 memoirs that he worked on the construction of the *Guadalupe* after finishing work on the *Santa Barbara*. He described the former as measuring "99 and 90/100 tons, was a topsail schooner and carried about 150 tons." White said she was built expressly for the mission to use for trade and shipping on the coast. However, Alfred Robinson, in his book *Life in California,* first published in New York in 1846, says the schooner was "of about 60 tons," and we are inclined to take his more contemporary word for the vessel's size. Robinson, a Bostonian, arrived in California in 1829 on the *Brookline* as supercargo's clerk, was naturalized and baptized, and married Ana Maria de la Guerra y Carillo, thus becoming linked to two important California families.

The *Guadalupe*'s head shipwright was Joseph Chapman, a Yankee seaman and jack-of-all-trades (primarily a blacksmith and carpenter) who had served an apprenticeship with a Boston boat builder, gone to sea, and was working in the Hawaiian Islands when he was pressed into service by the French freebooter Hippolyte de Bouchard. Chapman, suspected of piracy, was taken prisoner at Monterey in 1818 but eventually freed and allowed to remain in California, where he was universally liked by the Hispanic population and the friars at the missions. In 1822, having renounced his American citizenship and become a Catholic, he married into the wealthy and aristocratic Ortega family of Refugio Ranch near Santa Barbara. His wife's name was Guadalupe, after the patron saint of Mexico.

Indians at the San Gabriel Mission, taught to carpenter and caulk by Chapman, helped build the *Guadalupe* and another mission schooner, the sixty-ton *Refugio*. Alfred Robinson noted that Chapman, during his residence in California, had "acquired a mongrel language; English, Spanish and Indian being so intermingled in his speech that it was difficult to understand him," adding that "Father Sanchez, of San Gabriel [Mission] used to say that Chapman could get more work out of the Indians with his unintelligible tongue than all the *mayordomos* put together." A number of the Indians may have been from Catalina Island, although baptismal and other records that could prove their birthplace verge on nonexistence. Nevertheless, it is known that Indians from Catalina and the Channel Islands made their way or were taken to San Gabriel and Santa Barbara Missions during this dark period in coastal Indian history. The white man had arrived, and the natives never recovered from their "domestication."

Captain Dennis Holland built this replica of a late-eighteenth-century fore-and-aft rigged trading schooner of 1770 from plans in the Smithsonian. Named *Pilgrim,* her length is 83 feet on deck, with a sparred length of 114 feet and a 24-foot beam. She carried charter parties out of Newport Beach, California.

White noted that the *Guadalupe* was put under the command of William A. Richardson, an Englishman by birth, who arrived in California in 1822 as mate on the whaler *Orion* and later became captain of the port of San Francisco, owner of the Sausalito rancho, and husband of Maria Antonio, daughter of Comandante Ignacio Martinez. Richardson was said to be a skillful sailor, yet to him goes the dubious honor of wrecking the schooner *Josephine* on Catalina Island in 1832 — the island's first reported shipwreck. This may have resulted from a northeasterly wind that blows into the north-facing coves. Details are nonexistent, but Alfred Robinson mentions that a Mexican schooner was "wrecked on the island of Catalina. She had been taken into one of the harbors, for the purpose of 'heaving out.' When the gale commenced, she was unprepared to get under way, and soon a heavy swell rolled in, which drove her on the rocks." Richardson made his home in San Gabriel at the time but is said to have made trading trips up and down the coast in different vessels.

The San Gabriel Mission, founded September 8, 1771, as Misión San Gabriel Archangel, was administered efficiently and productively during this period by genial Father Jose Bernardo Sanchez who, in 1827, was elected president of the California missions, a position he held until 1831. San Gabriel had vast vineyards and orchards and the largest winery in California. Three grape presses and eight stills made wine and *aguardiente,* a potent brandy. Some 25,000 cattle and sheep grazed on the mission's immense acreage. Trade with visiting merchant vessels in sea otter pelts, cattle hides, horn, tallow, and wool, helped enrich the mission treasury.

Father Sanchez's entrepreneurial spirit was noted by J.J. Warner in his *An Historical Sketch of Los Angeles County* when he said: "The minister at San Gabriel . . . aided and encouraged William Wolfskill, Nathaniel Pryor, Richard Laughlin, Samuel Prentice and George Yount to build a schooner at San Pedro, which was employed by the Americans named in the hunting of sea otter." Pryor, Laughlin, and Prentice, you will recall, were part of the convivial group assembled at Antonio Rocha's house after the *Danube* went aground in 1828. Yount arrived from New Mexico in 1831 with Wolfskill's trapping party, liked what he saw, and stayed. As otter hunters, this group of Americans made an impact on Catalina's natural ecological balance, but they were a small group and stayed only a short time before moving on to mainland ranches and business interests.

Those first California-built schooners, the *Santa Barbara, Guadalupe,* and *Refugio,* were harbingers of later vessels that came to be known as Pacific Coast schooners, a tradition that persisted for seventy-five years. The majority, built in northern California, were topsail schooners carrying square yards on the foremast and fore and aft sails on the remainder. The fashion persisted longer on the Pacific Coast than on the eastern seaboard. Research by nautical historian John Lyman, as detailed in his *Sailing Vessels of the Pacific Coast, 1850–1905,* disclosed that a total of 480 schooners, two- to five-masted, were built on the West Coast during that fifty-five-year period (p. 21). Also built on the coast during the same period were 105 ships, barks, barkentines, brigs, and brigantines. Coastal shipping, lumber, and trade with the South Pacific, Australia, the Orient, and the United States were the major commercial enterprises.

3 San Pedro Channel

San Pedro Channel is about 17 miles wide between the mainland, Point Fermin, to Point Vicente, and Catalina Island. Current observations have been made 7 miles S of San Pedro Breakwater. Two periodic currents occur at this location: a tidal current, and a daily current apparently due to a land and sea breeze. Both are rotary, turning clockwise, and each is weak, having a velocity of 0.2 knot.
UNITED STATES COAST PILOT, June 1986

There was barely a stir of wind as the *Herald Bird* cleared the twin jetties of Newport Harbor. We set a southwesterly course, pointing the Bird's bows at an invisible destination twenty-seven nautical miles across the San Pedro Channel toward an area of small coves, generally known as White's Landing or the Long Point area. The ocean swells were long and lazy. Unless the weather gods turned frivolous, there would be no wind worth hoisting sails to until the appointed hour of freshening, about 1300 (1:00 P.M.). Estimated visibility across the misty channel was about seven miles. This morning I made our traditional cruising breakfast: browned smoked sausages wrapped in buttered warm tortillas with Coleman's English mustard — an international cholesterol delight. Each is wrapped in a paper towel, to catch the inevitable drippings, and passed out along with hot coffee in mugs with nonslip bases. We've named this breakfast the "Helmsman's Friend," for it is easy to eat it and steer at the same time.

San Pedro Channel, along with the adjacent Gulf of Catalina, Santa Barbara Channel, and Outer Santa Barbara Channel, has been called the channel of many weathers. It is not uncommon to begin a cruise to Catalina in a dead calm and encounter unanticipated nasty weather in midchannel. An early yachtsman, Los Angeles attorney and bank president J.A. Graves, who cruised in his thirty-eight-foot gasoline launch *Pasqualito,* built in 1899 by Joe Fellows of San Pedro, had this to say about the San Pedro Channel: "It [*Pasqualito*] was a very seaworthy boat and we crossed the channel to Catalina many times, but we never should have done so. No small boat without sails should ever be caught in the middle of that channel, as frequently storms come up quite unexpectedly, and if one's engine were to be put out of commission, the boat would, without doubt, be swamped" (Graves 1928, p. 338). Graves' warning is still valid. The channel can become rough enough to endanger large yachts, sail or power, not to mention small boats improperly designed for deep water cruising. I know of one small sailboat of about twenty-two feet, built with an opening in its stern on which to hang an outboard motor, that was pooped and sunk in the channel by a high following sea. Despite the fact that a bulkhead was built forward of the outboard engine, large waves astern caused the sea to "siphon" over the bulkhead and overwhelm the boat. Until a few years ago, skippers had no way of knowing the state of midchannel weather. The National Weather Service did not monitor conditions within the midchannel wind line: its radio weather reports were based on shore-positioned observations, which could be misleading to those planning channel crossings. It might be calm near shore and whooping it up in midchannel without anyone knowing unless they ventured out there.

In 1982, Robert Allan, a former commodore of the prestigious Newport Harbor Yacht Club and a U.S. Navy meteorologist during World War II, launched a campaign to establish an official weather station on an oil drilling platform about nine miles off the coast of Huntington Beach. The platform, one of several now in the area near the steamer lanes, was owned by Shell California Production Inc., a subsidiary of Shell Oil Company. Allan enlisted my journalistic help to promote the idea and talked it up among local yachtsmen. With the added efforts of a Shell executive, William Devereaux, the Los Angeles office of the National Weather Service agreed to install sensing equipment monitors on the platform. The equipment, donated by Shell at a cost of $5,000, relays wind speed and direction to NOAA (National Oceanic and Atmospheric Administration) Weather Radio, the Weather Service's twenty-four-hour reporting station in Oxnard, transmitted from a tower on Mount Wilson, Los Angeles.

The operation quickly proved its usefulness to commercial fishermen, the Coast Guard, state Fish and Game patrol boats, tugboats, commercial shippers, and, of course, yachtsmen, and convinced the Weather Service to install additional automatic reporting stations on several offshore buoys and the east end of the Long Beach breakwater. The "channels of many weathers" are potentially safer now because of better weather foreknowledge, but the gods who rule over this watery domain are capricious and loath to reveal their intentions. Thus, unknown perils still lurk that can catch a mariner unaware. One such danger is the rogue wave.

We encountered only one rogue wave during our nearly thirty years on the *Herald Bird,* but that was enough. For weeks afterward, lying awake in the night, I'd think of that giant wave moving relentlessly down on us and shudder with fear. It had come upon us from the southwest, seemingly out of nowhere, as we were nearing the mainland. The sea was confused, peaking up in the pyramidal waves we call "witches' hats." So evil and uncomfortable was this witches' sea that I altered course to mitigate its influence and headed toward Corona del Mar, east of Newport Beach. I dropped the *Bird*'s sails and was motoring up the coast into the wind when a monstrous wave suddenly appeared. I quartered the *Bird*'s bows toward the wall of water, which I estimated to be at least eighteen feet high, and we climbed up its face. Reaching the foaming crest and surmounting it, the *Bird*'s propeller cavitating as we started down the other side, I saw to my horror another great wave rolling behind it. The trough between the two seemed frighteningly narrow.

"Hold on!" I cried to Marjie, "We're going to bury." Everything loose in the cabin flew about when we reached the bottom with a dreadful thump, blue water sluicing over the deck from stem to stern. Miraculously, the *Bird*'s prow did not bury but rose cork-like to climb the second, slightly smaller wave. And then it was over, as suddenly as it had begun, and we were motoring home again, a pair of wet, thoroughly shaken mariners. Later we learned that a tsunami warning had been issued after an earthquake somewhere out in the Pacific. Could that have caused our rogue wave?

Waterspouts are another perilous plaything of the sea gods. In prudent response to NOAA Weather Radio's warning of waterspouts, we have laid over until the next day rather than chance an encounter with those cyclonic whirling dervishes. Fortunately, waterspouts and rogue waves are infrequent in the channel, as are Mexican hurricanes, which usually have lost their massive force by the time they reach our waters. Briefly, our predominant stormy weather patterns consist of southeasters, northeasters, southwesters, and northwesters. A true southerly is rare.

Here follows a boater's almanac of weather for the southern California coastal waters:

JANUARY THROUGH MARCH: When he was loading hides in 1835–36 as a foremast hand, Richard Henry Dana Jr. considered the southeaster to be the bane of our coast. Southeasters' favorite months are roughly January through March, although there can be exceptions. One of them was the hurricane that invaded southern California September 20, 1939, wreaking havoc everywhere, driving boats ashore, and taking lives. Southeasters may shift to west or northwest with gusts exceeding thirty knots. Swells from the southwest to west–northwest may range from four to six feet, with high surf. Such swells are generated by intense storms quite a distance from the coast. If there is rain, this is the time of year it is most likely to arrive.

APRIL THROUGH MAY: Weather fronts are less frequent and not as active as earlier. Occasionally there is rain; coastal fogs and low clouds are the rule. Winds are not usually over twenty knots.

JUNE: Normally no frontal weather occurs. Low, long-period swells from the southwest to west–northwest are not infrequent, along with occasional southerly swells, two to five feet, from early season storms moving off the Mexican coast. Cloud or fog pockets often collect around islands.

JULY THROUGH SEPTEMBER: Frequent night and morning fog or low clouds, clearing in the afternoon. Tropical air, with high humidity, moves up the southeast. There are occasional long swells caused by storms south of the equator, but they do not seriously affect boating.

OCTOBER THROUGH NOVEMBER: Short rainy periods and delayed "Indian summer" heat spells with one or two days of northeasterly or Santa Ana winds reaching thirty to forty knots below coastal canyons.

DECEMBER: Weather fronts become more active. Santa Ana or northeasterly winds become more frequent and may extend out over coastal waters reaching thirty to forty knots. Expect occasional dense night and morning coastal fogs and a few long-period swells from southwest to west–northwest from distant Pacific storms. (Weather information from Emil S. Kurtz, *Southern California Weather for Small Boats.*)

Some words of warning are in order about Santa Ana winds, a name associated with the Santa Ana River valley, one of the favored routes of these dry northeasters on their way from the mountains to the coast. These winds can threaten vessels in the popular coves along the northern (mainland-facing) side of Catalina Island, whether moored or at anchor. When the air turns hot and dry, the barometer rises, and you can see the mainland clearly, beware! The appearance of a dust cloud over the sea on the horizon is fair warning to cast off moorings or weigh anchor and get out to sea. When Santa Anas reach the island, dangerous waves can build up in the shallow water of the coves.

Many yachtsmen seek the protection of the southern or backside coast of the island. Reference to that excellent publication, *Chart Guide,* by Ed Winlund, will dis-

COURTESY DOUG BOMBARD

close a few, very few, relatively protected places on the north-facing coast where a small vessel may shelter during a severe Santa Ana. Get the hell out, if you can, is our best advice.

I have been on this channel off and on since childhood, and have seen many wonderful things upon it. This channel still has life in it, despite man's abuse, and any person who says a slow passage across is boring suffers from what I call "a freeway mentality in the fast lane." It seems to be a sickness of modern civilization to want to speed from one place to another, without heeding that which is in between. It is the sailing that counts, as my yachtsman friend, the late Hale

A northeasterly, or Santa Ana, wind sweeps large waves into Avalon Harbor. Strong Santa Anas occasionally blow from the mainland across the San Pedro Channel during fall and winter months, making the northern-facing island coves unsafe.

Field, used to say, and it is there in the "in-between" that nature reveals herself in infinite ways: schools of tiny anchovies frothing the sea, great whales passing, seabirds feeding, frolicsome porpoises, fish that fly, and thresher sharks and swordfish propelling themselves out of the water as though shot from cannons.

Once Marjie and I saw a marlin leap at least a half-dozen times, clearing the surface of the sea completely before falling back with mighty splashes, a magnificent white and blue projectile against the morning sun, arousing in us awe and joy at the sight. On another morning, a windless one in the spring, we decided to have breakfast off the coast before cranking up the "iron sail" (the engine) and heading for the island.

I was below, making a second cup of coffee, and Marjie was finishing a cup in the cockpit. Suddenly we heard a massive sigh, a cavernous exhalation of air. I leaped up, joining Marjie on the deck. A great gray whale, its enormous back mottled and barnacle-encrusted, had risen beside us, less than twenty feet away. He (or she) seemed twice our length. In leisurely fashion its great eye inspected us, this curious, quiet little vessel floating freely with the current. Apparently satisfied, the leviathan slipped gently beneath the sea and we could hear the water close softly over it. Marjie was pointing at it, stunned and speechless, a rare occurrence for her.

Encounters like these remind us of a penetrating observation by naturalist Henry Beston, in *The Outermost House,* that "animals are not brethren, they are not underlings; they are other nations, caught with ourselves in the net of life and time."

Before we "raise" Catalina Island (a mariner's word meaning "I see it"), I must correct an impression I have given about the capriciousness of the sea gods who rule over this channel. I wrote of their ways out of whimsy, mixed with awe of the unknown. Now I must amend this impression for the benefit of the hard-headed rationalists among you. I must tell what is true, leaving poetics out of it. The sea may be cruel, perplexing, relentless, unappeasable, awesome, and terrible or it may be tranquil, docile, beautiful, and in every way friendly to those who venture upon it in their puny boats. But it is never in itself unpredictable, abnormal, or capricious.

Unpredictability, abnormality, and capriciousness are merely value judgments by those of us who observe only the effects of the sea upon us and are ignorant of the causes. The sea responds to its own profound laws, which are little understood by humans. It is man's responses to the sea that are quixotic. Yet we are learning all the time. Scientists with their instruments are probing, measuring, relating, and collecting data so that, in time, man will understand the sea's multifaceted moods. With this knowledge will come understanding of new ways to cherish and husband the great oceans and their creatures, for truly the sea is in every man's blood, and to destroy the living sea is to destroy man.

4   Born in a Cataclysmic Stew

To those who "go down to the sea in ships" on the Southern California coast, the islands which are strung along the shores from fog-swept San Miguel, near Point Concepcion to Los Coronados, appear like off-shore Sierras. When the coast range of California was thrust up, and the great sea bottom became Los Angeles, there was, in all probability, a general upheaval all along the coast, and another Sierra endeavored to take shape and form about eighteen miles out at sea.
CHARLES F. HOLDER, *The Channel Islands of California*

For sixty years I was comfortable with my ignorance of the geologic origin of Catalina Island. I believed the island was once attached to the mainland by a land bridge originating on the Palos Verdes Peninsula. I believed that eons ago a seismic convulsion destroyed the land bridge, stranding mainland flora and fauna on the island. This theory was easy to believe. After all, weren't there foxes and ironwood trees endemic to modern Catalina that were reported to have lived on the mainland thousands of years ago? And, of course, in clear weather, anyone on the western part of the island can look across the channel and see Palos Verdes, some seventeen miles away. At night the lights, even automobile headlights, appear so close it seems as if you could reach out and touch them. This sense of geographic intimacy made the land bridge theory easy to accept.

It was disabused one day by Terrence D. Martin, former resident naturalist for the Catalina Island Conservancy, which owns and manages sixty-six of the island's seventy-five square miles. Martin's job was to roam the island; observe its geology, wildlife, and plants; and contrive ways to restore native vegetation and maintain its critical ecological balance. Over lunch, Martin patiently explained the currently accepted, but new to me then, tectonic plate theory of Catalina's origin. Later he sent a copy of his book, *Santa Catalina Island Adventure,* which, he said in an accompanying letter, should "help elucidate some of the topics we discussed."

The book offered a dramatic explanation of continental drift and plate tectonics, theories that help explain the earth's face, its movements, and its history, as well as unraveling some mysteries of life and its distribution on our planet. Martin believes that about 100 million years ago the continental plate, on which Catalina is located, lay somewhere off the coast of Baja California. The plate moved westward until it collided with the Farallon plate of northern California. A slow-motion collision occurred beneath the sea's surface, creating a cataclysmic stew of sea, steam, molten rock, and sediment. Evidence of that violent encounter is still visible at Ribbon Rock on the island's southerly or windward side.

"It must have been an awesome collision," Martin said. "Hard basalt crumbled; other rocks bent like taffy; the North American plate actually rose as the Farallon plate was driven underneath it — a process known as subduction. Sediments and basalt fragments, scraped from the advancing Farallon plate, accumulated on the hanging wall of the continent or were carried as much as twenty miles beneath the earth's surface."

The very structure of the rocks was changed by the immense heat and pressure, transforming some sediment to marble and bending layers into bizarre shapes. Martin said the debris scraped off by the collision formed the barely submerged embryonic island of Catalina, while the molten material jammed beneath the continent helped lift up the Sierra Nevada. (So Charles Holder's poetic interpretation of Catalina's origin, written a century ago and quoted at the beginning of this chapter, was pretty much on the mark.) Sometime between twenty and five million years ago, in the late Miocene period, the block on which Catalina rests moved about 100 miles north from its earlier location near the present Baja California border and rotated sixty degrees clockwise to reach its present position.

"In addition, the island was subjected to vertical movement and changes in sea level, changes that are still occurring. Thus, Catalina was once larger than it is now. A mile or so seaward from the present shore and eighty feet beneath the sea lies a vast, wave-cut terrace with valleys once cut by streams. This terrace is the remains of an ancient shoreline. Further uplift and down drop, along with changes in sea level have altered the island's size at various times," Martin said, adding there is evidence that the island may have turned around on its base twice during its most active, formative period. What's more, Catalina is unique to itself geologically, with little or no relationship to the other Channel Islands. To this day the island is rising, the rise exceeding the erosion.

Because of its origin and isolation, "everything on Catalina had to cross the channel to get there," Martin said. Everything had to be brought there, by birds, wind, the sea, modern man, and, of course, by the Indian population that inhabited the island at least 6,000 to 7,000 years ago.

During Catalina's formative period, the piece of land that is now the northern Channel Islands broke off in a block from the Santa Monica Mountains and moved about fifty miles laterally to the west. This one great island rose, broke apart, and formed the northern islands (San Miguel, Santa Rosa, Santa Cruz, Anacapa, Santa Barbara, and San Nicolas) when the seas became elevated during glacial warming. That is one theory, anyway. Another proposes that a volcanic archipelago emerged off southern California's coast, thus creating six of the Channel Islands, and that Catalina, the tectonic plate "floater," moved into line as the seventh island. Whether a land bridge from, say, Point Conception or Point Mugu to the early super island ever existed is still an unanswered question.

To solve satisfactorily this geologic mystery is like trying to complete a jigsaw puzzle minus pieces lost millions of years ago. So we shall content ourselves with the pragmatic view, the confirmable obvious, by pointing out that there is a roughly spaced chain of islands, continuously sculpted by the forces of nature. San Miguel

Island is located at the western extremity, some twenty-five miles off Point Conception. San Clemente Island, an eighth, lying forty miles off Dana Point, is the eastern end of the chain.

In between these two, going westerly, are the islands of Santa Catalina, about eighteen miles off Point Fermin; Anacapa, about eleven miles off Ventura; Santa Barbara, about forty-two miles off Point Dume; San Nicolas, the farthest out, about fifty-three miles off Port Hueneme; Santa Cruz, about twenty-one miles off Santa Barbara; and Santa Rosa, about twenty-two miles off Gaviota.

The islands lie along the great California bight, a kind of huge bay, if you will, extending from Point Conception to the Mexican border. The shore of this big dip of a bay lies in an east–west direction, a geographical fact ignored by highway engineers whose freeway signs direct motorists north or south from Santa Barbara to San Diego. There have been times upon entering a freeway that I became confused about which way to go because I knew where magnetic north and south were. The islands are south and the coastal mountains north. San Diego is east, Los Angeles is west.

5 Catalina Discovered

Then there was the Terrestrial Paradise, which had found a place on the ancient maps, and was looked for in America by the Spaniards of the early sixteenth century.   CHARLES E. CHAPMAN,
A History of California: The Spanish Period

Our course at 230 degrees magnetic has taken the *Herald Bird* to Long Point, widest part of Catalina Island, about one-third of the distance between the East and West Ends. Long Point is a craggy headland, its feet in a sea of such depths that even the mighty swordfish, bluefin tuna, and albacore found it a hospitable place to feed. At least, such was reported by old-time anglers who hooked up off this point where two currents meet and fought these fish on rod and reel along this shore of coves. Alas, I speak of recent history, barely seventy years ago, before overfishing and pollution diminished the ecosystem's food chain.

We motor to the largest of the coves, White's Landing, and pick up a mooring off the longest sandy beach on the island. Beyond the beach a group of young campers' tents occupies the shoreward edge of a broad valley, once the site of a large Indian village. (Since this particular visit, a forty-six-year-old lease of the camp by the Girl Scouts was voluntarily terminated in 1993. There are now no Girl Scout camps on the island. The camp and its facilities were taken over by the Glendale YMCA, which also continues to operate Camp Fox in Button Shell Cove just west of here. The San Diego Yacht Club has leased space for a shore facility immediately east of the former Girl Scout camp.)

Beyond the valley's head and over the first range of hills looms the 2,010-foot peak of Black Jack Mountain, exceeded in height only by the island's Mount Orizaba at 2,125 feet. Lesser peaks, bearing such names as Torquemada, Timms, Dakin, Whittley, and Banning (named for people important to Catalina history), range in height from 1,300 to 1,800 feet. There are about eleven mountain peaks altogether. We say "about" because there are dozens of high land masses that could qualify as mountains elsewhere. The island is really a complete range of mountains, its base in the valleys of the deep. All but the rockiest of peaks and headlands wear a mantle of emerald green grasses in the spring, but the rest of the year the island dresses in tawny burnt ochre, accented by dots of dark, gray-green chaparral: scrub oak, toyon, sage, cactus, Saint Catherine's lace, manzanita, stone crop, and dusty miller, clinging to the coastal bluffs. Some 400 native California plants grow on the island, one of which, the Catalina ironwood, is a living relict of forests that have not existed on the mainland for 20,000 years. The spring-fed canyons are lush with cottonwoods and sycamores and, in the spring, resplendent with a variety of wildflowers. It is the soul-healing balm of an unobstructed geological past and the living presence of descendants of ancient flora and fauna that help make this island so hauntingly beautiful.

We plan to moor here for at least four days, resting while shucking off layers of mainland problems and tensions before beginning our cove-by-cove rounding of the island. After a day or two of doing little more than eating, sleeping, reading, and polishing the tarnished brass of kerosene lamps, clock, and barometer in the cabin, we begin counting the hours on sea time. Sea time is a mysterious phenomenon that transforms hectic, overcrowded mainland hours into long, golden interludes of contentment. Several hours, even a day may pass without conscious awareness of time's passage. This is one of the blessings of the immemorial sea in its calmer moods. Snugged up in a cove, we are content to sit in the cockpit beneath a sun awning and simply observe the marine environment around us. Harbor watching is what we call it, studying anything that moves: curious seals, scurrying anchovies flecking the sea, soaring gulls, clownish brown pelicans plummeting with great splashes after unsuspecting fish, sleek ravens pumping their ebony bodies through the sky, and especially, the arrivals of other boats and the mooring and anchoring techniques used on nearby vessels.

By now the holy calm has possessed us and we are experiencing the strange wonder of this hallowed condition. Canoes paddled by the campers, gliding silently except for a coxswain's infrequent count, become in our imaginations the canoes of the ancient race that lived here. An armada of Spanish ships could ghost into this scarcely wind ruffled bay, and we would readily accept the truth of such a curious illusion. Such visions of the past are not without historical foundation. Our armada is very old, arriving here seventy-eight years before the *Mayflower* landed at Plymouth Rock and only fifty years after Columbus stumbled upon this continent. We see a high-bowed, stern-castled vessel, its square sails and lateen sail aft luffing and ready to furl as the anchor is lowered. She is named the *San Salvador* and is flying the banner of a *capitán general* from her fore-topmast. Also called the *Juan Rodríguez* or *La Capitana* by her men, she is a galleon of 200 tons, about 100 feet in length. The second ship is *La Victoria,* a smaller square-rigged vessel of 100 tons or more, which has decks but is uncastled and miserable to man in heavy weather. The third vessel, *San Miguel,* is a *bergantín* or *fragata,* a small boat or launch propelled by oars or sails, carrying a single mast, a lateen sail, and auxiliary power from thirteen pairs of oars. She serves to ferry parties ashore to fetch water and wood and to scout safe passageways for the larger ships in unfamiliar harbors.

These three vessels constitute the small armada of Juan Rodriguez Cabrillo on its 1542 voyage of exploration under orders from the Viceroy of Spanish Mexico, Antonio Mendoza. In all there are about 250 men aboard these vessels as well as basic provisions for two years, including wine, olive oil, hardtack, beans, salt meat and salt fish, garlic, dried fruit, cheese, live cattle and other live animals, iron work, oakum, and hempen ropes. In addition, the *San Salvador,* owned personally by Juan Rodriguez Cabrillo, carries several pieces of small artillery. The vessels are stocked with *arquebuses* (matchlock guns usually fired from a support) and crossbows, used for close combat at sea and ashore.

The date the armada discovered this uncharted and unnamed island (insofar as the Spanish were concerned) was October 7, 1542. The vessels anchored here for a morning's investigation ashore, then headed across the channel to what is now San Pedro. Juan Rodriguez Cabrillo marked and named this island after his flagship, *San Salvador.* La Victoria is the name he gave the island to the south across the Santa Barbara Passage, the island we know as San Clemente.

Unfortunately, the full, original description of Juan Rodriguez Cabrillo's voyage has been lost for 400 years, if it ever existed at all. However, several versions and attestations with confusing omissions and generalizations have come down to us. They are apparently the only descriptions of the voyage, which was actually a reconnaissance, not a planned voyage of exploration. One translated narrative describes what is almost certainly Juan Rodriguez Cabrillo's landing on Catalina Island:

> … They anchored at one of the islands and went ashore with the boat to see if there were people; and when the boat came near, a great number of Indians emerged from the bushes and grass, shouting, dancing and making signs that they should land. As they saw that the women were fleeing, from the boats they made signs that they should not be afraid. Immediately they were reassured and laid their bows and arrows on the ground and launched in the water a good canoe which held eight or ten Indians, and came to the ships.
>
> They gave them beads and other articles, with which they were pleased, and then they returned. Afterward the Spaniards went ashore, and they, the Indian women, and all felt very secure. Here an old Indian made signs to them that men like the Spaniards, clothed and bearded, were going about on the mainland (Bolton, p. 24).

The old Indian might have been referring to the expedition of Hernando de Alarcon, which was coordinated by sea with Vasquez de Coronado's exploration, ascending the Colorado River in small boats after voyaging up the Gulf of California, now the Sea of Cortes. It may be that the Indian was referring to another branch of Coronado's expedition, one headed by Melchor Diaz. This group marched overland to the Colorado and into the Imperial–Mexicali Valley and might have seen the mountains of California, although they didn't reach them. At any rate, the adventurous Spaniards were very visible, exciting the native people and setting tongues wagging. To Indian eyes these bearded men on horseback must have been as astonishing as a group of Martians would be to us. Word of their presence traveled all the way to the coast where Catalina Indians trading with the mainland exchanged gossip along with their goods.

Juan Rodriguez Cabrillo's armada left no tangible evidence as to where it initially anchored at Catalina, but historians have suggested that it may have been off what are now White's Landing, Avalon, Empire Landing, or the Isthmus. All four had sizable native populations at that time. We happen to favor White's, but who can be sure? At any rate, it is clear that members of the armada came to know Catalina well during the nine months they spent sailing up, down, and around all the offshore islands, exploring everything but sometimes simply seeking shelter from an unexpected, dangerous wind. It may seem odd to contemporary seamen, snugly moored in man-made harbors and marinas, that Cabrillo spent so much time nosing around the offshore islands. The reason was that 450 years ago nearly all anchorages in bays and bights became untenable during times of nasty weather, necessitating a move to a safer anchorage or putting out to sea. An exception was Catalina's natural, all-weather anchorage at Catalina Harbor on the southerly side of the Isthmus or Isthmus Harbor northerly of that low neck of land. While not safe in all weather, Isthmus Harbor was vastly better than most of the other refuges on the Channel Islands and the mainland.

A vessel could ride out winter's storms comfortably in Catalina Harbor and to a lesser degree in one or another of Isthmus Harbor's coves. A true southerly, fortunately rare, was the only real danger in Catalina Harbor. Even a northeasterly blowing over the Isthmus did not create large waves there. The island's present Avalon Cove, open to the northeast, was a good anchorage in southwest and southeast weather and offered passable protection in northwest weather, but could be a deadly anchorage in a northeasterly. (It still is.) The important fact is that 450 years ago and through most of the nineteenth century there were only three protected all-weather natural harbors along the greater portion of the Upper California coast. They were San Diego Bay, Catalina Harbor, and San Francisco Bay.

6 Cabrillo's Grave Mystery

Historian Harry Kelsey told us he regards the Juan Rodriguez Cabrillo "tombstone" as just another incised rock. There have been a number of them found on Santa Rosa Island and sent to him, each with different markings. In fact, we found an obviously manmade, scratched shingle near a rocky outcrop on Catalina's Isthmus Beach and sent it to Kelsey for a paperweight. The small slabs may have originally served as "tally boards" for the Indians or had some sort of ritual significance.   RICHARD AND MARJIE BUFFUM

The controversial JR stone (Juan Rodriguez Cabrillo), found on Santa Rosa Island, was believed to have marked Cabrillo's grave, but now seems doubtful. Later evidence indicates the explorer may have died on Santa Catalina Island.

It seems clear to us that Catalina Harbor was the place where Juan Rodriguez Cabrillo's armada wintered in 1543. On January 3 of that year, Juan Rodriguez Cabrillo died from complications of an injury and was buried by his officers and crewmen near Catalina Harbor. The statement sounds reasonable enough, doesn't it? It is easily understood, but certainly not accepted by all who have puzzled over the mysterious location of the explorer's grave site. Let us navigate cautiously through the shoals of this tantalizing mystery.

Among the places suggested as possible burial sites are Cuyler Harbor on San Miguel Island, Becher's Bay on Santa Rosa Island, and Prisoners' Harbor on Santa Cruz Island. Speculation about Becher's Bay peaked in 1972 when a sandstone artifact, thirteen and one-half inches long by four and one-half inches wide, inscribed with the initials JR, possibly the letter C, a stick figure, and other scratchings, came to the attention of anthropologist Robert F. Heizer at the University of California, Berkeley. The two-inch-thick sandstone piece, unearthed in 1901 on Santa Rosa Island by Philip Mills Jones during archaeological investigations, was, and still is, housed at the Lowie Museum of Anthropology at UC Berkeley. It is believed to have been Cabrillo's grave marker, hastily inscribed by the heavy blade of a seaman's knife, possibly while hostile Indians were held at bay by armada crewmen (see illustrations: Heizer 1972, pp. 60–64).

Curiously, a rocky outcropping at the mouth of a small occupation cave across the ravine from Mills Jones' Santa Rosa campsite has similar incisions on its face, including the stick figure (ibid., p. 63). Could this mark Rodriguez Cabrillo's grave site? A knowledgeable amateur epigrapher, who deciphers ancient inscriptions, thinks so. Wayne Kenaston Jr. of San Diego claimed in an interview that the epigraphs are symbols of "ancient Portuguese" writing giving Cabrillo's name and death date.

Be that as it may, San Miguel Island also has its advocates, who base their conclusions on interpretation (or misinterpretation) of early sailing records and phonetic translations of Chumash place names. There is even a commemorative granite cross on Dead Man's Point above Cuyler Harbor, but it was erected in 1937 by the Cabrillo

Civic Club of California at the behest of Herbert Lester, an early resident of the island. Lester, who called himself the King of San Miguel, sought for years to effect a change of name from San Miguel to Cabrillo Island. A more balanced approach might be that Juan Rodriguez Cabrillo sailed by this island off Point Conception, possibly stepping ashore briefly, but it seems an unlikely refuge for his fleet since Cuyler is open to winter's winds. Even a modern yachtsmen's guide notes that "San Miguel is notorious for its strong NW winds which... can reach 50 knots... [the] weather is unpredictable and dangerous" (Fagan, p. 103). Becher's Bay on Santa Rosa Island or Prisoners' Harbor on Santa Cruz are both north facing and decidedly no improvement as winter refuges.

These considerations cause us to accept the educated opinion of W. Michael Mathes of the University of San Francisco, a leading scholar of early Spanish exploration. Dr. Mathes is convinced that the small, engraved sandstone shingle is the authentic marker of Juan Rodriguez Cabrillo's grave. And Dr. Mathes isn't bothered by the fact that the marker was found on Santa Rosa Island because it could have been taken there from any of the other islands by Indians or even later by white men.

This was also Dr. Heizer's opinion, and he believed it "is highly probable we have here the stone which was carved in 1543 and set over the grave of Cabrillo, the first European to explore the California coast...." Yet he expresses some reservations:

> No scientific tests known to us can throw light upon the age, genuineness, identity of the engraver, identity of the person whose initials are incised, or precise place of origin of the stone or its inscriptions. The geology of San Miguel and Santa Rosa Islands is so similar that the source of the sandstone cannot be proved to be one or the other island, and in any case there was abundant intercourse between the several Channel islands and with the mainland, so that objects of all sorts could have been carried from one island to another. Among these transported pieces could have been the object which I believe may have been the grave marker of Juan Rodriguez Cabrillo, a special object in the eyes of Indians and one endowed with the "ceremonial" aura deriving from its being a relic of the first contact of the Chumash Indians with Europeans.

This brings us to Harry Kelsey, retired chief curator of history for the Los Angeles County Natural History Museum and research fellow at the Huntington Library. Dr. Kelsey, who has delved into unpublished original documents in Guatemala, Mexico, Spain, Portugal, the Netherlands, Austria, England, and the United States, places the explorer's burial on Catalina Island – a historically revolutionary conclusion! The facts are detailed in Kelsey's book, *Juan Rodriguez Cabrillo,* published by the Huntington Library, San Marino, in 1986.

According to the book, sailors Lazaro de Cardenas and Francisco de Vargas, testifying after their return from California, referred to the island of San Salvador (Catalina), calling it the most important island discovered on the expedition and headquarters for the Cabrillo fleet. Vargas and Cardenas testified that the fleet wintered on Catalina, despite resentment of the Spanish presence by the Indians. Vargas recalled that "all the time the armada was in the Isla Capitana the Indians there never stopped fighting us." Around Christmas Eve "the captain sent a party ashore and the Indians attacked," the testimony continued. The soldiers, outnumbered and sorely pressed, called out to the ship for help. Juan Rodriguez Cabrillo, determined to rescue them, quickly gathered a relief party and was rowed ashore.

"As he began to jump out of the boat," said Vargas, "one foot struck a rocky ledge, and he splintered a shinbone." Somehow dragging himself ashore, "the captain general refused to leave the island until all of his men were rescued," Kelsey wrote. The fatal accident might have occurred on rocks at today's Wells Beach, a small bight on the northwest shore of Catalina Harbor, where there was a source of fresh water used by early ships. Kelsey found conflicting evidence as to the nature of Cabrillo's injury. Was it a broken leg, arm, shoulder, or collar bone? Vargas insisted it was a shattered shinbone. "The witness knows this," Vargas testified, "because he was right there."

Juan Rodriguez Cabrillo was taken back aboard ship, where the surgeon tried to treat the wound, but the injury could not be helped with the medical knowledge then available. The wound became morbid, then gangrenous. Nearing death, Cabrillo called in his chief pilot, Bartolome Ferrer, and turned command of the armada over to him. On January 3, 1543, Juan Rodriguez Cabrillo died and was buried on the Isla Capitana (San Salvador). "Because he died here," Cardenas said, "the island retained the name Capitana."

The fleet remained on the island until January 19, attempting to reach the mainland for supplies for a renewed journey to the northwest. Violent winds in the channel prevented the ships from making their way ashore, however, and forced them to return to San Salvador. They sailed around the islands for several days in search of refuge, even stopping in the lee of Santa Cruz, the island they called San Lucas, but stormy seas forced them to slip their anchor cables and run for the open sea. Several times the ships became separated, and each ship's crew thought the other ships were lost. Eventually, after heading northwest again, the fleet, its supplies nearly exhausted, sailed back to Navidad on the coast of Mexico, arriving there April 14, 1543. California and its islands had been discovered and the expedition was a success, for it determined there was no great attraction on the northwest coast at the time, at least in the Spaniards' view.

If Cabrillo had lived to return to New Spain he would have been in serious financial difficulty for although he had amassed considerable wealth in land and mines during his twenty or so years in the New World, much of it was spent provisioning his California armada. Such expeditions were quasi-commercial ventures, similar to other exploratory, trade, and colonizing enterprises of the time. Financial risk was considerable, but the rewards, if realized, could be great.

After the armada's return, California and its southern islands were on the map, but in haphazard and confused form. Juan Rodriguez Cabrillo was essentially a military man, good at giving orders and leading men, but technically unqualified to chart and explore. Subsequent maps derived from the voyage suffered detailed, navigational inaccuracies, according to Dr. Mathes, who doubts that Cabrillo sailed farther up the coast than just above Point Pinos. After studying the welter of post-voyage testimony and supposition, he believes that accounts of Cabrillo's island-hopping are true, but that the place names and locations used are confusing. Above Point Conception matters become surrealistic. Can you believe a 200-mile voyage in one day, probably against the prevailing northwesterlies, in a sailing vessel? Dr. Mathes asked. Of course not. But such a statement is to be found among the remaining "records" of Juan Rodriguez Cabrillo's voyages, he said.

It was Sebastian Vizcaino in 1602 who first accurately put the islands and coast of California on the map, as well as many of the place names still used today. Modern cartographers would be astonished at the relative accuracy of Vizcaino's maps.

7   Strangers over the Horizon

The anchor heaves, the ship swings free, The sails swell full. To sea, to sea!
THOMAS LOVELL BEDDOES (1803–1849), *Sailor's Song*

After Cabrillo's voyage, mysterious strangers from over the horizon became more frequent visitors to the island, although their visits were still uncommon. Evidence of early foreigners on Catalina was unearthed more than a century ago by Charles F. Holder, enthusiastic fisherman and naturalist, during archaeological investigations in various areas of the island. Holder uncovered Italian beads, bell clappers, files, iron mattocks, and copper wire in the Indian graves he searched.

"The iron mattocks were evidently highly valued as they had been carefully wrapped in cloth and buried with their [Indian] owners; the cloth had literally turned to iron," he wrote about an 1887 excavation at the Isthmus (Holder 1910, p. 28). With Mexican Joe (Jose Presiado) and Dr. William Channing of Boston, he trenched through four or five layers of burials. The upper ones contained European artifacts, the lower ones had no metal, "nothing but stone, bone and shell implements, showing that the natives had no bartering with the whites and [that the graves] ante-dated Cabrillo," Holder said.

At least one foreign vessel in dire need, the *San Buenaventura*, a longboat or *viroco*, was aided by Catalina Indians in 1595 after it limped by sea from northern California with only a store of acorns to feed the crew of shipwrecked, stranded Spaniards. Commanded by the Portuguese-born Manila pilot Sebastian Rodriguez Cermenho, the *San Buenaventura* had been assembled at Drake's Bay, above San Francisco, to explore the shore and locate a protected harbor while the galleon *San Augustin* stayed offshore in safer, deep water. But on November 30, 1595, the *San Augustín* blew ashore in a storm and was wrecked east of Point Reyes, losing most of its valuable cargo and all of its provisions.

Cermenho bartered with the local Indians and obtained what food he could, but unfortunately, the food consisted mostly of acorns and acorn mush. By the time the *San Buenaventura* sailed into Catalina waters, the Spaniards were so hungry they killed a dog they had with them and cooked and ate it, even eating its skin. The next day two Indians brought aboard a dozen fish and a seal, for which Cermenho gave them some woolen blankets and some silk, salvaged from the galleon. Cermenho asked them, as well as he could, to bring more food, but when the Indians returned to the ship, they brought nothing to eat. The Spaniards managed to catch about thirty fish, which they cooked and ate before sailing on to San Clemente Island and down the coast, still foraging along the way. Despite the lack of food and water and increased illness of the crew, the little *San Buenaventura* arrived at Navidad on January 7, 1596 — a remarkable voyage for any century!

As mentioned in the last chapter, the most successful voyage of discovery as far as naming and charting the Californias was the 1602 expedition of Sebastian Vizcaino, a moderately successful merchant and explorer already familiar with the galleon route. In 1596 he led an expedition from Acapulco to La Paz, naming the latter for the peaceful Indians encountered there. Returning to New Spain he was ordered by the viceroy to explore the coast from Cape San Lucas to Cape Mendocino, employing two ships of moderate size and a launch that could sail near the coast for close-up observations.

On May 5, 1602, Vizcaino sailed from Acapulco on his flagship, *San Diego,* accompanied by the *Santo Tomas* and the launch, *Tres Reyes.* A lengthy list of sailing instructions had already been given Vizcaino in Acapulco by the viceroy of New Spain, Gaspar de Zuniga y Acevedo, Conde de Monterey. Vizcaino was instructed to proceed directly from Acapulco to Cabo San Lucas, weather permitting, and to sail as close to land as possible, employing the launch to enter bays and rivers from Cabo San Lucas to Cape Mendocino (Mathes, p. 58).

A few of the other instructions were to take solar readings during the day and stellar readings at night; keep a log of directions, time, winds, landmarks, and other such data; note the presence of firewood and ballast stone; take soundings; chart the coast without going inland to arouse the Indians; and call a council of officers when problems arose. This is but a small sample of the instructions, which are detailed in the Mathes book mentioned above.

Aboard the ships were some 200 carefully selected men, sailors and soldiers, most having been enlisted in Mexico City. The Acapulco to San Diego voyage against storms and contrary winds took six months. It is amazing to think of the infinite times these clumsy square-sail vessels were forced to tack and wear around while beating up the coast, due to their lack of maneuverability. My friend, boat designer Lyle Hess, figured out that as these ships zigzagged up the coast on long tacks, they made about one and one-half nautical miles for each six miles they sailed. General comparisons may be made between the sailing ability of the Spanish galleons and the late-eighteenth-century His Majesty's bark *Endeavour,* skippered by Captain James Cook. The square-rigged *Endeavour,* broad of beam and barrel hulled, averaged three knots. She would sail no closer to the wind than eighty degrees and typically wears rather than tacks, thus making leeway every time she turns.

The fleet arrived in San Diego November 10. After staying there ten days to explore, chart, sound, and rest from the exhausting voyage, make repairs to the vessels, and take on fresh water, the fleet set sail, sighting Catalina four days later, on the twenty-fourth. Because it was the day of Saint Catherine, Vizcaino named the island Santa Catalina. He arrived and anchored on November 27, 1602, delayed en route by strong head winds.

Our guess is that Vizcaino's ships initially put down their hooks at what is now White's Landing. You may do your own guessing, for the illustration marked Lamina 29, Isla Catalina (Enrico Martinez, 1603) is the first relatively accurate chart of Catalina ever made. The cartographer, actually a German named Heinrich Martin, who arrived in Mexico in 1589, redrew the map from draft charts made by Vizcaino's on-board first cosmographer, Geronimo Martin Palacios. The little drawings of anchors on the chart indicate places where the fleet anchored. The first anchorage is shown as being near *rancherías,* that is, groups of native huts. Both the Avalon and White's areas had, at the time, large Indian settlements. There is no doubt about the second anchorage: it is Isthmus Harbor, labeled here as "Puerto de Santa Catalina." Modern Catalina Harbor is marked *ensenada,* meaning cove or small bay. The word *pueblo* near the Isthmus translates as a town or village of the natives.

It is interesting to note that little Santa Barbara Island and distant San Nicolas are included on this sheet, as well as an area that appears to encompass San Pedro, Wilmington, and Long Beach, labeled here "Ensenada de S. Andres." Apparently the area was only briefly observed as there is no anchor indicated. The large ovoid black mass east of Point Fermin, labeled "Isla Raza de Buena Gente" (literally "Island of a Race of Good People") is certainly not the former Deadman's Island in San Pedro Bay, for that was much smaller. There was once a large Indian village near San Pedro, and historian Mathes, who obtained this photograph from the original documents of Vizcaino's charts in Seville, feels as we do that the big mass is the illusion of another island that can be seen today by mariners crossing a slightly misty San Pedro Channel. "That other island," as my wife and I call it, has apparently confused mariners for centuries. It is really the Palos Verdes Peninsula. The illusion of "that other island" was even commented upon in the *Coast Survey Directory* of 1858. The writer cautions captains of passing vessels not to mistake the Palos Verdes Peninsula for an island that appears to be projected against the coastal mountains.

Together with his officers and advisors on this important voyage, Vizcaino had along three Carmelite friars, including Father Antonio de Ascension, second cosmographer, whose diary was for many years among the best known of the original

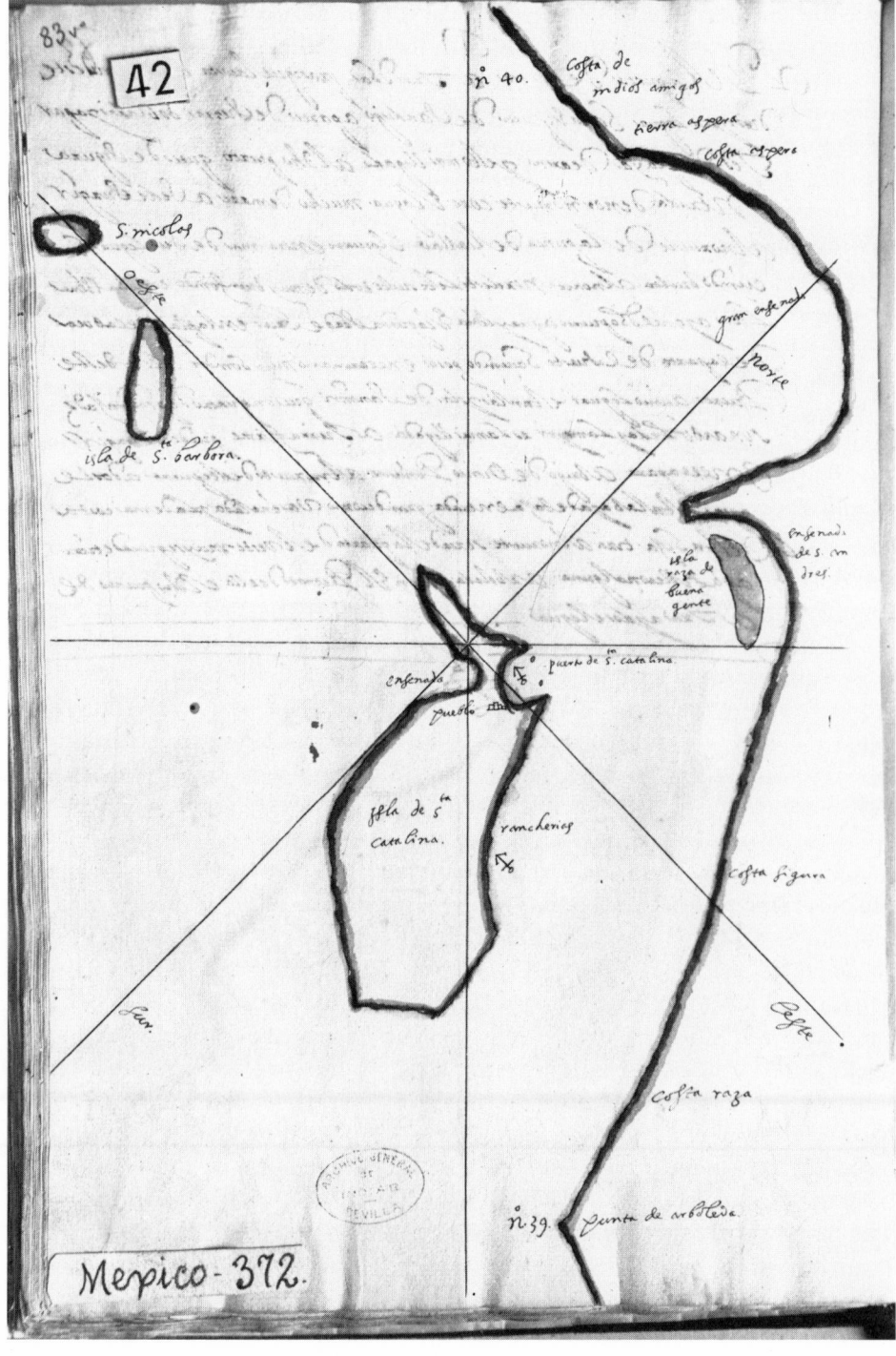

This first chart of Santa Catalina Island was drawn in 1602 by Sebastian Vizcaino's cosmographer. As indicated by the anchors, his galleon put down a hook at what appears to be today's White's Landing, where there was a large Indian population, and at Isthmus Harbor, also with an Indian village or *pueblo*. Vizcaino named the island Santa Catalina. Dr. Michael Mathes photographed the chart at the Archivo General in Seville, Spain.

sources. The following translation from the *Coleccion de Diarios y Relaciones para la Historia de Los Viajes y Descubrimientos*, published by the Instituto Historico de Marina, Madrid, 1944, was done for me by David E. Reyes, a fellow journalist on the *Los Angeles Times*. The paraphrases are mine.

The diarist, Vizcaino, relates that before the flotilla set down anchors "in a good cove" (either Avalon or White's Landing) on November 27, 1602, they were met by "many fine Indians in wooden canoes of cedar and pine. There were about fourteen or fifteen Indians in each canoe and they came close to our ships without fear." The Indians came aboard, after securing their canoes to the vessels, and "they appeared very content at having seen us."

The natives guided the flotilla to the anchorage and, using sign language, invited the Spaniards to their village. Vizcaino or the "general," as was his title, gave the Indian guides gifts, then he and a small party went ashore. On the beach a large number of native men and women greeted the Spaniards "with toasted sardines and toasted fruit, something like *camotes*," a kind of sweet potato. The Indians showed them a fresh water source, although it was far from the beach. This suggests White's, for a spring-fed stream flows down the canyon behind the first range of hills on the west and into White's Valley. There, in heavily wet years, it makes its way to the sea on the western edge of the YMCA (former Girl Scout) camp. Otherwise, in dry or moderately dry years, the stream disappears underground upon reaching the valley.

Vizcaino's men erected a canvas lean-to on the beach the following day and the priests said mass. More than 150 Indians, male and female, attended and "they marveled at the altar and at the image of our Lord Jesus Christ." The diary says the women were dressed in "seal skins" (which may have been sea otter) and "they are very modest and you can see the bashfulness in their faces, and they were thieves (both sexes) because anything they saw, if we were not paying attention, they would take." However, the Indians were said to be a friendly and agreeable people who bartered amicably. Bartering consisted of trading old clothes of the soldiers and crew for seal skins, abalone shells, nets, and cleverly twisted ropes of some natural fiber. The writer adds that the Indians have dogs "like the ones in Castilla," and we cannot help but wonder if these might instead have been domesticated little gray foxes, endemic to several of the Channel Islands. However, both dog and fox bones have been found in archaeological sites.

There was a lunar eclipse, and the following day an east wind came up. On the twenty-ninth, the eve of San Andre's Day, the flotilla weighed anchor and sailed westerly before the wind up the island's coast to a harbor recommended by the Indians. The Indians had said in sign language that "up ahead on the same island there was a good port," and that there were homes there and food to eat. At 4:00 P.M., the flotilla arrived at Isthmus Harbor. "And they guided us with the canoes, entering the port that is all one could wish for as to convenience and security."

There was a town by the beach and more than 300 men, women, and children assembled to greet the Spaniards.

8 Drake on Catalina

When [Sir Francis] *Drake returned to England in 1580 he turned his records over to Queen Elizabeth and they have not been seen since. No one knows what happened to these records . . .*

JUSTIN M. RUHGE, *Drake in Central California 1579,*
Unraveling One of California's Great Historical Mysteries

Having anchored in Isthmus Harbor, Vizcaino and his party went ashore, and the Indians "greeted them with embraces and took them to their homes." The Indian women were pronounced attractive by the diarist. Vizcaino gave them beads, and the women in return gave him cactus fruit, willow baskets filled with a grain "like maize," and fresh water in pliable reed flasks, tarred on the exterior to make them waterproof.

Vizcaino walked across the Isthmus to what is now Catalina Harbor "to see the other side of the coast." On the way "he found a very clean valley," possibly beyond the southeast foot of the hill on which the old Banning house now stands, and he discovered an effigy that was described as "a demon with horns and without a head, a dog at its feet and many children painted around it." The Indians attempted to prevent Vizcaino from stopping but he refused, and fashioning a crude cross from sticks, he scratched the name of Jesus on it and placed it atop the effigy. He informed his hosts that the cross was good and from heaven, but that the idol was a demon. At this the Indians "marveled." (This we interpret as exclamations of polite bewilderment by the natives, for the language barrier, admitted later by the diarist, was certainly profound.) The diarist then unctuously assumed that the Indians would "easily renounce the idol and receive our holy faith."

Another account, by the Franciscan historian Juan de Torquemada, tells how the Spaniards came dangerously close to straining friendly relations with the Indians. It must be explained that Torquemada was not on this voyage; he was a friend of Antonio de la Ascension and later paraphrased his account, stating that some soldiers with crossbows in the Vizcaino shore party shot and killed two plump ravens that were within the circle containing the idol, provoking the Indian guides into loud laments. Ravens, plentiful on the island, were considered sacred by the Indians. Torquemada, however, said he believed "the devil was in these crows and spoke through them." He added that the birds were so tame they would snatch fish from the hands of the women and children, who dared not resent the attack (Holder 1910, p. 18).

Vizcaino was shown two pieces of figured China silk by the Indian women and learned through sign language that the cloth had come from people like him who had Negroes with them and whose ship had foundered in a strong wind and sunk some distance ahead. Vizcaino apparently believed the wreck to be nearby and hoped to be shown the place by the Indian guides, but a heavy fog prevented his search.

There exists evidence that the references to Negroes and figured silk indicate that the ship was one of those sailed up the coast by Sir Francis Drake to about thirty-three degrees north latitude, where the Channel Islands were located on the Spanish maps of the period (Kelsey 1990, p. 454). According to testimony by John Drake, Sir Francis' relative who was on the voyage, one of the ships was the *Pelican,* renamed the *Golden Hind* or *Golden Hinde.* The other was a bark captured off the coast of Nicaragua and later abandoned at Nova Albion," seemingly with the dozen or so crewmen she had on board (ibid., p. 455).

Historian Kelsey conjectured that this abandoned bark may have been the ship Vizcaino heard about at Catalina in 1602. "According to an Indian woman who still had two pieces of 'Chinese damask' given her by one of the men, the ship had run aground and broken up on shore somewhere north of the main village," Kelsey said.

The location of the shipwreck could have been anywhere along Catalina's West End from Eagle Reef to Indian Rock and on to Land's End. There is published conjecture that a Spanish vessel (a Manila galleon) struck a rock and sank westerly of Ship Rock in the late sixteenth century (Winlund, 12th ed., p. M4, and Daily 1990, p. 44). Nevertheless, Vizcaino apparently found no trace of it during the five days he spent on the island. On December 1 his ships left the Isthmus, sailing to San Pedro (San Andres) and then northwesterly up the Santa Barbara Channel past the other Channel Islands. Vizcaino not only named the channel but left in his wake other place names that have remained. They include San Diego, in honor of his flagship; Point Conception (Concepción); Monterey Bay, after Conde de Monterey de Alcala, viceroy of New Spain, the Santa Lucia Mountains, and the Carmelo River.

About forty-two men died from disease, chiefly scurvy, before the ships returned to Acapulco on March 21, 1603, after a harrowing voyage (Griffin, p. 73). This remarkably important voyage of exploration produced a total of thirty-six draft charts, the first of their kind, and sailing directions that for the most part were in use for nearly 200 years.

In summation, historian W. Michael Mathes commented thus:

> A historical figure gains importance not by his actions alone, but by their influence upon history as a whole. Sebastian Vizcaino certainly falls within this category and, relative to early California history, may readily be considered as the founder of the region. While his predecessors gained a limited knowledge of the area, Vizcaino's knowledge of California included both the Gulf and Pacific coasts, as well as the North Pacific Basin.
>
> Furthermore, none of Vizcaino's predecessors urged so strongly the settlement of California, nor contributed more permanently to its cartography. Thus, in importance, Vizcaino ranks with Francisco Vazquez de Coronado

and Juan de Onate in New Mexico, and Hernando de Soto in the Mississippi Valley as one of the great early figures of the northern borderlands of New Spain.

It is a curious quirk of historical myopia that while monuments and parks have been named for his predecessor, Juan Rodriguez Cabrillo, few monuments bear the name of Vizcaino. Almost all the major place names along the California coast were given by him — a fact seldom remembered.

For nearly eighty years after Vizcaino charted the Californias, Spanish mariners were privy to a great amount of navigational information that they had no intention of sharing with other nations, especially the English, their arch rivals during the bloody buccaneering days of the late 1600s. Spanish captains during that period (and later) had orders to jettison all charts and sailing directions if their ships were captured. In 1681, however, *El Santo Rosario* was captured off Peru by an English pirate ship, the *Trinity,* and a "great book full of Sea-Charts and Maps" was taken (Thrower). This book, a Spanish *derrotero,* was of immense value to the English because it contained information the Spanish had kept secret from other nations since the days of Columbus. The secret out, these Spanish charts and sailing instructions, combined with those of the English, were the forebears of those subsequently published for general circulation.

Vizcaino's Monterey, destined to become the capitol of Alta California, languished, virtually not visited by Europeans for more than a century and a half after its discovery. Then on the third day of June, 1770, Monterey's Indian inhabitants gazed in wonder as the galleon *San Antonio* anchored in the bay and as its sailors, together with Spanish soldiers led overland by Don Gaspar de Portola, gathered around an oak tree to participate in the consecration of the second mission in Alta California. The ceremony at the site of San Carlos Borromeo Mission was led by Father Junipero Serra, who only a year before established the first Alta California mission, that of San Diego de Alcala, at San Diego.

Why a geographical leap of 650 miles of untracked terrain within a year? It was made to establish a firm foothold in the huge territory all but ignored by Spain until the threat of occupation by British and Russian fur traders and explorers who were nosing in and out of bays from Alaska to northern California.

Twenty more missions were to follow during a span of fifty-four years. The missions, presidios or forts, and subsequent ranches were the foundation of Alta California's economy, struggling in the beginning but becoming increasingly wealthy as trading vessels and sea otter hunters from several nations invaded the waters of the mainland and the offshore islands.

9 The Wool Boom

To a close shorn sheep, God gives wind by measure
GEORGE HERBERT, *Jacula Prudentum* (1640)

We remain moored off White's Landing longer than planned. Sea time exerted its relaxing effect on our schedule. Why rush to begin our counterclockwise circum-navigation of Catalina's fifty-four miles of coastline? Actually it was an important delay, for there had been explorations ashore in order to verify the validity of some historical occurrences referred to in our onboard notes and reference materials.

Robert L. (Bob) Cranton, once caretaker of a Girl Scout camp here and a former Avalon sheriff's deputy, was graciously cooperative in our historical search. He transported us in his carryall over the island's dusty roads to points of interest. Where we couldn't ride, we hiked with knapsacks carrying sandwiches and water. Bob's wife, Lorraine, who cooked for the camp, favored us with ample portions of a delicious "mud pie cake" she'd created, using eggs from their domesticated ducks. On one hike we startled one of the island's shy tiny foxes. It quickly retreated into the chaparral. On another, a bison rose suddenly from a nearby dust wallow, fright-ening us into a hasty withdrawal.

White's Landing from the sea is a wide sandy beach with a group of small build-ings and tents and a large valley rimmed by several sizable mountains. A pier bisects the beach and extends out over the water with a float at its seaward end during sum-mer. Camp, pier, and small boats on leased property ashore once belonged to the Los Angeles Girl Scout Council, which offered a variety of water-oriented activities, mostly during the summer months.

To our left or east around a protruding rock cliff is a picturesque little cove called Moonstone, with a steep, rocky beach, a couple of buildings tucked among tropical vegetation, and a small pier. This, the island facility of the Newport Harbor Yacht Club, was named for the opaline gemstones that once abounded here. Early tourists transported by Avalon's Meteor Boat Company vessels used to gather the translu-cent stones and take them back to Avalon where, for a small sum, one of the gift shops polished them. Moonstones must have been extremely popular early sou-venirs; we have searched for them in vain.

To our right, the westerly end of White's Landing beach, is a small oasis of palms and picnic tables, the shore facility of the Balboa Yacht Club. It is a truly historic location, an area that once bustled with an extensive mining operation.

Under David M. Renton, general manager for William Wrigley Jr., mining was begun in 1924 high on the slopes of Black Jack Mountain where ore containing galena, lead, and zinc was discovered. A 400-foot-deep vertical shaft was drilled on Black Jack, and a four-mile overhead bucket conveyer system was constructed over the rough terrain to take the ore to a flotation mill built on the beach. Its massive concrete foundations are still visible. A pier served as a shipping point for ore concentrates that were sent to smelters in the San Francisco area and overseas to Belgium. The flotation mill was capable of processing 100 tons of ore a day. To keep it busy, ore from the Renton Mine above Pebbly Beach near Avalon was also barged to White's.

Ore from Black Jack originally assayed at around $450 a ton, but by May 1927, a 50 percent drop in the market price of lead and zinc eliminated the profit from milling raw ore. "It would look to me as if we had better leave our ore where it is until such time as it can be manufactured at a profit," Wrigley wrote to Renton at the time.

Soon the mill and tramways were sold and the mine's surface plant dismantled. Shafts and adit portals were fenced to keep intruders away from dangerous places. Underground workings were flooded and caved in. A walk on the beach today still reveals at the western end the boarded-up entrance to an adit tunnel dug horizontally by two hard rock miners in 1926. The adit penetrates the hill to about 150 feet.

Hunting for moonstones was a popular pastime at Moonstone Cove west of White's Landing.

"All that remains is a memory of a valiant effort during which... 519,412 tons of ore were mined," concluded mining engineer Alan Probert in an article on the mining history of the island in 1984.

One day, while we were weighing anchor in about sixty-five feet of water some thousand feet off the Balboa Yacht Club beach, we discovered a souvenir of that historic mining project. I was working our little hand-operated winch and Marjie was tailing, that is, coiling the retrieved anchor line on deck, when something fouled our anchor. The winch couldn't budge it and the anchor rode went straight down from the bow over the anchor. Finally, after considerable exertion with the winch handle, the mysterious object broke loose and began to rise. What was it, we wondered, as a dim shape appeared below the surface? Perhaps an old Spanish anchor (hopefully) or a piece of an airplane that was said to have crashed in the cove years ago? More pumping on the winch handle ensued, and then the thing hung slightly above water from our bow. Our rode had snagged a rusty old mining cart, resembling a massive wheelbarrow. It was impossible to haul it on board. A helpful harbor patrolman came over in his boat, disentangled our catch and let it plunge back into the deep where it awaits another unlucky mariner.

The name "White's" for this place extends to sometime before 1893, for it is clearly indicated on a map of that date (Doran 1964, Appendix), and C.F. Holder mentions White's Canyon in the 1910 edition of his *Channel Islands of California*. It is believed by some that White's Landing derived its name from mispronunciation of the name of Frank Whittley (or Whitley), a stockman who had buildings and corrals here and on the Isthmus as early as the 1850s. The word "landing" in the place names of the island usually indicates a cove where livestock were landed or taken off.

Another clue to the naming of the cove and valley came from Eloi J. Amar, manager of the Mauer Cattle Company from 1915 to 1953. Amar believed the area was named for a herder, August Blanc (or White), who worked for the Frank Whittley mentioned above, and for George R. Shatto, an early owner of Catalina Island. Amar said that Blanc established his sheep camp in this valley many times during the late 1870s (from oral history by Eloi J. Amar in files of the Santa Catalina Island Company [SCICO], May 1, 1962).

As for Frank Whittley, he was a true sheep baron, a man of power and influence in the nineteenth century, not to be confused with the sometimes reclusive squatters and sheepherders. A handful of sheep and cattle barons, including Leopold Harris, James A. Johnson, John Johnson, Benjamin S. Weston, William S. Howland, Spencer H. Wilson, Walter Vail, and C.W. Gates, dominated about 90 percent of the island from the mid-1800s into the early part of the twentieth century. They operated with valid leases from the island owners. Estimates of the stock population pasturing on the island in the 1860s run as high as 22,000 sheep, 4,220 cattle, and 15,000 goats (Doran 1964, p. 92). Trade in wool, mutton, and goat (goat meat sold during the gold rush was represented as mutton) was the dominant business for many years. Corrals for shearing wool were established at several locations including the Isthmus, Middle Ranch Valley, and Avalon.

The California sheep industry dated back to the Spanish mission days but reached a period of unparalleled prosperity following a disastrous drought in the mid-1860s coupled with a demand for wool created by the Civil War. Cattle, which had earlier grazed on the vast ranches, died by the hundreds during the drought and were replaced by the hardier sheep.

"Wool production rose from 5½ million pounds in 1862 to more than 22 million pounds in 1871," wrote Robert Glass Cleland in *From Wilderness to Empire*. "Profits in the industry were enormous, often running from fifty to a hundred per cent a year; and, like almost everything else in California, sheep farming was carried out on a scale undreamed of in Eastern or Midwestern states."

Sheared wool from Catalina was shipped to a wool depot in Wilmington owned by E.M. McDonald of Wilmington and J.E. Perkins of San Francisco. The depot was a 180-by-40-foot warehouse erected by the government during the Civil War as part of the Drum Barracks complex. It had the capacity to store 2,000 bales of wool. Wool was graded, repackaged, and sold on commission from the depot.

"The enterprise meets with the cordial endorsement and cooperation of the wool growers of this section... This year it is confidently believed that over

Because of close-cropping, the result of overgrazing, sheep were banned on the island during Wrigley's ownership. This scene is at Catalina's Middle Ranch early in the twentieth century.

8,000,000 pounds will be shipped from these two points [Wilmington and Anaheim]," asserted the *Los Angeles Star* of March 28, 1874.

To the right of White's is a rocky point extending into the bay and effectively separating White's from Hen Rock Cove with a rocky shore and protective rocky cliffs. The cove derives its name from a huge angular rock at water's edge, shaped rather like a domestic chicken. It appears particularly hen-like in the raking sunlight of late afternoon. Passing around two dome-shaped, guano-covered rocks and a slide area with thick kelp beds inshore, we come to Button Shell Beach. (We have not found any button shells either). The lessee here is the Glendale Family YMCA, which runs year-round, water-oriented activities for young people and adults, male and female. Next to a steep headland, 545 feet at its highest elevation, are several moorings and anchorage for ten in sand. The headland is Long Point, which marks the widest part of the island, about seven and a half miles shore to shore. A flashing white light, a warning to mariners at night, is mounted on the outermost point at a height of seventy-one feet.

The calming arm of Long Point protects White's area coves from west to northwest winds, and there is good protection from southwesters at Hen Rock and Moonstone Coves. During southeasterly weather, the swell in these areas can make moorings uncomfortable. Small craft are advised to move around Long Point and anchor in quieter coves. As with all the island's northerly facing shores, strong north to northeasterly or Santa Ana winds can be extremely hazardous.

The camp at Button Shell Beach was founded in 1924 by Frank L. Fox of Glendale, who saw its inherent possibilities as a camp site for the Glendale YMCA. He put together a crew to clear the unimproved land and built the foundation of what has been more than three-quarters of a century of island camping, appropriately named Camp Fox. During World War II the facility was used to train Navy Seabees. The camp has had many improvements since its founding and is now attended by 15,000 young people a year, many coming from other southland YMCAs, according to Bob Driffill, chief executive officer of the Glendale YMCA.

On the eastern side of the Long Point headland is a small cove, no more than 200 feet across, known locally as Pirates Cove. It is a favorite locale of skin and scuba divers, including those at Camp Fox, since there is a lush submarine garden growing among the crevices and submerged boulders. A tunnel-like cave extending completely through Long Point just above the shoreline has occasionally been used in television productions. Local legend says that this tunnel, supposedly a result of nature, was a place where ancient pirates hid their loot, and more recently, bootleggers their booze, for its mouth is above the high-tide line and accessible by a short climb. However, an examination of the head of the little cove below the tunnel's mouth reveals the presence of disintegrated concrete footings or piers, offering a clue to both the origin and use of the tunnel.

The mystery was solved for us by the late Joe Guion, longtime island resident, who was born in 1898 in Mt. Vernon, New York, and came to Avalon with his parents about 1912 when he was fourteen years old. The tunnel through Long Point from Pirate's Cove to Italian Gardens was man-made, Guion said, by "a big Irish promoter" named Joseph McAfee, owner of the Catalina Excursion Company in Avalon and a former employee of Baldwin Locomotive Works in Philadelphia. Starting from a natural cave, McAfee had the tunnel blasted through the point for tourists. One of McAfee's several launches brought sightseers from Avalon to a McAfee-built wharf in Pirate's Cove where they disembarked, walked through the tunnel, and emerged on a McAfee-built porch on the westerly side of the point, overlooking Italian Gardens. It was a great place for taking snapshots, Guion said. An early travel brochure, circa 1919, called this a trip to "Neptune's Cave." An oldtimer, Edward T. Rinehart of Avalon, recalled that there was the beginning of a cave here before McAfee improved on nature. According to "If I Were a Fish," an undated pamphlet written by Miles Overholt, there were three caves here: Neptune Cave, the Mermaid's Swimming Pool, and Spook Cave, one leading into the other and each "more weird and beautiful than the other."

One of McAfee's other projects was the first flying fish boat, the original *Catalina Flyer,* a sixty-five-foot square-stern motor vessel that carried about 100 passengers. McAfee got the idea for this popular attraction while out in a boat one night during the period of the Bannings' ownership of the island. Shining a flashlight on the water, he watched the flying fish soar across the water, attracted by the light. The phenomenon became a commercial success for McAfee — for a while. When William Wrigley Jr. became the island's owner, he insisted that McAfee give him

10 percent of the receipts from the *Flyer,* according to Guion. McAfee refused, pointing out that Wrigley didn't own the sea. Wrigley then arranged to have two flying fish boats built, the *Hermosa* and the *Betty O,* and went into competition with McAfee. But the *Catalina Flyer* was faster, outrunning Wrigley's boats to Lover's Cove and other places the flying fish frequented, Guion said. In 1924, Wrigley had the present *Blanche W* built. She was faster than the *Catalina Flyer,* and McAfee threw in the towel.

The *Catalina Flyer* was used during the day for sight-seeing cruises around the island. Guion was her captain for seven years, making about a hundred circumnavigations a year during the busy summer months. Guion's shoreside interests were focused on the Avalon Boat Stand Company, also known as Joe's Rent-A-Boat, which he incorporated in 1927. It was still in business in 2002, operated by his son Jay and headquartered on the Pleasure Pier.

On a recent stag cruise with younger members of our family and a few of their friends on other boats, we witnessed the "herding" of millions of anchovies by a school of voracious barracuda at Pirate's Cove. The anchovies were swimming around in a huge compact ball, and the barracuda, in a feeding frenzy that caused them to strike at any lure we put in the water, would swim rapidly to the edge of the churning mass of anchovies and pick off their quarry. Here we saw the truth of the appellation given to barracuda: "cowboys of the sea." We enjoyed plenty of barracuda filets that evening for dinner.

Between Moonstone and Button Shell Coves, a distance of a little more than a mile, there are about ninety moorings. Outside the mooring areas there is good anchorage in sand in water ranging from 12 to 114 feet deep. A few words may be in order for those not acquainted with the process of picking up an island mooring. First, find the harbor patrolman (look for his patrol boat) for a mooring assignment. Then cruise slowly behind the row of mooring buoys or cans, find the assigned can (they are numbered), and go slowly, bow first, toward the can and halt forward motion so your first mate or friend, who is already on the bow, can quickly pick up the stick (also called a wand) and haul it on board. The skipper then reverses the engine so the boat stops dead in the water. This enables the bow person to haul the attached light line aboard, followed by the heavier line with an eyesplice on the end. The mooring line is then run through a chock on the bow of the boat and cleated.

If conditions (such as adverse currents or strong winds) prevent this process from succeeding, don't allow the first mate to hang onto the wand or line very long. A boat is heavy, and pulling against it may cause muscle strain or, worse, a tumble overboard. It's best to let go of wand and line, wait a few seconds so the boat's propeller doesn't get fouled on the line, then go around and try the whole thing again.

Once the bow line is cleated, the cross line, or sand line, is handed alongside the vessel toward the stern. Haul on this line until another eyesplice of heavy mooring line emerges from the water. Secure the looped line to your stern cleat and you are moored. Sometimes a fore and aft mooring is intended for a vessel that is larger or smaller than yours. In either case, simply secure the sand line to the stern of your boat and don't strain trying to haul in the eyesplice. A vessel secured too snugly fore and aft will surge to and fro in a little swell. Easy does it, with a bit of slack. And don't forget that the tide rises and falls.

All moorings except those controlled by the City of Avalon were patrolled and maintained by Doug Bombard Enterprises (DBE), headquartered at Two Harbors at the Isthmus (as of 1997). Mooring assignments and the collection of fees are handled by harbor patrolmen at each of the coves who will, when necessary, assist with picking up a mooring. Harbor Patrol boats are radio equipped and may be contacted on VHF radio, Channel 9. The same channel is used by shore boats in Avalon Bay and Isthmus area coves. The majority of the moorings, incidentally, are privately owned, originally bought or leased from the City of Avalon or other island entity such as DBE and still maintained by them, although owners pay maintenance charges. Owners have priority on use of their moorings, but must reserve in advance.

We now begin our circumnavigation of Catalina Island. Casting off the mooring lines we wait cautiously while they sink to the bottom, then engage the gear that turns the *Bird*'s propeller. Clearing a propeller fouled by a cross line is an unwelcome underwater chore and an embarrassment to the skipper. I know. We've done it, and that water can be chilly, especially in winter. I carry a dive mask on board for just such emergencies.

10   Mysteries of Origin

Nature is a rag merchant, who works up every shred and ort and end into new creations.

RALPH WALDO EMERSON
The Conduct of Life (1860)

On the other side (western) of Long Point is a coastal indentation less than a thousand feet in length with a broad sandy beach and rocks. This is known as Italian Gardens, after the Italian fishermen who once made abundant hauls of sardines for bait here, although the entire coastline between Long Point and Twin Rocks is generally designated as Italian Gardens. The area nearest Long Point offers fair refuge from the southeasterly swells sometimes caused by hurricanes and storms off Mexico. The bottom here is sandy but kelp strewn, and afternoon chop should be expected. There are no moorings, but there is anchorage for two or three modest vessels in about thirty feet of water.

We now head westerly for Goat Harbor, a desirable shelter during southeasterlies when the White's area is disturbed by high waves and surge. On the way we pass two unnamed small beaches along the stretch east of a large landslide called Devil's

Slide, which reaches a height of 497 feet. At times, large rocks above the slide area hurtle into the sea with a thunderous roar. In calm weather there is fair anchorage off the beaches in sand for half a dozen boats at depths of twenty-seven to ninety feet. Beware of partly submerged rocks that cover and uncover with the tides, and of scattered kelp.

Be aware too of a strong but invisible current that parallels the shore. Unaware that it existed, we once anchored here and swam ashore to beachcomb. After a short rest I decided to swim back to the boat alone, leaving Marjie ashore to enjoy the sun. It was a foolish thing to do. The current caught me, my strength quickly waned, and although I nearly reached the *Bird*'s stern, I couldn't make it. The current started to carry me down the coast while Marjie watched helplessly from shore. Fortunately some recreational divers passing by in a big inflatable noticed our predicament, motored over and pulled me on board, then fetched Marjie from the beach and took us out to the *Bird*. They continued on their way, and we learned an important lesson: bathers in unfamiliar water should travel as a team with one rowing a hard dinghy or inflatable. We will always be grateful to those strangers.

Past the slide are the aptly named Twin Rocks, and just beyond them a bay, about 500 yards wide with two beaches, the whole a place of beauty with the name of Goat Harbor. There are no moorings, but there is good anchorage for five to ten boats in five to forty feet on sand. The area is largely unprotected from northwest winds, and one should take care that anchors are not resting on kelp, which can cause them to drag.

The larger of the beaches, to the left or east, is spaciously sandy, with a spectacular view up a canyon accented by peaks and trees, reminiscent of a mountain landscape. On the heights, adjacent to a craggy peak, are a few stands of Catalina ironwood, now an endangered species. Around the turn of the last century this beach was a favorite landing place for wild goat hunters. A steep trail up the valley and across to middle ranch began here, and building materials for the ranch and Eagles Nest Lodge were landed and packed across the hills on burros.

The rocky beach to the west, covered at high tide, gives way to a steep, mountainous slope, peaking at about a thousand feet. Until recently it was the locale of a dramatic sight: the descent of the feral goats. In late afternoon dozens of these wild creatures used to appear at the top, then slide and sidestep their way to the bottom like a living avalanche, raising a cloud of dust. The purpose of their breathtaking descent seemed to be to lick salt from the rocks and loose kelp on shore. Thus, Goat Harbor was well named at some long-ago time.

Although Terrence Martin noted that every living thing on the island had to have been transported here at some time and in some way, history fails to reveal the arrival of the first goats. They probably arrived by ship and were brought by Spaniards, but whether they came with early explorers, with later traders, or even with the ecclesiastics intending to convert the natives, we don't know. It has been suggested that the goats arrived accidentally as a result of a shipwreck, but they may have been put ashore intentionally by a ship wanting fresh meat when it returned to the island after a voyage of exploration or trade. We know that nutritional disease was common among mariners before refrigeration, and as a possible preventive, early ships carried live domestic goats as part of their provisions. They released a few at nearly every oceanic island they visited, relying on goats' frequent breeding periods to develop large herds. At the time, of course, nobody was concerned about their destructive grazing habits, anymore than they worried about similar habits of sheep generations later.

Casual and then organized hunting helped control the burgeoning goat population. In fact, goat hunting was a popular pastime a century ago when a Banning Company advertisement in the *Los Angeles Times* offered Catalina's "wild goat shooting," fishing, and the "phenomenal stage ride." Earlier, during the gold rush, commercial hunters shipped wild goat meat to San Francisco.

For many years Catalina mariners, sipping their end-of-the-day libations, enjoyed the sight and sound of the goats, often watching them on the hills above the coves through binoculars. Yet in the early 1990s, people became aware that something wasn't fully what it used to be, namely the ubiquitous bleating of the goats, the sight of their astonishing agility on the perilous slopes, the plaintive cries of the kids for their mothers. The island's goat herds, present for more than a century, have been reduced annually since 1989 by gunshot from helicopters or rounded up and shipped to the mainland as part of an ongoing effort of the Catalina Conservancy to restore the island's once abundant population of endemic plants. There are, however, a few goats left on the island that have escaped this fate.

Lamentable as the reduction of goat herds may seem, it must be understood that they, along with their former grazing partners, sheep and wild pigs (the bulk of the latter brought from Santa Cruz Island to help control rattlesnakes), did, over the years, severely damage the native flora. Even Catalina's famous bison herds have been reduced to what is hoped to be a "manageable" size, excess animals being rounded up from time to time and shipped to the mainland.

In a small way we were party to the liberation of another species on the island during a spring cruise several years ago. When we were about ten miles from the mainland, a little yellow and gray speck of a bird appeared out of nowhere and circled above the *Herald Bird.* It seemed to want to come aboard to rest, but was undecided whether it was safe to do so. Exhaustion finally overcame the tiny creature, which we named Daisy, and it came to rest on our foredeck. Daisy was so tired I was able to catch her, and she cuddled in the warmth of my hand. Moments later a companion of the same species fluttered aboard. It was stronger and seemed more masculine so we named it Irving. We had no idea what kind of birds they were, but they didn't seem to be seabirds. We offered them bread crumbs and water, and soon they became bold enough to explore the cabin, fluttering about and finally coming to roost for a much-needed rest. Daisy chose the edge of a basket on a shelf and tucked her head beneath a wing. Irving, head erect, perched on a string hammock in which we stow clothes.

Having rested, Irving became sociable, fearlessly perching on our shoulders and heads and hopping inquisitively about the cockpit. When we neared the island, Irving suddenly flew off toward the land, but the trauma of being lost at sea was fatal for Daisy. She didn't wake up. We later learned from a local ornithologist that these tiny, canary-like creatures were called Wilson's warblers and were tragically off course during their annual migration from South America to nest in the Pacific Coast foothills. We also learned that it is not uncommon for land birds, whether lost at sea or blown off course by storms, to take refuge on passing vessels.

Speculation about the arrival of rattlesnakes on Catalina, perhaps eons ago, suggests that they were early, perhaps reluctant, "mariners," transported on fallen trees on which they had slithered to escape a storm-swollen river. A strong wind, perhaps a Santa Ana, blew their "vessel" across the channel.

Mysteries of island origins abound. Catalina's tiny gray fox, the largest weighing only about five pounds, is another enigma. These beautiful little creatures number about 750, according to Terrence Martin, who made a study of them several years ago. They are also found on San Clemente, Santa Cruz, and San Miguel Islands, which may offer a clue to their origin. About 20,000 years ago, these volcanically created islands are purported to have been a long mountain range extending offshore from Point Conception and forming an arm that protected an inland sea. It is believed that normal-sized gray foxes wandered over to this mountainous peninsula and, as the sea became deeper at the end of the Ice Age, were stranded on the islands that had become separated by the rising water. Over time, due to inbreeding and natural selection, the island foxes became smaller and smaller as they adapted to their limited environment and forage.

Now imagine, if you will, early men from Catalina Island, exploring and trading from their canoes as was their custom. Catalina, being geologically unique, had no little foxes, but the Catalina natives saw foxes on the other islands and thought they were adorable little things, especially the tiny pups, which could easily be tamed. The Indians thought they would make nice pets, perhaps companions for their children, so they made a trade for a few of them and paddled them home to Catalina. None of this can be proved, of course, but there is a poetic ring of truth to the theory. After all, bringing a baby animal home for a pet is a very human thing to do, and obviously early men were as human as we are.

An amusing story about Catalina's little foxes was related by Charles F. Holder in 1910. The story concerned a man who caught foxes, cut the tails off, and then released the animals. "Whether he expected [the tails] would grow again I do not recall," Holder wrote, "but he secured a large number of brushes in this altogether savage way. In time a guileless naturalist came to Catalina, so the story goes, and began trapping foxes. One or two without tails was mere chance, but several foxes without tails meant something; and it is said that the tail-less fox of Catalina Island was described as a distinct species."

As for the island's deer, its wild burros, its white-footed and harvest mice, its squirrels, quail, partridge, and other birds, animals, and insects, we shall not attempt to solve the mysteries of their origins over the past millenniums. At least we know how, where, and when one little Wilson's warbler got to the island.

11   Here Looms Gibraltar

*The moon governs everything, the fish, the whale, the crops, the tide —
even women. Everything!*   ATHNEAL OLLIVIERRE,
from Horace Beck's *Folklore and the Sea* (1973)

It's a short cruise, slightly over a half mile westerly, to the looming bulk of Little Gibraltar, a great rock 270 feet high from its base in the sea, resembling its namesake in the Mediterranean. A sandy beach about 600 feet long extends eastward from the rock. For some reason unknown to us, the area is named Cabrillo Beach. Is this another legendary landing place of the Spanish explorer, another enigma of this island of ancient mysteries?

In the prevailing winds from west or northwest this is an excellent anchorage. The bottom is sand, affording good holding, and the water sufficiently deep immediately off the beach so that a stern anchor can be embedded on the beach while the bow anchor rests in thirty to fifty feet of water. There are no moorings, but there is room enough for about five boats at anchor, fore and aft. If possible, anchor several yards off the beach, close to a small rock outcropping next to Gibraltar. This position gives the best protection from WNW winds. In fact, during the slightest breeze from this direction, one can clearly observe an unruffled arc of water, smooth as a mill pond, reaching from the end of Gibraltar. This is an agreeable place to hole up in for a day or two, surrounded by the holiness of all that is natural: the soft radiance of the night sky as one stands on deck before cuddling into an early bunk; the great ancient rocks, their bases purling in the wash of the restless sea; wild calls of seabirds and the huff of a seal as it surfaces.

"There, on the sea, is a man nearest his own making, and in communion with that which he came, and to which he shall return," Hilaire Belloc wrote in the 1920s while cruising aboard his beloved *Nona*. "For the wise men of very long ago have said, and it is true, that out of the salt water all things came. The sea is the matrix of creation and we have the memory of it in our blood."

The cabin of a boat, especially that of a fairly deep-draft sailboat such as the *Bird,* is like a womb, a cozy, protected enclosure to which a person can retreat in peace. My wife and I cherish our evenings in this small cabin where oil lamps glow softly, a little kerosene stove warms deliciously, and the ship's clock on the bulkhead chimes away at half-hour intervals, no longer a tyrannical sentinel commanding us to punctuality, but an accompaniment, only half heard, to the song of the eternal sea.

And, of course, there are the tides. Anyone who has spent much time on the sea knows that the average interval between high tides is about twelve hours and twenty-five minutes. The level of the water mass is nearly always rising or falling, as if the plug was pulled periodically in a gigantic bathtub and then, after a decent time, the water was pumped back in again. The scientific explanation of what causes the tides is even more wonderful than that. The tides, they say, are caused by the gravitational effect of the moon and sun and, to a slight degree, other planets and stars. The surface of the sea's individual particles, it is said, respond to this gravitational attraction. Now, how any mortal figured out such an explanation is quite beyond our comprehension. The bathtub interpretation we can understand — but the idea of this vast conglomeration of particles on the sea's surface, each a mere droplet of water, responding individually, yet in unison, like iron filings, to the bidding of the magnet of the infinite universe fills us with awe. We do not understand it; we cannot get our puny intellect around it. Can any man honestly claim to really understand this great mystery? It is celestial poetry beyond belief.

Now, consider the surge. It may be related to tides but we cannot find much scientific explanation of its cause. There are instances when it is kicked up by a faraway Mexican hurricane, proclaiming its presence with swells from the southeast and roiling many north-facing coves. In such cases, the surge lasts for several days. But the surge that deeply puzzles us is the sudden one of short duration. The boat is lying in a protected cove and the water is sleeping peacefully, that is, rising and falling gently like the bosom of a slumbering maiden. Then all at once the water begins to move in a billowing or swelling manner, as though it had a nightmare. One wave follows another for minutes, then they stop as suddenly as they began.

Early one morning before sunrise, I experienced one of these mysterious surges. Sleep had left me so I crept up on deck to have a smoke and look around while Marjie slept. The *Bird* was rising and falling gently. Anchor lights on other boats were almost motionless. Then suddenly, the surge came, rocking the *Bird* roughly from side to side. There was no explanation for it. In vain I strained my eyes toward the dark horizon to see if there were signs of a passing vessel, of anything that might have caused the motion. But there was nothing. The surge continued for perhaps four minutes, one wave following another with sharp regularity, the anchor lights dancing erratically. Then it subsided. We have experienced other short surges like this from time to time, and wondered what caused them. Do passing comets briefly interrupt the tidal schedules by rousing the droplets? The idea may be farfetched, yet unexplained phenomena abound in the universe.

The time at anchor during the day is convenient for observing rituals. Over the years, certain ways of doing things on board have become pleasant, but strict, rituals, and "my way" has become cast in a rigid mold. Everything on our boat must be in its place and arranged in a certain way: the bow anchor must be stowed thusly; the canvas awning must be put up thusly (even to the kind of knots used to secure it); the halyards must be coiled and hung onto the horns of the cleats on the mast just so. If a well-meaning guest on board does one of these things in another way, I am disturbed until I can unobtrusively do it over "my way."

To take such matters a little further, I am uncomfortable unless all loose lines are tied off neatly. During boot training at the island's Isthmus during World War II, our Coast Guard instructors impressed upon us apprentice seamen that we must never leave any sloppy "Irish pennants" dangling about. I hope this racial slur about a people who historically are excellent sailors has been dropped by now. Alas, this derogatory reference to the Irish has remained with me for half a century. Such is the power of early prejudicial conditioning.

Having unburdened myself of these musings, which seem appropriate to this placid anchorage, we prepare to weigh anchor and motor on to Ripper's Cove, earlier known as Pot Hole Harbor, a distance of less than a mile and a half. The origin of the name Ripper's Cove is another of the island's mysteries. We know only that there is ancient treasure to be found here inland from the reef that separates Ripper's from Empire Landing to the west. The treasure lies in the Valley of the Ollas (pronounced oy-yahs). The area inland has also been referred to as Potts Valley, and indeed, pots of all sizes were quarried here by the ancient Indians. As Blanche Luella Trask, an early islander, wrote in 1906: "There are tiny pots small enough to have been used as a child's bowl and others too heavy for a white man to lift!"

A double bowl, six inches long and carved from steatite, forms one of the domestic utensils of the Catalina Indians.

The pots, made of naturally occurring steatite or soapstone, were an important commodity for the island Indians, as was the unshaped raw material. Both were traded between the islands and with Indians on the mainland. The stone was easily worked and favored for cooking as it could be heated over fire without breaking and was a good conductor of heat. It was carved by early artisans into pipes, beads, ceremonial bowls, arrow shaft straighteners, flat rectangular plates with a hole in one end called plaques, and charming small effigies of canoes, birds, and sea mammals. The latter are thought to have had religious significance and to have been used by shamans as charms or ornaments of power.

To make an *olla*, the craftsman shaped an exterior form while leaving a base attached to the bedrock. The olla was then cut free at the base and removed so the interior could be hollowed out and the exterior smoothed. Sometimes the rim was decorated with incised designs or shells inlaid in asphalt. The Indians' tools included hard slate chisels, hafted stone hammers, quartzite picks, and scrapers. Paul Schumacher, who was commissioned by the U.S. Government and sent huge collections of artifacts to the Smithsonian Institution and Peabody Museum in the 1870s, counted around 300 steatite quarry pits on Catalina, some as much as fifteen feet in diameter and five feet deep. The Valley of the Ollas is the largest of all. Parenthetically, similar quarrying and manufacturing techniques are said to have been used by the Scandinavians of Norway and Sweden during the Viking period.

As the circles indicate, this site in the Valley of Ollas, inland from Empire Landing, was a major production site for steatite cooking pots.

There is an anchorage at Ripper's for some ten vessels of moderate size using fore and aft anchors in sand in nineteen to thirty feet of water. Here, with the Valley of the Ollas ascending inland, we meditate on the ancient inhabitants of this island. Once a proud, self-sufficient people, they began to suffer from introduced European diseases during the first quarter of the nineteenth century. At the same time, their economic base of trade with items manufactured from steatite began to erode. Many of those who survived these twin blows to their society gravitated voluntarily to San Gabriel Mission in search of security. Here they were joined by Indians of the coastal region of what is now Los Angeles County. Santa Barbara Mission received its share of neophytes from the northerly Channel Islands and the surrounding mainland, and San Juan Capistrano Mission attracted the Indians of San Clemente Island and perhaps some from Catalina.

The Indians were given religious instruction and introduced to new trades, such as carpentry, stone masonry, and agriculture. Although they arrived freely, once they were baptized they were no longer free to renounce their conversion nor were they permitted to return to their homes. Instead they were required to live the rest of their lives at the missions, and if they tried to escape, they were forcibly returned (McCawley). Because of their presence at San Gabriel Mission, these Indians became known as Gabrielinos. The Gabrielinos shared a common linguistic heritage. It was Shoshonean or Takic. The Catalina Islanders spoke the language of the

San Gabriel Mission figured prominently in Catalina's history for many years. This is the mission as it appeared in an 1832 painting by Ferdinand Deppe. Note the Indian house at right.

Takic family of Uto-Aztecan stock, and were closely related to the mainland Gabrielino or Tongva people. But they were unrelated to the Chumash, the native occupants of the northern Channel Islands and coastal mainland from Malibu to San Luis Obispo.

The Chumash belonged to the Hokan language family. The name Chumash derives from the word *Michumash,* a name given to Santa Cruz islanders by those on the mainland. Its meaning has been guessed at as "those who make shell bead money" from the word *alchum,* meaning money. The Chumash name for Catalina was *huya.* Significantly, it meant "steatite," attesting to the importance of the island's soapstone and soapstone products to the early native cultures of southern California (from an interview with Janice Timbrook, a senior associate curator of anthropology at the Santa Barbara Museum of Natural History).

As already mentioned, the Gabrielinos and the Chumash were seagoing people. Their skills as boatmen as well as their boats were admired by the European explorers, who noted that the Indians had developed sophisticated boat building techniques. So before moving on to Empire Landing, we'll examine in depth their unique wood-planked canoe. *Tomol* is the correct name of a plank or strake canoe in the Chumash language, but not in the speech of the Catalina Islanders. For them *ti'at* is the word that has been recorded for the planked canoe in the Takic language, according to anthropologist Timbrook.

12　Brotherhood-of-the-Canoe

Favorable geography, climate and abundant nature made living conditions in what is now Southern California as attractive to prehistoric Americans as it is to today's inhabitants.

CARL S. DENTZEL, Director, Southwest Museum (1962)

At its peak, the native population of Catalina Island probably numbered about 2,500 men, women, and children. Unfortunately, baptismal records from the San Gabriel Mission offer scant evidence of Catalina place names in the Takic language. However, *Pimu 'nga,* one of several versions of the word, has come down to us as the native name for Catalina Island. A Catalina Indian would have been known as a *Pimuvit,* old Gabrielinos agreed when interviewed early in the twentieth century, but the name somehow evolved into the Spanish *Pipimares* or *Pipamares,* perhaps a descriptive reference to the fact that they smoked pipes (*pipas* in Spanish) and went to sea (*mar* in Spanish).

The Pimuvits or Pimu were both feared and revered by mainland Gabrielinos, according to historians and anthropologists. Mainlanders "found something uncanny, even sinister, in the isolation granted their tribesmen by the rough water of the channel. Although brisk trading went on between them, and the mainland had learned from the religious genius of the men of Santa Catalina many elements of their vigorous *Chungichnish* cult, it was whispered that while the shamans of the mainland might kill their enemies with poison, those of the islands were fierce wizards who used wolves to carry out their lethal designs," reported Bernice Eastman Johnston in *California's Gabrielino Indians,* a publication of the Southwest Museum. Furthermore, the Pimuvit "knew better" than those on the mainland and could "prophesy truly." It was even believed that the islanders lived two or three hundred years and were so strong they could bend trees.

The Spanish explorers admired the Indians' skill as fishermen and marveled at their remarkable planked canoes. The Indians caught sea lions and large fish with bone harpoons lashed to willow rods and fished from their boats using finely wrought abalone shell hooks and bone gorges on tightly twisted lines of bull kelp and fibrous plants. Fish nets were also used, tied of the same materials.

Although the art and craft of tomol construction seems to have reached its peak in the Chumash area of Santa Barbara and Ventura, there was clearly a cultural exchange between the Chumash and the so-called Gabrielinos of the islands, the only tribes in California that had planked canoes. The tomol may have evolved from the dugout canoe, made from a single large log, but seems to have had no exact counterpart anywhere in the world. In a nonderogatory sense the tomol was a patchwork vessel, constructed of many short planks, usually of redwood or pine which had drifted down the coast on the heaving breasts of northwesterly storms. The only large wide board was used for the bottom of the tomol. Building a tomol, which took about fifty days, required sophisticated craftsmanship and a high degree of skill, especially with the simple stone and bone tools employed (Hudson, Timbrook, and Rempe 1978).

The building method was similar to today's construction of plywood boats over removable molds. For the tomol, logs were split into planks or strakes with bone antlers, then worked with hand adzes of hafted clam shells, requiring frequent sharpening. Stone scrapers served as planes and were used to bevel lateral edges of planks and ends of shorter planks before fitting, tarring, and lashing. To bend boards, the Indians dug a pit, waterproofed it with fire-hardened clay, filled it with water, and then brought the water to a boil with heated rocks. Sometimes wood was buried in wet sand with live coals and hot rocks in the hole. When the planks were heated they were either bent around a form until they cooled and dried or were forced into position on the hull against an improvised half mold. The planks were then lashed in place over the single plank bottom and tarred. Stone drills were employed to pierce the planks so that strong cords of vegetable fiber, two- or three-ply, could lash the strakes at prow and stern. When completely dry, tarred, and lashed, the boat was turned upside down, and caulking of dry tule hearts was forced into its seams with a wood or stone caulking chisel.

For finishing, tar or asphaltum was heated to boiling in an olla, then brushed into the seams. Fastening pegs, a kind of trunnel, were also employed. Interior gunwale battens to strengthen the hull and retain its shape were pegged into place, and a crosspiece was set in amidships. The completed tomol was scraped with abalone shells, smoothed with pieces of dried sharkskin, then painted with a mixture of hot tar, pine pitch, and red ochre or hematite. The tar or asphaltum used for tomol building was not the soft variety often washed up on beaches but was a harder variety, dug or mined on the mainland. Hard tar such as that still exists in a deposit near Santa Paula, on the road to Ojai. It was a valuable commodity for early seagoing people, being formed into cakes and sold or traded among the channel villages. It was also taken to the islands, where none existed, and exchanged for steatite or otter skins. In addition to boatbuilding, tar was used for waterproofing baskets and as an all-around adhesive.

Decorations on a tomol's bow and stem posts as well as the vessel's traditional four "ears" were often inlaid with pieces of abalone shell. "Ears," made of board, were added to dress up the top edge of the gunwale and so that the tomol could cut through the waves well. Viewed from above, they resembled the tails of fish.

The strengthening cross member amidships is said to have had a hole in it to accommodate a compass stone, with a sundial-like vertical stick. Some anthropologists discount the use and practicality of a compass stone in southern California, even though Chumash interviews attested to its use. Doubters claim that a compass stone would only be useful on sunny days when Indian paddlers could steer for clearly visible landmarks, but this is not necessarily true. Even today when there is full sunshine in midchannel, the islands and mainland can be shrouded in mist. A compass is very useful on such occasions. The compass stone, according to Chumash interviewees, was a round rock, painted red. Painted lines, approximating the top northern half of a rude compass, radiated from the center of an east-west baseline. The southern half of the rock was not painted. A nine-inch-long stick, inserted in a hole in the center of the rock, cast a shadow in relation to the sun. Obviously, directional calculations had to be made from time to time in relation to the sun's passage, and native knowledge of ocean currents and wind direction entered the calculations.

Care was taken to make tomol passages during the windless, early morning hours. Experienced paddlers using double-bladed paddles could make from five to seven knots, which would take them across the San Pedro Channel in about five hours. To establish paddling rhythm, they sang or chanted. It is unrecorded how far back in history these remarkable vessels go, but Cabrillo noted them as early as the sixteenth century.

Indians of the Channel Islands and nearby mainland coast seem to have coexisted peaceably for millennia before the arrival of the white man. They shared resources, had a simple system of trade or barter, lived in comfortable thatched homes with pole or whalebone frames, sang, danced, made music with simple instruments, and enjoyed an abundance of readily available food. Their religion was complex and animistic, relating people to the natural world about them. These Indians had no agriculture, and did not raise domestic animals. They had no need of either, since there were abundant natural resources. They bathed in salt water, and in fresh when it was available, using certain herbs as soap. Their villages had ceremonial areas, living areas, and other areas set aside as graveyards.

Not much is known about the political systems of early coastal and island Indians, except for a group called Brotherhood-of-the-Canoe. This possibly unique group united all people associated with canoes, regardless of tribe or village, and members pledged to help each other whenever necessary. Members of the Brotherhood were among the elite in California Indian society, often being accepted as part of a chief's extended family. One of the Brotherhood's most important functions was that of transporting natural and manufactured goods between the islands and mainland and overseeing their exchange. The Brotherhood appears to have had a monopoly on sea trade, at least until the white traders arrived. And even then, in the early years of Spanish and Yankee traders, otter skins were often obtained in trade from the seagoing Indians.

A connection can be made between the ultimate demise of the sea otter and the Indians. Captain Jonathan Winship Jr., of the O'Cain, trader and otter hunter, will serve here as a convenient historical example of the defeat of the native population. In 1806, Captain Winship's 280-ton O'Cain out of Boston, plying Pacific waters as far north as Alaska, had aboard 100 Kodiak hunters and 50 bidarkas, the hunters' skin-covered canoes. "Working in cooperation with the Russian American Company which furnished the skilled native hunters in return for half the skins taken, Captain Winship was leaving parties of Aleuts at various points along the coast, and would pick them up later together with the skins they might have taken," wrote the late maritime historian John Kemble, a professor at Pomona College, Claremont, California. The Aleuts were reputed to be a fierce lot who murdered and carried diseases to the more peaceful island Indians. There is a story that the Aleuts almost wiped out the native population of San Nicolas Island in the early 1830s. Otter-hunting Aleuts took possession of the women of the island and killed every man and male child (Thompson and West, p. 91).

Similar fateful forces seem to have been at work on Catalina in the early 1800s. Something terribly frightening prompted the island Indians to forsake their ancestral home in the sea for the constraints of mission existence on the mainland although only a few of the once large Catalina population made their way to San Gabriel Mission. Disease claimed the island Indians, but they could not grasp what was happening to them and blamed strange, malevolent spirits which could not be appeased. The promise of Catholic salvation appeared to offer protection from a disaster they could not comprehend.

In the end, they were a doomed people. The Catalina Gabrielino "no longer seemed, to their equally diminished tribesmen of the mainland, the fierce wizards who had once fared across the rough channel waters from the mysterious stronghold of their island home," Bernice Eastman Johnston wrote. "They were mild, quiet and aloof, and quite soon they disappeared [almost] entirely... as they had some years earlier from their beloved 'mountains which are in the sea.'"

A story recorded by anthropologist John P. Harrington relates that an old Chumash in Santa Barbara told his fellows: "Everything we have has been taken away from us. We have lost our rights in this land. I will go where you will never see me again. I am going, for all is gone, and I do not want to stay and see you suffer. I go."

And he went to sea in his little tomol and was never seen again.

13 Empire Builders

At the north end of our old house, my grandfather's house in Wilmington, Father,
for the fun of it, built a beautiful bar with columns of different colored marble.
Later on, when the city took over grandfather's house in Wilmington for
Banning Park, they moved the bar down to the Episcopal Church and made
the altar out of it.   HANCOCK BANNING JR., 1970, speaking of
serpentine marble quarried at Empire Landing

At Empire Landing there is anchorage for about twenty vessels in 24 to 108 feet of
water on a sandy bottom. As usual, mind the kelp, and be aware of the island's prevailing west-northwest winds and those from the north. They can turn the area into
a cool and lumpy anchorage in the afternoon.

Empire Landing was named for Walter L. Vail's great Empire Ranch near Tucson,
Arizona, and was part of a large spread (most of Catalina Island) used by Vail and his
partner, stockman Carroll W. Gates, to range cattle during the last part of the nineteenth century. Exactly when Vail and Gates initially brought livestock to the island
is unclear, but in 1891 Gates was secretary to the Empire Land and Cattle Company,
and in 1894 the partners had a contract with the island's owners, William, Joseph
Brent (J.B.), and Hancock Banning to "lease the whole of Catalina Island" except for
certain portions "for the purpose of pasturage." The annual rent of $2,000 entitled
Vail and Gates to run stock over 95 percent of the island's 45,820 acres.

The contract exempted 2,233 acres, more or less, from the grazing rights. The
exemptions were in parcels, mostly touching beaches, including White's Landing,
Johnson's Landing, Cherry Valley, Isthmus Cove, Swain's Landing (Toyon), Little
Harbor, Avalon, and Piedracitas (Pebbly Beach). Also exempted were 200 acres of
cove and canyon at Gallagher Beach, which had been set aside by the Bannings for a
partridge shelter. The Bannings issued permits to hunt on the island and, according
to the lease, were "stocking it with deer, grouse and other game birds and animals."

The contract gave Vail and Gates the right to drive their stock into seven existing corrals in various parts of the island and to a "convenient shipping point on the
beach, together with the right to use said corrals and beach for shipping purposes
and for handling and shearing said stock." Prior to the lease, dated June 20, 1894,
there had been growing discord between the Bannings' successful resort operation
and frequent incursions of livestock. There had also been problems with diverting
water for livestock, the erection of fences and corrals and the proximity of recreational hunters to the livestock. The lease was drawn up to spell out the rights of all
parties.

Vail began the original Empire Ranch in 1876 southeast of Tucson, Arizona, on
part of a small Spanish land grant. Originally a 160-acre "mescal ranch," it was ulti-

mately expanded to more than a thousand square miles, one of the largest cattle enterprises in Arizona's history. Walter Vail's first two partners, Herbert R. Hislop and John N. Harvey, were young Englishmen of good family, who soon tired of the wild west and the cattle industry. In 1879, Edward L. Vail joined his brother in the Empire business. By 1880 the Vails had more than 5,000 cattle on Arizona's Empire Ranch. They branched out into mining and continued to add neighboring ranches to their own.

But by 1890, the cattle industry in Arizona was facing a day of reckoning. Many cattlemen had overstocked their ranches when economic and range conditions were favorable, and this in time led to gradual deterioration of Arizona's virgin rangelands. When the rains refused to come in the early nineties, many ranchers suffered severe losses. In 1890 the railroads contributed to the disaster by raising rates. The cost of shipping to eastern markets threatened to bankrupt the shipper.

According to a 1982 book published by the University of Oklahoma Press (Sonnichsen), "Walter and Ed Vail of the Empire Ranch stayed solvent by reviving the practice of trail driving and walked their herds to California at a considerable saving." On their return to Tucson, Vail and his foreman met with area ranchers and convinced them of the feasibility of shipping "by hoof." The railroad "read the signs correctly and restored the old rates." The Vail and Gates cattle appear to have arrived on Catalina at about this time, but whether they were shipped by rail or driven overland is a question we have not been able to answer with any certainty. We have been told that Vail leased the Warner Ranch from former Governor John Downey; this would have been a convenient stopping place for cattle driven overland, while those shipped by train arrived in Los Angeles and from there were shipped by boat to Catalina.

At any rate, the lease with the Bannings ended in 1896, the proximity of people and cattle apparently never totally resolved. In 1901, the Vail family with J.V. Vickers bought Santa Rosa Island from the A.P. More heirs of Santa Barbara to use as a cattle ranch, barging the animals to and from the mainland. Stock operations on Santa Rosa, originally started in 1844, continued until 1980 when Santa Rosa became part of the National Park and National Marine Sanctuary. The sanctuary includes Anacapa, Santa Cruz, Santa Rosa, San Miguel, and Santa Barbara Islands, and was authorized by Congress to protect the unique natural and cultural resources of the area, including the islands' surrounding six nautical miles of ocean and kelp forests. This unusual marine park provides habitat for many kinds of marine flora and fauna ranging from microscopic plankton to the blue whale, generally considered the earth's largest living mammal.

Around the time Vail moved his operations to Santa Rosa Island, Phineas Banning's youngest son, Hancock, established a serpentine marble quarry above Empire Landing and west of the ancient Indian steatite quarry in the Valley of the Ollas. In about 1902 he brought heavy equipment, including steam boilers and a derrick, from the mainland to work the marble. Large blocks of serpentine were drilled with steam and broken loose by driving in wooden pegs. This split the marble into large chunks without cracking the pieces, and these were then loaded onto a two-wheeled rig that was hauled down the steep hillside to the beach by a team of four horses.

The derrick then "picked it up and put it on the river scow," Hancock Banning Jr. recalled in 1971 during an oral history interview for the Powell Library, University of California at Los Angeles. "The old Sacramento River scow took it across to the mainland. Southern Pacific would pick it up at Wilmington and take it to Naud Junction. That's where our marble works were." Naud Junction, named for Edouard Naud, a pioneer Los Angeles pastry baker who had a wool warehouse nearby, is just northeast of the present Union Station. Hancock Banning Sr. had a coal yard at Naud Junction, and his brother, William Banning, had a stable there for his horses and coaches. William was famous for his exciting stagecoach excursions on Catalina, which will be detailed when we reach Little Harbor.

Hancock Banning Jr. completed tape recording a historically valuable history of Catalina in 1970 for the University of California, Los Angeles. The son of Hancock Banning and grandson of Phineas Banning, he is pictured here at age eighty in 1972.

Serpentine marble from the Empire quarry found its way onto the facades of several early Los Angeles buildings and was used to frame the original aquarium in Avalon, with the glass fitted in to prevent saltwater corrosion. The facade of the old Catalina Hotel in Avalon, built by George Patton, father of the famous World War II general and uncle of William Banning, was of Empire serpentine. The hotel was lost to fire.

An imposing altar largely of serpentine from the Empire Landing quarry contrasts with the simple elegance of the stave-type structure of the mission church of St. John's and Holy Child in Wilmington. This altar was formerly a buffet in the Phineas Banning house nearby, and was donated by the Banning family in 1925. The church was built in 1883 by several members of the Banning family. Two stunning stained glass windows memorialize Phineas Banning and a daughter, both of whom had died before the church's founding. The church was originally built at 422 Avalon Boulevard (then called Canal Street), near the Banning home. In 1943 the building was moved to 1537 Neptune Avenue where it serves members of St. John's Episcopal Church and Holy Child Philippine Independent Church.

Some of the serpentine was turned on a lathe into thin-walled cups by Frank Carey, manager of the quarry and marble yard, and some was made into bookends and paperweights that were sold commercially. When William Wrigley Jr. bought the island in 1919, the serpentine quarry operation was closed on the grounds that it was financially impractical. The last commercial quarrying of serpentine marble and steatite was done by Hancock Banning. Collectors seeking these island artifacts might recognize them by their dark green color and mottled appearance. Serpentine marble is a rock consisting of hydrous magnesium silicate.

Connolly-Pacific Company, headquartered in Long Beach, has operated a rock quarry at Empire, west of the serpentine area, since 1937. Previous quarry operations, also under lease with the Santa Catalina Island Company, were carried on by

American Cement and earlier, beginning in the early 1900s, by Graham Brothers. All of the buildings at Empire Landing, including the permanently installed mobile homes, are owned by Connolly-Pacific, which also has quarried rock at the island's East End, near Pebbly Beach, since 1933.

When passing the worked cliffs of the Empire quarry, mind the two large offshore buoys at the western end. The outer buoy is located about a thousand yards from shore.

14 Spelunking in Blue Cavern

The cave had two openings, the small entrance leading into a large bay around the point. The canoe was urged along the rocky shores, while the Spaniards were not three hundred yards away watching for the wreck to float out, thinking that the craft had been ground to pieces in the hole in the wall.

CHARLES F. HOLDER, *The Adventures of Torqua* (1902)

From Empire Landing past the quarry to Blue Cavern Point is a distance of a little more than three nautical miles. Here, in the cliff face at water's edge, are three caves: Perdition Cave, Spouting Cave, and Blue Cavern, the latter being the largest and most spectacular. The entrance to Blue Cavern is wide and high. Charles F. Holder described his exploration of the cavern in an 1897 article for *Scientific American*:

> At the entrance the water is so deep that the largest ship could thrust the tip of her bowsprit into the cavern, and [it is] of rich blue, telling of great depth . . . Pushing a boat in, one is surprised to find a small tunnel branching off to the right — the real cave. The writer entered this in a small boat one day when the tide and sea were low, and penetrated it without difficulty. The water was about six feet deep, over a perfectly level floor covered with pebbles and seaweed, while here and there could be seen the sparkle of the pearl of the abalone.
>
> The sides were too narrow to use oars, and the wall so low that every wave that came rolling in through the tunnel lifted the boat unpleasantly near the roof, showing that at very high tide, when the wind was fresh, the attempt to enter the Blue Cavern might be accompanied with some danger. By standing up and pushing the boat by hand, using the sides and roof, the passage was easily made for about one hundred and fifty feet, the boat suddenly coming out around a point some distance from the main entrance. For unknown centuries the waves have been working at this cave, gradually eating it out, with the result given.

Holder's experience in the cavern led him to employ its setting for the dramatic escape of two teenage Spaniards, Raphael and Arturo Velazquez, and a Catalina Indian, Torqua, from their pursuers in his fictional tale, *The Adventures of Torqua*. In

Holder's story, set in the late eighteenth century, the youths are about to be transferred from San Juan Capistrano Mission to another on the "borders of the land." Rather than make the move, the trio escapes at night by paddling across the channel to Pimunga (Catalina) in a canoe "cut out of a big pine log which had drifted down from the unknown north." Just as they reach the island, the boys notice they are being followed by a large canoe filled with men from the mission, some armed Spanish soldiers, and an Apache "skilled in following the enemy." They escape by darting suddenly into the mouth of the Blue Cavern. To the Spanish officers, the boys' canoe "seemed to strike the abrupt wall and be swallowed, [and] she disappeared as though the rock had opened and closed over her." The boys emerged from the cavern's small opening to the east, for the passage describes an arc, and went on to further exciting adventures.

Enterprising souls may still explore the Blue Cavern, for it remains nearly unchanged except that the passage is minutely larger than in Holder's day, due to tidal scouring. A young harbor patrolman at the Isthmus told us that he had ventured into the cavern in a Boston Whaler. His comment was an enthusiastic, "It's really neat!"

After rounding the Blue Cavern headland, the panorama of Isthmus Cove is visible, a large bay about two and a quarter miles wide at the entrance, narrowing to about a thousand yards at Isthmus beach. When we approach Isthmus Cove from seaward, Ship Rock, which stands sixty-six feet above water a little more than a mile offshore of the cove, presents a profile and coloring suggestive of a large ship under full sail. Baring at three feet at mean low water is a reef extending a little more than 100 yards from the rock's southeastern face. The reef doesn't show at high tide, but can be dangerous. Give it plenty of sea room. Mounted on Ship Rock is a white warning light, at an elevation of seventy-five feet.

Long before the light was installed, there was an amusing story related about the schooner *Eagle* out of Boston, a pioneer trader on the California coast. During September 1821, the vessel's master, Captain Eliab Grimes, took a party ashore at the Isthmus to obtain fresh water. A gun fired from the schooner caused Grimes to hasten back aboard. A strange sail had been sighted at sea, and the crew feared it was a Spanish ship looking for the *Eagle,* for Grimes was bent upon escaping the heavy tariffs levied on "foreign" goods landed along the coast. Grimes was among the first of a long parade of so-called smugglers, which they were from the reigning government's standpoint, which used Catalina as a cache. The *Eagle* had sailed with $10,000 worth of goods, loaded by its Boston agents in the Hawaiian Islands, to sell or trade along the Pacific coast, chiefly for sea otter skins. The *Eagle* set sail promptly to escape the Spanish ship. Next day she ventured cautiously back to the Isthmus, only to find that the strange ship was in the same place and "certainly fixed there for ages past." Closer investigation proved it to be a large pinnacle rock "a considerable distance from shore and when the sun reflected on it, it had the appearance of a ship under full sail" (Ogden, pp. 81–83).

Captain Grimes may have had a premonition. According to an appendix to William Heath Davis's *Seventy-Five Years in California,* the *Eagle* in 1822 was "seized by the government for smuggling, Aug. 1st, and sold at auction at Santa Barbara, Nov. 8th." This time it was the Mexican government that seized and sold the *Eagle,* for, on April 11, 1822, the Mexican flag had been raised over Monterey, capital of Alta California. Grimes, incidentally, returned to Honolulu where, from 1835 to 1839, he was engaged in general trade, importing goods from Boston and annually sending out three American brigs for sea otter hunting along the coast of California. Grimes earlier made voyages "all over the Atlantic Ocean, commencing before the mast." In about 1841 he obtained a grant of land near Sacramento where he raised cattle until his death in 1848.

A low, small, flat island, unlighted, is located about a half mile from Isthmus Cove, slightly more easterly than Ship Rock. This islet, known as Bird Rock, looks as if it is covered with snow. When the wind is right, it becomes very clear to the nose that this is not snow, for it has been claimed as a roosting place by seabirds for centuries. A contemporary wag, however, once had bumper stickers printed that read: "Ski Bird Rock."

This rock was earlier called White Rock Island, and it was under that name that Frew Morton of San Francisco acquired it in 1929 with some old Valentine scrip, although at the time William Wrigley Jr. believed he owned all of Catalina, including the offshore rocks, according to Santa Catalina Island Company (SCICO) archives. Somehow this guano-covered islet, though of visual and unmistakable olfactory presence, had been omitted for nearly a century from the chain of title conveyances to Catalina's owners. (Ship Rock, however, was included in the legal title.) Morton is said to have paid $138 plus expenses for the 50,000-square-foot rocky marine plateau which, at this writing, is still under private ownership, not that of the SCICO. Owners of the rock, which occasionally is used for filming commercials, are Michael and Ann Caffey of Eugene, Oregon. They inherited a two-thirds interest from Caffey's father, Frank, and purchased the remaining third from the estate of Pearle Kirchmann of Belvedere, California, after her death in 1987.

Mrs. Kirchmann was given the one-third interest in White Rock Island in 1938 by her husband, Henry Kirchmann Jr., as a whimsical birthday gift. In 1925 he was one of three men who discovered that Wrigley's title included all land outside Avalon and all rocks and islets around the island, except for Bird Rock. Kirchmann's partners were Frew Morton and William Warmington. They acquired the islet four years later using Valentine scrip to pay for it. Their agreement was that ownership would be in Morton's name, with the others furnishing money for taxes. Morton and Warmington apparently lost interest and sold out to Caffey in the late 1920s. A Robert P. Tracy was at one time among Bird Rock's owners.

Valentine land scrip received its name from Thomas B. Valentine, founder of a pioneer San Francisco printing establishment in the early 1850s. Valentine possessed a shrewd eye for real estate, and managed to acquire a former Mexican rancho near Petaluma, which was also claimed as public land by the U.S. government. Taking advantage of the U.S. Land Commission's recognition of private land claims originating in the Spanish and Mexican periods, Valentine was involved in lengthy legal proceedings. The U.S. Supreme Court ultimately ordered compensation to Valentine for the Petaluma rancho claimed by the government. Compensation was in the form of certificates of location issued by the General Land Office, which entitled Valentine to select compensatory acreage from surveyed or unsurveyed public land equal in area to the Petaluma rancho. These certificates, which were also issued to others under similar circumstances, became known as Valentine scrip.

What Valentine didn't use himself, he sold. Speculators bought some, hiking the price. Scrip became too dear to be used on admittedly public lands, so owners began to seek out forgotten places or "sleepers" — areas overlooked by government surveyors or with questionable titles. Such, apparently, was White Rock Island.

15   J. B. Banning, Tree Planter

Isthmus Cove, on the north shore about 6 miles eastward from the western end of the island, affords shelter for small vessels in southerly weather but is dangerous in northwesterly weather. A wharf has been built to about 12 feet of water, and other improvements are in progress and contemplation with a view of making a summer resort.   UNITED STATES COAST PILOT, 1903

After rounding Blue Cavern Point and entering Isthmus Harbor, one must keep well to the east of a nearly invisible reef, marked at night by a buoy flashing a red light and by other buoys, unlighted, during the day. This is Harbor Reef, a roughly oval hazard about 1,300 yards wide, its highest point baring two feet at mean lower low water. The reef lies about 250 yards southerly of Bird Rock. Vessels approaching from the north should bear west of the reef.

In the past few decades there have been dozens of groundings on Harbor Reef by unwary or incautious yachtsmen. It is possible that the first recorded grounding occurred in 1543 when Cabrillo's armada, its captain dead, began its homeward voyage. One of the ships attempted to run into a harbor at San Salvador (Catalina), scraped across a reef, and was nearly lost, according to historian Harry Kelsey, with whom we discussed the matter. Evidence of the location of that long-ago grounding points strongly to Harbor Reef or possibly to Eagle Reef, between Lion Head and Howland's Landing, west of the Isthmus. Another potentially hazardous reef, this one above Howland's, extends nearly the length of Emerald Bay. This hazard, Indian Reef, is more visible, however; the craggy marker at its eastern end is known as Indian Rock.

Tall palms lining the beach at the head of Isthmus Harbor were barged over from

J.B. Banning planted a forest of young eucalyptus trees on the Isthmus to minimize afternoon wind and form the basis for a new resort community called Cabrillo in the early 1900s. Damaging winds and a lack of water killed the trees, making Cabrillo an unrealized dream. This view faces north; Bird, or White Rock lies at the Isthmus Bay entrance.

the mainland in the 1930s by the landscaper of William Wrigley Jr.'s Pasadena home, long after Wrigley acquired the island. Other palm trees were planted by early movie companies to enhance the South Seas feeling of their films. But everlasting credit for early tree planting at the Isthmus, Avalon, and other parts of the island must go to Joseph Brent (J.B.) Banning, who seems to have been a self-appointed "Johnny Eucalyptus Seed." A son of Phineas Banning, the early developer of the San Pedro–Wilmington harbor, J.B. (then called Joe) grew up in his father's Wilmington mansion and shared Phineas's pleasure in planting the hardy, fast-growing eucalyptus as a windbreak on the barren plains of the Los Angeles basin. The seeds, about the size of acorns, were originally brought to Phineas from Australia by ship captains, along with a variety of other necessary goods.

"Sea captains used to bring these seeds up," recalled Hancock Banning Jr., a grandson of Phineas, in a 1971 interview for the UCLA Library, "and [grandfather] planted a great many of them around Wilmington because there weren't any trees there… What a horrible place it was because sand was blowing all over the place. No trees, no shrubbery, just a bare plain. Very different from what it is now with all those eucalyptus trees."

When Phineas's sons formed the Santa Catalina Island Company (SCICO) in 1894, "they planted some [eucalyptus] at the Isthmus, Emerald Bay, Johnson's Landing, and then at Avalon," Hancock Banning Jr. recalled. "Wherever my Uncle Joe [J.B.] went and stayed very long, he planted trees. It was a wonderful thing."

Around the turn of the twentieth century, the Banning family spent a few years trying to develop the Isthmus as a resort where, as owners of the island, they controlled all the land, as opposed to Avalon, where a previous island owner had sold lots. The Bannings felt that Avalon had become "a sort of honky-tonk place" with too many stores and too many tourists. Their attempt to develop the Isthmus into a high-class, genteel resort (called Cabrillo on a few old maps) failed. The nearly constant wind discouraged visitors, even after J.B. Banning planted a forest of young eucalyptus trees as a buffer. The wind "spoiled the swimming from about eleven o'clock in the morning usually until sundown," Hancock Jr. said, and the forest was stunted because of wind and lack of water. The present J.B. Banning house on the hill had (and has) improved wind protection. J.B. built a curving stage road to it and had the entire hillside planted with a variety of trees, including conifers. He had his own gasoline-powered electric generating plant and a water well, and trees on the hill received better trimming and watering than those on the flatlands.

The pier at the head of the fairway between moorings was initially constructed in 1903 by the Banning brothers as part of the "Cabrillo" development. The pier was shortened by 150 feet after World War II, and floats were employed to assist landing the passengers from cross-channel vessels and from other craft. Today there is a float where fuel and water can be obtained and dinghy docks for yachtsmen and their guests. The harbormaster's office is on the pier.

Isthmus Harbor, Catalina Harbor, and the coves east to Moonstone and west to the far end of Emerald Bay fall under the jurisdiction of the Catalina Mooring Service, operated by Doug Bombard Enterprises, whose owners are Bombard and his family. The mooring service keeps the moorings in good repair year-round; the men aboard its *Kingfisher II* tender are especially busy when winter storms pull the floats out of alignment and tangle their lines. (See the Afterword for changes in jurisdiction.) A harbor security officer patrols the coves, assigns moorings, and, as previously mentioned, collects fees for use of the moorings. Moorings in these areas are on tidelands Bombard leases from the state of California. Interestingly, Bombard also holds state tidelands leases on Parson's Landing near the West End and for Little Harbor on the windward or southern side of the island. There are no moorings in either of these areas and, of course, anchorage is free, as it is in all coves. Bombard, a yachtsman himself, believes in protecting certain anchorages from the encroachment of moorings.

Businesses at the Isthmus (or Two Harbors) include a restaurant (Doug's Harbor Reef Restaurant and Saloon), the Two Harbors campground, the Banning House Lodge (now a bed and breakfast inn), the Two Harbors General Store, and repair facilities. Also on site are Baywatch paramedics and Los Angeles County Sheriffs deputies. Headquartered here are Safari Tours, conducted by a naturalist who explains the island's natural history and flora and fauna, and Safari Bus Service, which connects the Isthmus with Avalon. All enterprises at Isthmus Cove and Two Harbors are operated by the Bombard family, which includes Doug and his wife,

Audrey, and their children, Randy, Greg, and Doreen (McElroy). The family also created a separate company, the Catalina Channel Express, that operates a fleet of fast passenger vessels between the mainland (Long Beach and Los Angeles harbors) and the island (Two Harbors and Avalon).

Bombard, born in Avalon in 1926, was sent to the Isthmus in 1956 by the SCICo to develop camping and yachting in an attempt to make the enterprise (then operated by the SCICo and called Catalina Camp and Cove Agency) self-sustaining. At the time there were tents and small cabins at the Isthmus, a general store operated jointly by several Avalon merchants, a restaurant and snack bar run by Press and Gerry Taylor, and both gun and archery hunting seasons. Moorings were provided by the Isthmus Mooring Service, owned by Burt Grove and Ralph Baker.

By 1975, Bombard had successfully redeveloped Two Harbors and was ready to operate on his own. He leased the Isthmus from SCICo and formed Doug Bombard Enterprises (DBE). The small cabins of early days now house DBE employees, who number as many as 180 in the peak summer season. Some DBE employees are on personal cruises and live aboard their own boats. As he developed the Isthmus, Bombard added such amenities as an ice machine, public showers, a Laundromat, and a dive shop. He also originated the West End Cruising Club, which has a full calendar of races and other events during the summer. A previous agreement with the Catalina Island Conservancy enabled Bombard Enterprises to conduct hunting parties on the island for deer and wild pigs until 1996. No firearms were allowed; all hunting was done with bow and arrow and only with possession of applicable hunting permits, local and state.

The South Seas character of Two Harbors inspired early motion picture companies to film such epics as *Mutiny on the Bounty* and *Rain* on location there. In the early 1930s, Isthmus Harbor Beach was known as "Papeete Beach" because above the sand there was a settlement of one-story thatched bungalettes catering to a fluctuating summer population. This South Sea island effect extended to other structures used as sets in the silent film *Sadie Thompson* (1928), starring Gloria Swanson and Lionel Barrymore, and a remake of the story in sound, titled *Rain* (1932), with Joan Crawford and Walter Huston. The movie set for Christian's Hut, from the *Bounty* movie, became an Isthmus landmark and popular bar until it burned down, with some other buildings, in the late 1940s. Actually, much of the *Bounty* was filmed at Catalina, on the San Pedro Channel, and at the Craig Shipyard in Wilmington where storm scenes were enacted dockside, the ship rocked by hawsers and deluged with water shot from fire hoses and blown by airplane propellers. The replica of the *Bounty* was built at the shipyard on the hull of an old schooner. Adapted from a best-selling trilogy based on the true story of the *Bounty* by Charles Bernard Nordhoff and James Norman Hall, the MGM film was released in 1935 and starred Charles Laughton, Clark Gable, and Franchot Tone. *Mutiny on the Bounty* is available on videocassette and still makes for an exciting evening. The island was such a convenient and attractive movie location that more than 200 films were shot there from 1911 to 1977, according to Catalina Island Museum records.

Until recent years, the Isthmus was a popular retreat for the movie colony, who either came on their yachts or stayed in cottages ashore. Among the better known early stars who enjoyed life at the Isthmus were Preston Foster, John Wayne, Richard Arlen, John Weismuller, James Cagney, Victor McLaughlin, Errol Flynn, Oliver Hardy, Stan Laurel, Ward Bond, and director John Ford.

At the lower part of the road leading to the Banning house is the home of Doug and Audrey Bombard. It has an inviting garden, both visually to humans and nutritionally to the island animals who feed on it: deer, buffalo, and wild pigs. The Bombards accept this munching, rooting, and pawing invasion as a small price to pay for living in an island paradise with a magnificent view of both harbors. Below the Bombard home is a little red schoolhouse with a cupola on top, a gift of Cliff Tucker, wealthy retired Long Beach businessman and yachtsman, and his wife, Marybelle, who became concerned about the grueling three-hour, round-trip bus ride the Isthmus children had to take to attend elementary school in Avalon. In 1958, Tucker shipped $7,000 worth of playground equipment to the people at Two Harbors, then offered to build the community a $90,000 one-room schoolhouse.

COURTESY NEWPORT HARBOR NAUTICAL MUSEUM AND SHERMAN LIBRARY

This replica of the HMS *Bounty*, pictured in Long Beach Harbor, sailed in the movie *Mutiny on the Bounty,* starring Clark Gable and Charles Laughton, the bulk of which was shot on and around Catalina.

"That's when I learned how hard it is to give away money," Tucker commented to us. "Here I was, offering to pay for everything, but the Long Beach Unified School District, which had operated the schools on the island since 1923, didn't care. Finally I convinced Superintendent Tom Giugni to come to Two Harbors and take a ride on that bus..." Thus the school was built. It opened in September 1987.

Near the school at the crown of the Isthmus is an ancient, rambling one-story building. This is the Civil War Barracks, one of the few remaining wooden structures in California from that period. The next chapter will examine its historical significance.

Meanwhile, starting at Blue Cavern Point, we will cruise in a clockwise direction and visit the coves in Isthmus Harbor. The first is Big Fisherman, which, in 1889, was simply named Fishermans Cove, without a possessive apostrophe. The *Pacific Coast Pilot* of that year notes it is "275 yards wide and the same distance deep; and on account of the reef and rock off its entrance is an excellent shelter for small craft in all weathers." The cove was used extensively by fishermen and others during the days of pure sailing more than a century ago because in the rest of the Isthmus a ship might "experience difficulty in getting out, as there is always a swell setting in and the wind blows in flaws and eddies round the hills," according to the *Pilot*. These historic weather and sea patterns still exist, but "getting out" is no longer a problem with the universality of engine-powered craft.

Today the shores of Big Fisherman Cove contain the buildings of the Philip K. Wrigley Marine Science Center, formerly the University of Southern California (USC) Catalina Marine Science Center. The facility was renamed in 1992 to recognize the enormous contributions to the facility made by the late P.K. Wrigley, son of William Wrigley Jr. and a former president of the SCICo. The gifts began in March 1965, when 5.3 acres of land at the cove were given to USC for a marine science center. A month later, USC and the SCICo entered into a seventy-five-year lease of forty acres of surrounding property to serve as a buffer zone against future encroachments or development. The laboratories were completed in 1967. In 1972, an additional 8.77 acres were given to USC for the construction of housing and a food service complex at the Science Center. Just three years later, 3,200.88 shares of participating preferred stock of SCICo were donated to the university by Wrigley and his sister, Dorothy Offield. Other stock was willed to USC by Wrigley, who died April 11, 1977, at the age of eighty-two.

Built at the Isthmus for the movie *Mutiny on the Bounty,* Christian's Hut is seen here during World War II. It was destroyed by fire.

As a result of its holdings, USC receives about $27,000 annually in dividends for the development and maintenance of the center, along with other outside science-related gifts and grants (*Water Lines,* vol. 7, no. 2, 1992). Wrigley's generous gifts were predicated on his belief that the island offered an ideal location for research and teaching programs in the fields of marine biology, submarine geology, oceanography, and related subjects conducted by the university.

Moorings in Big Fisherman are private and may be used only in emergencies. Offshore about 100 yards and running from Blue Cavern Point to the chalk cliffs near Little Fisherman Cove is a Marine Life Refuge, dedicated in 1989 and set apart by marker buoys. Diving in the kelp beds in the refuge is permitted, but anchoring, fishing, spear guns, and collecting are not. The State Department of Fish and Game uses the refuge as a nursery and conducts research on island fishes, stocking them in hopes of replenishing the fish resources which are becoming, or have become, depleted.

Next on our cruise around the harbor is Little Fisherman Cove, which has camp-sites with beautiful views; the Isthmus town site; Fourth of July Cove, once the site of Banning family holiday picnics; and last, Cherry Cove, ending at a prominent headland called Lion Head. Over the years, Cherry Cove's shore has been leased from the island's owners by the Boy Scouts. As for available moorings, in numbers Little Fisherman's are combined with Isthmus Cove's to total about 249, with anchorage for about 100; Fourth of July has some 42 moorings but no anchorage; and Cherry has about 103 moorings, also with no anchorage.

Harry Houdini, famous escape artist/magician, and heroine are seen in a publicity photograph from the film *Terror Island,* largely made on Catalina Island in the fall of 1919.

A Civil War map of the Isthmus designates but two inlets: Fisherman's Bay and Fourth of July Bay. Apparently these place names were bestowed by early miners or stock-men and have remained in place (with variations) for more than a century. Fourth of July Cove appears to be a snug harbor, its hills offering protection from most prevailing winds. We found out otherwise when we moved there from Hen Rock Cove after hearing on the radio weather station that a strong northwesterly was expected. About midnight, when we had settled in, an unnatural still-ness kept us awake until suddenly we were beset by fifty-knot, gale-force winds, which continued to howl until dawn. The cove's water looked as if it were being stirred by a giant hand, sending spray almost to the top of the surrounding cliffs. Our tethered inflatable dinghy rose and fell in the air like a huge kite, and outside the cove's entrance, a larger dinghy than ours, complete with outboard, turned over and skittered behind the pitching yacht to which it was tied.

The gale finally died, the sun came out, and we agreed it would have been much wiser to have stayed put at Hen Rock, sheltered by the protective arm of Long Point.

16 Two-War Barracks

Union soldiers from the Civil War and Coast Guardsmen from World War II slept in this building. And so did I in 1943 as a U.S. Coast Guard apprentice seaman. RICHARD BUFFUM

The white-trimmed, barn-red wooden building sprawling across the highest point of the Isthmus is a true historic structure built during the Civil War as barracks to house a company of Union Army infantry. Material for construction of the building and others later razed was shipped to the Isthmus from a wharf at Drum Barracks near Wilmington. This extensive Union Army complex was established in 1862 on thirty acres of land made available by Phineas Banning and his business associate, Benjamin D. (Don Benito) Wilson. Drum Barracks was the military supply headquarters for southern California and Arizona, and the contract to transport these materials to the island was awarded to Banning.

The military took possession of Catalina Island on January 2, 1864. Under the command of Captain B.R. West of the Fourth Regiment, California Volunteer Infantry, one subaltern, eighty enlisted men, and an assistant surgeon from the First California Cavalry were sent to the island and encamped near Isthmus Harbor, at the time called Union Bay. A week later the assistant adjutant-general, Richard Coulter Drum (after whom Drum Barracks had been named), instructed in a letter that a certain building owned by Charles Enoch Huse of Santa Barbara "be turned over for the use of troops sent to that place" and that "the general directs that the officer in command will see that no damage is done to the building (Tompkins, pp. 115–18)." Huse, a bilingual attorney originally from Massachusetts, was an ardent Union supporter who made his early living in California as interpreter for Judge Joaquin Carrillo, who spoke little English.

How Huse came to own a building at the Isthmus we do not know, but he may have acquired it as payment for trying to unscramble one of the jumbled land titles of the period. After all, Thomas Robbins, Jose Maria Covarrubias, and Albert Packard, the first three private owners of Catalina, were Huse's fellow Santa Barbarans. At any rate, California land titles were so muddied and confused during the Civil War that even the State of California could not give satisfactory deeds to its public lands, according to historian Robert Glass Cleland. And when Lieutenant Colonel James F. Curtis of the Fourth California Infantry reported to San Francisco from Drum Barracks on January 12, 1864, he said that "nothing definite was ascertained of the title to the island [but] the occupants all acknowledged the United States Government as owner." Colonel Curtis added that the "U.S. district attorney for the southern district of California should possess reliable information regarding ownership."

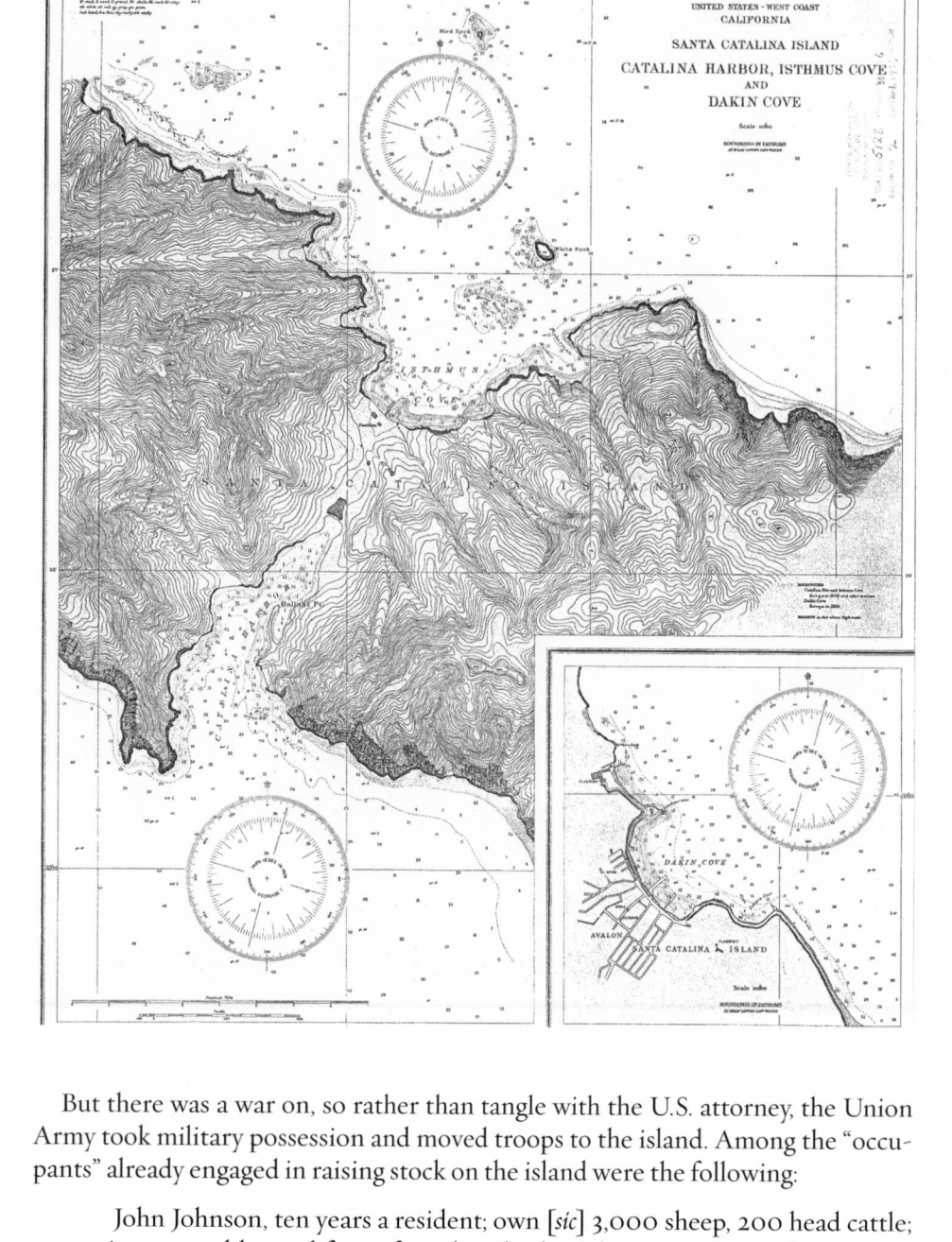

This U.S. Coast and Geodetic Survey of Catalina Harbor, Isthmus Cove, and Dakin Cove dates back to March 1927. The townsite is named Avalon.

But there was a war on, so rather than tangle with the U.S. attorney, the Union Army took military possession and moved troops to the island. Among the "occupants" already engaged in raising stock on the island were the following:

John Johnson, ten years a resident; own [*sic*] 3,000 sheep, 200 head cattle; raises vegetables and fruits for sale. Charles Johnson, brother of above; ten years residence, 100 mares and colts. Spencer H. Wilson, five years a resident, 12,000 sheep, 10 head of cattle; principal occupation, cutting firewood for sale. William Howland, six years' residence; 3,000 sheep. Benjamin Weston, 2,000 sheep. Juan Cota, 400 head cattle. Francisco Guerrero, eight years a resident, 2,000 sheep. Swain Lawson, 10 head cattle; owns a small vessel employed about the island.

Curtis omitted the names of Frank Whittley and D.B. Diltz, Esq., who were mentioned as occupying Isthmus land in an earlier report, and probably a few others.

In addition to the people raising stock, there were about seventy miners at work in companies that mostly had "been incorporated since the 21st of December [1863]" when apparently word got out that only miners with incorporated companies would be allowed to remain on the island. About thirty of these miners were said to be encamped at Fourth of July Bay near a place where mines of galena had been discovered and where copper, silver, and gold were said to exist. But, cautioned Colonel Curtis, "Whether the ledges will pay to work is being solved. With the contradictory evidence upon the point I could reach no conclusion."

It was necessary for the miners at Fourth of July Bay to haul fresh water in casks by skiff from Howland's

Catalina Harbor was the backdrop as Coast Guard "boots" drilled at the Isthmus during World War II. In the pictured guardhouse, the author often wondered what he would do if a Japanese submarine showed up.

Landing. Other springs existed in the area, but Major Henry Hancock reported in November 1863 that while "there is no abundance of wood and water, the supply of both is adequate to all present and perhaps future demands." Nevertheless, the supply of fresh water continued to worry the military. Before and after the garrison was established on the Isthmus, various suggestions were made including sinking a well forty to fifty feet deep, cutting a road "to Mr. Diltz's well," using a well near the camp "for washing and culinary purposes," and bringing water "from the spring on the mountain" by pipe, for a distance of six to eight miles. Captain B.R. West, commander of the Fourth Regiment, suggested at the end of January 1864, "that an accurate survey be made by a civil engineer at the earliest possible moment" so that pipes could be installed to bring the elevated spring water to the post. "This is the best . . . and only mode by which the garrison can be sure of a permanent supply of good and wholesome water," he concluded.

Whether this survey was actually done is difficult to say because a month later, in February 1864, Brigadier General George Wright, commander of the Department of the Pacific, requested the Department of Interior to turn Catalina into an Indian reservation where hostile Indians from the District of Humboldt, above San Francisco, could be removed. The Indian war there occupied sixteen companies of troops, and it was felt that if the Indians could be captured and removed, "at least twelve of these companies [could be] withdrawn for service elsewhere." It was also pointed out that the island was a "very desirable place for an Indian reservation" because it had "wild goats and other game in abundance, plenty of wood and an inexhaustible supply of fish and pure fresh water." This was not the first time the island had been considered as a refuge for Indians. In 1804, according to H.H. Ban-

croft, Father Estevan Tapis, president of the California missions, "desired to found a new mission on Limu or Santa Catalina Island, with a view to convert the naked and superstitious, though friendly, natives, who were not disposed to join a mission on the mainland, yet caused the friars trouble by their intercourse with the Channel neophytes." Father Tapis noted that an "island establishment would be a most effective means of checking contraband trade," predating by a half century the Civil War views of the U.S. military (Bancroft, vol. 2).

This Civil War barracks still stands on the crown of the Isthmus.

The reservation plan soon died, canceled by the Departments of Interior and Indian Affairs for the stated reason that no money was available for establishing a new reservation and that such a move would impose undue hardship on the Indians. The move was also unnecessary. The crisis in the Humboldt District was over.

The public was told that the military occupation of Catalina was taken to forestall a Confederate attempt to seize the island and establish a privateer base that could intercept ships and shipping. Considering the extent of Confederate sympathy in southern California at the time, the official presence of Union troops probably discouraged some Southern sympathizers from taking matters into their own hands. The Isthmus garrison was soon abandoned. The troops were withdrawn from the island in September 1864.

Nearly a century would pass before another conflict, World War II, would reactivate the old barracks. It served as housing for sailors of the U.S. Coast Guard, which employed the entire Isthmus as a recruit training base or "boot camp" from July 1942 until September 1945. Seamen, coxswains, quartermasters, and gunners mates were trained at the Isthmus that, like other military areas on the island, was leased from the Santa Catalina Island Company (SCICO).

In early January 1943, I was an apprentice seaman here, being indoctrinated for six weeks into the mysteries of signal lights and flags, knot tying (I can still tie a mean bowline on a bight), helmsmanship, rowing so-called whale boats with several pulling stations, and other salty arcana of sailoring. The lovely 161-foot schooner *Goodwill,* built in 1938, was our training vessel. Her beam was thirty feet, her draft fifteen-feet three-inches; her sail area was 29,000 square feet. The *Goodwill* was then painted a dreary gray, but I remembered her years earlier when owner Keith Spaulding, an iron magnate, sailed into Avalon Bay; she was gleaming white with highly varnished mahogany and a nattily attired crew. That memory heightened my satisfaction with standing at her big wheel before the binnacle and learning to steer a proper compass course during boot training. Alas, well after my being mustered out of service, the *Goodwill,* then owned by a Southland syndicate, was returning to Ensenada from the Galapagos Islands when she foundered on the Sacramento Reef near Cedros Island on May 25, 1969. All hands perished in the accident.

During World War II, U.S. Coast Guardsmen stationed at the Isthmus trained in Catalina waters aboard the schooner *Goodwill.*

We boots were quartered two bunks high in every room of the old Civil War barracks. It is a minor miracle that its ancient wooden floor, also painted gray at the time, survived rotting from the watery, sudsy onslaught of the vigorous swabbing we apprentice seamen were required to give it weekly before it was inspected by the white-gloved commanding officer. He, it should be added, did not reside in the barracks but was quartered with the other officers in a privileged aerie, the Banning House.

Day and night, in small watch units, we Coast Guardsmen guarded Two Harbors against possible attack and invasion by Japanese submarines which, according to residents of Catalina who saw them, did lurk in the channel, surfacing at night to recharge their batteries. Among the Japanese submarines sighted was a pack of three off Silver Canyon, near the southeast end of the island. They were spotted by the Los Angeles County Fish and Game vessel *Grego*. She beat a hasty retreat, being armed only with a 30-06 Springfield rifle (Doug Bombard interview, 1990).

Many nights when I was on duty alone at a little sentry shack at the head of Catalina Harbor, I wondered (and still do) what I would have done if an enemy sub had appeared. I was armed only with a holstered Smith and Wesson revolver and six rounds of ammunition. I probably would have run like hell to rouse the garrison which, unfortunately, was as inadequately armed as I. I think our Civil War ancestors were better off. They at least possessed a twelve-pound field gun with proper ammunition. It was transported to Union Bay by a vessel that brought troops and supplies, anchoring in about fifteen feet of water 150 yards off the beach. The field gun was installed in a commanding position on high ground.

17 Banning's Western War

Banning in early times could ride farther with less fatigue than any man I ever knew, notwithstanding he was never a lightweight. He could also drive a stage, six-in-hand, faster and over rougher roads and over places where no roads existed than any driver who ever cracked whip or pulled the ribbons.

MAJOR HORACE BELL,
Reminiscences of a Ranger (originally published in 1881)

Although California furnished more than 15,000 volunteers for Union service during the Civil War, Confederate sympathizers are estimated to have numbered more than 30,000, many of them residing in southern California. They were "in large part *Californios* who had been persuaded that a new government would speed up their land claims and that squatters and other lawless trespassers would be dispossessed," noted Richard Pourade in *The Silver Dons.* "Arms were kept ready and ammunition [was] stolen from Union depots in the expectation of guerrilla warfare."

One victim of the period's partisan feeling was Charles Enoch Huse, the bilingual Santa Barbara lawyer mentioned in the previous chapter. An ardent Union man, Huse was confronted outside his home in Santa Barbara one day by a lynch mob of Confederate supporters calling for his death. Henceforth he had to hire bodyguards to accompany him whenever he went outdoors (Tompkins, p.117).

More than one vessel, ostensibly headed for Mexican or South American ports, managed to slip away from California waters to prey upon Union commerce in the Pacific. Guerrilla bands sometimes interfered with the shipment of bullion through the mountains. Indeed, during the four years of war, the air was full of plots by southern adherents intent on destroying the Union and supporting the Confederacy. An armed fleet of six Union ships and a thousand men patrolled the coast from Alaska to Panama in an attempt to protect the coast from Confederate raiders. Camp Drum became Union military headquarters for southern California in January 1862, under the command of Colonel James Henry Carleton. Volunteers from Camp Latham at Playa del Rey were moved to a tent city, located about a mile northwest of the center of Wilmington, near Banning's busy wharf. Also posted at Camp Drum were volunteers from other California posts and regular Union army units heading east.

The wet winter of 1861–62, with heavy rainfall, cold winds, and blowing sand which followed, pointed to a need for permanent buildings at the camp. Construction began in late 1862, and by September 1863, the post was complete, consisting of a thirty-acre parade ground, a residence for the base commander, junior officers' barracks, an adjutant's office, five troop barracks, two large stables, and nine other buildings. Transfer of title to the land from Phineas Banning to the federal government was dated October 31, 1863, six weeks after the buildings were finished. Title to additional land from Banning and his partner, Benjamin Davis Wilson, was transferred in February 1864, and a third piece of land was transferred to the government by Banning in February 1865. Total land conveyed to the government was just less than sixty acres. Drum Barracks served as a major staging area for troops and supplies bound for much of the West. It was an active and crowded post until the end of the Civil War. Although Banning and Wilson conveyed the barracks property to the government for the duration of the war, it was not transferred back to them until 1873. At auction that year the partners bought the remaining government buildings for $3,551.

Competition for government trade was keen in the 1860s, according to Harris Newmark, a successful merchant and friend of Phineas Banning, who said in *Sixty Years in Southern California* that "energetic efforts were made by merchants to secure their share of the crumbs, as well as the loaves, that might fall from Uncle Sam's table." One of the "loaves" was certainly the establishment of Camp Drum and Drum Barracks at Wilmington for, wrote Newmark, "the government not only spent over a million dollars in buildings and works there, and constantly drew on the town for at least part of its supplies, but provisions of all kinds were sent through Wilmington to troops in southern California, Utah, Yuma, Tucson and vicinity, and New Mexico." Government supplies were shipped to these far-flung inland areas on great wagon trains run by employees of the indefatigable Banning.

Phineas Banning was born in 1830 at Oak Hill Farm near Wilmington, Delaware; arrived in California in 1851; and soon went to work for the firm of Douglas and Sanford in the highly competitive freight business between San Pedro and Los

Angeles. Later he joined the freighting firm of Temple and Alexander, making enough money to buy out Temple and become the partner of George C. Alexander. Inside of two years the firm of Alexander and Banning had 500 mules, 40 horses, several stages, and more than 30 heavy freight wagons. Banning not only managed the business but often drove the stages himself. His ambition, according to historian John W. Robinson, "was not only to dominate commerce between San Pedro and Los Angeles, but [to] cover the whole Southwest."

When young Harris Newmark, recently arrived from Europe, first encountered Banning, later a close friend, he was astonished by Banning's appearance. Knowing "that this gentleman was a forwarding merchant, I had expected to find a man

dressed in either a uniform or a Prince Albert, with a high hat and other appropriate appurtenances," Newmark wrote. "I knew absolutely nothing of the rough methods in vogue on the Pacific Coast, [and] there stood before me a very large, powerful man, coatless and vestless, without necktie or collar, and wearing pantaloons at least six inches too short, a pair of brogans and socks with large holes; while bright-colored suspenders added to the picturesque effect of his costume" (Newmark, p. 23).

Banning started hauling freight for the Army in 1854, beginning with building supplies for Fort Tejon. That same year the California Steam Navigation Company was incorporated, and small steamships began to call regularly at San Pedro. Two years later, with Alexander and Banning stages and wagons traveling regular routes to Fort Tejon, Salt Lake, and Fort Yuma, Banning was aware of the need for better transfer facilities. He persuaded fellow businessmen John G. Downey, Benjamin D. Wilson, and William Sanford to purchase with him 2,400 acres of Rancho San

Phineas Banning was the "father" of Los Angeles Harbor.

Pedro from Manuel Dominguez with a view toward converting the estuary into a first-class harbor. The partners did not want to invest large sums of money in the proposed landing, however, so in 1857, Banning purchased back from his partners 640 acres of sheltered land back of Rattlesnake (now Terminal) Island and began plans for a new town and wharf. The new town, initially named New San Pedro, was later renamed Wilmington after Banning's birthplace in Delaware.

With customary speed, Banning hired a surveyor, laid out the town, and began work on a home for his family along with warehouses, corrals, a canal, and a wharf. He had a channel dredged for shallow draft vessels from Deadman's Island through the marshland to his landing at the head of the bay, and on September 25, 1858, the first passengers and freight were landed at the new Banning wharf in Wilmington.

When, in 1864, Banning built his Greek Revival home, now a residence museum in Banning Park, it stood virtually alone near muddy tide flats. To the east of his wharf and warehouses lay Mormon Island, on which, during the Civil War, a volunteer Mormon cavalry unit established a small shipyard, giving the area its name. Later Banning founded a shipyard on the island where many vessels vital to both Catalina's cross-channel commerce and to his Wilmington Transportation Company's tug and lightering enterprise in Los Angeles Harbor were built. The island is now connected to mainland Wilmington by Fries Avenue. Early in the twentieth century, William Wrigley Jr. constructed the Catalina Terminal just west of the Banning property for his company's excursion trips to Catalina Island.

Banning's close friendship with Brigadier General Winfield Scott Hancock, a West Point graduate later nominated for U.S. president, began in 1859 when Hancock was sent to establish a supply depot for the Army Quartermaster Corps of the Southwest near Los Angeles. The quartermaster's depot was eventually located in Wilmington, from which Banning's stage lines shipped supplies and materials to at least seventy military posts scattered throughout the West and Southwest. Banning, always a strong Union supporter, received the contract for constructing Fort Yuma, just across the Colorado River. He also undertook another project for the Union Army: construction of an aqueduct to bring fresh water from the San Gabriel River to Wilmington, a distance of eight miles.

Banning continued to make harbor improvements needed to unload increasingly heavy military supplies. He was also contractor for the first telegraph line between Los Angeles, Wilmington, and Yuma in 1861, the same year the Civil War began.

An estimated 7,000 Union troops passed through Drum Barracks between 1861 and 1871, when it was deactivated. The only remaining standing structure of the barracks is one of the junior officers' quarters, a white frame building at 1052 Banning Boulevard. It was preserved by the Thomas Keaveney family as a home and boardinghouse until it became a state historical monument and Civil War Museum in 1986 under the auspices of the Drum Barracks Society and City of Los Angeles. The museum is located about a block south of the General Phineas Banning Residence Museum in Banning Park at 401 East M Street, Wilmington.

Banning's partner in the Wilmington land deeded to the government was Benjamin D. Wilson, known widely and affectionately among the Californians as "Don Benito." A native of Tennessee, he came to Los Angeles in 1841, engaged in trading, became the first county clerk and first mayor of Los Angeles, and served two terms as a U.S. senator. Mrs. George S. Patton Sr. was the youngest daughter of Wilson. The Pattons' son, George S. Patton Jr., famous five-star general of World War II, lived in Avalon as a youth.

18 Sea Otter Wealth

The sea otter feeds on muscles [sic] and other bivalvular shell fish — He descends and brings up one of these fish, and also brings two stones of convenient size to the surface of the water — He then turns over upon his back, [and] lays one stone upon his breast, and placing the muscle upon the stone, with the other stone, he breaks the shell of the muscle in pieces to obtain the fish within.

GEORGE C. YOUNT, *Chronicles of the West*

Through no fault of its own except that it grew a luxurious fur coat, that playful, tool-using mammal, the sea otter, did as much as, if not more than, the gold rush to determine the commercial and social destiny of California. In the process, that rare small marine mammal of the northern Pacific coast, officially *Enhydra lutris,* came close to extinction.

The sea otter's long travail began with the third voyage of Captain James A. Cook, the great English navigator. After discovering the Sandwich (Hawaiian) Islands in January 1778 (this Polynesian-inhabited Hawaiian group he named after the head of the British Navy, Lord Sandwich), Cook reached the North American coast at about forty-four degrees, near the latitude of present-day Eugene, Oregon. He then proceeded northward to Nootka. His voyage of exploration helped seal the fate of fur-bearing mammals along the coast from Alaska to Baja California, and heralded the later arrival by land and sea of the Yankee hunter, trapper, and trader, along with others interested in trade or settlement: the English, Russians, and French.

During Cook's voyage, furs picked up from the natives for a few trinkets were disposed of in China "at such good prices as to open the eyes of merchants to the possibilities of the fur trade," observed Charles E. Chapman in *A History of California, The Spanish Period.* "The result was a swarm of European vessels, particularly English ships, on the northwest coast in the last fifteen years of the [eighteenth] century... exploration in the Pacific was gathering momentum."

Although Spaniards in California had been aware of the presence of sea otters, they apparently paid little attention to them until about 1780, after the missions had been founded and the presidios established. Then missionaries and soldiers began to purchase otter skins from local Indians for a few *reales* each. Otter furs found their way to the Orient on the Manila galleons, and through Russian fur traders who purchased skins from natives on the Aleutian Islands. Trade in sea otter furs was given a boost in 1784 by the published account of Cook's voyage, which mentioned sea otter trade as a potentially lucrative enterprise. That same year the Spanish government entered the otter trade on an extensive organized basis. New Spain (Mexico) had a continuing need of quicksilver for use in its gold and silver mines. China had ample supplies of quicksilver, and sea otter skins were highly prized by the Chinese. There developed a rather short-lived two-way trade. The San Blas vessels which annually brought supplies to California missions and presidios, obtained valuable sea otter skins there before returning to New Spain.

Sea otter skins went by sea to San Blas and were sent overland to Mexico City, where they were dressed by experts, packed in special mothproof boxes, and taken back over the hills to Acapulco. Then the skins were shipped by galleons via Manila to Canton. Containers of quicksilver obtained in China in exchange for the furs arrived in New Spain from 1789 to 1793. But there were problems in obtaining enough skins in Alta California. Mission Indians were unskilled otter hunters, and the padres lacked a suitable means of paying the Indians. Adele Ogden noted that the "Indians would not take to otter hunting unless they were compensated for their labor" and it could not be expected "that the padres would further a project unless they could see that it contributed to the welfare of their charges."

Still, the "fur rush" was on and prices for the skins escalated. A worried Spain tightened its hold on the Californias and sought to keep foreigners, including Russians and Americans, out of its waters. Despite Spain's efforts, the first "Boston vessel" arrived on the coast in 1796, and the Russian American Fur Company began to extend its activities into California.

It has been reported that in Canton, Cook's seamen received as much as $120 for a single prime pelt. While this may be an exaggeration, profits could be enormous, even with an average price of about forty dollars a pelt in the first quarter of the nineteenth century. One New England trader bought more than 300 skins from Indians at a cost of two yards of cotton cloth apiece. Similar skins then sold for twenty-three dollars each in Canton. Another shrewd Yankee received $8,000 worth of furs in exchange for a rusty iron chisel (Cleland 1930, p. 9). Despite (or because of) the competition, Spain continued its efforts to control the fur trade. Most were focused on the northwest, but small collections of sea otter skins began to be made in Alta California. To that end, Father Lasuen in 1791 requested the mission padres to continue obtaining otter skins, which could be sent to New Spain on the annual San Blas supply ships. There they could be sold for good prices.

The padres were good merchants, keeping stores at the missions to supply the wants of the Indians as well as the Californians on the ranchos. They took in payment tallow, hides, furs, and horn. They "traded with fur hunters and gave, in exchange for skins, goods and also gold and silver coin.... When they made purchases from vessels trading on the coast, they exhibited good judgment in their selections and were close buyers," wrote William Heath Davis in *Seventy-Five Years in California.*

Although early sea otter hunting was done by native Aleuts, hired by the Russians, American hunters and trappers coming overland began to hunt the profitable sea otters, sometimes in cooperation with the mission fathers. Some of these adventurous men were important to California history, others to the history of Catalina Island.

In 1830, George C. Yount, a hunter and trapper from North Carolina who had come overland from New Mexico with William Wolfskill's party to trap beaver on the San Joaquin, learned that "an animal called the Sea Otter abounded on the coast and on the islands contiguous to the seashore" (Camp, "The Chronicles of George Yount," p. 99) and that the gathering of otter furs had "sometimes been made lucrative." This important news was relayed by Padre Jose Bernardo Sanchez, amiable priest and genial head of the San Gabriel Mission (founded September 8, 1771), during the two weeks Yount and Wolfskill stayed at the mission after their long overland journey.

Described by his contemporaries as a man "who loved good eating, hearty living and practical joking" (W.W. Robinson 1948), as well as a "great sportsman and capital shot with rifle and fowling piece," Father Sanchez was completing a term as president of the California missions when he encouraged his visitors to build a small schooner for sea otter hunting and offered to help finance the endeavor. Included in the group of hunters were Nathaniel M. Pryor and Richard Laughlin, who had trapped with Yount on the Gila River in 1827. With Indian help and the guiding hand of Joseph Chapman, an American who had arrived in California with the pirate Bouchard in 1818, the men built the thirty-ton schooner *Refugio*, which they launched at San Pedro in 1831. The *Refugio* was named for the Refugio ranch near Santa Barbara owned by Chapman's in-laws, the Ortegas.

San Pedro port, such as it was, and San Gabriel Mission, thirty miles inland, were closely linked in those early days. San Pedro was the mission's main link with the outside world. An adobe hide warehouse, then the only building at the port, was owned by the mission under Father Sanchez and used as a storeroom for cattle hides and otter pelts ready for shipping, as well as a place to do business with supercargoes, those roving merchants from incoming ships. Constructed in 1823 for William Hartnell and Hugh McCulloch, English hide and tallow traders from Lima, the adobe was transferred to the San Gabriel Mission in 1829.

Yount, Wolfskill, Pryor, Laughlin, Samuel Prentice (of the ship-wrecked *Danube*), and others sailed far and wide along the coast and its neighboring islands in search of sea otters, nearly exterminating them in the course of a few years. In the early days, hunters commented on the abundance of otters, Yount describing them as "laying upon the surface of the water, near the land, in groups of several hundred together" (Camp, "The Chronicles of George Yount"). Numbers were reduced when virtually uncontrolled hunting eventually reduced the breeding stock, and an even greater decimation occurred after the 1840s when the Yankee hunters and traders introduced the efficient gun to supplement the spear utilized by the Indians and Aleuts. Estimates vary widely, but it is thought that around one million pelts were harvested from Alaska to Baja California between 1741 (the beginning of the Russian period) and 1911, when an international moratorium on sea otter hunting was enacted. Ottering, as it was called, continued into the 1840s, when California became part of the United States, although it was gradually supplanted by the hide-

and-tallow and whaling industries in importance. Then, of course, came the gold rush, which, for a time, eclipsed everything in California.

The gold rush seems to have reminded an aging Yount of an underwater outcropping of quartz with gold in it on Catalina Island that he had seen while hunting sea otter years earlier. Yount returned to Catalina several times, but could not relocate his treasure. Neither could others, but we will deal with Catalina gold in a later chapter.

In southern California, most otters were found around the kelp-rich islands of the Santa Barbara Channel: San Nicolas, San Miguel, Santa Cruz, Santa Rosa, and Santa Barbara, and to a lesser extent, Catalina and San Clemente, but smaller populations were found in mainland waters near Santa Barbara, San Pedro, and San Juan Capistrano. When the hunters left off seafaring and hunting marine mammals, many settled in California, becoming landowners and leading citizens.

In Los Angeles, Wolfskill became a horticulturist, raising some of the first commercial oranges; Pryor had a vineyard and walnut trees and became a *regidor* or city councilman. Laughlin was at one time a trader at San Pedro, supporting himself by carpentry and hunting and eventually owning a vineyard on Alameda Street. Other sea otter hunters included J.J. Warner, founder of Warner's Ranch, and Benjamin D. Wilson, Phineas Banning's partner after whom Mount Wilson is named. Samuel Prentice spent most of his life on Catalina Island, hunting and fishing and dreaming of buried Spanish treasure there. George Nidever, along with Isaac J. Sparks and Lewis T. Burton, became a leading citizen of Santa Barbara.

It was Captain Nidever who made history by rescuing the legendary lost Indian woman from rugged San Nicolas Island in July of 1853. She had eluded discovery for eighteen years, subsisting on fish, seal, blubber, and whatever she could forage. The woman was among the last twenty natives of San Nicolas Island who had assembled on the beach there before boarding the Mexican schooner *Peor Es Nada* (Worse than Nothing), to be removed to the mainland. At the last minute the woman believed her child had been left behind and asked to return to the village and rescue it. She was allowed to go, but while she was absent, a strong wind began to blow. Fearing for everyone's safety if they waited any longer, the rescuers sailed without the Indian woman, running *Peor Es Nada* before the wind and landing the Indians at San Pedro. The schooner intended to return to San Nicolas, according to Nidever (Ellison) but was ordered to Monterey and then to San Francisco where *Peor Es Nada* capsized, although her crew was saved. As the years passed, people who knew the story assumed that the lone Indian woman on San Nicolas had perished.

Nidever, who ran sheep on San Miguel Island, went to San Nicolas in 1852 in search of sea gull eggs and discovered signs of human habitation, as well as footprints, but was forced to leave because of a gale. The following year he returned, but again was driven off by a gale. Later, in the spring of 1853, Nidever returned to San Nicolas, found the woman, and took her to Santa Barbara where she became a great curiosity for the few remaining weeks of her life. Despite efforts of Nidever and the padres, no one was found who could understand the woman's language or speak to her, although, Nidever said, "she expressed a great many ideas by signs, so plainly that we readily understood them." The rescued woman was judged to be in her fifties. In 1928, a tablet in memory of the unknown mother was placed on a Santa Barbara Mission wall by the Daughters of the American Revolution.

When George Yount came ashore permanently, he used another of his skills. He introduced shingle roofing and siding into California. Having explained the process of making shingles to the Mexican general, Mariano Vallejo, Yount hand-split shingles and applied them to Vallejo's house in Sonoma. The general was so pleased at having the first shingled house in the two Californias that he gave Yount, in payment for the work, two square leagues of land (about five square miles) in upper Napa Valley. Yount, the first white man to occupy that valley, became influential in the changeover from stock raising, which required huge amounts of land to succeed, to regular crop production and horticulture on a large scale. He died in 1865 at the age of seventy-one, having donated land for the northern California town which bears his name, Yountville, from his large Caymus Ranch.

While the earliest hunters obtained their sea otter skins by bartering with the natives, the Russians saw this as risky and not as profitable as it might have been. The next attempt to take otters in waters controlled by the Spanish government involved a contract system, in which Boston ships contracted with the Russians in a California hunting experiment. Under this approach, the Russians supplied Aleuts (natives of the Aleutian Islands) with *baidarkas* (portable boats of skins stretched over wood frames), and a Yankee captain transported both by ship to the rich sea otter waters to the south. Skins obtained by the natives were divided equally, with large profits made on both sides. The system worked for nearly a decade, but eventually the Russians preferred independent hunting expeditions, where they did not have to divide their profits. The first of these went to Bodega Bay, where temporary buildings were erected. A second expedition went to San Francisco Bay, and it was decided to establish a permanent hunting base at Fort Ross, which the Russians had already designated as a supply base.

From these bases, Russian ships, with their sharp shooting Aleuts, began a systematic slaughter of sea otters. The Aleuts were sometimes left for months on the islands, with food and water and women to prepare the food. Then they were picked up by the Russian vessels and returned to the Russian bases or left off at another island. The sea otters were hunted so assiduously that before long they were cleared off the northern California coast between Trinidad and San Francisco Bays (Rolle, p. 106). The hunters even sailed to San Pedro and the Channel Islands seeking pelts.

The Russians built a few large ships at Bodega Bay, and they were among the first vessels launched in California, along with those constructed in the Santa Barbara and San Pedro areas. Unfortunately, the Russian ships were of unseasoned lumber, so they didn't last long. Russian vessels wintered and were repaired at Bodega Bay, and goods were stored in warehouses there. At Fort Ross, eighteen miles to the north, there was a community of about 400 people, including Aleuts and their wives. In 1841, the Russians and the Russian American Fur Company, experiencing serious financial losses and problems from a growing number of American settlers, abandoned Fort Ross (Rolle, pp. 165–66). They left behind some place names: Fort Ross, a derivation of Russia; the Russian River; and Mount St. Helena, named for the Empress of Russia. They also left a small vessel, some farming equipment, a few cannons, and other armament, which were bought by John Sutter of gold rush fame.

Along with commercial fur hunters of other nationalities, the Russian and Aleut hunters nearly eliminated the sea otter population. When an international moratorium on hunting them was enacted in 1911, only about 1,000 to 2,000 otters remained along the entire Pacific coast, from the Bering Sea to Baja California. The California Fish and Game Department estimates there were more than 300,000 in the same range in the early 1800s. Today these attractive, playful mammals, ranging in size from 86 to 102 pounds, may be observed sporting and feeding among the bull kelp in protected water offshore at Point Lobos State Reserve, four miles south of Monterey, and at Pacific Grove nearby.

19   The Yankee Vanguard

The link between California and Oahu, "the crossroads of the Pacific," was especially close, and the adventurous, profit-seeking sons of New England who dominated the three-cornered trade between the Atlantic seaboard, California and Canton, molded the destinies of both countries.

ROBERT GLASS CLELAND,
Foreword to *China Trade Days in California*

The late maritime historian John Haskell Kemble, professor emeritus of history at Pomona College, Claremont, California, was convinced that the first Yankee ship to come ashore on Catalina Island for repairs was careened at the Isthmus rather than at what is now Avalon Bay, as was previously assumed. Furthermore, it was not Avalon Bay that was once named Port Roussillon, but the Isthmus, with its three good coves, all with beaches suitable for careening a vessel at low tide. The Yankee vessel was the 175-ton Virginia-built brig *Lelia Byrd,* two-masted and square-rigged. The year was 1805 and the master of the ship was William Shaler who, with his partner, Richard Jeffry Cleveland, had purchased the *Lelia Byrd* in 1801 in Kiel, Germany, both intending to become what were termed "merchant captains." With equal shares in the enterprise, the twenty-eight-year old partners, each with considerable sailing experience, drew lots to determine their positions aboard ship. Shaler won the title of master and Cleveland became supercargo or business agent (Pourade 1962 and Teller 1960).

In Hamburg the partners met a young Polish exile, Count John De Roussillon, inviting the amiable nobleman to become their third partner on a trading voyage to Valparaiso, Chile, and San Blas, Mexico. At San Blas the partners spent six months trying to arrange for the disposal of $10,000 worth of goods and the purchase of 1,600 sea otter skins recently arrived from the Californias. It was De Roussillon who helped close the deal; his charm and ability to play the flute won over a Spanish official who eventually allowed the Yankees to trade their cargo and secure the otter skins. Unfortunately, the count became seriously ill and went to Mexico City where he died in 1803 at the age of twenty-eight. Two years later, when Shaler took the *Lelia Byrd* to Catalina for repairs, he "took the liberty of naming [the harbor] after my much respected friend, M. De Roussillon."

On the earlier trip, the vessel acquired a new topmast at San Blas, took on supplies, and filled its water casks. A rumor reached the partners that a great many sea otter skins were available at San Diego, so they headed the *Lelia Byrd* north. On March 17, 1803, they passed the Spanish fort on Point Guijarros (near present-day Ballast Point on Point Loma), its nine-pound cannons directed toward the harbor entrance, and put down their anchor. The next day they had difficulty with an arrogant Spanish official while trying to purchase otter pelts, the upshot later being termed the "bloodless Battle of San Diego." No great harm was done either to the battery on shore or to the traders, although the *Lelia Byrd* suffered damage to her sails and rigging and a few small holes in her hull, which were temporarily patched with oakum.

The vessel then sailed up and down the coast in search of furs, meeting a few other Yankee traders before going on to the Hawaiian Islands and Canton where the accumulated skins were sold at a comfortable profit. Cleveland left for Boston in January 1804, on another ship, the *Alert,* with Captain Caleb Winship. On board, he wrote, was "an invoice of silks of about fifty thousand dollars, belonging equally to my friend Shaler and myself. The result of this, with that of my former voyage, and my interest in the *Lelia Byrd* would amount to about seventy thousand dollars . . . clear of debt." One would think Cleveland, only thirty-one at the time, might have come ashore and retired from the sea, but that was not to be. Two years later, in 1806, he put to sea again, trying to make up losses caused by several poor investments. Shaler, meanwhile, had sole command of the *Lelia Byrd.* He traded his cargo of Asian and European goods along California's sparsely populated coast, but on May 1, 1805, was forced into the harbor at Catalina when the *Lelia Byrd* became so unseaworthy that she required pumping every ten to fifteen minutes to remain afloat.

Two months earlier, Shaler wrote, he "paid a visit to the island of Santa Catalina, where I had been informed by the Indians that there was a good harbor. We remained there a few days only to ascertain the point. We found the harbor every thing that could be desired, and I determined that, after collecting all the skins on the coast, I would return to it and careen the ship, which she was by this time greatly in want of." (This and the following quotations are from Shaler's "Description of California," first published in 1808 in the *American Register,* vol. 3 and reprinted in Appendix B of Robert Glass Cleland's *A History of California: The American Period.*)

Shaler stated (incorrectly) that he "was the first navigator who had ever visited and surveyed this place," seemingly unaware of the Spanish explorers who preceded him. He went on to say that he "warped the ship into a small cove," possibly Big Fisherman, Fourth of July, or Cherry, then landed the cargo "and everything moveable, under tents that we had previously prepared for their reception. The Indian inhabitants of this island, to the amount of about 150 men, women, and children, came and encamped with us, and readily afforded every aid in their power."

Shaler's impression of the Indians who inhabited the "shores and islands of the canal of Santa Barbara" was highly favorable. He said they "seem to be a race of people quite distinct from the other aboriginals of the country. They are a handsome people, remarkably sprightly, courteous and intelligent, and display great ingenuity in all their arts." Shaler mentioned the Indians' fine canoes of small "pine" boards, "sewed together in a very curious manner; these are generally capable of carrying from six to fourteen people, and are in form not unlike a whaleboat; they are managed with paddles, and go with surprizing [*sic*] velocity. They besides make a great variety of curious and useful articles of wicker work, and excellent pots and mortars of stone."

Having beached the *Lelia Byrd* at high tide, her careening — heaving her down on one side with tackles at low tide to clean and repair the bottom — proved to be a daunting task. The brig's bottom was in "a most alarming state; the worms had nearly destroyed the sheathing, and were found to be lodged in the bottom planks." The keel and sternpost "were nearly reduced to a honeycomb." Once, when hoving her farther out from shore, she upset and filled with seawater. After steady pumping, bailing, and the application of quantities of lime burnt on the beach together with tallow and oakum held down by stones until "the mass had consolidated," Shaler decided that since by then the ship leaked only slightly, she was fit to reenter the trade.

> By the 9th of June, the ship was again rigged with a jury mizen-mast [*sic*], our cargo on board, and we were again ready for sea. On the 12th, we bid adieu to our Indian friends, and left Port Roussillon with the intention of running down the coast, and, if we found the ship not to leak so much as to be unsafe, to run for the Sandwich Islands, where I determined to leave her, and to take passage in some north-west fur trader for Canton.

The *Lelia Byrd* reached Hawaii without mishap, was sold to King Kamehameha I, later entered the opium trade, and eventually rotted away on Whampoa Beach. The *Tamana,* a smaller vessel obtained in trade from King Kamehameha I, was sent back to the California coast with the remainder of Shaler's cargo, under the direction, Shaler wrote, of "Mr. Hudson, a young gentleman who had long (since Valparaiso)

With Isthmus Bay in the foreground and Catalina Harbor in the background, the Civil War barracks can be seen on the crest of the Isthmus in this Banning-period (1891–1919) photograph. Judge J.B. Banning built the wharf in 1903.

been my companion and assistant." Hudson, then twenty-seven, was already familiar with Isthmus Harbor, calling it Port Roussillon in 1806 as he entered the harbor "with the rock in the entrance to the bay," probably an allusion to Bird Rock. "At 11 o'clock we entered the bay, where we before careened the ship and came to." This seems a clear reference to the careening of the *Lelia Byrd.*

Hudson, whose full name was John Thomas Hudson, had sailed the *Tamana* earlier that day from San Pedro where, he said, he acquired 510 skins for $1,200 in cash, the rest in goods. He had steered "for the west end of the island" where he arrived on May 12, 1806. Hudson's words are found in a rare handwritten log book, catalogued as "The Journal of the Schooner *Tamana,* from Woahoo (Sandwich Islands) to the Coast of America," kept by John T. Hudson for the years 1805 to 1807 (call number HM 30491) in the collection of the Huntington Library, San Marino, California. Before his death in February 1990, John Kemble told us about this logbook. He had been working on a history involving Hudson and the *Tamana.* With Peter

Blodgett, then assistant curator of western manuscripts at the Huntington Library in attendance, my wife and I spent a spellbound afternoon studying this priceless manuscript, from which the excerpts below were copied.

Upon anchoring in a cove "on the west side of the bay," possibly today's Fourth of July or Cherry Cove, the schooner's sails were unbent and the yards sent down. A large tent was erected "on shore for the reception of the goods."

Tuesday, May 13, 1806 — "In the morning early commenced landing goods and skins, etc. I got them all on shore before dinner. In the afternoon, the water, and had a clear ship. Got down the caboose [cookroom or kitchen on deck of a merchant-man] ashore and took up my quarters in the tent with the goods and skins."

Captain Hudson had his personnel problems, which were duly noted. He suspended from duty Charles Peterson, first mate, "in consequence of his abusive language." Hudson got into a scuffle with Peterson when the latter refused to give up the log book. Peterson was intoxicated, Hudson wrote, a not uncommon problem aboard vessels of the period.

The crew gathered wood on shore and burned lime in a kiln they apparently built. Three days passed before the tide was high enough to haul the schooner on shore. On Thursday the fifteenth, a Mr. Hinckly, second mate, went in a canoe to the east side of the bay and got six barrels of fresh water, which he filled out of "several holes." In the afternoon the men were engaged in tanning skins, and a party went "wooding." The carpenter and one of the islanders (a native) came down with "the flux" (dysentery). The afternoon weather was drizzly, with a light breeze. On the seventeenth, the *Tamana* was in readiness and was hauled high on shore. The carpenter "was bled" for he was pronounced no better.

On the eighteenth, at daybreak, the schooner lay high and dry. "Worms had taken possession of her sheathing and entered in every place where there happened to be rubbed off areas." These areas were patched. From Tuesday, the twentieth, through Monday, June 3, the men were engaged in refloating the vessel, taking on a ton of ballast, water, skins, and the principal part of the goods; painting her, working on sails, and blackening the spars.

The carpenter, who had been bled several times, seemed to be better. He hauled up the "fish," a piece of timber shaped like a fish and used to strengthen a mast or yard, to the topsail yard. The bower anchor was put out. And, because the weather was cloudy and drizzly, they waited for the paint to dry while "the canoe went afishing." One crewman went gunning after partridges and "fell in with a sow and two sloats we left there the year before," and a "fine fair boar" was shot. The rigging was set up, with the fore topmast yards, new sail bent on along with the mainsail. The Indians, whom they considered their friends, were visited. For some reason, Hudson reports, most of the Indians had left the island before their arrival, and no women were to be seen. On June 3 they "hove to" and "towed her out into the breeze today with boat and canoe," and the vessel departed for San Pedro.

Earlier that year, in February, the *Tamana* had made an unscheduled visit to Port

Roussillon for about five days, waiting for soldiers from the Santa Barbara presidio to leave San Pedro so the *Tamana* could sail back and resume trading with the padres on the coast. Hudson found many of the Indians ill and a number dead. Apparently the white man's diseases had begun to take their toll among the native population. Hudson engaged one of the Catalina Indians to paddle to San Pedro in his small canoe to deliver a letter. He did not disclose the letter's content or addressee in the logbook.

Port Roussillon was visited again on January 31, 1807. The wind was light so the boat had to tow the *Tamana* in for three miles. Wood was growing scarce, Hudson reported, and so, apparently, were sea otter skins. They went to the Indians' village to "visit old acquaintances," one of whom sold them one otter skin. Another visit was made to Port Roussillon in early April 1807. At San Buenaventura, where the ship had taken 100 skins aboard, Captain Hudson met up with Captain William H. Davis of Boston from the ship *Mercury* — "14 month out" — and the captains agreed to sail together to Catalina where they could conduct business unmolested by Spanish customs officials. On Sunday, April 12, 1807, the ships sailed together past Anacapa and Santa Barbara Islands, heading for Catalina's West End. On the fourteenth they anchored in the bay at the Isthmus, where the two masters traded part of their goods and otter skins, Davis to take what he wanted to Canton.

Unfortunately, Hudson did not possess the shrewdness or aggressiveness of Shaler and Cleveland, and fared poorly in his "sales made among the missions and barter with the Indians." Nor did Hudson have much success collecting from the missionaries "any part of the sums due from them for goods, with which Mr. Shaler had credited them, though the hope of recovering these had been a considerable inducement in expediting this vessel," Cleveland said in his *Narrative of Voyages and Commercial Enterprises,* published in 1850.

After visiting most of the California missions and navigating the coast for a period of five to six months, Hudson still had not made any important sales. With his patience and that of the crew exhausted, and with provisions running low and otter skins scarce, Hudson returned the *Tamana* to the Sandwich Islands. Earlier in 1807, Hudson had sold the *Tamana* to Pavl Slobodchikov for 125 prime and 25 second-size otter skins, worth perhaps $3,000 on the Honolulu market. Slobodchikov was a trusted friend of Alexander Baranof, the Russian American Company's governor in Alaska (Kemble 1969). Slobodchikov and three other Russians sailed with Hudson back to the Sandwich Islands where the new owner took possession at Honolulu. *Tamana*'s career after her sale to the Russians was a short one. She was renamed *Nikolai* and sailed from Honolulu to Sitka. In the autumn of 1808 she was dispatched for California but was wrecked at the mouth of Gray's Harbor, Washington. Hudson proceeded on to Canton where he took passage to Boston on the *O'Cain,* arriving on June 14, 1808. On July 18 he committed suicide in Providence, Rhode Island (ibid.). The published report of his death said he had appeared insane for many days.

Shaler went on to become United States consul at Algiers, and in 1828 was appointed consul at Havana, then one of the best-paying offices in the government service (Teller, p. 210). He promptly invited his former partner to join him as vice-consul, which Cleveland accepted. Shaler died in Havana in 1833 during a cholera epidemic. Cleveland, unable to succeed Shaler as consul for political reasons, returned to the states, dying in Danvers, Massachusetts, in 1860 at the age of eighty-seven.

20   Unstoppable Commerce

Had the shipper been compelled, under a more stringent administration of the law, to pay the full amount of duties, he could not have made a fair profit out of the business. Moreover, he would have been compelled to charge so high a price for his goods that it would have been a severe tax upon the rancheros who required them.

WILLIAM HEATH DAVIS, *Seventy-five Years in California*

Since 1768, San Blas, near Tepic on Mexico's mainland coast, has been a small, mosquito-infested shipbuilding port and supply center. San Blas had ready access to the populous areas of Jalisco and contact via Guadalajara with Mexico City, the viceregal capital of New Spain. The port, known as San Blas de Californias, was a point of outlet for all products leaving California in legal trade. Furs from the northwest debarked from there, along with agricultural products from Alta and Baja California.

What is important to the Channel Islands and the southern California mainland was that San Blas became a department of the Spanish Navy from which armed vessels patrolled the Pacific coast as far north as Nootka Sound (Thurman, pp. 14–15). Fortunately for the Yankee, Russian, and English ships intent on trade and the purchase of sea otter skins, the Spaniards had too few warships patrolling too much territory to be an effective deterrent to outside trade.

After Mexico successfully revolted against Spanish rule in 1821 (although it was some time before word of this reached Alta California), Mexican authorities, like the Spanish, attempted to exclude foreign maritime traders and placed a ban on sea otter hunting by foreigners. Exorbitant tariffs were imposed, as much as 100 percent of the value of landed goods from the Sandwich Islands, the United States, and Canton, much to the dismay of mission fathers and California residents who were heavily dependent on such goods for survival. No better firsthand description of traders and their methods for escaping or reducing the exorbitant tariffs can be found than in Richard Henry Dana Jr.'s *Two Years Before the Mast*. The brig *Pilgrim* was anchored off San Buenaventura in early November of 1835 and Dana described what he saw:

The other vessel which we found in port was the hermaphrodite brig *Avon,* Capt. Hinckley, from the Sandwich Islands. She was fitted up in handsome style; fired a gun and ran her ensign up and down at sunrise and sunset; had a band of four or five pieces of music on board and appeared rather like a pleasure yacht than trader; yet, in connection with the *Loriotte, Clementine, Bolivar, Convoy,* and other small vessels belonging to the Consul and other Americans at Oahu, she carried on a great trade — legal and illegal — in otter skins, silks, tea, specie, &c.

The second day after our arrival, a full-rigged brig came around the point from the northward, sailed leisurely through the bay, and stood off again for the south-east, in the direction of the large island of Catalina. The next day the *Avon* got under weigh, and stood in the same direction, nominally bound for San Pedro. This might do for the marines and Californians, but we knew the ropes too well. The brig was never again seen on the coast, and the *Avon* arrived at San Pedro in about a week, with a full cargo of Canton and American goods.

This was one of the means of escaping the heavy duties the Mexicans lay upon all imports. A vessel comes on the coast, enters a moderate cargo at Monterey, which is the only customhouse, and commences trading. In a month or more, having sold a large part of her cargo, she stretches over to Catalina, or other of the large uninhabited islands which lie off the coast, in a trip from port to port, and supplies herself with choice goods from a vessel from Oahu, which has been lying off and on the islands, waiting for her. Two days after the sailing of the *Avon,* the *Loriotte* came in from the leeward, and without doubt had also a snatch at the brig's cargo.

To import or export something in violation of customs law is, of course, smuggling, but one must understand the historical circumstances that encouraged, even necessitated, smuggling along the Pacific Coast during the periods of Spanish and Mexican rule.

At the heart of the problem was the physical distance from and apparent disinterest of both Spanish and Mexican governments in the welfare of those living in the far-flung pastoral settlements of Upper California. The missions eventually flourished thanks to the unceasing efforts of the padres; the secular ranchos succeeded after they began to breed cattle on their vast acreage, but aside from what was grown or produced by the Californians, there was almost nothing available to furnish homes, equip the large establishments, and clothe the ranchers' ever-growing families.

Referring to the Mexican period (1822 to 1848), William Heath Davis, who had firsthand knowledge of such matters, said that it was considered "no disgrace for a merchant to evade the revenue laws to such an extent as he thought proper to take the risk, some doing so more than others." Pointing out that smuggling was never discussed among the merchants or made public in any way, Davis noted that "there was a kind of tacit understanding that this was the general custom, and it was all right and proper to get as many goods in free of duty as possible, and it was encouraged by the rancheros themselves, as many were not solicitous of assisting the remote general government of Mexico by payment of exorbitant taxes in duties upon the necessaries of life required of them."

In many respects the hide and tallow trade resembled the fur trade of the earlier period and throughout the Mexican period constituted California's chief contact with the outside world. It was also, according to historian John Walton Caughey, "a natural outgrowth of the earlier traffic with the Boston fur ships, natural because of the commercial connections already made and because the New England boot and shoe factories offered the best market for California's most abundant export commodity, cowhides."

Cattle raising flourished in the half century after the first herds were introduced by the Spaniards but, Caughey noted, "these were typical Mexican range cattle, wide-horned, long-legged, small-bodied, wild, and well able to forage and fend for themselves. The tough beef they afforded was a staple food of the province . . . [but] at the end of the Spanish period Californians could not begin to consume all the beef that was produced; they used only the choicest cuts [as food]."

At the missions and on a few ranchos a small amount of leather was tanned and hides were worked up into rawhide, which was widely used on the ranches, as well as for furniture. Tallow was tried out from the carcasses for candle and soap making, but again, supply exceeded demand. Small quantities of tallow were sent to San Blas before 1810 and some was sent to Lima in 1813. But the real start of the hide and tallow trade was at the beginning of the Mexican period when Hugh McCulloch and William E.P. Hartnell, representatives of the English house of John Begg and Company, arrived from Lima and negotiated with the prefect of the missions for a long-term monopoly of the mission trade in soap, suet, lard, horns, wine, hides, and tallow. These were the same men who arranged for building, in 1823, the small adobe warehouse at San Pedro, later given to San Gabriel Mission.

William Heath Davis estimated the astonishing volume of hides and tallow traded or sold on the coast from 1800 to 1847. Using a figure of 200 vessels extrapolated from a total of 600 arrivals "of all sizes and nationalities," he allowed each vessel 1,000 hides, exported annually, and arrived at a total of 9,400,000 hides for the forty-seven-year period, as well as 18,800,000 *arrobas* of tallow. An arroba is an old Spanish unit of weight equal to about twenty-five pounds. In exchange the ships imported from the east a tremendous variety of goods: carpeting, cotton handkerchiefs, broadcloth, velveteen, flour, sarsaparilla, lemon syrup, almonds, tobacco, rice, sugar, coffee, tinned salmon and oysters, pruning knives, iron trypots, coffee mills, tacks, nails, corks, soup tureens, crockery, wooden pails, cart wheels, sheep shears, corn brooms, carpenter's tools, iron horseshoes, ribbon, wood flooring and boards . . . the list goes on and on.

It was said that articles sold in California cost 300 percent more than their coun-

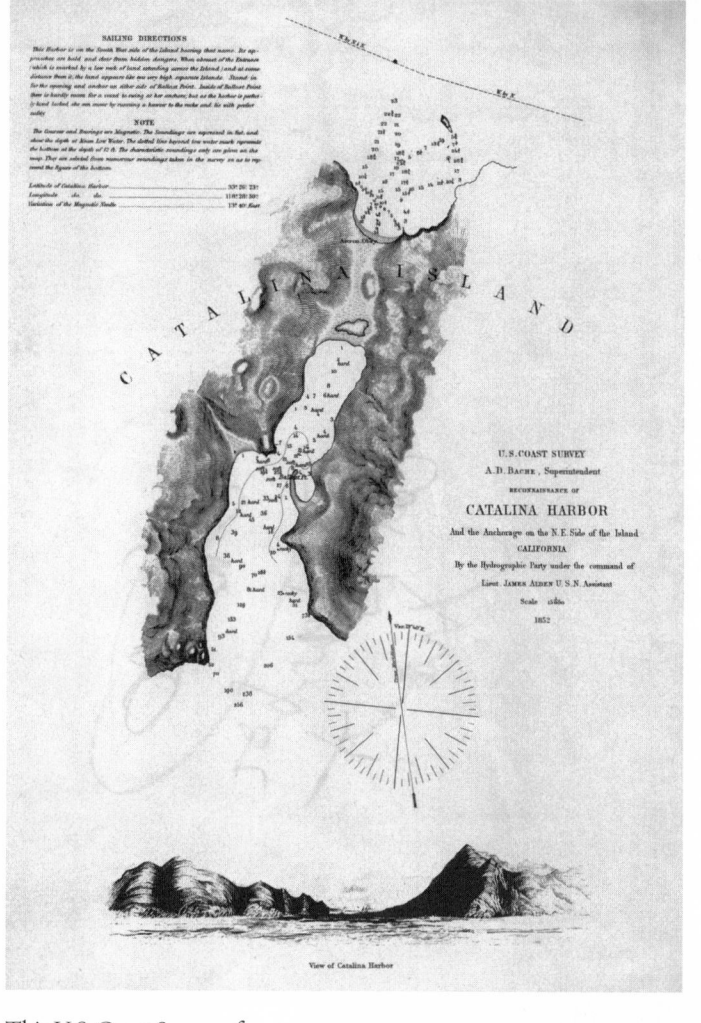

This U.S. Coast Survey of Catalina Harbor was the first and only chart of Catalina Island at the time of its survey, 1852. The emphasis was placed here, rather than on the rest of the island, because Catalina Harbor was a safe anchorage in nearly all types of weather, as opposed to almost all other anchorages in southern California. Detail of chart is opposite.

terparts in the East. Shipping expenses accounted for part of the inflation; excessive duty, when collected, added to it. So, at times, did the cost of taking goods to the Sandwich Islands before bringing them to California. Honolulu at that time had only a 5 percent duty on goods brought in from elsewhere, so it formed a convenient way stop for a number of merchant traders. Out of the way as it may seem to us, prevailing winds made Honolulu an easier port of call than California for vessels that had rounded Cape Horn. It was also a convenient stopping place for vessels returning to New England from Canton.

We have no means of identifying all the vessels that sought shelter during heavy weather, were careened for repairs, or held "smuggled" cargo on Catalina during the first half of the nineteenth century. They left no visible marks on the water of the coves, nor any on land that have lasted. Today they are ghost ships, long vanished, their names surviving only in scattered logbooks and the few narratives left behind. Among them were the schooner *Eagle* in 1821, which was mentioned in Chapter 14, and the ship *Courier* in 1826. Both American vessels encountered difficulties with the authorities while trading on the California coast.

The *Courier,* out of Boston with William H. Cunningham as captain, frequently visited Catalina Island from 1826 to 1828. Captain Cunningham attempted to improve facilities for coastal trade by establishing a kind of trading station at what is now Avalon. This shore base is described in the *Log of the Courier, 1826–1827–1828* by Captain Cunningham, taken from the original manuscript in the Peabody Museum, Salem, Massachusetts. Cunningham referred to this harbor as "Sachem Bay," possibly after the ship *Sachem,* a pioneer in the hide trade with Boston in early 1822 when California ports were briefly opened to free trade (Bancroft, vol. 2). Cunningham noted that "Sugar Loaf" lies NNW, ½W from where the *Courier* was anchored. These compass bearings coincide with the location of the towering rock of that name which once formed the western headland of Avalon Bay. It was blasted away in 1928 to make way for the Casino.

The *Courier*'s log for October 30 through November 20, 1826, records: "Landed hides and salt and lumber, built a house and three vatts [*sic*], dug two new wells and cleaned an old one. Done considerable business with the Russians and others in the Seal skin line. Took in ballast, etc. Landed Wm. G. Vincent with three men, with directions for salting and curing Cattle hides and Seal skins…"

Mexican governor Jose Maria Echeandia, displeased at learning of the onshore facility, ordered Cunningham to vacate the island. Cunningham complied in the fall of 1827 after salting 3,000 hides and 3,000 seal skins that were taken aboard, along with the rest of the property Cunningham and the *Courier*'s owners had had at the facility: tallow, spars, house, provisions, and other articles. The brig *Waverly* arrived and took off lumber belonging to the storehouse, which William G. Dana, master of the *Waverly,* purchased from Cunningham. The brig *Harbinger* landed some hides. Another brig, the *Banyon* of Boston, was anchored in Isthmus Harbor at the time, according to the log.

And so it transpired that vessels often came and went from Catalina, exchanging cargoes, careening, salting hides, all in defiance of Governor Echeandia's subsequent order banning foreign vessels from visiting Catalina. According to Bancroft, about a hundred American, English, French, and Russian vessels touched the California coast during this period, many undoubtedly anchoring at Catalina by reason of rest, safety, or smuggling. A few vessels were confiscated by Spanish and Mexican authorities.

There exists a mysterious presence that can be sensed on quiet nights in Catalina's coves. Listen closely with a sharpened inner ear, for it is sensed rather than heard. This old island, largely as it was two centuries ago, harbors ghosts that whisper to those who are removed from the mainland's bustle and strife. Heed us, they whisper, for we speak of continuity with the past, of departed people and vessels, large and small. We were here, we are still here, may be heard in the sea's murmur.

The answer to the question of how these vessels managed to navigate safely along the Pacific coast is that they had access to Spanish and English charts, obtained by whatever means possible. These were eventually augmented by French and Yankee explorers, who recorded information on maps they drew themselves or noted on maps drawn by professional cartographers. Even so, there were serious navigational problems. In 1852, with the California gold rush under way, Richard D. Cutts, Esq., assistant U.S. Coast Survey, aboard the U.S. surveying schooner *Baltimore* lying in San Francisco Bay, complained in a letter to the superintendent of the survey in Washington, D.C., about the absence of accurate charts covering the coast from Panama to San Diego. Pointing out that the English had made some surveys but that they were "unconnected, and thus deficient in the most important element," Cutts said "that the inaccuracy of the charts is the cause of great anxiety to the captains and owners of the steamships and other vessels plying this coast."

Cutts added: "There are very few of the captains who cannot recount some hair-breadth escapes; — some have been ashore; — and all this risk due to the fact that this headland, or that bay, is thirty or forty miles distant from the position assigned it on the chart. Existing rocks and islands are not down at all, and some far distant from the coast-line. Indeed, it is the practice of some of the best sailors to keep in sight of land or hug the coast, rather than trust to a straight course taken off from the present charts."

Cutts accurately foresaw the future value and importance of trade along the coast. He predicted that nearly half a million American citizens, either coming or going, would have traveled along the poorly marked sea track to California before the end of 1852.

A coast survey of the route from Panama to California, without the elaborate geodetic operations which were confined to American waters, was completed a few years later. As for Catalina, it was not until the island's economy began gearing for tourism in the late 1880s that Avalon Harbor, then known as Dakin's Cove, became sufficiently important for the Coast and Geodetic Survey, the former Coast Survey, to publish a description of it along with the Two Harbors area. Sailing instructions were included. The survey was published in 1889, two years after the establishment of Avalon. That year the *Pacific Coast Pilot* stated: "A topographical survey of the island has been made by the U.S. Coast and Geodetic Survey, and the topographical and hydrographic sketches of the anchorages have been published. The whole island and its relation to the mainland and the other islands are well exhibited in the Coast Survey chart from San Diego to Santa Monica."

According to the Library of Congress's Map Division, the earliest chart in its collection showing the whole of Catalina Island and its relation to the mainland from San Diego to Point Conception was published in 1890. Subsequent charts in various scales were published in 1915, 1917, 1927, 1929, and 1935, and continued to show the island in relation to the mainland. Astonishingly, it was not until early in 1936 that the first edition of a chart that detailed and covered the full island, without depicting the mainland (No. 5112), was published by the U.S. Coast and Geodetic Survey. We are indebted to Jim Flatnus of the Map Division, who helpfully sorted through the chart collection to determine this for us.

Before 1890, charts that showed only Isthmus Cove and Catalina Harbor were published, attesting to the Two Harbor area's importance to early mariners. Dakin Cove (Avalon) is first mentioned in the annual report of the Superintendent of Geodetic Survey for 1878 but, as stated, there is no charted detail.

21 From Lion Head to Howland's

In obedience to orders I have directed the removal of the corrals and buildings on the isthmus. The owners have removed some and will the balance as soon as they possibly can. The corrals we have used to store forage in and stable mules, and find them very convenient for such purposes, if you would be pleased to let them remain. But the fence extending down to Catalina Harbor is in the way...
CAPTAIN B.R. WEST, Fourth California Infantry, in a letter to Lt. Colonel J.F. Curtis, Drum Barracks, January 17, 1864

And so onward toward the west. Having rounded Lion Head, the steep promontory that protects Cherry Cove, we putter up the coast under power, keeping rather well inshore. To the north is Eagle Reef, a good 800 yards seaward. Its highest point is three feet underwater, marked with a warning buoy and a flashing light. Lying east to west, the reef is about 450 yards in length. Before reaching Howland's Landing, a scant nautical mile and a quarter from Lion Head, we pass two charming coves, graven from the cliffs, first Little Geiger Cove and then Big Geiger Cove.

Little Geiger has one mooring, Big Geiger none, and both are leased by mainland yacht clubs. The mooring in Little Geiger is the descendant of one put down in 1925 by the late George L. Geiger of Long Beach and his father. This long-vanished mooring, consisting of a Douglas fir float and scrap metal anchor linked by a metal cable from the Venice oil field, marked the first cove on the island formally leased by the Santa Catalina Island Company. Geiger family vessels that moored here in the early days included *Whitecap,* built in 1929, and *Daisy R.,* built in 1931, both sailboats. In those unregulated days, no formal approval was required to put down a mooring in Isthmus area coves.

Here in Little Geiger today, the island facility of the Offshore Cruising Club of Pacific Palisades overlooks the cove from a stilted onshore aerie. Nearby, in Big Geiger, the Blue Water Cruising Club of Long Beach has leased the shore facility since 1953. George Geiger was an early club member and commodore, and it was he who invited world-class British sailor Eric C. Hiscock to anchor his *Wanderer IV* in the cove in the early 1970s. Big Geiger, the only Catalina cove Hiscock touched, is described in his *Sou'west in Wanderer IV.* While *Wanderer IV* was at Big Geiger, several club members produced know-how, parts, and tools to repair the engine and expedite her visit to other Channel Islands,

From Big Geiger it is only about 500 yards before the opening to the spacious valley at Howland's Landing. The shore is leased by Catalina Camps (for boys and girls), whose general office is in Playa del Rey. It was founded in 1926 as Catalina Island Boys Camp. A private pier extends from the shore. Moorings in the cove and a shore facility are owned by the Los Angeles Yacht Club. Here are about forty moorings and a small anchorage.

Located at Howland's is a historic well that produced excellent potable water for more than a century. After 1863, miners, some seventy of them living at Fourth of

COURTESY DON MEADOWS COLLECTION, SHERMAN LIBRARY

July Bay, as it was then named, preferred obtaining fresh water from the Howland well because water in their cove was of inferior quality. Today a new well drilled farther up in the canyon serves Two Harbors, the old well having become tainted with salt water. Fresh water for early settlers was also available at Isthmus Cove, where there was a spring, and from an area near Big Fisherman's, which had a well. D.B. Diltz, Esq., had a house and a freshwater well in a ravine southwest of the Isthmus during the Civil War period. Diltz also had a

Howland House at Howland's Landing, pictured here circa 1920, is thought to be where the first white boy was born on Catalina.

wool storehouse and wharf on the tip of Ballast Point where livestock was loaded and offloaded. The location of the Diltz house and well at Catalina Harbor is known as Well Beach. A pier and a concrete ramp for the seaplanes that used to fly in here mark the location (Doran, 1980 and 1964).

Howland's Landing commemorates the home of one of the island's earliest settlers, Captain William Robert (Roberti) Howland, born in 1820 in Portugal. With a brother, Caleb, he shipped to New England where both boys were adopted by a family named Howland, according to Alberta Howland Lumbard of Glendale, California, William R. Howland's granddaughter. During an interview in 1992 she said that her grandmother, William Howland's wife, was Sarah Ann Simmons, an Englishwoman who had lived in Australia before marrying "grandpa" when she was sixteen. The couple had eight children, most of them born on Catalina.

Mrs. Lumbard was uncertain of the year in which Captain Howland, former master of a three-masted schooner which hunted for whales off the California coast, settled on Catalina Island. Using as a basis the official military report on the occupation of the island, however, Howland would have arrived in 1857 or 1858, for in January 1864, he was said to have been a resident "for six years" and to own 3,000 sheep. When the barracks were constructed at the Isthmus to accommodate the military, Howland agreed to move the fence of one of his corrals to the eastern slope of Catalina Harbor. Howland's extensive flocks ranged over much of the island, Mrs. Lumbard said, adding that at one time he shared grazing rights or was a partner with Phineas Banning in a sheep enterprise. As late as 1886, a year before the town of Avalon was laid out, Howland had a small building there for storing wool when his sheep were sheared at Descanso Bay, just west of Timms' Landing. A hard-water well at Descanso was used to water the sheep.

James Lick of northern California observatory fame became interested in Catalina in the early 1860s, primarily because of persistent reports of great mineral wealth on the island. He bought a share in the island in 1864 and additional portions during the next few years. By the time Lick owned the whole island he had become disappointed at the lack of minerals and offered to sell the island to Howland for $8,000, but Howland declined, believing the price too steep. A few years later Howland offered to buy the island for $50,000, but his offer was rejected by the Lick trustees, who by then were handling Lick's properties.

While moored at Howland's, we went ashore to seek Howland's legendary fig tree, reputed to be the largest in southern California. The tree shaded the Howland family's house and, in later years, sheltered youngsters attending camp there. We couldn't locate it, however, and when asked, Mrs. Lumbard said the tree had been taken down a few years before our visit, having become weakened by insects and old age. She said the huge tree began as a cutting, planted to commemorate the birth of William Percival Howland in April 1865. William is believed to have been the first white boy born on the island.

During the Howland years, the motor vessel *Edith* transported sheep, wool, and some cattle back and forth across the channel from Howland's Landing to Wilmington. "Grandfather used to say the cattle swam across," Mrs. Lumbard said. By that he meant that the bovines were "lashed to the sides of the boat" while the sheep rode high on the deck, she explained. The cattle were too big and heavy to take on board; they would have swamped the boat.

For a few years the Howlands' eldest son, Joseph Garcia Howland, attempted to run sheep on Santa Rosa and San Nicolas Islands, but the terrain and weather were discouraging and the project was abandoned. Joseph went to the mainland where he ran a successful feed and grain store at Main and 96th Street in Los Angeles.

San Clemente Island, however, was a beneficial place, and in the late 1880s, William R. Howland moved his sheep and family the eighteen nautical miles out there to the south, leasing it from the government (Windle, p. 139). After Howland's death in 1888 the San Clemente operation was run by his son, Charles Taggart Howland, and several brothers, who operated as the San Clemente Wool Company. Charles F. Holder, the writer-naturalist-fisherman, described the operation in 1910 as "one of the best conducted sheep ranches in the country, its eighteen or twenty miles laid out in various ranches." Charles Howland, with a long lease on San Clemente Island, "is developing the water, damming up the cañons at great expense, planting it with spineless cactus and various trees... Visitors must obtain permission from Mr. Howland before landing...," Holder said. Howland was also breeding horses that took the steep trails "as a matter of course." Charles eventually had 15,000 sheep on San Clemente, cropping the short grass of the island. He also grew wheat and barley on the island by a dry farming method of his own; the scant supply of water was reserved for the stock and domestic purposes.

The patriarch of the family, William R. Howland, and Frank Whittley, another large-scale sheep rancher, seem to have gotten along well together on Catalina, sharing at times land and corrals on the Isthmus and other island locations. Whittley lived on the Isthmus after 1850, where he also had his own corrals. A Whittley son, Thomas, later a sea captain, was four years old when the family settled on Catalina, bringing with them sheep that had been driven up from Mexico. With them came Jose Felice Presiado, "Mexican Joe," born in 1843, later one of Avalon's more famous professional boatmen, before the gasoline launch supplanted the rowboat for trolling. It was Mexican Joe (as he was always called) who Charles F. Holder engaged to row him fishing in Jose's heavy, broad-beamed yawl from one end of the island to the other (Holder 1910).

As a boy Jose was described as "wild and climbing and always after goats." Marco R. Newmark wrote that the colorful Presiado "never went to school; he was never in an elevator; he never used a telephone but he did know Catalina. As he himself expressed it, 'If there is a tree on the island I do not know, it must have grown last night,'" claimed an article in the *Los Angeles Morning Herald* of October 30, 1903. Joe also guided goat-hunting parties.

We now take a very short motor around the headland to Emerald Bay, its water remarkably blue and clear and filled with moorings.

22 Emerald Bay

A popular skin-diving anchorage, with 97 moorings. The five to ten boat anchorage area is limited (sand). A 200-yard fairway with depths of 12 to 24 feet between moorings leads into the bay. Many small outboard boats use this bay, which should be used in settled conditions only.

BRIAN M. FAGAN, *Cruising Guide to California's Channel Islands* (1983)

Here, on a well laid out farm and in a neat little house inland from the beach at the bay's westerly end, the island's first white girl was born in 1856. She was Louisa Behn, daughter of Johann Behn and his young Mexican-born wife, Pabla. John (or Johann), a native of Baden, was said to have been a member of the Workman party from New Mexico in 1841 and, according to historian Bancroft, to have been an otter-hunter and trader in Los Angeles in 1844. Harris Newmark said Behn had a grocery business in 1848 at the northeast corner of First and Los Angeles Streets. Selling his business and retiring in 1853, Behn came across the channel and established a farm here at Emerald Bay, probably encouraged by his brother-in-law, Frank Whittley, who had sheep ranch holdings at the Isthmus and later at White's Landing. Both men exercised squatter's rights or more specifically, preemption, a preferential right of purchase given to actual settlers on presumptive government land. By the preemption act of 1841, Congress gave settlers who staked claims in advance of government surveys a priority to buy claims at a minimum official price of about $1.25 an acre. Once established, the settlers (often erroneously called "squatters") could sell the claims to others.

By association, this crystalline cove became known as Behn's Harbor. Behn, often known as "Old Ben," died December 6, 1868, in Los Angeles; in 1873 his daughter Louisa married H.W. Stall, a German, founder of the Los Angeles Soda Water Works.

The name of a much earlier settler here failed to survive as a name for this cove, although his presence generated a venerable Catalina legend. The person was Samuel Prentiss or Prentice, who came here to live sometime in the mid-1830s. We have written of Prentiss before: he was one of the seamen who walked away from the wreck of the brig *Danube* on Point Fermin in 1828. A native of Rhode Island, Prentiss had joined the *Danube*'s crew in Lima, Peru, after deserting an American man-of-war in South America.

Having hunted sea otter with George Yount and others on the *Refugio* around the Channel Islands, Prentiss seems to have harbored a private dream of rich buried treasure on Catalina. His dream had been fired by an old Catalina Indian chief named Turei he had befriended at San Gabriel Mission — or so goes the legend. Chief Turei reportedly told Prentiss about Spanish gold buried on the island by pirates. According to the generally accepted story, the old chief drew a crude treasure map for Prentiss, but the map blew overboard while Prentiss was sailing from San Pedro to Catalina in a small boat. Prentiss is said to have spent the rest of his life digging beneath hundreds of trees on the island in search of the treasure — but to no avail. He remembered there was a tree on the map, but not where the tree was located.

Anyway, that's the popular yarn. Mrs. Sarah Howland, widow of Captain William Howland, early settler at Howland's Landing "around the corner," could only confirm that Prentiss, an unlettered bachelor, had built himself a cabin at the west end of Johnson's Landing on Emerald Bay. Interviewed in 1903 for the *Annual Publication of the Historical Society of Southern California,* Mrs. Howland recalled that Prentiss was called "Old Sam," and that he was a hunter and trapper who hunted and fished for a living until his death on Catalina in 1854. She was mute about his treasure hunt.

In the early 1900s, J.B. Banning erected a stone grave marker of Samuel Prentice on the site of a wooden marker at Johnson's Landing. "Arrived in California 1824. Died on Catalina 1854." Clearly, the marker has been defaced.

Prentiss's grave is indicated by a stone monument erected by J.B. Banning, although the site was originally marked by a simple wooden memorial surrounded by dark brown pickets. A writer for San Francisco's *Daily Alta California,* who visited the site in 1864, "looked upon it and sighed . . . wondering if the lonely occupant's days had been spent in toiling, mining — or busy trade." The writer said, with proper Victorian sentimentality, that he "envied the lot of the sleeper, and passed on to the shore to hold communion with the deep, dark, rolling restless sea"(Doran 1980).

Another place name surviving to this day is Johnson. James Charles Johnson came to this cove about 1854 with his brother, John, using much of the island to range livestock. Between them the brothers had 3,000 sheep, 200 cattle, and 100 mares and colts. The same 1864 article in the *Daily Alta California* mentioned above reported that "Mr. Johnson's ranch . . . is now so well stocked with sheep and cattle, that he furnishes the Government and citizens, from his shop on the Isthmus, with beef and mutton, at from eight to ten cents per pound." Thus the beach area became known as Johnson's Landing, a name it retains today.

There is some evidence that the bulk of ranch management at the West End was handled by James Johnson, while John ranched in the large valley inland from Dakin Cove or Timms' Landing, now Avalon. Timms' Landing on the island was developed by Augustus W. Timms around 1849 and included a small wool warehouse, corrals for sheep shearing, and a flock of sheep. Timms also owned and operated a landing bearing his name at San Pedro: it was "Timms to Timms" as sheep and tourists were shipped across the channel.

On Catalina, the most efficient communication between the West End and eastern portion was by boat: it was about thirteen nautical miles from Johnson's Landing to Timms' Landing: the route by horseback over inland valleys and along steep trails was decidedly more arduous and time consuming.

An additional place name at Emerald was furnished by Spencer H. Wilson who, according to some papers in the Banning family, lived on the island after buying John Behn's sheep ranch in partnership with E.N. McDonald. Wilson had been foreman of Phineas Banning's wheelwright shop in San Pedro before Banning moved his business to Wilmington. McDonald had been foreman of Banning's blacksmith shop on the mainland. Wilson, who may have had business ties to Timms as well as Banning, took Major Henry Hancock of the Union Army on a seventeen-ton sloop, the *Ned Beal* or *Beale,* from the Port of San Pedro to Catalina on a reconnaissance of the island to ascertain its resources and advantages from a military standpoint. The sloop, with John Brown as master, arrived at Fishermans Cove in Isthmus Harbor the afternoon of November 22, 1863. Also on board were two enlisted men of Company C, Fourth Regiment Infantry, California Volunteers.

Following Wilson's guidance, the reconnaissance covered coves from Goat Harbor around the island to Little Harbor, poking into "Wilson's or the old John Beghn [*sic*] Harbor," Major Hancock reported to Lt. Colonel James F. Curtis, commanding, at Camp Drum, Wilmington. Among Major Hancock's conclusions was the fact that "the island, and more especially that particular portion of it, to wit, the said isthmus with its adjacent bays, is capable of becoming a vast military and naval depot of a long reach to the Pacific Coast, and in the hands of an enemy possessed of a respectable navy might become of infinite annoyance and incalculable prejudice to the Government. Wherefore it would seem of vital moment that in the way of coast defense a small force with a few guns should be permanently stationed there at once to prevent the possibility of its falling into the power of a maritime enemy" (Doran 1964).

Who else but marauding Confederate ships which might be attracted by the lure of California silver and gold to finance the war against the army and navy of President Lincoln? Not only that, Catalina's purported gold rush was shifting into high gear.

Major Hancock referred to the sloop *Ned Beal* as being owned by Spencer Wilson, a point about which we have some reservations. The *Ned Beal* and the sloop *Pioneer* were said to have been built on Catalina, possibly at Timms' Landing. If so, it is probably an instance of geographical confusion — was he referring to Timms' San Pedro or Timms' Catalina? Yet the *Ned Beal,* the *Pioneer,* and another small vessel, the *Rosita,* have been reported as being owned by Timms. He employed them in his cross-channel transport business. To keep his sheep watered in drought periods (of which 1862–64 was a severe one), Timms sailed across the channel with cargoes of 200 to 300 barrels of water, sufficient to last for three months (from an article by Genevieve Farnell-Bond in the *Los Angeles Times,* February 14, 1914).

Possibly the *Ned Beal* was Wilson's vessel, for he was a sheep baron with 9,000 head on the island, his ranch headquartered in the spacious valley that bore his name behind Johnson's Landing. Perhaps the vessel was leased to Timms by Wilson, or leased to Wilson by Timms. We suspect, but cannot corroborate, a business arrangement of some kind between the two men.

While Major Hancock was conducting his reconnaissance with Wilson, a pair of speculators, Colonel R.I. Shipley and William Hazeltine, were preparing to stake out a forty-acre plot on the tableland of Wilson's Valley (Doran 1980). They planned to build a fine city there about a half mile from the beach and name it Queen City, metropolis of the mining district of Catalina. The project got as far as a lot of stakes in the ground before the Fourth Infantry California Volunteers unceremoniously took possession of the whole island and prepared to send everybody back to the mainland. That was the end of Queen City. Fortunately for the miners with valid claims and for the legitimate stockmen, the Union army withdrew its eviction notice on February 19, 1864, although stockmen were cautioned to make no

While a catch of fresh abalone in shells, harvested by Sanford Smith, Marjie's diving son, dangles over the port side to be kept fresh before cleaning and pounding, the authors lounge in the cockpit of *Herald Bird* at Emerald Bay.

improvements, and mining work had come to a standstill. Meanwhile, a schooner, the *Jessup,* was fitted out as an armed vessel with a pivot gun with carriage, for the use and supply of troops on the Isthmus. And the barracks were under construction.

Emerald Bay is the last and contemporary place name for this lovely cove with exquisitely clear and blue jewel-like water. It is easy to see how it got its name, but we don't know when that occurred. It is enough to look over the side of the boat and imagine we can reach and touch the bottom, twenty-four feet down.

Before heading westward again, a few words of advice. The tall spire of rock to the east that heads the lightly submerged reef seaward of the bay affords an excellent place to moor. Also, the mooring buoys close to the eastern headland and southerly of the spire give protection from northwest afternoon winds. Again, a severe northeaster here can be dangerous, and strong westerlies can make the area uncomfortable enough to send boats around to Howland's for shelter.

23   Yount's Gold Rush

All that glisters is not gold —
Often have you heard that told
SHAKESPEARE, *Merchant of Venice*

Legend has it that in the early 1830s, George C. Yount discovered at low tide on Catalina Island a ledge of gold-bearing quartz that he was never able to find again, despite returning to the island three times to search for it, the last in 1854. From this slim thread the whole cloth of Catalina's 1860s gold rush was woven.

Yount, originally a beaver hunter and trapper, went after the lucrative sea otter with William Wolfskill and others, sailing around the islands on the schooner *Refugio,* built at San Gabriel Mission. On one of these expeditions in 1832, Yount reported finding a gold-bearing ledge while hunting close to shore from a pulling boat. He broke off a piece of the quartz, but it fell overboard while he was transferring from the small boat to a larger vessel. It does not appear that Yount set much value upon his discovery at the time, but the later discovery of gold at the Kern and Colorado Rivers and the San Gabriel placers apparently stirred his memory. When he couldn't find gold on his return trips to the island, he told others about it and the rush was on.

Adding to the confusion about Yount's "gold" is the fact that Yount's published memoirs (Charles L. Camp, *The Chronicles of George Yount*) place the golden ledge on San Clemente Island, where Yount also hunted sea otter. We are inclined to agree with historian H.H. Bancroft who said that several of the old trapper's experiences were "embellished by others" and have "no foundation in fact."

Some believe that Yount's gold was at Arrow Point, about a nautical mile west of Emerald Bay, but those diving for abalone and lobster in the area's strong currents have yet to find a trace of the precious metal there. There was a mine at Fourth of July Cove called the Argentine, which could only be worked at low tide because otherwise it was completely out of sight, according to Mrs. Sarah Howland, quoted in a Southern California Historical Society paper in 1903. Could this have been Yount's ledge? Or perhaps it was the Gem of the Ocean Mine that Yount found. Mrs. Howland recalled that the Gem was blasted for ore, but that the "blast stopped all future expectations, as water, instead of ore, now filled the mine." We do know, however, that Augustus Timms and Benjamin S. Weston, along with five other partners, held claim to the Argentine mine beginning in 1863 and sold their interest a year later to one Cortland Wood of San Francisco (Deeds, Hall of Records, L.A., Book 6, 1864, p. 462, courtesy of Flora Baker, San Pedro). Weston, about whom we'll write later, ran sheep on the island, as did Timms.

At least one other sheep man seems to have been drawn to the glitter of precious metal. That was Martin Morse Kimberly who, with Daniel E. Way, staked out a claim or two and helped establish the San Pedro Mining District, the boundaries to "include all the islands of the county," according to Harris Newmark. Kimberly arrived in San Francisco from Connecticut in 1851, bought the schooner *Cygnet,* and came to Santa Barbara in 1852, trading up and down the coast. For a while Kimberly had sheep on Santa Cruz Island, then moved to San Nicolas Island which he found "ideal for sheep raising" until the drought of the mid-1860s. At this point he hopefully turned to mining, then returned to Santa Barbara where he operated a store until 1871. He took to the sea again, becoming a moderately successful otter and seal hunter.

Summing up the mining picture on Catalina, which was extensively mined for part of the Civil War period, mining engineer Alan Probert noted to us in 1982 that "gold is a scarce accessory mineral on Santa Catalina, almost a trace element. All of the published accounts of a gold strike at sometime in the past are purely apocryphal," he said. "I'm not saying that gold does not exist there, but that it has never been found is true." And Probert made a thorough historical study of the matter.

No gold, perhaps, but there was silver in variable amounts, and thereby hangs a romantic tale, the lost — and then found — legendary mine of Stephen Boushey, sometimes spelled Beauche, Boushay, and Bouchette, among others. Catalina history has been confused by the existence of two Bousheys, Stephen and Santos Louis, both Frenchmen. Santos Louis Bouchette arrived in California around 1828, married, and became known for his vineyard in Los Angeles. He was survived by his widow, who continued to reside in their mainland home after his death on October 23, 1847.

The Boushey (or Bouchette) Small Hills mining claim above Johnson's Landing was filed by Stephen Boushey on April 7, 1864, seventeen years after Louis Bouchette's death. It was said to have produced ore assaying at between $200 and $800 a ton, mostly silver with some gold. According to the stories, Stephen Boushey, after becoming a wealthy man, took a trip to the mainland one day, and in Los Angeles encountered a lovely French dancer, with whom he was instantly smitten.

After they were married, Boushey took his bride to Catalina, but she disliked the isolation and primitive life of a mining camp. To pacify her, Boushey had a fine house constructed up the canyon from Johnson's Landing at Emerald Bay, filling it with imported furniture and a large French plate glass mirror. Mrs. Boushey's loudest complaint had been that there was no proper mirror on the godforsaken island. That there was such a house, lavishly furnished, is true. When the Banning family owned the island, the deserted house was often visited by tourists, and it is recorded that one merrymaker, in his cups, fired a pistol at the mirror to challenge the superstition of seven years' bad luck. Fragments of the mirror and frame were taken to Avalon where, it is claimed, they were lost in the disastrous fire of 1915. A grass fire eventually destroyed the remains of the ransacked house.

Much earlier, in the spring of 1876, the story has Boushey blasting shut the entrance to his mine to hide it forever, loading a pile of silver ore aboard a small sailboat, and ostensibly heading for San Pedro with his French wife. No mention is

The flotation mill at White's Landing processed ore from the Blackjack Mine and other island locations. It was abandoned in 1927.

made of their reaching San Pedro, but a rumor developed that they sold "silver ore" in Baja California.

Reality isn't quite as colorful, but Remi Nadeau in *City-Makers* notes that Stephen Boushey went to Los Angeles in early 1873 and enlisted the financial support of F.P.F. Temple, president of the city's leading bank. Together they organized the Cerro Gordo Water and Mining Company, with a capital stock of $200,000. They contracted to build a steam pumping plant and a ten-mile pipeline to introduce drinking water to Cerro Gordo, ten miles away in Inyo County. The treasure came in the form of freshwater for the miners laboring at Cerro Gordo. With mines, miners, furnaces, and mule teams operating to the utmost, Cerro Gordo in 1874 sent 5,290 tons of silver ingots to Los Angeles.

Prospecting for gold, silver, lead, and other minerals continued sporadically on the island from the Civil War period through 1927. During William Wrigley Jr.'s ownership, D.M. Renton managed mining operations and rediscovered the Boushey mine using modern equipment and an old compass survey of the area. The workings were originally quite extensive — some eight hundred feet of adits. Lead in great quantity was found plus a small amount of silver, but not a trace of gold. The location is in Cherry Valley, near Howland's Landing. The mine is now closed.

Mines at Silver Canyon near the southeast end of the island and the Renton Mine easterly of Pebbly Beach on the island's north shore, both of which we'll encounter later on our cruise, and Blackjack Mine above White's Landing fairly round out mining activity on Catalina.

24 To Land's End and Around

Avoid the reeking herd,
Shun the polluted flock,
Live like that stoic bird
The eagle of the rock.

ELINOR HOYT WYLIE

From Emerald Bay, after clearing Indian Rock reef (a popular marine garden for divers), we pass a small bight, its mouth hardly more than 300 yards wide. This is known locally as Doctor's Cove, a place where boating physicians wishing privacy can retain proximity to the Boy Scout camp where they care for, when necessary, youngsters camped at the landing. They put down hooks in about eighteen feet of water. It is a short run of three-quarters of a nautical mile from Doctor's Cove to the headland of Arrow Point, its red peak at 329 feet.

Rounding Arrow Point is like testing the water with your toes. If it's going to be rough at the West End, you get the message just past Arrow Point. Here, except on calm mornings, the great rolling swells come sweeping from the Hawaiian Islands, unobstructed over the vast expanse of ocean. We have seen swells up to ten feet in otherwise pleasant weather, turning us back to Emerald Bay or Howland's. From Arrow Point west it is approximately two-thirds of a nautical mile to Parson's Landing, recognizable by its red cliffs and a great rock to the east side of the bay, its base in the sea and its face tortured by an ancient seismic thrust. West of here a sloping valley one-third mile wide extends inland for half a mile. One may anchor off the beach in about thirty feet of water by first penetrating the thick kelp bed which rims the cove. The kelp provides a quiet anchorage and fairly waveless access to the beach in a dinghy. Public camping is permissible ashore, and there is a freshwater spring above the beach, except in dry years. There are no moorings.

There were once several small cabins here, used by miners and stockmen. The landing was named for Nathaniel Parsons who lived here in the 1880s in a small stone house he built for himself. Ernest Windle, in his island history of 1931, said that Nathaniel had a twin brother, Theoples, who lived in Avalon. Louella Blanche Trask, naturalist and author who lived in Fisherman's Cove in 1895, recalled in a 1906 article in the *Los Angeles Times* that Captain Parsons frequently rowed around Catalina, occasionally rowing to San Clemente Island or out to little Santa Barbara Island. Known affectionately as "Uncle," Parsons took early relic hunters to San Clemente and San Nicolas Islands, although the vessel used is unclear.

Blanche Trask thought nothing of walking from the Isthmus to Avalon and back in one day. She left Catalina in 1915 and died in San Francisco in 1916. Her published work about her beloved Catalina included "The Heart of Santa Catalina," an article in *Land of Sunshine,* a monthly magazine about California and the Southwest edited by Charles F. Lummis. She wrote in the September 1897 issue that for a few months each summer, Catalina's "little tented city of Avalon spreads its white wings to shelter thousands of people who come and go without learning anything about Catalina. The remainder of the year, save for a handful of inhabitants left over in Avalon, [the island] is quite alone."

Ms. Trask said that at the name Catalina

> thousands will see again the crescent bay dotted with boats, the beach with bathers, and the white city of Avalon. But this is not Santa Catalina. It is only what man has done toward bringing her into touch of his own moods and ways. Her real self lives on unmoved upon the heights — the heights so full of mystery and beauty, seldom seen by any.
>
> The highest peaks stand looking down upon the dead craters; bare and desolate mountains of over-burnt rock — rock somewhat comforted, perhaps, by the brilliant lichens of green and orange and red and lavender carelessly draped about them by the hand of Time, like Oriental scarves.
>
> Now and then a bald eagle, its white head and tail gleaming in the sunlight (and where else is there such sunlight?) descends to rest upon some tip-top ledge. The goat trails run to the very summits, and these lonely peaks are the real homes of the goats.

Blanche Trask's description of the island remains essentially valid today, save for the intrusion of hikers and campers under the enlightened jurisdiction of the Catalina Conservancy (see Chapter 40). The untouched wildness of the island makes a vivid impression as we motor the *Bird* against a gentle westerly from Parson's, the last refuge, to the tip of the West End. The nearly three-mile passage carries us by Stony Point, Lorenzo Beach, Black Point, and "foul rocks," according to the chart. The latter, known as Johnson Rocks, are marked by kelp and water boils.

Until recently, the land harbored herds of wild goats, skittish in their solitude. They scattered in fright as a small party of us flew low over this wilderness, known as Land's End on the charts, on a whale-watching flight sponsored by the American Cetacean Society aboard the Goodyear blimp several years ago. This area was the domain of the American bald eagle until the 1950s when it became extinct here and on the other islands because of a lethal combination of pesticides such as DDT and trigger-happy hunters.

Earlier seamen remembered eagles perched on the rocky pillars of the West End and Eagle Rock nearby, scanning the sea for fish to feed upon. Although we have not seen eagles here, it is a possibility, for thirty-three of them were introduced on the island several years ago in a noble experiment. Under a joint program of the Institute for Wildlife Studies and the Catalina Conservancy, a pair of eaglets was hatched from the first mature mated pair. The young eagles and others brought to the island are being monitored and protected, at least initially, in lofty cages in the island's

This is the desolate West End of Catalina Island. The outcropping in the sea at right is Eagle Rock.

interior. The program includes an attempt to reestablish the peregrine falcon.

Ruben V. Vaughan, one of the vanished clan of charter boatmen who had stalls on Avalon's Pleasure Pier before World War II, recalled in his 1961 *Doc's Catalina Diary* a nest of eagles on top of the large rock which comes into view upon rounding the West End: "Never has this rock been known without eagles nesting thereon, probably because it is a safe place and the abundance of sea-life around this rocky shore affords unlimited food for these ernes."

Vaughan marveled at the ability of the "sea eagle" to dive from great heights and "skim along at possibly a hundred miles an hour with talons open to grab a fish, then rise gracefully up into the air again." Often, while trolling flying fish as bait for marlin from his fishing vessel *Popeye,* Doc Vaughan had seen "the fish skittering so much [and] the eagles bothered me to such an extent that I had to slow down to let the bait sink beneath the waves. That way they could not catch it, for I have had them grab it and pull the bait right off the hook."

We've gone around the West End several times. Invariably this primal headland evokes a sensation of foreboding — and fascination. This rocky prow of Catalina thrust into the Pacific remains unmarked by man, save an automatic light that winks by night at seventy-six feet of elevation to warn off mariners, and the usual painted marker. The prow of the island is a bleakly attractive place, with ribbons of opposing currents extending from it, even on the calmest days. It seems haunted by specters, for over the centuries the West End has claimed vessels to its offshore deeps. A diver once showed us a silver doubloon reputedly from a Spanish galleon that had gone down in 1598 near Arrow Point, long before there was anything to warn off ships. Over the centuries, other vessels collided with the unseen rocks (Winlund, 11th edition, 1986).

We do not know how many lives the West End has claimed, but we were acquainted with two men who dramatically escaped this headland's baleful influence in early 1982. They were Robin A. Edwards, then thirty-seven, and Richard Larson, thirty-one, experienced divers who had rounded the West End in their thirty-four-foot, diesel-powered fiberglass cruiser, heavily laden with 4,000 pounds of sea urchins harvested off the southern side of the island. A northeasterly was blowing off the mainland, and the vessel was in danger of being overwhelmed by waves cresting up to ten feet. Because of the heavy cargo, the boat became unmanageable and broached, lying broadside to the waves in the trough of the sea. In this perilous position she had taken on water and was in danger of capsizing. Both men hastily donned wet suits. As they jumped overboard, the vessel turned over and began to sink.

Edwards said afterward that he watched the boat go down slowly, her lights still burning as she slipped from sight in the deep. It was early evening; the night was clear. The lights of Point Fermin and Point Vicente on the mainland shone brightly and Edwards estimated they were about ten miles from them. Drawing upon deep wells of stamina and courage, the men swam doggedly against the wind-whipped sea for nearly fifteen hours, finally hauling themselves from the water onto a buoy near Point Fermin. Exhausted, they instantly fell asleep, riding the buoy like harbor seals. Around noon they were rescued by a passing tugboat. Reviewing the ordeal Edwards told me, "We didn't talk about dying. We would not allow ourselves to think about it. We just kept on swimming."

Others have swum the channel, but not under such lonely, harrowing circumstances. History records the Wrigley Ocean Marathon on January 15, 1927; the race began at the Isthmus, with 123 swimmers entered. Point Vicente was the destination. Each swimmer was accompanied by a rowboat containing his trainer, an observer, and an oarsman. A powerboat carried a physician, relatives, and friends. Newsmen had their own vessels, and the ss *Avalon* served as the official convoy craft. In total, the flotilla accompanying the swimmers numbered about 300. George Young, a Canadian, waded ashore on January 16, the only contestant to finish the twenty-two-mile swim. He was in the water nearly sixteen hours. Young was awarded the $25,000 prize. Two plucky women who had to be forcibly removed from the sea were awarded $2,500 each as consolation for "their courage." The event was never repeated. Wrigley feared a tragedy might occur.

Other swimmers continued to cross the channel on their own, including Florence Chadwick, who made the swim in less than fourteen hours in 1952, and Greta Anderson, who swam the channel round trip in just over twenty-six hours in 1958. Later round-trip swimmers broke her record. They were Penny Dean, who made the swim in twenty-plus hours in 1977. That same year, John York did it in sixteen and a half hours.

In 1927, forty-nine rowers raced their boats from Long Beach to Avalon for a $1,000 prize. The winner, Frank Hagney, completed the pulling race in five hours. Since then, other swimmers, motor boaters, sail boaters, aqua planers, paddle boarders, and kayakers have braved the channel or circumnavigated the island in a variety of races.

We round the West End without mishap and enter the outer Santa Barbara Channel. If we were to position our stern just off the island's point and steer due west we would raise little Santa Barbara Island, about one mile in width and twenty nautical miles away. As it is, the *Bird* is running down the opposite side of the West End, heading about 120 degrees magnetic southeast under sail, with a following sea on her stern quarter. Our destination for the day is Catalina Harbor, six and three-quarters nautical miles away. We have passed Whale Rock and are passing the previously mentioned Eagle Rock, a towering gray monolith 300 yards offshore. No nesting eagles — yet!

Our thoughts turn to Albert Strange's cautionary advice, reported in *Wooden Boat* magazine, "always keep a bit in hand," as we give ample clearance to Eagle Rock. Strange was an English boat designer, yachtsman, and artist of the Victorian era whose advice to mariners is as valid today as it was when he gave it in 1901:

> Always 'keep a bit in hand' — a bit on the weather side — a bit of room to swing clear in harbor — a bit to spare when cutting things fine across shoal patches — a bit of cable to slack out if necessary. In fact, always have a bit to spare of everything you know you will want the most.
>
> Do not drive your boat too hard. Press her to gain a point, but don't press her all the time. Canvas and sail her with seamanlike judgment and you will get as far as the man who drowns his craft and wears himself out, while you will be fresh and dry and he will be well salted and very damp.

Strange developed the cruising canoe yawl and other small, simply rigged cruising sailboats that could be single-handed in an era when most yachts were large and heavily canvassed. The canoe stern, trademark of his most successful designs, became known as "the Strange stern" (*Wooden Boat,* last quarter, 1985). In this century, America's great boat designer L. Francis Herreshoff ("father" of the *Herald Bird,* we remind you) again popularized the canoe yawl with the admirable twenty-eight-foot *Rozinante* which figured importantly in his book, *The Compleat Cruiser.*

Sailing along this rugged, precipitous shore about a quarter of a mile out puts roughly forty-eight fathoms under our keel. (A fathom is a unit of depth equal to six feet.) This depth of at least 288 feet conceals from us the vast, wave-cut terrace with valleys once cut by streams. Geologists tell us that it is the remains of an ancient shoreline (Martin). One of the most dramatic and beautiful geological edifices on the island is Ribbon Rock, about three nautical miles from Land's End. The gray-and-white tilted bands of volcanic quartzite between layers of metamorphic material give Ribbon Rock its distinctive appearance, rising 782 feet from the sea. Here we gaze upon the awesome record of 120 million years of geologic history.

Adjacent to Ribbon Rock to the northwest is Iron Bound Cove with an opening nearly one-third mile wide. It is an exposed but fairly secure anchorage in about fifty feet of water. Romantic if somewhat unreliable tales of smuggling have been circulated over the years relative to this cove and Lobster Bay, sometimes called Smuggler's Cove, near the entrance to Catalina Harbor. The coves may have been used by early traders to conceal their vessels from Spanish and Mexican authorities; they did at least provide refuge from occasional strong northeasterlies.

Ribbon Rock is a geologic upthrust, 782 feet high, on the south shore of the island.

There are indications that these coves and others on both sides of the island were used to a moderate degree from 1919 to 1933, during Prohibition. Prohibition began with the Eighteenth Amendment to the Constitution, which prohibited the manufacture, sale, or transportation of intoxicating liquors. It was followed almost immediately by the Volstead Act (after its congressional sponsor, Andrew Volstead of Minnesota) which enabled the government to enforce the act. The Volstead Act, which went into effect January 16, 1920, legally defined intoxicating liquor as "any beverage containing ½ of 1% alcohol," thus including wine and beer.

Prohibition kept the U.S. Coast Guard busy at sea intercepting illegal "rum-running" vessels, impounding their boozy cargoes, arresting captains and crews, and testifying against them in court. The Coast Guard seized literally thousands of vessels engaged in transporting liquor into the U.S. by sea. Lawmen ashore were equally busy battling the illicit traffic, which was dominated by bootleggers, gangsters, and racketeers, aided and abetted by many otherwise law-abiding citizens who wanted their alcohol when they wanted it. Prohibition was about as effective as ordering the tide to stop rising.

Coast Guard Commander Malcolm F. Willoughby, in his *Rum War at Sea,* noted that "rum" and "rum running" were generic terms, broadly covering all intoxicating beverages including "demon rum." "Liquor smuggling along the coasts of Washington, Oregon, and California never attained the volume or big business aspects of that in the Atlantic," Commander Willoughby said. The West Coast was not as heavily populated as the East so did not attract as many smugglers. "Practically all of the seaborne liquor for the Pacific Coast was run in from British Columbia, mostly from Vancouver."

Mexican territorial water also had rum runners hovering offshore, mostly "rum ships" loaded with scotch whisky. Hancock Banning Jr. reminisced about an English flag vessel lying "quite a ways out to sea" off Santa Barbara. He said he and some friends on the steam yacht *Cricket* (named for Phineas Banning's earlier *Cricket* that sank around 1900 off San Pedro) approached the English vessel and found she was loaded with "Peter Dawson's scotch whisky in beautiful stone crocks with red ribbons tying on the fancy corks." They took a few cases aboard the *Cricket,* Banning recalled in his oral history. Banning doubted that rum runners used any of the islands, including Catalina, very much, noting that rum was in such great demand, "if you had a cache of rum, why, the fishermen would find out about that. You'd go back to get it and it wouldn't be there."

Most contraband and liquor was off-loaded from large "mother" vessels at sea, then transported to mainland ports in fast, specially outfitted small powerboats capable of outrunning the slower Coast Guard vessels. Some supply vessels may have hidden temporarily in the coves on Catalina's "back side."

25　Catalina Harbor

When abreast of the Entrance (which is marked by a low neck of land extending across the Island) and at some distance from it, the land appears like two very high separate islands. Stand in for the opening and anchor on either side of Ballast Point. Inside of Ballast Point there is hardly room for a vessel to swing at her anchors; but as the harbor is perfectly land locked she can moor by running a hawser to the rocks and lie with perfect safety.

U.S. Coast Survey of Catalina Harbor, 1852
(first government chart of the island)

Having traversed the seven nautical miles from the West End, lowered our sails and started up the *Bird*'s engine, we enter Catalina Harbor between the two headlands: Catalina Head on our port (with a flashing light at 400 feet elevation) and, to starboard, Ballast Point, keeping about 150 yards off either side. The entrance is 800 yards wide; avoid Pin Rock, 100 yards offshore of the eastern point.

Although there is ample room to anchor in sand, we pick up a mooring (some ninety-nine of them here) in the well-sheltered inlet, whose nearly treeless hills roll away from both east and west shores, with the low neck of the Isthmus ahead to the north. Mount Torquemada's 1,336 feet rise to the west in contrast to the head of the harbor that is shallow, its shore exposed at low tide. One cannot help but wonder how many vessels were careened here over the centuries, and by whom. This history-hallowed port is probably — if one accepts historian Harry Kelsey's conclusions (which we do) — the place where explorer Juan Rodriguez Cabrillo met his death in 1543.

As late as 1910 there were, at the undeveloped village of Cabrillo near here, Chinese divers who gathered abalone and caught sharks valuable for their oily livers. Abalone, long considered a delicacy by the Chinese, were dried and shipped to China in huge quantities for a tidy profit. Americans of the period had yet to acquire an appetite for the strange sea mollusk, as one writer expressed in *The Overland Monthly* of May 1893: "When alive the abalone is a pound or less of very unpalatable looking black life: and dried, it looks and feels like the heel of an old boot." The writer seems not to have sampled fresh abalone, trimmed, filleted, pounded, and quickly sautéed — a modern gastronomic delight. Over-harvested and withering and dying from a mysterious malady — perhaps pollution or a virus — the mollusk, at this writing, is selling for forty to fifty dollars a pound retail, when it can be found. Yet it was not always so. Huge middens of brittle shells attest to the Indians' fondness for the abalone, and within memory is the sound of hollow thumping on the foredecks of nearby vessels, attesting to a diver's prowess in prying a few off the submerged rocks. Alas, that tenderizing thumping with a meat hammer is a sound seldom heard anymore.

In this view of Two Harbors, the white shape in Isthmus Harbor is Bird Rock, with part of its reef visible. In the distance is Catalina Harbor.

The Chinese in California helped develop a thriving commercial fishing industry, beginning with the arrival of a small band of immigrants during the 1840s. By the end of the century Chinese fishing villages dotted the state from the Sacramento River delta to San Diego, causing one 1898 visitor to report: "Chinamen have large villages, some of them more like small cities, along the shore, whose inhabitants are wholly engaged in catching, drying and shipping fish to China" (McWilliams, p. 87).

It can be said, however, that the abalone, today a scarce, expensive, and treasured culinary delicacy, remains a symbol of the prejudice directed at California Chinese at the end of the nineteenth century. One of the principal indictments against the Chinese by the very provincial Caucasian residents was the Orientals' obvious fondness for shellfish, especially abalone. This was regarded as "conclusive evidence that they were subhuman and had the tastes of animals," remarked author McWilliams. Added to this "obvious" peculiarity were the "facts" that the Chinese spoke an outlandish jargon, refused to adapt their customs and lifestyle to that of the U.S., regarded China as the land of the blessed, worked with a patience and industry beyond comprehension, practiced strange vices, wore pigtails, kept entirely to themselves, and thrived under standards of living no white could endure (Cleland 1930).

Yet by the 1870s, when the California Chinese population had reached an estimated 49,277 (Rolle) and there was serious unemployment in the mines and cities, the white laboring class began to accuse the Chinese of undercutting wages and depriving them of work. But the powerful railroad and mining interests needed cheap labor, and lured still more Chinese from Hong Kong and other seaport cities. Promises of riches and opportunity were made by a group of wealthy Chinese entrepreneurs known as the Six Companies, headquartered in San Francisco.

In 1882, the United States closed the door to Chinese immigration, opening it a decade later with certain exceptions. It was during this closure that Catalina and San Clemente Islands became way stations for the illicit smuggling of Chinese to the mainland. Charles Holder described the process in his *Channel Islands of California,* published in 1910:

> Twenty years ago I landed at San Clemente Island and found that a clever old Chinese genius was carrying on a twofold business, making it pay both going and coming. The old Chinaman was a smuggler, but on the surface he was an abalone fisherman. He made his headquarters on San Clemente Island, a place rarely visited in winter. Some one who owned a little schooner brought Chinamen up the coast from Mexico and landed them at San Clemente — an easy thing to do when the government had only one revenue cutter on the coast, and that up north all the time. As soon as the men were landed they began to collect abalones, and the day I stumbled on their camp they had hundreds piled up in heaps — shells and meat. Upon seeing me a number of men ran for a big tent. I ran after them, and when I reached the tent I threw open the fly. They were a demoralized lot of smugglers. I laughed, and that raised their spirits; they had taken me for a revenue officer.
>
> The abalone shells were shipped to Germany, the meat went to China. Every week, I fancy, a few Chinamen were sent over to the mainland in an old junk that was always drifting up and down the channel. At night she would drift inshore; a boat would be sent into some convenient spot, the Chinese would

land, and by the next day they would have walked the twenty miles to Los Angeles and were lost in the local Chinatown. The old junk would run into San Pedro in the morning, and her Chinese crew, with certificates, would land the crop of abalones, after which they would sail again for San Clemente.

One of the more horrifying descriptions of human smuggling was related by Hancock Banning Jr. in his oral history. It concerned three brothers in San Pedro, owners of a vessel named the *Sampson* that had "a pretty good engine in it" and was used to bring human cargo from Mexico to California. The brothers were paid $200 to $500 a head for the Chinese by the Chinese colony or "whatever it was in Mexico... to get these guys in, get [them] to Chinatown [in Los Angeles] and get lost," Banning said. If a revenue cutter came in sight of the *Sampson*, "they'd bring the Chinamen up on deck, one by one, for fresh air. They had everything fixed, put a weight around their ankles and overboard they went," thus destroying the evidence of human smuggling. The story had been related to Banning by the *Sampson*'s engineer.

Coves of Iron Bound Bay, Lobster Bay, and the beach at China Point served as temporary refuges for Chinese deposited there by seagoing ships and awaiting transportation by smaller vessels which then smuggled them across the channel to the mainland. Windle noted in his history of Catalina that although the contraband Chinese were supposed to be "under cover," they had considerable freedom at Lobster Bay. There was said to be a well-defined trail from the bay around Mount Torquemada to Catalina Harbor. Presumably it was traveled by the illegal immigrants who, awaiting transport to the mainland, went to visit, eat, gamble, and exchange news with their brethren, the Chinese fishermen working at Cabrillo (Windle).

As fishermen, the Chinese were unexcelled. Carey McWilliams estimated that by 1870 the California Chinese exported $1 million worth of abalone annually, and a decade later their annual shipments of dried shrimp to China totaled $3 million. A campaign to oust the Chinese from the lucrative fishing industry began as early as 1860; a measure imposing a special tax on them was levied and there were obstructive regulations on the mesh size used for shrimp nets (McWilliams). But the Chinese stoically persevered, operating clandestinely when necessary. After the 1890s they were driven from the industry, first by Italians, later by the Portuguese, Japanese, and Yugoslavians.

Holder mentioned the entry of Japanese into the Chinese abalone industry, seeing several working on a double-ended boat while he was drift-fishing for albacore near Catalina. He said they dived like seals for the abalone, warming themselves between dives beside a brick fireplace in the stern of their boat. This was long before the era of wetsuits. These men, Holder lamented, were "black pearl and abalone shell hunters, one crew out of numbers which have so thoroughly plucked the entire Pacific coast that there is little left for the American whenever he opens his eyes to the value of the fast-disappearing mollusk." Mind you, that was written in 1910.

Today, despite regulatory efforts by the California Department of Fish and Game, hordes of sport scuba divers, not to mention commercial divers, carry on the old tradition of systematically reducing the abalone population on the mainland and the islands. The coves of Catalina are nearly bereft of this lovely ear-shell, the *Haliotis* of science.

Holder noted that tons of the iridescent shells — when ground and polished becoming a beautiful mother-of-pearl — were sold to Germany. There, in the "child-labor homes and factories of Vienna they are made into a thousand peculiar things and sent back to Catalina and other tourist resorts for sale," Holder said. He also mentioned an abalone-shell-polishing enterprise on the island, the shells purchased from Japanese entrepreneurs at both the Isthmus (Cabrillo) and Avalon.

Snugly moored for the night in "Cat Harbor," as it is familiarly known, my wife and I speculated on the mysterious history of the *Ning Po,* whose scant remains, not carried away by souvenir hunters, lie underwater in the inlet between the curved arm of Ballast Point and the harbor's eastern shore. Possibly built in 1806, a date that is uncertain, in China, the *Ning Po* was a massive Foochow pole-type junk, 138 feet in length with a 31-foot beam and a 15-foot draft. She weighed 291 gross tons. Her topsides were elaborately carved and colorfully painted in red, green, blue, yellow, and other bright colors. "Particularly noteworthy were her glaring oculi, black eyeballs bulging on a white background, one on each side of the flaring wings of the transom bow – eyes which to the Chinese mind enabled the craft to sail safely across the waters" (Don H. Kennedy, "The Infamous *Ningpo* [*sic*]" in "The American Neptune").

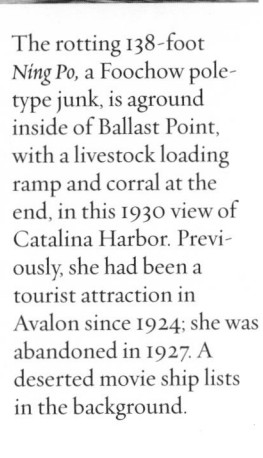

COURTESY NEWPORT HARBOR NAUTICAL MUSEUM, SHERMAN LIBRARY

The rotting 138-foot *Ning Po,* a Foochow pole-type junk, is aground inside of Ballast Point, with a livestock loading ramp and corral at the end, in this 1930 view of Catalina Harbor. Previously, she had been a tourist attraction in Avalon since 1924; she was abandoned in 1927. A deserted movie ship lists in the background.

On February 17, 1913, the master of a steam schooner off the Santa Barbara light reported a curious sighting: a large Chinese junk. It was the *Ning Po*. She had completed a 7,000-mile passage from Shanghai, having barely survived two typhoons. She had been purchased in China by William M. Milne of South Pasadena with the intention of using her as a tourist attraction. And attract tourists she did, at San Pedro and San Diego Harbors and finally at Catalina in Avalon, Lovers' Cove, and Catalina Harbor. *Ning Po*'s island sojourn began in 1914 when the Meteor Boat Company acquired her. Prominent in the company were Watson Hubbard, a Los Angeles auto dealer, and Charles Lockard, who ran Meteor's glassbottom boats at the island and later was with the management of the Los Angeles Angels baseball team. At the height of her popularity in the Avalon area she served as a restaurant with entertainment. Various romantic (and bloody) tales told about her enhanced her tourist appeal. It was said she had been a pirate ship, a slaver, a prison ship (158 pirates and smugglers were reputedly beheaded on her deck), and a rebel vessel in two Chinese revolutions. An article in the *Los Angeles Times* (February 19, 1913) commented that the *Ning Po* had "more past than a chorus lady." By 1927 she lay virtually abandoned at anchor within Ballast Point, while souvenir hunters gradually stripped her of her substance, including camphor-wood, teak, mahogany, and ironwood. Teredos, tides, and skin divers further demolished her until nothing visible remains today.

We have avoided identifying many of the island's shore facilities, many on land leased to southern California yacht clubs by the Santa Catalina Island Company, because the SCICo is reviewing its lease holdings with plans to develop "more environmentally sensitive, year-round uses" of the coves, according to Paxson H. Offield, company president (*Los Angeles Times,* July 5, 1992). In 1996 there were thirteen mainland yacht clubs with leased shore facilities on the island, exclusive of Avalon, which has the Catalina Island Yacht Club and Tuna Club.

And that which is here today may not be here tomorrow. The Boy Scout camp, located at Johnson's Landing on Emerald Bay since 1925, is an example. In the early 1990s the Scouts nearly lost their lease to the Cousteau Society, which had been invited to develop a marine science center and resort at that location. The project was eventually canceled by the Cousteau group, although it did not explain why. However, Scout leaders and company officials later met to work out a compromise that would free Emerald Bay for development and give the Scouts a new site on the island.

We must mention the California Yacht Club (CYC), headquartered in Marina del Rey, because one of its founders carried a name important to Catalina history: Ben S. Weston, grandnephew of the Ben S. Weston of Ben Weston Beach and Point, to which we will sail soon. Ben Weston of CYC was a Star Class sailor; CYC built the first three Star sailboats in 1922, the year it was organized. CYC's Catalina facility is on the northern tip of Ballast Point, named in the 1852 Coast Survey and presumably long before that.

Anchored in Catalina Harbor in 1902 is Hancock Banning's forty-seven-foot racing schooner, *La Paloma* (in foreground). Banning organized the Catalina Yacht Club at the Isthmus in 1893. It was disbanded in 1914. The schooner was built by Phil Alward of Wilmington for Banning.

Both shores of this narrow, crescent-shaped sand bar are covered with sea-smoothed pebbles and rocks of various composition, primarily granite, quartzite, and sandstone. How did they come to be here? One legend says that sailing vessels careening in the shoals of the harbor off-loaded and replaced ballast here. Another story says the sandbar was riprapped by sheepherders to prevent erosion of an early causeway used to run sheep from corrals to a loading ramp at the end for shipment to the mainland. That such a ramp existed is well documented, but neither story satisfactorily explains the mystery of so many rocks. They represent a distributional feat of no mean magnitude. Perhaps they got there through the mysterious work of that champion mover of all things: nature.

The other structure on the eastern shore, opposite Ballast Point, belongs to the Del Rey Yacht Club of Marina del Rey. The club was founded in 1952; the facility on Catalina was dedicated in 1972.

On our first cruise to Catalina Harbor some years ago, we plotted a prudent course after studying the National Oceanic and Atmospheric Administration's chart of the island, a chart showing the entire island. But this was not always the case. The first closely detailed government chart, dated 1852, was of "Catalina Harbor And the Anchorage on the N.E. Side of the Island," and was the only chart available. This again emphasizes the importance of these two harbors to early mariners on the California coast. The 1852 chart was made after a reconnaissance by a hydrographic party commanded by Lieutenant James Alden, U.S.N., for the simply named agency, the U.S. Coast Survey. The chart has a lovely hand-drawn and engraved profile of the approach to Catalina Harbor, delineating its geographic features and showing two tiny ships of the period. The view and topography were drawn by W.B.

McMurtrie, lettering was by E.F. Woodward, and engraving by A. Rolle and G. McCoy. Such charts are coveted by collectors, especially the one featuring a drawing of Anacapa Island by James McNeill Whistler, famous American painter and etcher, who worked for the Coast Survey for a brief time. The hydrographic charting agency, then headquartered in Washington, D.C., became the U.S. Coast and Geodetic Service and is now the National Ocean Service, National Oceanic and Atmospheric Administration (NOAA), located in Rockville, Maryland.

When one is moored here it is interesting to realize that in this water, in this harbor, and among these hills, the steamer *Active* anchored, ready for the reconnaissance of the Isthmus. And a year before, the U.S. Revenue Service's brig *C.W. Lawrence* put down her anchors, en route from San Francisco to San Diego, apparently doing preliminary work for the coastal survey. From a copy of the *Lawrence*'s 1851 journal, provided by the former Nautical Heritage Museum in Dana Point, we learn that as the vessel approached the entrance to Catalina Harbor, a cautious Captain A.V. Fraser ordered her to lay off while he went aboard a small boat to ascertain the capacities of the harbor and take soundings. Fraser found the harbor safe and "determined to anchor," but once anchored, the brig touched bottom at low tide. A kedge anchor had to be employed to work her off at high water. The following excerpts are from the *Lawrence*'s logbook:

> Tuesday January 7th 1851 Crew employed during the day securing ship, cleaning fire arms, making nippers for the messenger [binding a rope to the anchor cable to ease heaving up the anchor] and other necessary ship's duty. Served 34 rations...
>
> Wednesday January 8th Capt. Fraser engaged both morning and afternoon in making observations to determine the latitude and longitude of the harbor of Santa Catalina Island...
>
> Thursday January 9th During the day Capt. Fraser engaged triangulating the Bay and Harbor of Santa Catalina...
>
> Friday January 10th, Capt. Fraser occupied throughout the day in continuing the survey of the harbor...
>
> Saturday January 11th Crew employed setting up the jib guys and rigging about the bowsprit, and at other necessary duty...

Sunday Captain Fraser was "continuing the survey of the harbor," and Monday he was "engaged completing the survey of the harbor."

On Tuesday, January 14, in foggy weather, the men "found on the Isthmus a man who was a soldier of the last war, having been attached to the New York Regiment of Volunteers who was looking for a place to locate himself, by name of Patrick McGill, entirely destitute of comforts of any kind. The officers and men gave their voluntary contributions. Capt. Fraser had a tent made and given him with a few other useful articles..."

Two days later McGill, "a citizen of the U.S. and late a volunteer in Col. Jonathan

The *Californian,* rigged as a topsail schooner with a sparred hull length of 145 feet, is a close representation of the *C.W. Lawrence,* a U.S. Revenue brig. She is seen here off Catalina Harbor.

D.J. Stevenson's regiment who arrived on the island the day before the vessel anchored in this harbor in a suffering condition and in want of the necessaries of life" was "supplied with 60 lbs. of pork, 40 pounds of bread, one hand of twine, one half gallon of oil, and to enable him to dig a well, a shovel and deck bucket, the crew and officers contributing one ration and supplying him with clothing..."

The following day, January 17, the *Lawrence* got under weigh at 8:00 A.M. "and stood out of the harbor, all drawing sail set before the wind" leaving on the beach Patrick McGill, waving bon voyage. How McGill got to the Isthmus is unknown, but a clue may be offered by a later entry in the *Lawrence*'s log when Captain Fraser asked the crew to determine punishment for one of their number who "had bitten a piece off the nose" and "stabbed in the face" another crewman. The crew agreed that the guilty man "should have the hair shaved close off on one side of his head, whiped [*sic*] at the gang way at the discretion of the Captn, and then turned on shore without either clothes or means, confiscating both for the use of" the injured party. This form of maritime punishment, varying in degree, was called "marooning" and was said to have originated among pirates on the Spanish Main. An instance of the marooning of two Catholic priests expelled from the Sandwich Islands because of prejudice against their religion occurred in January 1832. At that time a small brig entered San Pedro Bay, where the ecclesiastics were rowed ashore and then abandoned with two bottles of water and a few biscuits. An Indian hunting seashells found them, and they were taken to San Gabriel Mission where they were cared for (*Los Angeles Times,* October 31, 1897).

Poor McGill had opted for adventure in New York when he volunteered for the regiment, authorized by President Polk, to fight in the undeclared war with Mexico. But there was another purpose for the volunteers; their free journey west was a one-way trip, and they were expected to remain in U.S. territory as colonists when mustered out. What ever became of McGill is another Catalina mystery.

A re-creation of the *Lawrence* — 130 tons of her with a sparred length of 145 feet — was constructed in San Diego in 1983, under the sponsorship of the Nautical Heritage Museum. She is the *Californian,* designated as the state's official tall ship. Her builder and designer was Melbourne Smith, who also supervised construction of the ill-fated *Pride of Baltimore,* lost at sea during a goodwill world tour in 1986. The original *Lawrence,* built in Washington, had not long to live after leaving Catalina in 1851. Later that year she was wrecked near San Francisco. She was one of the most advanced "clipper" models of the time, rigged as a brig. The *Californian,* rigged as a topsail schooner, has graced island waters, as has another historic visitor, a replica of Dana's *Pilgrim.* Built in 1948 in Spain and remodeled during the 1970s, the 130-foot *Pilgrim* is owned by the Orange County Marine Institute and mainly serves as a nautical classroom for schoolchildren at her home port, Dana Point Harbor. The *Californian* is moored in San Diego Harbor and is the property of the San Diego Maritime Museum.

The regular drivers are only allowed to make the descent at a certain speed,
but I have taken it a number of times with Captain William Banning, one of
the owners of the island, and one of the most skillful amateur whips in America.
Then the six horses were 'let out' and the full delights of mountain coaching
were realized . . . All six were running down the incline, not prancing, but on
a dead run.   CHARLES F. HOLDER, *Life in the Open* (1906)

From Catalina Harbor it is three nautical miles southeast to Little Harbor, the next important port of call. We enter Little Harbor keeping well toward the shore of a steep, prominent headland on the east, called Indian Head Rock because to some it resembles the profile of an Indian. The outline is seen best after one passes the headland. When entering the harbor, keep clear of a reef that extends from the northwesterly shore one-third of the way across the mouth.

The reef is nearly covered at high tide. We round it carefully, passing behind to an anchorage between it and the sandy beach. This is an excellent anchorage, without moorings, for a maximum of fifteen boats in about fifteen feet of water. It is advisable to anchor fore and aft, bow facing the reef; fore and aft anchoring is mandatory when other vessels occupy the cove because there is insufficient room to swing on a single anchor. The cove is often crowded in summer. As we turn to enter Little Harbor there are two other designated harbors, Shark and Little Shark, between a pockmarked rocky promontory and the southeast cliff-lined shore. Both are unsafe anchorages and should be avoided. At times, large breakers crash onto their shores.

Little Harbor has a fine, calm beach, perfect for landing a dinghy. Beyond is a broad, sloping valley with a public camp that offers piped-in drinking water, cold showers, primitive toilets, and camping tables. Once there was a large Indian village here with clusters of domed shelters constructed of woven mats, animal skins, or brush over frames of whale ribs or poles. The settlement may have included a sweathouse, earth covered and partially subterranean, and a ceremonial enclosure near the chief's house. "The ceremonial enclosure was open-air, usually oval in plan, made with either a pole or whalebone framework and decorated with feathers and skins," according to *A Step Into the Past: Island Dwellers of Southern California,* a 1989 publication of the Department of Anthropology, California State University, Fullerton. Generations of archaeologists and amateur "pot hunters" have virtually stripped this valley, and others, of tangible evidence of early civilizations.

Going ashore in our inflatable dinghy, we hike up a winding dirt road that passes across the valley, the only thoroughfare connecting Avalon with the Isthmus. Reaching the summit, we can see the *Bird* at anchor, resembling a toy boat from this elevation. Around us, even in the roadbed, a vast display of gleaming abalone shell fragments indicates a layering of ancient maritime cultures. Here an excavation was conducted in the 1950s by archaeologists from the University of California, Los Angeles. Dr. Clement W. Meighan of the UCLA archaeology department said, in connection with that important dig: "Prior to the development of radiocarbon dating, we really had no idea of how early the offshore islands were settled by man. Comparison of the island finds with those of the mainland suggested an antiquity of a few thousand years, but no direct dating evidence was available. I obtained the first radiocarbon date for the Channel Islands in the 1950s — this date of slightly under 4,000 years ago was on the Little Harbor Site on Catalina Island."

COURTESY DOUG BOMBARD

Erected in 1894, these buildings at Little Harbor were on the coach road from Avalon to the Isthmus during Banning ownership.

Further archaeological study of the Channel Islands, Dr. Meighan said, seemed to indicate that they were visited by man at least 10,000 years ago, and that all the islands were settled and commonly visited between 6,000 and 8,000 years ago. These early men must have had boats, for there was no other way to reach the islands. There is speculation that the planked canoe dates back that far, evidence of continuing trade between the island Indians and those on the mainland.

All the islands shared similar shell fishhooks, mortuary customs, shell beads, and ornaments. However, Meighan pointed out, the southern islands, including Catalina, developed their own patterns and had some specializations that were rare or absent on the northern islands, namely, steatite effigies of fishes and whales, which were heavily concentrated on the southern islands. Virtually all steatite in southern California appears to have come originally from the extensive quarries of Catalina Island, largely in the canyon extending inland from Rippers Cove on the northern shore. Little Harbor is only four miles from this principal source of steatite. Meighan declared that steatite objects found at Little Harbor were of particular interest in dating the steatite industry and the growth of widespread and sophisticated exchange networks between the islands and the mainland.

During our hike from the Little Harbor valley we paused to examine some twisted old water pipes, rusty debris, and disturbed earth on the hillside. This was the site of the twelve-room Little Harbor Inn, built in 1894 and razed in 1931. The inn, a popular rest stop for tourists taking the stagecoach ride from Avalon to the Isthmus (and earlier from the Isthmus to Little Harbor), was a single-story, wooden structure with a deep surrounding porch where guests could lounge in the shade, admiring the peaceful ocean view. Arriving at the inn, tourists marveled that the cook always knew how many people to expect for dinner. It seems a code had been developed using signal flags, with various flags representing specific numbers. The coach driver would fly the flag denoting the number of passengers and thus the cook knew precisely how many were coming to dine.

In 1894, two years after the island was acquired by William Banning with his brothers, construction began on a coach road, the first leg running from the Isthmus to Little Harbor, a distance of eight miles. The Bannings also started building the Little Harbor Inn, managed by O.T. Fellows when it opened. An early magazine, *The Traveler,* opined in 1895 that the inn is "already a favorite rendezvous and the beautiful harbor with its twin coves is destined at no distant day to become a formidable rival to Avalon and vicinity." Implicit in this promotion was the Bannings' desire to develop the Isthmus and the island's western attractions into a resort equal to, if not eclipsing, Avalon.

The Bannings had experienced considerable difficulty developing Avalon as a semiprivate resort and anglers' paradise. Although they transported early tourists on ships of the Wilmington Transportation Company, formed in 1877 by their father, Phineas Banning, competition occurred when other companies attempted to run rival transchannel passenger boat service to Avalon.

Hancock Banning Jr., in his oral history, pointed out that the three brothers, Hancock (1865–1925), Joseph Brent (1861–1920), and William (1858–1946) owned the entire island, including the streets of Avalon, except for a few freeholder's lots in town sold earlier by George Shatto, the original developer of Avalon. The Banning Company was a holding company, largely for land, such as Catalina Island. The three brothers owned the Santa Catalina Island Company (SCICO) equally.

Characterizing the rival vessels as "tramp boats," Hancock Banning Jr. said that

> We were furnishing all the entertainment, including a dance hall and concerts by the Santa Catalina Island Marine Band, most of it free. Why should these people capitalize on our entertainment? … Our steamer fares were paying for it all [but] they [wanted] to take a free ride. We put up barbed wire fences and sea walls and we used fire hoses on them, scared them off the beach. My Uncle Joe picked up one man and threw him back in the water. He brought suit … We proved it was high tide when this man walked ashore and Uncle Joe threw him back in the water again. He was on our land.

This battle for legal property dominance lasted until 1909 when the Avalon Freeholders' Improvement Association was formed to establish order. With all the problems, it is not surprising that the Bannings became soured on Avalon and attempted to develop Little Harbor and the Isthmus, where the town of Cabrillo was to be built as a resort.

Most of the old coach road was built for the Bannings by Samuel Stephen

Farnsworth, contract engineer and father of the famous sport fisherman, George C. Farnsworth. The road from Avalon to Little Harbor was completed in 1903, linking Avalon with the Isthmus. Earlier, in 1894, a road was built from the Isthmus to Little Harbor. A road from Avalon to the summit was built in 1897, continuing from the summit to Eagles' Nest in 1898 and Eagles' Nest to Little Harbor in 1903 (Oliver Loud manuscript in the Santa Catalina Island Museum). Farnsworth designed the lower half of a figure eight, called the Farnsworth Loop, on a very steep grade near Avalon. It required at least three hours going by coach from Avalon to the Isthmus on the new road, but it was a vast improvement over the old trail which necessitated a laborious day's tramp by burro or on foot.

Captain William Banning poses with a model Concord six-in-hand coach in the background. He was an expert driver of similar full-size stages on the island road between Avalon and the Isthmus.

Although several automobiles had appeared on the mainland, they were impractical for the island, and it was not until 1914, when the road to the summit was widened, that the old Concord stages and their teams of horses were retired from service. An anecdote that was told by Hancock Banning Jr. illustrates the difficulty of driving "horseless carriages" on the coach road.

In 1903, Banning, his brother, and his sister were passengers of their father, Hancock Banning, in a 1902 Oldsmobile, the first automobile on the island. Their starting point was the Hotel Metropole in Avalon, where they obtained two large buckets of cracked ice. Their destination was Middle Ranch. The children were seated in the back, over a tank containing the engine's cooling water. About every two miles Hancock Jr. would shout, "Father, it's boiling again!" and Banning would stop, get the children out of the car, remove the back seat, take the lid off the water tank, and pour in melted ice water from one of the buckets. Finally reaching Middle Ranch, they spent the night, refilled the buckets, and made it back to Avalon the next day.

The Oldsmobile had come across the channel in the hold of the SS *Hermosa II*, and was unloaded at Avalon by derrick. The *Hermosa II* was also used nearly a decade later to transport a Packard to the Isthmus for Judge Joseph Brent Banning. J.B. was at the wheel in 1912 when the Packard made the run from the Isthmus to Avalon in an astonishing two hours and ten minutes. Ernest Windle, a breathless passenger on this trip, recorded the feat in his island history.

During the period of Banning ownership of Catalina, 1892 to 1919, stage coaching was *the* thrilling experience for visitors. Stages, drawn by six prancing horses, would draw up on the plateau above Little Harbor for a rest stop so visitors could enjoy the commanding view. Holder took the ride many times and enthused that "Captain William Banning is probably the finest amateur six-in-hand driver in the United States; to see him handle his famous team on the island roads, or anywhere in California, is something worth while [*sic*]..." And going down a mountain road when Banning "let them out" was "as near an aeroplane as anything could be." Most tourists were driven by George Greeley of Pasadena, who also owned the coaches, and earlier, by Tom Green. Recalling Greeley, who retired to a small Diamond Bar Ranch in Los Angeles County, Hancock Banning III of Balboa expressed his affection for him, adding that Greeley was "a wonderful, profane man and a great storyteller to us kids."

The coach road still traverses some of the deepest canyons on the island, affording a succession of awesome views of ocean and abyss, as breathtaking in modern vehicles as in a stagecoach, but without the roar of wheels on hard ground, the clanking of buckles and trappings, the snap of long lash, and shouts from the driver that only horses understood. Today's tour buses climb steeply out of Avalon, and the smaller trans-island vehicles leave from both the Isthmus and Avalon, offering sweeping views down canyons to the sea where vessels appear as tiny white punctuation marks on the blue.

Staging in Catalina's interior during the Banning brothers' ownership of the island was a popular tourist attraction during the second decade of the twentieth century.

A newer road passes the Airport in the Sky, paved from Avalon to this point and continuing to the Isthmus as graded dirt. This road approaches El Rancho Escondido, located where Cottonwood Canyon widens, then passes on to Little Harbor. The old coach road leaves the new road at Middle Ranch Junction on the ridge above Toyon Bay and meanders through Middle Ranch Valley. Beyond this is a narrow canyon where Eagle's Nest, an ancient wooden structure with a corral, served as an early stage stop and place where tired horses were changed for fresh ones. Set among cottonwood trees that line and canopy the road, the structure took its name from a pair of bald eagles who made their home in a nearby tree. In 1896, Eagle's Nest was the inland home of the island's hunting guide, D.A. Baughman. Early goat hunting parties departed from here.

Middle Ranch itself is an area of tilled land, now planted to hay but once a source of fresh fruit and vegetables for the former Hotel St. Catherine and Avalon. Homes housing employees of the Catalina Conservancy and a few stables are located here

The stage pauses on Indian Head headland, where the entrance to Little Harbor is on the immediate right and the entrance to Catalina Harbor beyond the coach. This is the southern or windward side of Catalina.

as well as a native plant nursery. The road passes Thompson Reservoir, which provides much of the domestic water for Avalon, then follows Cottonwood Canyon to the island's southern side where it climbs the Indian Head plateau. Due to severe storms in 1995, the Middle Canyon road now ends at Middle Ranch. Although the road runs circuitously along the West Summit to the Isthmus, a little west of Lower Buffalo Reservoir the old Coach Road takes off in a nearly straight line over a steep hill to the Banning House at the Isthmus. This historic stretch, a narrow track, is in disrepair and virtually impassable.

We must not overlook El Rancho Escondido (the Hidden Ranch) with its pastures, corrals, and tile-roofed, whitewashed buildings on about 1,500 acres. This ranch had been a dream of Philip K. Wrigley, son of William Wrigley Jr., long before its development began in 1931. Design of the ranch is attributed to Malcolm Joseph Renton, who joined the SCICo in 1929 following his graduation from Stanford University. Renton was named a vice president in 1931–32 and served as corporate secretary in charge of development until his retirement in 1975. He died at age eighty-nine in 1997.

Malcolm Renton's father, David M. Renton, was vice president and general manager for William Wrigley Jr. until Renton's death in 1947. He was a successful lumberyard owner and building contractor in Pasadena when he attracted the favorable attention of Wrigley after the latter's purchase of the island in 1919. Under D. M. Renton's creative management, the island became a nationally famous tourist attraction. Renton and his son, Malcolm, worked together for eighteen years.

Architecturally, El Rancho Escondido reflects P. K. Wrigley's desire to introduce a Spanish or early-California theme to the island and to buildings constructed in Avalon. The motif was continued in outdoor tourist entertainment and in the attire of island employees who dealt with the public, from dock workers to the tour bus operators. Philip Wrigley believed strongly in the development of the island's interior. He said it seemed obvious to him that if Catalina were ever to come into its own, people must be able to get away from the few blocks near the bay in Avalon and the "very limited number of coves on the channel or mainland side, as they represent a very small portion of the total area" (Wrigley 1952).

Concord stages meet near Little Harbor on the old coach road prior to 1914, when some paving began.

Horses left to run wild after the stage operation closed were rounded up to become Rancho Escondido's original stock. Wild palominos from New Mexico were added, followed by Arabians. The Arabian horse is a species, not a breed, with a known history of more than 2,000 years, a "small, very tough horse that can get along very well on a minimum of feed and water," according to P. K. Wrigley (ibid.). A gray Arabian stallion named Kaaba, bought by Philip Wrigley and his wife, Helen, became the foundation sire of their Catalina Arabian horses, which were initially bred with the palominos and other ranch horses. The Wrigleys' decision to specialize in purebred Arabians was based on the fact that they "ate no more and occupied no more space than mixed breed horses" (ibid.; Wrigley-Rusack). Over the years the ranch's specialization in Arabians garnered an impressive number of champi-

Tour buses in the 1920s filled up fast after the old coach road was widened and partially paved. Dakin Bay and Sugar Loaf can be seen in the background.

onships at horse shows throughout the country. Today, tour buses stop at El Rancho Escondido where passengers are treated to an exhibit of saddles and trophies, as well as a chance to see the prize-winning horses in an equestrian show in the arena.

Despite rising operating expenses and taxes that, after World War II, drained the slim profits of the ranch and other island operations, Philip Wrigley's dream of broadening public appreciation of the island as a whole began to be realized in 1972 with the creation of the Catalina Conservancy. There will be more about that when we reach Avalon.

27 The True Ben Weston

He was not run off the island during the Civil War period. He was not a squatter. He had a lease to run sheep.

MRS. HARVEY (SALLY) SOMERS,
great-grandniece of Ben S. Weston

It is about one nautical mile from Little Harbor, past Sentinel Rock, to Ben Weston Beach. We make no attempt to land here, simply lying off for a good view, because the anchorage is not safe. There are primitive camping facilities in the canyon; concrete bunkers, abandoned after World War II, can be seen on shore.

The identity of Ben Weston or, more fully, Benjamin Stone Weston, seems to have been an enigma to previous Catalina historians who generally categorized him as an old "resident" or "squatter" who ran sheep in the canyon bearing his name and lived a hermit's existence in a little stone house built above the nearby beach. The historical truth, and we are indebted to Mrs. Harvey (Sally) Somers of Balboa for it, is that Ben S. Weston was a successful rancher who settled in the Torrance area on a 4,000-acre ranch bought with a partner for twenty-five cents an acre in the early 1850s. Born in Salem, Massachusetts, in 1832, he was a sailor before turning to ranching. He was aboard a vessel engaged in trading along the Pacific Coast and making voyages to and from the Sandwich Islands and Canton when the vessel visited Catalina, thus acquainting him with the island, according to Mrs. Somers.

Weston and his partner, Nathaniel A. Narbonne, also born in Salem, Massachusetts (in 1827), secured a lease from James Lick, owner of the island from 1864 to 1874. Mrs. Somers, a great-grandniece of Ben S. Weston, has a receipt from Lick showing that Weston paid him twenty dollars in gold for the privilege of running 3,000 head of sheep on the back side of the island, now Ben Weston Canyon. The sheep were brought back to the mainland and placed on a 4,000-acre range near Torrance, an area that was once part of the vast Sepulveda Ranch. Narbonne had also been a sailor, arriving in California in 1849 to seek gold. He died in a ranch house fire in 1881; a high school in Lomita is named after him, according to Edna Marinella, a librarian at Narbonne High School. Weston spent most of his days on the mainland property, called the Weston Narbonne Ranch, devoting his time to sheep and cattle husbandry and field crops. He maintained several hired hands on the island. A bachelor, Weston died in 1905 at age seventy-three and is buried in Wilmington Cemetery near the Phineas Banning residence and museum.

Mills Landing, part of the Weston property on Catalina Island, was named after Hiram and Warren Mills, who had an interest in San Miguel Island in the early 1870s before they transferred their interests to the Pacific Wool Growing Company, which was based in San Francisco. The Mills brothers also ran sheep on

Anacapa Island and at one time forwarded animals from Mills Landing there.

The concrete military bunkers at Ben Weston Beach stand as grim reminders of World War II, after the Japanese air attack on Pearl Harbor in Hawaii December 7, 1941. The United States declared war against Japan the following day. Two weeks later, on December 24, Catalina transchannel steamers were taken off their run, the result of a fortuitous early decision by the Santa Catalina Island and Wilmington Transportation Companies. Coincidentally, a Japanese submarine had shelled and sunk a lumber ship, the *Absaroka,* within sight of the San Pedro breakwater the day before the trip was cancelled (Alma Overholt, *Catalina Islander,* August 24, 1944; Bob Wells, *Independent Press Telegram,* Long Beach, April 19, 1959).

The late Joe Guion of Avalon said that sightings of Japanese submarines in Catalina waters were infrequent but alarming occurrences during the war in the Pacific, which ended with Japan's surrender on September 2, 1945. The end of the war was hastened by President Harry Truman's order for an atomic bomb to be dropped on the Japanese city of Hiroshima on August 6, 1945, followed by a second bomb on Nagasaki three days later. The last of the Axis resistance in Europe had terminated on May 8, 1945, when Germany surrendered. World War II was over and the atomic age was upon us, clutching the world in its ominous embrace.

Halting the runs of Catalina's transchannel steamers, wrote island historian Alma Overholt, "automatically cut the life-line of Catalina's one business — tourists and vacationers — and stopped the income of the SCI Company and of Avalon's business and property owners." The last scheduled means of transportation to and from the mainland were the Douglas Dolphins, boat-hulled seaplanes of the Wilmington Catalina Airline. The flights ended when the government took them over in May 1942. The government takeover also included the large, newly built Lockheed passenger planes, scheduled to touch down at the new Buffalo Springs airfield, known today as the Airport in the Sky, on a leveled mountaintop inland from Mount Blackjack.

The economic future of Avalon and of the entire island was decidedly bleak, and strong measures for survival had to be taken. SCICo officials succeeded in temporarily persuading the Los Angeles County Board of Supervisors, sitting as a Board of Equalization, to reduce property taxes by 50 percent. Company executives launched a successful campaign in Washington for the government to lease suitable areas on the island for use as training facilities by the Army, Navy, Marines, Coast Guard, and U.S. Maritime Service. An economic infusion resulted as thousands of armed forces trainees, with their families in some cases, spent their paychecks with Avalon merchants.

The military was spread over much of the island during World War II including the Army's U.S. Signal Corps on Mount Blackjack and other Army units at Cactus Flats near Ben Weston Beach, the U.S. Maritime Service and Navy at Avalon, and the Office of Strategic Services at Toyon Bay. The Hotel St. Catherine at Descanso Bay trained cooks; Marine Corps personnel were scattered in the island's canyons learning to scale cliffs and mountain summits; and, as mentioned before, the Coast Guard trained at Two Harbors. Blackouts were imposed by air wardens; identification cards were issued to island residents. The SS *Avalon,* operated by the Maritime Service during the war years, was painted gray, her windows and ports blacked out. She carried passengers and freight to and from San Pedro, but frequently had to lie off for several hours while the line of submarine nets protecting the harbors was opened (Malcolm Renton interview).

Naturally, ocean sport fishing was suspended for the duration and the famous Tuna Club in Avalon was closed, members gathering on the mainland for their annual meetings. My father, Harry Buffum, was president in 1942, succeeded by Joseph D. Peeler, Charles F. Jones, and Robert C. Mankowski, all famous anglers, during the war years. One of the club's best known members was off fighting in Europe: General George S. Patton Jr.

It was nearly impossible to get over to Catalina, according to Arthur N. Macrate Jr. of Long Beach, former Tuna Club historian. Special arrangements were made for any fish caught during this period to be officially weighed at Balboa on the mainland, instead of Avalon. According to club records, very few marlin and broadbill swordfish were landed during the war years and virtually no bluefin tuna of record. During those dark years, the old saying, "The next best thing to fishing is to sit and talk about it," held especially true for angling in Catalina waters.

28 The Clemente Monster

The sea never changes, and its works,
for all the talk of men, are wrapped in mystery.
JOSEPH CONRAD, *Typhoon* (1902)

Ben Weston Point lies three-quarters of a nautical mile easterly of Ben Weston Beach. We steer a magnetic compass course of 226 degrees from Ben Weston Point in the southerly direction of San Clemente Island; after a little less than two nautical miles we reach the twenty-eight-acre Farnsworth Bank, its highest elevation nine fathoms below the surface at mean lower low water. This underwater secret we cannot see is a designated ecological reserve established to protect a rare purple coral, *Allopora Californica,* which grows here in heads up to two feet in diameter. It is taboo for divers to take the coral.

We briefly troll a hand line with a feather jig over the bank, for it was purported to be good fishing ground, but have nary a strike. Doug Bombard, who fished commercially as a young man, said this bank once yielded great catches of albacore, but no longer. Actually, our fishing was done in memory of the late, great angler, George C. Farnsworth, who discovered the bank and named it after his father, Stephen

Farnsworth, engineer of the coach road. George Farnsworth fished the island's waters as early as 1902 in his vessel, the *Nestella*. Launched June 10, 1902, the *Nestella* was built in Avalon by J.E. (Pard) Mathewson. She was twenty feet long, with a five-foot-eight-inch beam, powered by a four-horsepower gasoline engine. "Uncle" John Nestell, an owner of the Meteor Boat Company in Avalon, fished with Farnsworth and had the *Nestella* built for him, with the understanding that Farnsworth would repay Nestell with profits from his charters (*Los Angeles Times,* June 12, 1902).

While trolling, my wife and I scanned the channel toward San Clemente Island, hoping for a glimpse of the mysterious San Clemente sea monster and wondering how we might react if we actually saw it. We doubted we'd be as calm as George Farnsworth seemed to be in a report made in the *History of the Tuna Club* of Avalon:

> On the way to Clemente one day [ca. 1920–21] with Mr. Paparinsky, I saw what looked like a boat with a sail on it. It was calm, though. I set out to see what it was; thought maybe it was someone broken down. It was possibly three miles away.
>
> We started out in its general direction; covered probably half the distance when it disappeared. We could see nothing, no sail, no boat; nothing at all. Well, we came to the Glory Hole... There ahead of us was the same thing; it looked like a boat with the sail up. I wondered how it could have got there ahead of us without our seeing it.
>
> We started towards it, but again, half way there, it vanished. Whatever it was stood 15 to 20 feet out of the water... The next time I saw it off the east end of Catalina. I seized the glasses and had a perfect view because we were running right towards it.
>
> Its eyes were 12 inches in diameter, not set on the side like an ordinary fish, but more central. It had a big mange of hair, about two feet long. We were within a hundred feet of it before it went down.
>
> I saw it afterwards several times, but never close like that. Lots of people said it was a sea elephant. Well, I know a sea elephant as far as I can see it. This was no sea elephant... Nobody will believe it, unless they see it themselves. But I did see it.

George Farnsworth was a large, ruddy-faced charter boatman who, according to those who fished with him, knew more about the migration of fishes and their habits than any man alive. He made a lifelong study of aquatic life around the islands, keeping a detailed journal of his discoveries that he planned to use in a book. Alas, the book was never written.

But Farnsworth wasn't the only person to sight the Clemente monster. One of the Tuna Club's most famous members, George C. Thomas III, a sober, hard-fishing gentleman of the old school not given to tall tales or exaggeration, also saw the creature. It was around 1924 or 1925, he reported, "and we were going to San

Clemente — George Farnsworth and I — on the old *Fairplay*." Thomas, in *History of the Tuna Club,* said they headed toward the east end of San Clemente on a calm, glassy sea. About eight miles off the coast of Clemente Island they saw a big black form, like the sail of a Japanese albacore boat.

"I said to George: 'What the hell's that?' He said: 'The Clemente Monster.' We went towards it. We got to within three-quarters of a mile. Then it went down."

It is recorded that "other Tuna Club members, withal a little shamefacedly, admit to having seen it. They know, however convincing their narrative of the incident may be, most of their listeners will be inclined to scoff and maybe mutter something about the Ananias Club."

Among others who swore they saw the Clemente Monster was Captain John Vitalich, who skippered for author Zane Grey on his boat *Frangipani.* Vitalich was a lad of fourteen in September 1927, when he saw the monster. He and his father were fishing for albacore in the channel when the monster surfaced about seventy-five yards to port. Vitalich, in *Incredible Fishing Stories,* compiled by Shaun Morey, described the mysterious creature as having large eyes, small ears, a long neck, and a head much like a horse. It was glossy black.

Most of the recorded sightings were in the 1920s, but at least one was reported earlier: angler and author-attorney Ralph Bandini described the monster he saw in 1916. He said it had "a great columnar neck or body, eight or ten feet thick and lifting 20 feet above the surface. Surmount this neck or body with a flat-topped, blunt reptilian head. On either side of the head place two huge, round and bulging eyes. I don't believe they were an inch under a foot and a half across, perhaps more... Two things stood out above all others: those enormous eyes and its unbelievably huge bulk. I never want to look at such eyes again. They were like the creations of a nightmare."

Bandini was trolling for marlin swordfish about a mile and one-half off the east end of San Clemente Island when he spotted "something big and black lifting above the surface." He was sitting on top of the vessel's cabin watching for fins. He observed the monster about a quarter-mile away with his seven-power field glasses.

In the *National Fisherman* magazine for June 1991, John Grissim reported:

> The head of a sea monster "as big as a submarine, like something out of prehistoric times," rose out of the water next to the purse seiner *Endeavor* near San Clemente Island... Capt. Sam Randazzo reported to the Coast Guard in an affidavit that he and his nine-man crew were at first reluctant to make a report for fear of ridicule. Randazzo said the crew was in the midst of pulling aboard the nets when "the monster reared its head out of the ocean only 15 feet from the boat, threatening to tear up the nets and capsize the boat."
>
> Reaching for his 30-30 rifle, Randazzo fired two bullets into "the ugly beast. We were close enough to hear the thud of the bullets in the monster's flesh. It didn't bleed, but instead, quietly submerged."

We have wondered where the monster — or possibly monsters, for it might have had a mate and offspring — made its home or lair. While studying a chart of San Clemente Island, we noted a warning to mariners of an unexplained magnetic disturbance generally located to the east of Pyramid Cove. It is a force that can cause a compass variation of as much as five degrees. Perhaps this magnetic disturbance emanates from the monster's ancient abode — a great undersea cavern with walls of lodestone or magnetite, possessing polarity. But our imagination runs away. We must limit this chapter to objective reporting.

In the fall of 1967, I interviewed Howard Wilson of Laguna Beach for my column in the Orange County edition of the *Los Angeles Times.* Wilson, a building designer in

Captain George Farnsworth swore to the validity of the Clemente Sea Monster.

that seaside community for thirty years, swore to me that he and his mother, Mrs. Grace Wilson, sighted the Clemente monster in 1927, when he was a high school student. This was the period when fairly frequent sightings were reported, most of them off the East End of Catalina or near San Clemente Island, but Wilson and his mother spotted the monster cruising about 400 yards off the Laguna Beach coast. It was moving in an easterly direction, Wilson said, and they watched it, enthralled, for about fifteen minutes from the bluffs above Aliso Beach where they lived. Wilson described the monster as brownish, more like the color of a wet seal. He said it had a camel-like head and neck, large eyes like dinner plates, and a neck that extended some ten feet above the surface of the sea.

"He looked at us and we looked at him," Wilson said. "It was a clear, cold day and his details showed up very well. There was no mistaking him for something else."

Wilson was no stranger to inhabitants of southern California's prehistory, a category in which he placed the Clemente monster, saying it was dinosaur-like. A few years after sighting the monster, he and a friend discovered a piece of an ancient human skull near what is now St. Ann's Drive in Laguna Beach. It was the now famous Laguna Woman, also known as the Laguna Girl. In 1967 Dr. Louis S.B. Leakey, the noted archaeologist, established the authenticity of the skull, carbon-dating it to about 17,000 years ago, one of the oldest human remains found in the Americas. The skull fragment (much of the original was lost during the carbon-dating process) is in a collection at UCLA.

Tales of sea serpents abound in myth and legend. Horace B. Beck, folklorist, sailor, professor of American literature at Middlebury College in Vermont, and author of *Folklore and the Sea,* said that in recent times sea monsters "have been noted frequently on the California coast, from Monterey and San Clemente Island clear north to British Columbia." All of them, he said, have been described in roughly similar terms: 40 to 70 feet in length, serpentine, dark in color — brown and gray — maned or at least possessing nubs along the neck, with a head like that of an eel, snake, lion, or horse, with very prominent eyes.

"No group of people has a corner on the belief in such unusual creatures. It is worldwide, running from the Orient through India and Africa to Greece, the entire Mediterranean and up into Scandinavia. Tales of serpents and monsters were popular even among the American Indians and Eskimos," Beck wrote.

A believer in sea serpents, at least in large and strange creatures of some kind, was the late marine biologist Roger Revelle of the century-old Scripps Institute of Oceanography, La Jolla, California. Dr. Revelle said, in a 1984 article in the *National Fisherman,* that there is a good possibility that large sea creatures similar to serpents have managed to survive sea pollution, environmental changes in the oceans, and the depredations of man by seeking the cold, black depths of less-traveled areas of the sea.

Tales of the Clemente monster seem to relate us to nearly forgotten mythology that harkens back to prehistoric times. The stories tie us to widely held beliefs of the early Christian era, of enchanted islands, of lands beneath the sea, of kelpies and merfolk of the Celts and Vikings. So strong was the concept of sea monsters that the Norse designed their ships to look like them, with dragon head and tail. And early maps and charts frequently were illustrated by legendary creatures rising from the depths.

This ephemera of mythology sometimes invades our dreams, even in this highly technical age. The ancient poetry of mythology, however submerged, exists in our racial memories. The Clemente monster struggles for belief in its reality. My wife and I would not have scanned the surface of the sea off Farnsworth Bank if that mysterious part of us had not wanted to believe that *something* was out there.

29   Around to the Other Side

> *Off Silver Canyon are the famous Black Sea Bass Beds where these monsters lived and were caught.* Stereolepsis gigas *is the scientific name for these giants which were exceptionally large. The Chinese deemed the fish a superior codfish and as a result, the Black Sea Bass were all destroyed within my time and memory.*   RUBEN V. VAUGHAN, *Doc's Catalina Diary* (1961)

The *Bird's* bows are now directed toward Avalon or, to put it more clearly, Avalon is our destination. We must loop around the island's east end to arrive at Avalon Bay, some fifteen nautical miles away. There is a fine northwesterly breeze and we sail a pleasant broad reach toward the east, the sea passing along our hull seeming to sing a homeward-bound song, for our circumnavigation will end at White's Landing. Meanwhile, we will pause at Avalon for a few days to sample the rich history of the only incorporated city on Catalina Island.

Off our port side we identify China Point, already mentioned in connection with early illegal Chinese immigrants, and Salta Verde Point with its startling vegetation in the otherwise barren coastline. Silver Canyon Landing is next, lying on the westerly side of the towering and easily identifiable Palisades. The area has long been used as a refuge by vessels when treacherous Santa Ana winds make Avalon Bay untenable. Silver Canyon, so named because silver was once mined in the canyon, is four and three-quarters nautical miles from the island's east end. There is an anchorage off the beach in twenty to seventy feet in sand, with Bulldog Rock offering some westerly protection. Landing is risky, with fewest breakers on the southwest side.

The treasure of Silver Canyon was recognized and mined at an early date, for in May 1846, Thomas O. Larkin, Monterey merchant, United States consul in the Mexican province of California, and a confidential agent for President James K. Polk, reported this to the secretary of state at Washington: "On the Southeast end of the island of Catalina there is a silver mine from which silver has been extracted... there is no doubt but that gold, silver, quick silver [*sic*], copper, lead, sulphur and coal mines are to be found all over Calif'a [*sic*] & it is equally doubtful whether under thier [*sic*] present owners they will ever be worked... Up to the present time there are few or no persons in California with sufficient energy & capital to carry on mining" (Gleason and Gleason 1978).

That situation proved to be temporary. An Act of Congress dated May 13, 1846, authorized the president of the United States to call for and accept the services of volunteers for the Mexican war, and on June 26, President Polk's secretary of war asked Colonel Jonathan D. Stevenson of New York City to organize a regiment of volunteers to tender their services "during the war with Mexico." When the war ended, the volunteers were to remain in California as colonists. According to Bancroft (vol. 5, p. 502), "No secret was made of the regiment's destination and prospective service... [although] there was perhaps no formal publication of the colonizing scheme. No volunteer dreamed of conflict with any foe: all regarded themselves as immigrant adventurers bound for a distant land of many charms, under the protection of government. There was but slight pretense of patriotism, and no fear of danger..."

Two years later, in January 1848, gold was discovered at Coloma, and the war with Mexico ended February 2 with the Treaty of Guadalupe Hidalgo, by which Mexico gave up claims to Texas and ceded New Mexico and California to the United States. By then there were, in part because of Stevenson's New York volunteers, already in California hundreds of young American men with "sufficient energy" to work the mines, and hundreds more followed. Some already had "sufficient capital to carry on mining": others got their start with mustering-out pay, heading as quickly as possible for the gold fields.

Larkin, it should be added, arrived in California in 1832 and built up an important commercial and trading business along the coast before becoming, in 1843, the only American consul appointed to Mexican California (Busch, see Phelps, p. 31). Larkin was sympathetic to the expansionists and their belief in "manifest destiny," i.e., that the United States must expand across the continent until it controlled the

Tourists onboard an overloaded small schooner near the turn of the twentieth century view Church Rock at Catalina's east end.

shores of the Pacific. As "confidential agent" to President James K. Polk, Larkin was to keep the president informed of political and military matters in the province, and to encourage Californians to seek independence from Mexico and look to the U.S. for advice and assistance. President Polk was determined to annex California to the U.S., by purchase or negotiation if possible, by conquest if all else failed.

The United States agreed to pay Mexico $15 million for the land it acquired under the Treaty of Guadalupe Hidalgo and to assume American claims against Mexico. Curiously, the treaty was silent about California's offshore islands, an oversight that has prompted Mexican ownership claims from time to time with, however, no serious consequences. California was admitted to the Union September 9, 1850.

Back to the present. We pass Church Rock, standing out from shore and resembling a great cathedral with lofty spires, then begin rounding the east end, an area where the sea has offered memorable catches for generations of anglers. Next come Seal Rocks, where great herds of sea lions frequently sport in the restless surf. Midway between Church and Seal Rocks is a flashing light at 212 feet, warning mariners of the east end.

One nautical mile from Seal Rocks is Jewfish Point, and above it the great chewed and blasted cliffs of a rock quarry, leased from the Santa Catalina Island Company (SCICO) by Connolly Pacific Company. We run by the area for a good mile and a half, heading ultimately for Avalon Bay. Jewfish Point is named for the California jewfish or black sea bass, which once lurked here as well as off Silver Canyon. David Starr Jordan, president of Leland Stanford Junior University, seemed in awe of these giant fish in his 1905 book, *American Food and Game Fishes,* written with Dr. Barton Warren

Angler T.S. Manning displays the 370-pound black sea bass, or jewfish, he caught on twenty-one-strand cuttyhunk off Catalina's east end on September 16, 1899.

Evermann, ichthyologist with the United States Fish Commission. They quoted Professor Charles F. Holder, Catalina's avid sports fisherman and naturalist, as saying:

> When hooked, the fish is away with a rush that has been known to demoralize experienced anglers. My largest fish [weighed] 276 pounds [and] was taken in a boat or skiff which weighed 125 pounds, and I was repeatedly almost jerked overboard by the struggles of the bass.
>
> When it was gaffed it jerked the gaff from my hands a score of times. It was impossible to take it aboard so we towed it five miles to port [Avalon], well illustrating how delightful the most arduous labor becomes when dignified by the term "sport."

Holder added that he had seen a 200-pound jewfish or black sea bass snap the largest shark-line like a thread and had seen "large specimens straighten out an iron shark-hook."

At the western end of the quarry at Pebbly Beach is what remains of the Renton Mine. On the steep mountainside, development of the ore bodies was undertaken from five adits, the highest at 1,085 feet above sea level, the lowest at 716 feet. Renton Mine ore ranged from 8 to 12 percent zinc with only $1\frac{1}{2}$ to 2 percent lead and between two and three ounces of silver per ton. Gold was not found. The mining history here and at other island locations, particularly White's Landing, was provided by mining engineer Al Probert.

Probert was amused by a lengthy story in a 1926 Long Beach newspaper which said that certain streets in Long Beach were "paved with Catalina silver." The story came about because a large quantity of rock excavated from the west side of the Pebbly Beach quarry had been sent to Long Beach for street improvements. The rock had an assay value of $300 worth of silver to a ton. This is how the Renton Mine was first discovered; it was then developed by David M. Renton, manager of the SCICo. Ore from the Renton Mine was sent down a cable tramway, then barged to White's Landing for processing at the flotation mill there. The mine was abandoned in 1927 when the worldwide market for base metals collapsed.

30 Pebbly Beach

When the well's dry, we know the worth of water.

BENJAMIN FRANKLIN (1746)

Ever since tourists were attracted to the island during the final decades of the nineteenth century, maintaining an adequate supply of potable water has been a recurring problem, particularly during periods of drought that plague southern California. In the late nineteenth and early twentieth centuries, natural wells and springs on the island were supplemented by containers of mainland water shipped across the channel in the holds of passenger vessels and on water barges. One such vessel was the steamer *Aquador,* a water carrier owned by the Bannings.

We are reminded of this because off our port side just past the rock quarry at Pebbly Beach is modern technology's solution to the island's historic water problem. It is the Southern California Edison Company's $2.1 million desalinization plant that produces 132,000 gallons of drinking water per day for the City of Avalon's 3,000 residents during times of drought. The plant went into service July 1, 1991, and was then the West Coast's first permanent municipal seawater desalting facility for potable water. The plant removes salt from seawater by forcing it through thin fiber membranes, a process known as reverse osmosis. Developers of the then-projected 330-unit condominium complex at the old airport site at Hamilton Beach helped bankroll the desalting plant in exchange for a guaranteed allotment of water.

The Edison Company is no stranger to the island. On November 29, 1962, this private utility company purchased the island's water, electricity, and gas systems. Prior to that date the Santa Catalina Island Company (SCICO) and Avalon's municipal departments had labored to maintain an adequate water supply. William Wrigley Jr.'s SCICO had engineered construction of a large reservoir, Thompson Dam, in Middle Ranch in 1923, along with improving other dams and wells on the island. In 1962, Edison, which gained rights to all of the island's groundwater, took over the maintenance and operation of Thompson Reservoir, which has a capacity of 326 million gallons. Water is conveyed to Avalon over an 800-foot summit by two pumping stations through eight miles of pipeline. As mentioned previously, the historic well of Civil War and mining days at Howland's Landing northwest of the Isthmus has been invaded by salt water, owing to a lowered freshwater table. Edison has sunk a new well farther up the canyon, in addition to developing several new wells in various locations around the island.

Alongside the desalting plant at Pebbly Beach is Edison's electric power station. Edison also has a facility here that converts liquid petroleum gas and sends it through a distribution system to homes and businesses. Thus, this island is the only place in southern California that cooks with Edison gas. Up from the beach is the municipally owned sewage treatment plant. In Avalon Bay there is a separate facility that pumps seawater for firefighting and flushing the city's toilets — part of a thoroughly enlightened system of fresh water conservation that other coastal parts of California may someday have to follow.

In 1901, under the supervision of J.B. Banning, the Santa Catalina Island Company installed the first electric light plant on the island, located up Falls Canyon inland and southwesterly of Avalon. A waterfall once tumbled into this canyon, which is jointly owned by SCICo and the city of Avalon. Falls Canyon was abandoned in 1947 when the Pebbly Beach plant became operational. For contemporary readers who take for granted the blessings of electricity, it should be noted that the island, its dwellings, and its businesses were illuminated by kerosene lamps and candles prior to 1901.

The *Princess,* a glass-bottom boat operated by Wilmington Transportation Company under the corporate umbrella of the Santa Catalina Island Company, approaches the Pleasure Pier at Avalon. She was launched in 1926.

Beyond these very necessary facilities at Pebbly Beach is the site of a small airport where flying boats once ascended a ramp from the sea. Today it serves as a commercial heliport. The present buildings, excluding a newly built air terminal, are all that remain of a manufacturing community that thrived here before World War II. Located here was the Catalina Clay Products Division of the SCICo, a tile and pottery factory started by William Wrigley Jr. and D.M. Renton to produce bricks, pavers, and roof tiles for the island (including those for the Casino) and provide employment for year-round island residents. Glazed decorative tiles, ceramic art pieces, and earthenware also were made here. The tableware, now sought by collectors, was originally sold on the island and later nationwide in leading department stores. Clay for the original ceramic products was obtained from clay pits found at various locations on the island. By the 1930s, the ceramic plant was called Catalina Clay Products.

According to Lee Rosenthal's excellent *Catalina Tile of the Magic Isle,* the plant may have started producing brick from island clay as early as 1923. Hollow tiles, patio tiles, and mission roofing tiles followed. By the early 1930s, the line of dinnerware and decorative pottery was being produced. The strikingly lovely and colorful glazed decorative tiles, seen today in many island locations as well as at Clark Hall, Pomona College, Claremont, California, and the Arizona Biltmore, Phoenix, Arizona, were manufactured here. The pottery operation closed in 1937 when the island ceramic company was bought by Gladding, McBean & Company of California. For a decade, until discontinued, Catalina tableware, gradually integrated with its Franciscan line, was made by Gladding, McBean.

Also at Pebbly Beach were a planing mill, furniture factory, paint shop, iron foundry, and blacksmith shop, enabling designers to combine pottery and tile products with wood and iron.

Between Pebbly Beach and Avalon are Abalone Point and Lover's Cove, set aside as a preserve for an undersea garden of waving plants and colorful fishes, viewed through the glass-paneled bottoms of excursion boats. The first glass-bottom boat was a rowboat, built in 1896 at the suggestion of Charles F. Holder and others including abalone fisherman Charlie Faggie (or Feige) of Avalon, who applied the principle of a box with a glass bottom which, when partially submerged, enabled a person to see clearly objects at considerable depth. Soon a fleet of these canvas-canopied pulling boats was available for hire. Captain J.E. (Pard) Mathewson built many of the early glass-bottomed rowboats, which had watertight "wells" set amidships and carried four passengers. The development of glass-bottom boats is peculiar to Catalina Island, author-artist Duncan Gleason claimed. However, they were also found in Florida at about the same time.

A forerunner of the side-wheeler, a stern-wheeler, was built in 1898 by P.J. (Bill) Waller, who operated the twenty-foot vessel with a bicycle propulsion mechanism. A glass-bottom catamaran was tried unsuccessfully in 1899, while the first side-wheeler glass-bottom boat, the *Mon Ami,* powered by a gasoline motor, appeared on the scene in 1902. A year later the *Lady Lou,* carrying twenty-five passengers, was put into service. Other side-wheelers followed: the *Empress,* the *Cleopatra,* the *Emperor,* and the *Princess.* In 1931, a new side-wheeler replacing those wrecked or sold was launched at the Wilmington Boat Works in Los Angeles Harbor. She was the *Phoenix.* Sixty-two years later (1993) she was still revealing to passengers the wonders of the undersea garden in Lover's Cove, as well as transporting them on summer dinner cruises along the island coast. In 1995, the *Phoenix* was sold, brought across the channel, and is used as an excursion vessel in Newport Harbor. Other builders of the early excursion vessels were Fellows and Stewart in Los Angeles Harbor and William Muller on Mormon Island, Wilmington.

In 1937, the first propeller-driven glass-bottom boat, the *Torqua,* was added to the SCICO fleet. A sleek fifty-six-foot passenger cruiser with two viewing cockpits and

An early side-wheeler, the glass-bottom boat *Cleopatra,* was built in 1906 and owned by the Meteor Boat Company, a competing excursion firm with the Bannings' island monopoly. A lawsuit settlement in 1907 permitted Meteor to continue operating until it was purchased by the Santa Catalina Island Company in 1920, then under William Wrigley Jr. ownership.

twin Hall-Scott gas engines in a separate compartment amidships, she could be altered to serve as a passenger coastal cruiser by placing wooden covers over the glass wells.

To preserve the scenic underwater grandeur and marine life, anchoring is prohibited in Lover's Cove and there are no moorings. Snorkeling is permitted, but not scuba diving. Taking or disturbing animal or plant life is prohibited in this roughly 500-yard-long cove, extending from Abalone Point to the Cabrillo Mole.

The *Phoenix,* launched in 1931, floats over the undersea gardens of Lovers Cove. The glass-bottom side-wheeler carried Avalon excursionists for sixty-four years until she was sold to a new owner in Newport Harbor.

Presiding on the rocks at the end of Cabrillo Mole is a realistic statue of Old Ben, a legendary sea lion bull that amused and sometimes frightened unwary swimmers. He even became a movie star in a 1914 Mack Sennett film, *The Sea Nymphs,* with Mabel Normand and Roscoe "Fatty" Arbuckle. The plot revolved around Mabel and Fatty trying to outswim, outdive, and outsubmarine Ben, who was supposed to be Miss Normand's pet sea lion. In the 1920s, Harry "Monk" Boosinger, one of several versatile divers who entertained glass-bottom boat excursionists, cavorted with Old Ben under the boats' viewing windows in Lover's Cove. Ben, whose weight was estimated at 1,750 pounds, is said to have died in 1926 after becoming entangled in a fisherman's net. His statue, created by Stanley Rosin, was given to the city of Avalon by Rosin in memory of his father, Bernath Rosin, an early Avalon resident. The sculpture was unveiled on the mole September 18, 1975.

We round Cabrillo Mole with Old Ben's statue on our port side and the Casino groin to starboard, both with flashing lights at twenty-one feet. Keeping the engine on, we slow to less than five knots as we enter the harbor, mindful of the floating traffic that becomes congested on holidays and during the summer months. We stop and await a harbor patrol vessel to approach and assign us to a mooring.

31 Avalon

*From the harbor you see this town of Avalon filling the canyon and climbing the
hillsides. It is all very clean, very white, very orange. The houses are of many
styles. They stand agreeably side by side. There is an esplanade, encircling the
beach, with palm trees growing at south-sea angles.*

W.W. ROBINSON, *The Island of Santa Catalina* (1941)

Avalon, the only city on Catalina Island, was incorporated June 26, 1913, in Los
Angeles County. It is about a mile square in size and, since 1929, has had a prominent and beloved landmark, the magnificent Casino, located on the west side of the
mouth of the bay. Visible from about eight miles at sea on a clear day, the huge
Casino is a white circular structure with a diameter of 178 feet and a height equal to
a twelve-story building, topped by a red-glazed tile roof.

From the shore of this natural, crescent-shaped bay, Avalon Valley slopes gently
upward for nearly two miles until it abuts East Mountain. On the other side of this
range lie the Palisades; at the northerly base of East Mountain is the forty-acre
Wrigley Memorial and Botanical Garden.

The town of Avalon nestles between the arms of two hills whose ridges extend to
the sea, protecting the bay in southeasterly and southwesterly weather and in northwesterly weather when the wind is not too strong. But there is no protection from
the dreaded northeasterly winds (Santa Anas) that have driven yachts ashore, help-
less amid high, ferocious waves that crash against the shore, sending spray soaring
to heights of twenty feet. This fearsome onslaught was mitigated slightly in 1967
when the moles at either side of the harbor entrance were completed. The west
mole near the Casino provides the most protection.

Avalon's buildings climb both hillsides. The splendid twenty-two-room mansion built in 1920 by Mr. and Mrs. William Wrigley Jr. commands the crest of the
easterly ridge, named Mount Ada for Mrs. Wrigley. It is now an elegant bed and
breakfast inn. It is said that Wrigley ordered his architect to build wherever the sunrise brushed earliest in the morning and the sunset lingered latest in the evening.
That spot is on the hillside 350 feet above the town of Avalon. On the opposite ridge
above the Casino stands a small white structure housing the Deagan Westminster
Chimes, Ada Wrigley's gift to the city in 1925. Sonorously, the chimes proclaim the
hour, half hour, and quarter hour, musical benedictions floating peacefully over the
entire area.

This idyllic setting was not always named Avalon. The name used by early Indian
inhabitants — for there was a large prehistoric town here — has been lost. The area
became known as Timms' Harbor and Landing in the mid-1850s when Augustus W.
Timms, a native of Prussia and an under-officer in the United States Navy during

the Mexican War (1846–1848), began running vessels here from his Timms' Landing in San Pedro. The 1878 U.S. Coast Survey sheet indicates a building of A.W. Timms situated near the shore of this cove, according to Charles Harrington, U.S. staff geographer, NOAA, in Rockport, Maryland.

In San Pedro, Timms' Landing or Timms' Point (sometimes called Timmsville) was a small settlement of shipping and forwarding establishments first developed in the 1850s. Included were warehouses, service businesses, a beach "hotel" in Timms' own two-story house, and a few other residences. The area handled most of the seagoing shipping until the early 1870s when the more aggressive Phineas Banning gained a monopoly on the lightering and freight-forwarding business of San Pedro Bay. Even so, Timms continued to hold onto his San Pedro land and a sheep-raising enterprise on Catalina Island, which he owned with partners.

In this view of Timms' Landing at San Pedro in 1873, Deadman's Island is visible in the background. Augustus Timms was among the first to run excursion vessels to a Catalina Island bay named after him for a time, now Avalon.

By the early 1880s Timms was transporting passengers to the future Avalon from his San Pedro landing aboard the schooner *Rosita* or one of his other sailing vessels, the *Ned Beal* and the *Pioneer.* He offered fishing, bathing, and primitive camping at his Timms' Landing on the island. Customers had to furnish their own provisions and camping equipment, but feed for their horses at Timms' San Pedro landing was included in the round trip fare of four dollars (Houston). Nonetheless, the highly competitive Banning, having established his Wilmington Transportation Company in 1877 (it was incorporated in 1884), was starting to monopolize the transchannel excursion business. As early as 1881, Phineas and his sons, William, Joseph, and Hancock, carried people to the island on a sailboat, rowing guests ashore to the beach.

Timms died in San Pedro on June 21, 1888, at the age of sixty-three. A few years before his death he donated four acres to the city to establish the San Pedro Cemetery, now named Harbor View Memorial Park, where he is buried. It is a pioneer cemetery overlooking the now underwater site of his old landing opposite today's Twenty-fourth Street at Grand Avenue. At Sampson Way and the Southern Pacific slip stands California Landmark Number 384, a monument commemorating Timms' Landing. It was dedicated May 29, 1993, by the San Pedro Bay Historical Society, according to Flora Baker, a past president of the society.

U.S. Staff Geographer Harrington generously gave a great deal of his time helping us ferret out place names for this book. Yet even he, with all the material in his archives, was unable to discover the origin of another name for Catalina's popular bay: Dakin or Dakin's Cove. Dakin Cove was the name of Avalon Bay on the charts for fifty-seven years, from 1878 until 1935. The Dakin name lingered on well after the bay and town were romantically named Avalon in 1887 when George R. Shatto became owner of the island. *Coast Pilots* up to and including the 1934 edition use the name Dakin Cove, remarking that it is "generally known as Avalon." The official change from Dakin Cove to Avalon was "due to a 1935 decision by the Board of Geographic Names," Harrington said. "On the nautical charts, Dakin's Cove appeared on the first edition of [Chart] No. 5100 in 1890, Dakin Cove was on the 1933 edition of No. 5101, and Avalon Bay on the 1937 edition of No. 5101." Even so, the 1942 *Pacific Coast Pilot* of the Coast and Geodetic Survey refers to "Avalon Bay, sometimes known as Dakin Cove…" An astonishingly persistent place name!

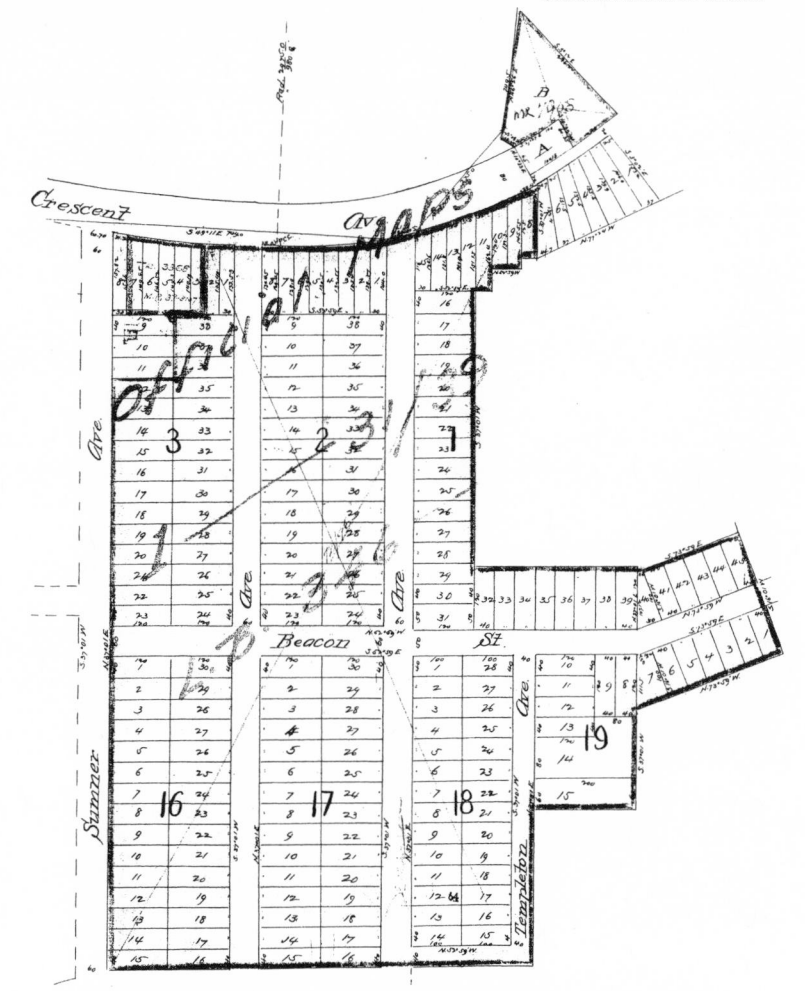

A section of a plat of the town of Shatto City — now Avalon — was recorded September 28, 1888, at the request of George R. Shatto. This section is bounded by Crescent and Sumner Avenues.

There is nothing in the records to show who Dakin was. Harrington speculated that he "must have been either a contemporary of Timms or else an earlier resident of the island…" Among the knowledgeable people we queried about the mysterious Dakin was the late Don Meadows, historian, journalist, botanist, biologist, and author of several books including *Historic Place Names in Orange County.* Don and his wife, Frances, lived in Avalon from 1927 to 1934, while he taught high school and she was a librarian. During a biological survey of the island sponsored by the Los Angeles County Museum of Natural History, Meadows discovered a rare spider that still bears his name: *Arachnis picta meadows.* The identity of Dakin eluded him, however, so he offered the wry suggestion that "Dakin was probably some guy standing on the beach when the Coast Survey people landed. They didn't have a name for the cove so they immortalized a mysterious stranger."

There is a mountain west of Avalon that still bears the name of the unknown islander, Dakin Peak, which has microwave equipment on it. And we offer some names, taken from *Descendants of Thomas Dakin of Concord, Massachusetts,* a microfiche from the Sutro Library, San Francisco. Dakins known to have been in the West during the period the bay was surveyed were mostly mariners and miners. Their first (and middle) names were Judson, John Hunting, Edwin, William Wallace, John Wentworth, George Nelson, William Henry, Hiram Henry, Henry Mumford, Hubbard, William Justus, and Isaac. There was even an early "Preserved Fish Dakin" listed, but much as the name appeals to us, we lean toward one of the mining Dakins, who may have been on shore during the island's brief gold rush in the 1860s.

Several earlier island historians included Port Rousillon as an Avalon Bay place name, believing that William Shaler careened his *Lelia Bird* there, but recent research has proved otherwise. Port de Rousillon, as we noted earlier, was at the Isthmus. In 1888, while making a plat of the proposed city, surveyors named it Shatto City after George R. Shatto, the new owner of the island. But that was quickly changed to Avalon by Mrs. Etta Marilla Whitney, Shatto's romantically minded sister-in-law and wife of Edwin J. Whitney, the island manager. Like a modern real estate promoter, Mrs. Whitney perceived a connection between the island's lovely valley and King Arthur's final resting place in *Idylls of the King,* written by the then contemporary popular poet, Alfred, Lord Tennyson:

> But now farewell. I am going a long way
> With these thou seest . . .
> To the island-valley of Avilion [Avalon];
> Where falls not hail, or rain, or any snow,
> Nor ever wind blows loudly; but it lies
> Deep-meadow'd, happy, fair with orchard lawns
> And bowery hollows crown'd with summer sea.

This bay has sheltered mariners for centuries; even the aboriginal inhabitants were a maritime people, traveling to other islands and the mainland by planked canoes. We suggest, however, that although many generations have visited here, a major change in the marine bioecology of our Pacific Ocean region came about because of a visit by a Maine-born Yankee, Charles M. Scammon.

The alteration began in 1857 when the surrounding hills were mantled in chaparral and the valley floor swept inland with few obstructions. The brig *Boston,* commanded by Captain Scammon, lay anchored in the bay, awaiting the arrival of a small schooner, the *Marin,* sent from San Francisco with extra men for a voyage to explore a purported whaling ground located on the west coast of Baja California (Scammon, introduction to the 1969 edition by Campbell Grant). This was the prelude to the slaughter of the California gray whale by thousands of whalers that drove these giant mammals to near extinction by 1937.

Scammon was to sail from "Avalon harbor" to discover one of the most prolific

calving grounds of this leviathan, the large lagoon in Baja California now bearing his name. The warm shallow water of Scammon's Lagoon and San Ignacio Lagoon, as well as many miles of protected water in and north of Magdalena Bay, becomes the world's largest whale nursery from January to March when these peerless navigators complete their annual 6,000-mile migration from the Bering Sea.

The gray whale population was estimated at 30,000 in the middle of the nine-teenth century. By 1964, the population had diminished to about 5,000. Commercial whaling off the California coast did not stop until 1946, even though the gray was supposedly protected by an international agreement made in 1937. The 1946 federal law prohibiting commercial whaling was followed in 1972 by the Marine Mammal Protection Act, giving complete protection to eight species of whales, including the gray.

Most of Scammon's Lagoon has been declared a whale refuge by the Mexican government, and vessels are forbidden to enter the area during calving season. Grays once existed on the Atlantic coast but have been nonexistent there since the

Before Avalon Bay became crowded with mooring cans, yachts swung on their anchors. Photographed from the top of Sugar Loaf Rock, the Hotel Metropole can be seen at the turn of the twentieth century.

In 1904 the SS *Hermosa II* approaches the steamer pier in Avalon. The Peter Gano house is in the foreground, and the Pacific Wireless station is on the hill in the background.

turn of the last century. A small group that wintered near South Korea is on its way to extinction, according to John Scholl, marine biologist with the California Department of Fish and Game in Long Beach. Scholl said some scientists believe that the Pacific Coast gray whale population may be increasing by as much as 11 percent a year. As of late December 1992, the gray whale was removed from the endangered species list, according to the National Marine Fisheries Service. However, the grays continue to be protected under the U.S. Marine Mammal Act, which prohibits harassing or killing them. At the time of the announcement, the agency estimated the gray whale population at 21,000.

In Captain Scammon's time, when whaling was done from specially designed rowboats twenty-eight to thirty feet long and about six feet wide, whales were killed by harpoon guns or by handheld harpoons or lances. The dead whale was cut up or flensed and secured to the side of the mother vessel by heavy tackle. Later the blubber was heated in the tryworks on deck to extract the oil. A forty-foot whale yielded about twenty barrels of oil.

Whaling vessels once abounded on the California coast. It is not known how many sought refuge and replenished water and wood at Catalina and other islands. The total of New England–based whaling vessels ranging the entire Pacific Ocean as of December 1828 was 118 ships and three brigs, according to Edouard A. Stackpole, in *The Sea Hunters: The Great Age of Whaling*. The majority hailed from Nantucket and New Bedford. The whaling period from the 1820s to 1905 embraced a highly lucrative phase of the industry for owners and investors. "The peak of American whaling came in 1846, when 678 ships and barks, 35 brigs and 22 schooners composed the fleet," Stackpole noted.

There was worldwide demand for oil for lamps (including lighthouses), for making spermaceti candles, and as a nonclogging lubricant particularly favored for watches and clocks. Whalebone was in demand for corset stays and umbrella ribs. Whaling ships began to appear in California vessel lists about 1825, with numbers increasing for a while, then dropping off at the time of the gold rush. Among the early whalers were the *Ploughboy, Apollo, Factor, Whaleman, Don, Washington, Paragon, Peruvian, Mercury, Charles, Cyrus, Moor, Franklin, Massachusetts, Orion, Minerva, Wilmantic,* and *Warren.* There were also a number of English whalers, attesting to the importance of whaling in those long ago days.

This account of whaling presages a bit of more recent history, an unforgettable experience I had as a boy while fishing with my father. As late as the fall of 1933, F.K. Dedrick's San Pedro whaling fleet was hunting off Catalina, San Clemente, and Santa Barbara Islands. The fleet had two "killer" vessels, the *Hawk* and the *Port Sanders,* with a mother ship, the *California.* It was one of these killer vessels that provided me, then a twelve-year old, with an unforgettable experience while sport fishing with my father on a charter boat out of Avalon. Somewhere between the island and the mainland, on long easy swells, I saw the sea run red with blood. A slaughtered gray whale had been secured to the side of a large, engine-powered vessel, and a man in the bow was preparing to add to the gore. He fired a stationary gun at another gray, and I watched with stunned fascination as a harpoon with an explosive head, its rope trailing like a comet's tail, drove deeply into the body of the whale. I didn't know that I was watching the death throes of a warm-blooded mammal nearly on the brink of extinction. I knew only that the sight made me ill, and I suddenly threw up.

In this panoramic view of Dakin Cove, the structure on the
right is the Holly Hill House, completed in March 1890 by
Peter Gano, an engineer and craftsman. The year is estimated at
1910. The town became Avalon in 1888, but the bay remained
Dakin Cove. The pier was built in 1909.

32   The Pleasure Pier

In gallant trim the gilded vessel goes,
Youth on the prow and Pleasure at the helm.
THOMAS GRAY, *The Bard* (1759)

We have been assigned a mooring in Avalon Bay two rows out from the historic Tuna Club. The bay has about eight rows of moorings for a total of more than 315 buoys, which fill it so completely that there is no place to anchor, nor is anchoring allowed. Once we have moored and settled in, I row our dinghy to the Pleasure Pier and tie it to the small float before going ashore. We row because we don't own an outboard engine, preferring exercise and quiet contemplation of the harbor to the speed, noise, and hassle of mechanically induced motion.

Blessedly, the old Pleasure Pier is still standing, for it is a place of pleasant memories for me. During the 1920s and 1930s I gazed in awe at the great fishes being weighed and photographed near the pier's end, longing to be big enough to catch one myself. I didn't know that this pier, off the foot of Catalina Street, had been constructed in 1909 by the Avalon Freeholders' Improvement Association. Nor did I know that it became known as the Boatmen's Pier when charter boatmen moved their lockers and stands to it from the beach in front of the old Hotel Metropole.

The days of the Boatmen's Pier during both the Banning and early Wrigley periods of island ownership were the glory days of sport fishing, a period when vast schools of albacore, leaping tuna, and other game fish abounded in nearby waters. It was also a time when the now legendary boatmen — Jose (Mexican Joe) Presiado, George C. Farnsworth, Harry Elms, H.J. Warner, Monte Foster, Parker Pence, Ruben (Doc) Vaughan, Loren Zane Grey, and R.J. Cope, to name a few — guided, instructed, and pampered their charterers into landing equally legendary piscatorial prizes.

Over lunch in 1977, Mrs. Gertrude E. Pence, widow of Parker Pence, a charter boatman, told me the story of Sam Rikalo, who sometimes fished with her husband during the depression years of the 1930s. Rikalo was a Serb who had settled in Avalon after World War I, married, and raised a family. He was a market fisherman, mostly for albacore, and occasionally took out charters. He was also a wine maker.

"Most of the Slavs on the island made their own wine and, of course, they were very popular during Prohibition," Mrs. Pence observed. The homemade wine of Rikalo and his compatriots became known as "Yellow Jacket Wine" because yellow jacket wasps were attracted into the wine during its fermentation. In fact, Yellow Jacket Wine was confiscated by revenue agents in Avalon's one major booze bust. Barrels of the stuff were rolled down the hill and their contents dumped into the bay, Malcolm Renton remembered. Rikalo and others claimed the wasps improved the flavor, and that Yellow Jacket had remarkable curative properties. Mrs. Pence believed that the wine saved Sam's life after a goat hunting accident.

"It was the custom for islanders to shoot a goat now and then," Mrs. Pence said, "and I cooked many a goat during the depression. Well, one day Sam went down the coast alone to get a goat, shot one and put it in his skiff. In trying to get his oar up — it was beneath his rifle — the gun went off and shot his lower left arm off," Mrs. Pence recalled. Sam managed to scull the skiff to his boat, cut the anchor rope, start the boat's motor, and head for Avalon, meanwhile stanching the flow of blood with towels and drinking red wine. At Long Point he hailed a fisherman who took over and brought a weakened Sam to Avalon. It was nip and tuck for a while at the hospital, but thanks to a host of blood donors in town, Sam pulled through. And everyone agreed that without the Yellow Jacket Wine, Sam wouldn't have made it. After that, Sam fished for albacore with his son, Martin, but it was too difficult with one arm and he gave up.

"Sam is gone now," said Mrs. Pence, "and I hope he is catching lots of fish where he is."

After World War II the Boatmen's Pier became more commonly known as the Pleasure Pier, Municipal Pier, or Green Pier (because it was and is painted green), reflecting the changing picture of sport fishing. After the war, larger and more efficient commercial fishing vessels from the mainland began to deplete the seemingly infinite marine resources, and most boatmen abandoned their stands because of a lack of charters.

The pier has always been owned and operated by the city of Avalon, but there have been differences of opinion about its permanence. Captain Eddie Harrison, who was born in Avalon in 1912 and died there in 1992, served as port captain for the Santa Catalina Island Company's (SCICO) pleasure boat fleet. He recalled the battle he waged to save the pier in 1967 when he was also chairman of the city's Harbor Committee. At that time, some members of the city council wanted the historic pier demolished to make room for forty to fifty additional yacht moorings. It was felt that these, like the ones located where the Steamer Pier once stood, would bring more revenue to the city. But for once, common sense and a feeling for historic preservation won out over the profits that were envisioned.

For thirty-five years Harrison was senior skipper of the glass-bottomed boat *Phoenix*, now retired. Also under his supervision was the long, narrow, wooden-hull flying fish boat *Blanche W*, built on Mormon Island in 1924 by William Muller. The boat still entertains passengers at night with the remarkable spectacle of hundreds of the fish soaring on long gossamer pectoral fins over the dark water. The searchlights that attract the fish are the original carbon arc lamps, Captain Harrison said. Both boats boarded their passengers at the Pleasure Pier during the summer. They were refurbished on the mainland each winter and were thus protected from damage by storms.

Harrison began working on the SCICO's boats at the age of fourteen and retired fifty-five years later. His father, Eddie Harrison Sr., had been the number one diver

Flying fish are attracted by searchlight on the *Blanche W* in this postcard illustration.

for the Meteor Boat Company's glass-bottom boats when William Wrigley Jr. purchased the Meteor Boat Company in 1919 along with the island. He stayed on as chief diver/deckhand of the fleet.

Among others on the pier in the 1930s were Joe Guion's Rent-A-Boat, successor to Captain Pard Mathewson's rental pulling boats; Victor Lytle's yellow U-Drive auto boats; the D'Arcy brothers' glass-bottom rowboats; Harry Diffin's sport fishing bookings; Arno's fish market; and a famous recreational attraction, gone since 1956 — a thrilling ride on one of the *Miss Catalina* speedboats. Nearly thirty feet long (twenty-nine feet, eleven inches), the speedboats were built to heavy scantlings to withstand the heavy pounding of waves endured during almost continuous runs in and out of Avalon Bay. Passengers boarded the *Miss Catalina*s on the east side of the Pleasure Pier and raced out to meet the SS *Catalina* and SS *Avalon,* circling the ships at fifty miles an hour, sirens wailing. Passengers on the vessels engaged in a frenzy of shouts and joyously waved greetings.

The Catalina Speedboat Company, incorporated February 2, 1922, was headed by Ed Deardon, owner of Deardon's Department Store in Los Angeles. Alfred Bombard, onetime mayor of Avalon and father of Douglas Bombard (until recently owner-operator of Two Harbors and founder of the Catalina Express Line), was part owner and manager of the speedboat firm. Wilbur S. White was secretary-treasurer.

In total there were six *Miss Catalina*s. The first four were designed by Hugh Morgan Angelman, best known today for his design and construction of the salty forty-foot Sea Witch ketches. Angelman's *Miss Catalina*s were built at the Wilmington Boat Works in Los Angeles Harbor, which he managed and partly owned. The last two *Miss Catalina*s were designed and built at Avalon by Al Bombard.

Firsthand knowledge of the history of the *Miss Catalina* era was provided to us by Doug Bombard, who helped build the last two in the company's shop on Whittley Avenue, then next door to the Carson Plumbing Company. Here, in his own words, is the story:

In 1921 when my father, Al Bombard, came to the island there was a fellow by the name of Clarence Richie who was operating two speedboats, one called the *Spearmint* and the other the *Doublemint*. They had Miller racing car engines and carried six to eight persons. When my dad and Vic Lytle came to the island they bought an old auto boat company. I was told they were steel boats in bad shape. So Vic and my dad began running the auto boats after fixing them up for the water.

My dad really loved working with boats and racing engines because he had a lot of experience with gas engines at the Beverly Hills race track before he came to the island. Within two or three years [he] became manager and part owner of the Miss Catalina Speedboat Company and had built *Miss Catalina* #1 and #2.

The boats were powered by V-12 World War I Liberty airplane engines that used to power the DH4 bi-planes. We had both Army and Navy versions of these engines, the only difference being the compression ratio, Numbers 1 and 2 ran pretty much through the twenties, and in 1931, *Miss Catalina* #3 was built, again designed by Angelman and built by him. About two years later *Miss Catalina* #2 was converted to what became *Miss Catalina* #4, with a more modern deck that resembled the #3 boat. *Miss Catalina* #5 was built in 1938 and *Miss Catalina* #6 in 1939.

The last two speedboats were designed by my father and built in our shop on Whittley Avenue. They were constructed of vertical grain Douglas fir [with] selected stock planking on the sides and bottom. The bottom was ⅞" planking and the sides ⅝" planking over oak frames. The transom and the decks were planked with mahogany, Philippine mahogany on the center decks and covering boards with Honduras mahogany. The screws were Everdu bronze, as were all the bolts used in the construction of the frames.

They were considered the latest thing going in 1938 and '39 and were very fast. We were able to take on most of the hot boats of that era and beat them, even sometimes with a full load of passengers.

One of the favorite trips with the customers was the steamer trip and it was so popular that we sold reservations sometimes a week or two in advance. When the two steamers were running, the *Avalon* and the *Catalina,* we could make as many as eight steamer trips with the two boats meeting each steamer twice with each boat.

Our first trip would leave the dock when the steamer was still over the horizon and we would go out and circle the boat, riding the wake, which was the

A *Miss Catalina* speedboat races past the end of the Steamer Pier in Avalon Bay in the early 1940s.

real fun part of the trip. We would first meet the boat, one on each side, with our sirens blaring and, of course, our passengers screaming, which was also quite a thrill for the passengers on the steamer.

We would cross over the boats, running side by side and riding the wake and then rush back to the Pleasure Pier to switch loads and make a second trip out to meet the steamer before it docked. We were always sold out on that trip.

The Miss Catalina Speedboat Company was liquidated in 1956. Contributing to its demise was the diminished number of tourists staying overnight in Avalon. Furthermore, operation of the steamers, partly because of trade union demands, was becoming too costly for a year-round schedule. Fortunately, two *Miss Catalinas* were preserved and restored at Lake Tahoe.

During the *Miss Catalina* heydays, Al Bombard carefully selected those who skippered the boats. Among them were Doug Bombard, Erv Mohler, Clark Sweet, Ray Nagle, Rudy Piltch, Frankie Albert, and Don McBain. McBain became the technician for the National Broadcasting Company which aired the big bands from the Casino during the 1930s and 1940s.

There has been some confusion over the *Miss Catalinas* being Chris Crafts. The reason is that the speedboat company also owned two twenty-eight-foot Chris Crafts that were used for charter work and trips between Avalon and the Isthmus and the mainland. The Chris Crafts also filled in during the winter when the *Miss Catalinas* were out of the water.

The company also had a thirty-six-foot, Liberty engine-powered water taxi built, using it to tow upwards of five people at a time on aquaplanes. "In the 1940s, aquaplaning, with two feet on a wide board, was popular, but we never used the *Miss Catalinas* for it," Bombard said "It died out with the growing popularity of water skiing."

A postscript on the Miss Catalina Company: Wilbur White, secretary-treasurer of the company and also a mayor of Avalon, had a son, William S. (Bill) White, who was born on the island May 7, 1922. Bill White, who contributed to the Miss Catalina story, has island roots extending to his grandparents, Arthur W. and Evaline White. The couple honeymooned in Avalon in 1890 in one of the tented cottages abounding at the time.

Not everything was speed-oriented on the Pleasure Pier. There was once a small fleet of lovely little wherries one could rent to row around the harbor. They began in the 1920s when Pard Mathewson designed and built a fourteen-foot spruce-planked-over-oak-frame pulling boat he called a "canoe boat." Built in Mathewson's small shop on the upper west side of Whittley Avenue, the boat featured "swelled seams." That is, instead of caulking between butted strakes, one edge of a plank was concave while a sister plank was convex. The two were fitted together and when the wherry was in the water, all of the strakes swelled, making the vessel watertight. For many years these graceful boats with hourglass-shaped transoms and three-foot beams could be rented for recreational rowing from Mathewson and later from Joe Guion's Rent-A-Boat, founded in 1927. Today Joe's son, Joseph E. (Jay) Guion, owns this more than seventy-year-old Pleasure Pier business.

A modern fiberglass model, named the Catalina Wherry, has three rowing stations and is molded from an original Canoe Boat. Nearly a dozen are in use today by islanders, among them Rudy Piltch, retired from the SCICo, and Jim Dittmar, formerly a Two Harbors employee. Piltch and Dittmar, both middle-aged, rowed their Catalina Wherries fifty-two miles around the island in four days in July 1993, stopping overnight in various coves.

"Rowing around Catalina Island is certainly not everyone's cup of tea," enthused Piltch in *Water Lines,* a publication of the SCICo. "For those who do, the rewards are plentiful. The ability to propel these small boats along the shoreline in silence and at a pace that allows each detail of the island's magnificent sea and landscape to be observed at close range is an indelible reward to be cherished."

Piltch also experienced a historic sighting while rounding the West End: three bald eagles and one young brown eagle, attesting to the success of the island's conservation program.

33　The Steamer Pier

Santa Catalina . . . is reached from Los Angeles in three hours by the ocean-going steamers Cabrillo *and* Hermosa *of the Wilmington Transportation Company (Banning Line), which ply between the island and the mainland, connecting with railroads out of Los Angeles, affording a trip across the Santa Catalina Channel, delightful in itself.*

Banning Company promotional pamphlet, circa 1910

Unless one is old enough to remember, it is difficult to imagine that before 1967 there were two important piers in the harbor — the Pleasure Pier discussed in the previous chapter and the much older Steamer Pier, which extended into the bay near the foot of Metropole Avenue. This venerable pier was lengthened, widened, and strengthened to a total length of 460 feet and a width of 60 feet during its eighty years of existence. Most of the enlarging was done by Carl Johnson, a Swede and an employee of the Santa Catalina Island Company, and his crew, which also built bridges in the island's interior.

A small wharf was originally built here in 1887 when the island was purchased by George R. Shatto, an early California real estate promoter after whom Shatto Street in Los Angeles was named. By October of that year, the Hotel Metropole on Crescent Avenue between Whittley and Metropole Avenues was nearly complete, town sites had been surveyed, and Shatto began promoting the island as a real estate venture and resort, aided by his friend C.A. Sumner, a prominent Los Angeles real estate agent. That first wharf was the grandfather of the Steamer Pier. Shatto purchased the 140-foot, 151-ton former coastal steamer SS *Ferndale,* built in 1880 by Palmer's Company of San Francisco. She docked at the pier on her weekly crossings with tourists and campers, many of them potential buyers of Shatto's small town lots.

Also using the wharf were several excursion vessels including the seventy-five-foot yacht *Aggie* out of San Pedro, but Banning's Wilmington Transportation Company (WTC) had a near monopoly of transportation to the island. Primary among its vessels was the 100-foot steamer *Falcon,* built in San Francisco in 1886, whose master was J.W. Simmie. The *Los Angeles Times* of the period published schedules of the *Falcon*'s weekly departures, which left the Southern Pacific Railroad Company's wharf at San Pedro "at 1 o'clock p.m., returning next day to connect with the 3 p.m. train." The train was owned by the Los Angeles and San Pedro Railroad, put through to Banning's Wilmington in 1869.

Phineas Banning's importance in the development of San Pedro Harbor began shortly after his arrival in California in 1851. A year later Banning formed a stage and freighting business with David Alexander between San Pedro and Los Angeles, and a year after that, Banning, Alexander, and the latter's brother, George, hosted a two-day Fourth of July party at San Pedro for 2,000 guests, according to Horace Bell in *Reminiscences of a Ranger*. Banning married Rebecca Sanford in 1854, and in 1857 decided to found the town of New San Pedro (later renamed Wilmington) and move his business there. By 1859, Banning had become so influential that he was able to host a festive outing to Catalina aboard the U.S. government ship sent to survey and chart the coast. The event was described by Banning's friend, merchant Harris Newmark, in his *Sixty Years in Southern California, 1853–1913*.

> Banning had invited fifty or sixty ladies and gentlemen to accompany him to Catalina, and at about five o'clock on a June morning the guests arrived at Banning's residence where they partook of refreshments. [This was not the splendid Greek revival house in Wilmington, which wasn't built until 1864.] Then they started in decorated stages for New San Pedro, where the host (who, by the way, was a man of genial temperament, fond of a joke and sure to infuse others with his good-heartedness) regaled his friends with a hearty breakfast, not forgetting anything likely to both warm and cheer. After ample justice had been done to this feature, the picnickers boarded Banning's little steamer *Comet* and made for the outer harbor.
>
> There they were transferred to the United States Survey ship *Active*, which steamed away so spiritedly that in two hours the passengers were off Catalina; nothing meanwhile having been left undone to promote the comfort of everyone aboard the vessel. During this time Captain Alden and his officers, resplendent in their naval uniforms, held a reception; and unwilling that the merrymakers should be exposed without provisions to the wilds of the less-trodden island, they set before them a substantial ship's dinner.
>
> Once ashore, the visitors strolled along the beach and across that part of the island then most familiar [the Isthmus]; and at four o'clock the members of the party were again walking the decks of the Government vessel. Steaming back slowly, San Pedro was reached after sundown; and, having been bundled into the stages, the excursionists were back in Los Angeles about ten o'clock.

Congress had designated San Pedro a port of entry, with a customs house, in 1854, and coastal trade increased, but it was not a safe harbor. Wilmington was safer and grew in importance after the first passengers and freight were lightered ashore there in September 1858 by Banning vessels. Meanwhile Banning began lobbying publicly and privately for a railroad to the harbor, but met with considerable opposition, especially in rural Los Angeles County. However, after several setbacks, the railroad was approved, financing arranged, and construction started. Southern California's first railroad, the Los Angeles & San Pedro Railroad, made a trial run to Wilmington on September 8, 1869. On board were Phineas Banning and his partner, Henry B. Tichenor, a wealthy San Francisco lumberman who owned a fleet of coastal steamships. The line opened officially on October 26 with a formal cere-

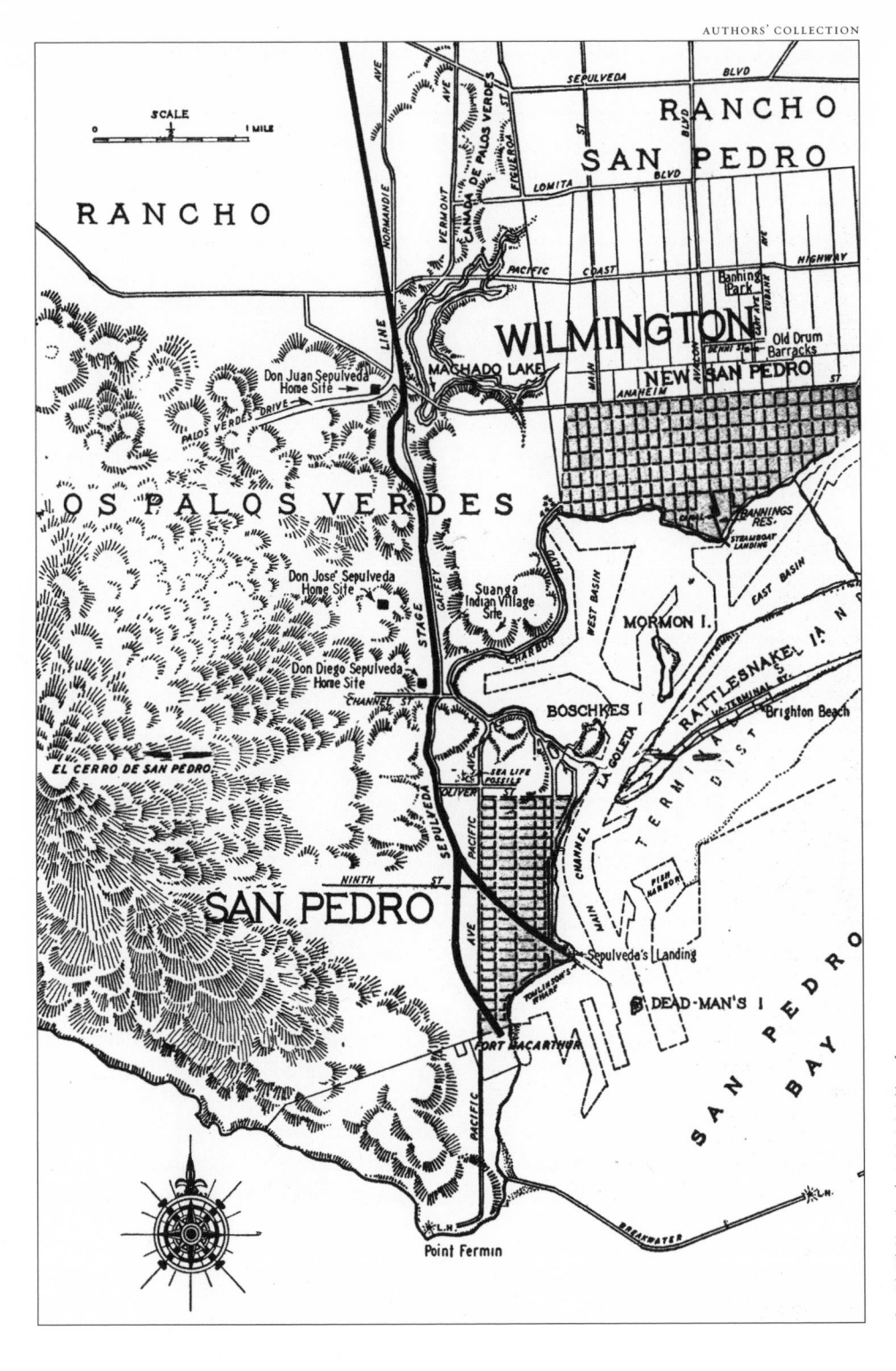

Three of the original islands in San Pedro Bay — Deadman's, Rattlesnake, and Mormon — can be seen with the outlines of the then-proposed harbor improvements. The breakwater has been built, dating the map at circa 1912.

mony, free excursions to Wilmington, and a dedication ball that night in the Los Angeles depot.

In those early days two trains daily made the run between Los Angeles and the Wilmington wharf, carrying both passengers and freight. Connections with coastal vessels anchored in the outer harbor were by lighter and small steamer. Silver and lead bullion from the rich Cerro Gordo mines in the Inyo Mountains passed through the port along with varied agricultural products of southern California. The L.A. & S.P. Railroad was linked with the Southern Pacific in 1873, the S.P. acquiring Banning's wharf, lighterage, and tug business when it acquired the railroad. Three years later the Southern Pacific sold the Wilmington operations back to Banning, and in 1877 Banning incorporated the Wilmington Transportation Company. The WTC, which was still in business, was acquired by William Wrigley Jr. when he purchased Catalina Island.

Wilmington became a legal port of entry in 1874, and an early breakwater between Rattlesnake and Dead Man's Islands, started in 1872 but constrained by engineering and financial problems, was finally completed in the winter of 1874. The work of San Pedro–Wilmington Harbor improvement was under way, but it would be more than twenty years before the final creation of a safe, deep water port that could serve ships of all sizes from all over the world.

It is appropriate, however, that Dana's "rascally hole" was finally rendered safe from southeasters by a breakwater that contains rock quarried on Catalina Island in 1899. It serves as a remindful monument to the vision of Phineas Banning and his sons.

34   The Two *Hermosas*

The mystery is why the fiery destruction of the first Hermosa *took place off Avalon on Independence Day when she was only fourteen years of age.*
WILLIAM OLESEN, Los Angeles Maritime Museum, San Pedro

Early Banning Company vessels such as the 147-foot side-wheeler *Amelia,* the 57-foot *Catalina,* the SS *Falcon,* and the SS *Warriors I* and *II* made the mainland to Avalon run on more or less weekly schedules. The number of island visitors increased measurably after the Bannings purchased the luxurious 133.5-foot SS *Hermosa.* Built by Hanson and Fraser of San Francisco in early 1888 for Hastings' Steam Navigation Company of Port Townsend, Washington, the *Hermosa* made her maiden voyage to Catalina in April 1889 and was soon making round trips to the island on Saturdays and Sundays. She also sailed Tuesdays and Thursdays, with overnight stays in Avalon.

The SS *Hermosa* was powered by a two-cycle compound engine installed by the San

The SS *Hermosa I,* the first luxurious transchannel vessel on the Catalina run, was purposely destroyed by fire off Avalon during the Independence Day celebration in 1902. She was replaced by the *Hermosa II,* which closely resembled the first *Hermosa.*

Francisco firm of Hinkley, Speirs, and Hayes. She had a width of 24.8 feet and a depth of 11.8 feet (National Maritime Library, San Francisco, *Lloyd's Registry of Shipping*).

The SS *Hermosa* was described by Dr. E. Henry Way of Riverside, California, who crossed from San Pedro to Avalon on April 11, 1889, and told of the trip a few days later in the *Riverside Press and Horticulturist:* "She is a very smooth-running steamer," he wrote. "And just built, has the Edison incandescent electric light and full electric bell system throughout. Her engines are high and low pressure; high pressure 16 inches, low pressure 32 inches with a 24-inch stroke." The new floating palace achieved a speed of eleven and one-half knots, was large enough to carry 375 excursionists, and had accommodations for seventy-five passengers, with berths and meals. "Her 'dining saloon' will seat at one sitting 56 [people]," Dr. Way noted. "To give you some idea how well her kitchen and pantry are fitted, I will say the steam table alone cost $250." Dr. Way was so impressed with the fine meals aboard the *Hermosa* that he gave the full name of her steward, Charles Counceleo, a Frenchman. The "pleasant" master was identified as Captain J.W. Simmie, former master of the steamer *Falcon* and a man familiar with the channel waters.

The steamer transported thousands of happy vacationers to the island, but for some reason unknown to us the Wilmington Transportation Company (WTC) decided to dispose of her after only fourteen years of service. The company contracted with master shipwright William August Muller to build an almost identical replacement, the SS *Hermosa II,* at their shipyard on Mormon Island. The second *Hermosa,* which was four feet longer and four feet wider than the first *Hermosa,* was launched in February 1902, after being christened with a bottle of champagne by

The SS *Hermosa II* docked at Avalon in 1904. Launched in 1902, the second *Hermosa* was built in the Banning yard by William Muller on Mormon Island, Wilmington, and carried guests who watched the first *Hermosa* burn almost to her waterline.

fourteen-year old Anne Wilson Patton (Nita), daughter of Mr. and Mrs. George S. Patton and sister of George S. Patton Jr., later to become the famous World War II general.

The *Hermosa II* embarked on her maiden voyage to Avalon on June 21, 1902, with Captain Hancock Banning at the helm and about 400 passengers on board. She made the crossing in two hours and thirty minutes and was said by her passengers to be smoother sailing and roomier than her predecessor. She made the Avalon run for two decades, being declared surplus about 1920 when she was sold to William Magio, who was affiliated with C. J. Hendry Company, a San Pedro ship's chandlery. She was then converted into one of the largest refrigerated tuna ships on the coast, serving until 1925 when she caught fire and sank off Baja California.

The first *Hermosa* also met a fiery death, but one carefully planned by her Banning owners as an important part of Avalon's 1902 Fourth of July celebration. After stripping her of salvageable Honduran mahogany and birdseye maple interiors as well as her engine and reusable fittings and appurtenances, her owners had her towed to sea about a mile off the entrance to Avalon Bay where the conflagration was to be "a magnificent spectacle," according to the *Los Angeles Times,* accompanied by the "enlivening music" of the twenty-two-piece Catalina Marine Band. "The

Hermosa appears much as she did while in commission," the *Times* added, "the parts missing being her masts and stack. The three decks are there, and there is lumber enough in her to make a great fire."

The Catalina Island Marine Band, underwritten by the Banning Company, was managed by Charles H. Porter and directed by Harold Kammameyer. The band entertained on the island for two decades, principally at summer concerts in the Greek theater built by Hancock Banning in 1904 on the eastern edge of Avalon just off Crescent Avenue.

A follow-up story in the July 6, 1902, *Times* reported that thousands gazed in "admiring awe" at the blazing vessel, watching the fireworks previously placed on her bursting in air while the new *Hermosa II* stood by, filled with spectators "mourning" the watery grave of the earlier ship. Many important guests from the Hotel Metropole were among those aboard the new *Hermosa II*. Papers of the WTC in the Huntington Library disclose that Hancock Banning dispatched several boxes of fireworks to Avalon for the conflagration, plus hams for the guests to enjoy. The next morning, the *Times'* report continued, the old vessel's hull seemed intact, although smoke was coming from the interior. The "anchor rope had burned and she was drifting westward."

The Bannings had planned to tow the hull to the Isthmus where it was

Assembled here in 1913 is the Catalina Marine Band, managed by Charles Porter and directed by Harold Kammameyer. Underwritten by the Banning Company, the band entertained for twenty years.

to be "beached and stripped of copper sheathing" to be sold as salvage. Then she was to be brought back and sunk in Lover's Cove "as an added attraction to the marine gardens." Unforeseen circumstances intervened. The old *Hermosa* drifted about five miles westward into the vicinity of White's Landing where she pounded on the rocks until the tug *Falcon* pulled her off and towed her back to Avalon. Once again she was set on fire, burning her entire length. Suddenly she sank with a hissing and a burst of steam. The *Falcon* gave three toots of her whistle as a parting salute, but the *Hermosa* surfaced again, bottom side up. This tenacity ended on July 6 when the *Falcon* towed the *Hermosa* across the channel to San Pedro Harbor. There more than $500 worth of copper sheathing was salvaged and the charred remains of the first large transchannel steamer were broken up (*Los Angeles Times,* July 7, 1902).

Incidentally, the good Dr. Way of Riverside was so impressed with Avalon that a year after his maiden voyage on *Hermosa I,* he was having a cottage named the Alham-

Under Banning owner-
ship, the Wilmington
Transportation Com-
pany's ss *Cabrillo* arrives
at the Steamer Pier. She
was built by William
Muller at Wilmington
and launched in 1904.

bra built there for his family. The Avalon and Catalina Hotels, he reported, had
been enlarged and improved. The main hotel, the three-story Metropole, with 108
sleeping rooms and a large dining room seating 200 people at a time, had added new
"ice houses . . . splendidly arranged, so that there is no trouble in keeping meats and
vegetables for days in perfect condition." Dr. Way appears to have been a gentleman
who traveled on his stomach.

Two years after the ss *Hermosa II* was put into service, another steamer designed and
built by William Muller at the Mormon Island shipyard off Wilmington was launched:
this was the 182-foot ss *Cabrillo,* Muller's crowning achievement. She had a wooden
hull, was thirty-two feet wide, and was sheathed in copper below the waterline. The
Cabrillo's sound design, meticulous construction, and heavy scantlings guaranteed her
longevity for fifty-five years, most of them on the San Pedro–Catalina run. Her luxurious joinery of Honduran mahogany was dramatically displayed in a grand staircase.
The *Cabrillo* was christened in June 1904 by Muller's eleven-year-old daughter, Sarah
Margarethe, later a popular mathematics teacher in San Pedro.

The SS *Avalon* steams past Catalina Island nearing Avalon.

The SS *Cabrillo* was flying the WTC's blue and white house flag with a capital "W" when William Wrigley Jr. bought the island in 1919. From that time on many people assumed the "W" stood for Wrigley, who, wanting to transport more people to the island than was possible on the *Cabrillo,* soon purchased the steel 269-foot SS *Virginia,* built in Cleveland, Ohio, by Globe Iron Works in 1891. She had served as a Great Lakes passenger steamer operated by the Goodrich Steamship Line. Under the direction of Captain William Banning, who went to work for Wrigley, the 1,186-ton vessel was converted to the SS *Avalon* at the Morse Dry Dock Company of New York and taken through the Panama Canal, arriving in Los Angeles Harbor in 1920. That same year the Steamer Pier in Avalon was extended and rebuilt by Carl Johnson and his crew to accommodate her.

At the same time, a terminal with indoor parking space for automobiles was constructed on the site of the old Banning wharf in Wilmington at the foot of Canal Street, berths 184 and 185, and Wrigley had the name Canal Street changed to Avalon Boulevard. Canal Street had marked the first channel dredged by Phineas Banning through the mudflats to his wharf. Avalon Boulevard led to the departure point of ships bound for Avalon and the point of their return from Avalon's Steamer Pier.

35　The Great White Steamer

*The 1974 season was the 50th year of service
between the Mainland and Avalon for the* ss Catalina.

Legend on a colored postcard of the ship in the authors' collection

Shortly alter the ss *Avalon* was put into transchannel service, William Wrigley Jr. ordered the building of the magnificent, steel-hulled ss *Catalina,* the island's most famous passenger vessel. When she was launched in 1923, an unprecedented era of tourism to the "magic isle" began. Certainly no one by the wildest stretch of imagination could have predicted the curious series of events that finally led to the *Catalina* lying today in what may be her final resting place: Ensenada, Baja California, Mexico.

Dubbed by her fans the "Great White Steamer," the ss *Catalina* was constructed at the Los Angeles Shipbuilding and Dry Dock Corporation in San Pedro. She slid majestically off the ways on May 23, 1923, ready for fitting to 1,800 tons. She was 285.2 feet long, her beam was 52.1 feet, and her draft, 18.8 feet. Her twin screws were driven by twin, six-cylinder, oil-fired, triple-expansion steam engines made by Hooven, Owens, and Renstscheer Company of Hamilton, Ontario, Canada. The massive engines generated 2,000 horsepower each at 110 revolutions per minute, driving her at a speed of sixteen knots. Michael Cropper, librarian at the Los Angeles Maritime Museum in San Pedro, noted that *Lloyd's Registry of Shipping,* which furnished the bulk of these statistics, gave her completion date as 1924, the year she made her maiden cross-channel run to Catalina. Her passenger-carrying capacity was 1,963.

During her first year of operation, the ss *Catalina* transported 391,190 people to Avalon, attesting to the great popularity of a Catalina holiday and Wrigley's skillful promotion. A peak year for the Bannings' Wilmington Transportation Company (WTC) was 1915 when the *Hermosa II* and the *Cabrillo* together transported about 150,000 visitors to the island. A telling commentary on our current inflated economy is the fact that from 1919 until 1923, a round-trip to Catalina cost only $4.25.

One tradition of welcome for the early steamers was the diving for coins thrown overboard by the arriving passengers. Judge Ernest Windle, editor and publisher of the *Catalina Islander* newspaper, called it one of the "most picturesque aquatic stunts." The boys "would often recover money thrown from the decks of steamers [even] after it had reached a depth of 30 or 40 feet," he wrote. "An expert diver could often collect as high as $30 to $40 a day, and frequently was so skillful in his work that he could recover and hold in his mouth, five or six coins at a time."

By 1913 several men had started to make a business of coin diving, often refusing to enter the water if the coins were less than a quarter. "They forced the smaller boys out of the game," Windle added, and their language sometimes became very abusive

The ss *Catalina,* the Great White Steamer, carried dance bands in her ball-room during her halcyon days. Among those bands were Ralph Capollingo's sextet and Don Ricardo's seven-piece group.

toward those who threw only small change overboard. This became such a problem that in 1914 the city of Avalon passed an ordinance prohibiting coin diving in Avalon Bay without a city permit. Then along came a fellow by the name of Jack Williams, a native of Portugal and a powerful swimmer, who greeted incoming tourists by "walking on water" while waving two American flags on staves, one in each hand. He had perfected a way of treading water perpendicularly so his shoulders were well above water and he avoided wetting the flags.

Unaware of the need for a permit (or perhaps the law was no longer being enforced), I spent many hours treading water and diving for coins in the early 1930s, among a swarm of other teenage boys. The vessel was the ss *Catalina,* and I went diving for pocket money. It was then the happy habit of my parents to rent a cottage in Avalon for several weeks each summer. I confess I was an aquatic inept and would have starved if survival had depended on my earnings from the water — even in those days when ten cents would buy a hamburger, and fried sea bass filets with rice and gravy cost only a dollar. The latter was one of my favorite repasts at the barn-like Boos Brothers' cafeteria, which had been on Crescent Avenue since 1916. It later became Childs' cafeteria.

When the Steamer Pier was dismantled in 1967 to gain space for additional yacht moorings, the ss *Catalina* was moved and docked on the outside of the newly constructed Cabrillo Mole where the famous vessel had problems with the waves and surge. Relics of her sojourn there are the massive iron bollards on the seaward side of the eastern mole. The *Catalina's* trips were discontinued for financial reasons in 1976, but she had carried an estimated 25 million passengers during her fifty-one years of service.

COURTESY SANTA CATALINA ISLAND COMPANY

Wilmington's Catalina Terminal was at the foot of Avalon Boulevard. Wilmington Transportation Company tugs are in the foreground with the ss *Catalina* at the dock.

World War II interrupted all routine crossings of the San Pedro Channel. Along with the *Cabrillo,* the *Catalina* was commandeered by the War Shipping Administration and relocated to San Francisco Bay for troop transport service. She served with honor, transporting a total of 820,199 troops across San Francisco Bay. This was more than any other army transport carried during the entire course of the war. The ss *Avalon* remained in Avalon/San Pedro under the jurisdiction of the U.S. Maritime Service.

After the war the vessels reverted to the WTC owned by the SCICO. The *Cabrillo* was sold as surplus. Ultimately, after an unsuccessful attempt to turn her into a restaurant, the *Cabrillo* decayed in Napa Creek of San Pablo Bay, above San Francisco. In 1969, a young nautical enthusiast, John Meyer, salvaged her bow bulwark and stern scroll carvings for exhibition at the Los Angeles Maritime Museum, San Pedro. As for the ss *Avalon,* the bulk of her was sold as salvage in 1960. The salvage company stripped her and scuttled the hull off Point Vicente, near Point Fermin of the Palos Verdes peninsula, despite objections of the U.S. Coast Guard. She lies there today, occasionally visited by adventuresome scuba divers, according to William Oleson of the Los Angeles Maritime Museum.

The ss *Catalina* was placed back in service during the summers by several different owners until 1975 when she became the pawn in a curious series of events. On a whim at an auction in 1977, a Beverly Hills real estate developer, Hymie Singer, bought the Great White Steamer as a Valentine gift for his wife, Ruth. He paid $70,000 for her, mooring her in Los Angeles Harbor. There she languished, gathering rust and enduring vandalism. She went adrift several times, endangering shipping and dismaying the U.S. Coast Guard, which wanted her out of the harbor.

Singer attempted to find a place for her as a tourist attraction and restaurant in various southern California ports, including Avalon, but nobody wanted her. The Great White Steamer had become a great white elephant.

In 1988, the SS *Catalina* was towed to Ensenada, where Singer entered into a joint venture with a Mexican capitalist. She was partially restored and converted into a floating restaurant, discotheque, open air bar, and shopping center at an anchorage dredged by the Mexican government for a yacht harbor. A snarl of litigation and financial problems halted the enterprise, but the *Catalina* remains in Baja, where vandals and rust are again taking their insidious toll. Her ultimate fate hangs in the balance.

Nevertheless, Catalina's tourism by sea continues to flourish. A variety of excursion vessels ply the channel to Avalon and to Two Harbors at the Isthmus. There is regularly scheduled service from San Pedro, Long Beach, Newport Beach, and Dana Point. Passengers have a wide choice of speedy vessels with catamaran hulls, barge-shaped hulls, sleek cruiser hulls, and mammoth ocean-going hulls, the last belonging to large cruise ships that anchor off Avalon Bay. Passengers from the cruise ships, which also visit San Diego and lower California, are lightered ashore in Avalon shore boats for a day of shopping and sightseeing. From time to time other boat companies have attempted scheduled service from Oceanside, San Diego, and King Harbor, but all were short-lived.

Smaller excursion vessels take turns docking at a couple of moderate-sized slips behind Cabrillo Mole, then move offshore to large buoys where they kill time until an appointed hour when passengers embark for the return trip to the mainland, an interesting game of "musical slips." It is a far cry from the days of a century or more ago when Banning Company vessels made the mainland–Avalon run on a weekly or less than weekly schedule.

One of the later excursion boats was the *Catalina Holiday*, owned by Phil Tozer, with homeport on the Balboa Peninsula, Newport Beach. She is seen here in Avalon on her maiden voyage, June 9, 1978.

William Muller Shipyard was located on Mormon Island, Wilmington. The sign, with the Wilmington Transportation Company's insignia on top, reads "William Muller Shipyard — Wilmington Transportation Co." This photograph is circa 1920.

William Wrigley Jr.'s yacht *Quest* is seen in the William Muller Shipyard in 1923. Designed and built by Muller, she was sixty-two feet in length, her beam was fourteen feet, and her draft five feet. Of wood construction, she was gasoline-powered. She was launched in 1922.

The home where master shipwright William Muller, his wife, Elsie, and their children — two sons and three daughters — lived from 1899 until 1948 serves today as headquarters of the San Pedro Bay Historical Society at 1542 South Beacon Street, San Pedro. The single-story house, complete with finely crafted African gumwood interior trim made by Muller, has been relocated to its present site overlooking the old Timms' Landing area.

RICHARD AND MARJIE BUFFUM

William August Muller, born in Altenbruck, Germany, in 1865, came to the United States in 1886, working in several Pacific coast shipyards before joining the Bannings' Wilmington Transportation Company (WTC) in 1898. William Banning hired the thirty-three-year-old master cabinet maker, ship's carpenter, and sailor from the Fulton Iron Works of San Francisco. Muller was personally retiring, a private man with an artist's temperament. Shoddy workmanship could provoke him to sudden anger, according to Hancock Banning's oral history. Yet despite his temper, "he was awfully good to us children," Banning said. "He'd show us how to build little boats and that sort of thing." Muller also taught the Banning boys the importance of sharp tools and, once they were old enough to understand the inherent dangers, showed them how to use, sharpen, and hone the tools.

Over the years Muller built, rebuilt, and repaired numerous vessels at the Banning shipyard on Mormon Island, among them the tugs *Warrior I* and *Warrior II*. The first *Warrior* was brought down from Washington in the 1880s to work in the

COURTESY JOHN (JACK) GRAHAM

The *Clara* was Wilmington Transportation Company's and Los Angeles Harbor's first tugboat. She is pictured here in 1854.

harbor, but also carried passengers to and from Avalon until she was retired in 1901. She then became a seaman's bethel or chapel, managed by Charles Parr, a Christian preacher. The chapel was located on a mud flat near Terminal Island, finally rotting away and becoming part of a landfill project.

Warrior II, with a more commodious cabin on her 134 feet, was built and launched by Muller in 1901 and used for work in the harbor as well as cross-channel excursions. Between vessels, Muller's impeccable craftsmanship was used in building sturdy Concord coaches that were pulled by six horses on Catalina for the Banning brothers. About 1912, when the gasoline motor tug *Listo* was completed and launched on Mormon Island, *Warrior II* was taken to Avalon where Captain Hancock Banning had her superstructure, along with that of the *Falcon,* converted into a unique house. The structure still stands at Third Street and Descanso Avenue in Avalon.

The gasoline-powered tug *Listo* revolutionized WTC operations in San Pedro Harbor. The simple economy of the gasoline engine, which does not have to keep a constant steam pressure and requires a smaller crew, heralded the end of steam-powered tugs (*The Compass Rose,* Los Angeles Maritime Museum, summer 1991). During the last fifteen years of his illustrious career, through 1926, Muller

COURTESY JOHN (JACK) GRAHAM

created a fleet of eight diesel-powered tugboats for the WTC. In 1922, Muller designed and built for William Wrigley Jr. his magnificent sixty-two-foot yacht *Quest*. Made of wood and gasoline-powered, the *Quest* was manned by a nattily uniformed master and crew.

A personal aside involves the *Quest*. One of the major disappointments of my boyhood was the time my maternal grandfather, E.C. Denio, a Long Beach corporate attorney, refused to board the *Quest,* although her gangplank awaited us and her captain was standing by. I was with my grandfather and asked for an explanation. I recall him saying that he did not wish to become obligated to Mr. Wrigley in this instance, even though he had offered us a ride to Avalon on his lovely private yacht. Instead we boarded the SS *Cabrillo*. I learned only recently that Grandfather Denio represented the Graham Brothers, whose rock quarry on Catalina at the time was leased from the Santa Catalina Island Company. Apparently some serious negotiations were being conducted with Wrigley's company.

The steam-powered *Cricket* was Wilmington Transportation Company's third towboat in Los Angeles Harbor. She was built in 1864 by William Muller in Banning's Mormon Island shipyard, Wilmington. In 1883 this fifty-foot vessel was under command of William Banning, master; Andrew Young was chief engineer.

Muller also had built the fifty-foot *Cricket* for Hancock Banning in 1903 and the ninety-five-foot steam yacht *Campanero* for William Banning in 1910. Vail and Vickers had commissioned the Muller yard to build the auxiliary schooner *Santa Rosa Island* in 1904 and the 125-foot steam schooner *Vaquero,* both used for their cattle and sheep operations on the offshore islands.

Muller's Mormon Island shipbuilding of such Catalina vessels as the SS *Cabrillo* underwent a change during the United States' involvement in World War I (April 6, 1917, to November 11, 1918). Six box-shaped wooden cargo vessels, 281 feet in length with a forty-foot beam and twenty-six-foot depth, were built at Mormon

Island under contract with the U.S. Shipping Board Emergency Fleet Corporation. Called Ferris-types after their designer, Theodore E. Ferris, the vessels were part of this nation's war effort against Germany, whose submarines took their toll on allied shipping. Some 400 such vessels were built in various yards across the country, including a less successful Hough-type with a vee bottom. Muller supervised a crew of fifty men building the Ferris-types for the Ralph J. Chandler Shipyard Company, on about nine acres near the southwesterly end of Mormon Island. This parcel had been purchased from the Bannings. The Chandler yard, which began production August 1, 1917, was primarily bankrolled by Harry Chandler, then president and publisher of the *Los Angeles Times,* and Moses H. Sherman, a business associate. Ralph Joseph Chandler, a nephew, had been raised in the Harry Chandler home. The

Chandler Shipyard continued in business until 1921 when its affairs were closed. Muller then returned to his own boat building business at the familiar site on Mormon Island at the northwesterly edge of the island. Before 1919, Muller was superintendent of the Banning yard. After that he ran the yard under the name William Muller Shipbuilder.

Upon Muller's death in 1936 at the age of seventy-one, the shipyard fell into disuse. Before then, however, powerful political forces had been at work to alter the management of Los Angeles Harbor. It began when the city of Los Angeles found a way to control the entire shoreline of the harbor. By 1912, aiming to create a harbor district, the city had extended a strip annexation about twenty-two miles long and a half-mile wide from Los Angeles to the junction of San Pedro and Wilmington. With the new harbor district in place, the city and the port commissioners began to exert pressure on all freeholders of shoreline properties, claiming the land did not belong to them because it was on state-owned tidelands. Therefore, they said, freeholders must enter into a lease with the port authorities or vacate their property. By 1919, the takeover was complete except for obstinate Banning heirs who refused to knuckle under.

From 1929 until 1933, ten Los Angeles deputy city attorneys worked on the settlement of the port's $3 million Mormon Island tidelands suit against the Banning estate and the Pacific Borax Company, which by then had constructed a large borax refining plant and wharves on the old Chandler Shipyard site on the western side of the island. A simplified explanation of the suit involved the plaintiff's claim that

Captain William Banning's ninety-eight-foot wooden yacht, the ss *Companero,* was built in 1910 by William Muller at the Bannings' Mormon Island shipyard. Powered by a 150-horsepower, two-cycle steam engine, she was sold to William Wrigley Jr. in 1919. Renamed the *Alma* under later ownership, she was wrecked off Portuguese Bend in the late 1920s.

The SS *Cabrillo*, built by William Muller at the Banning yard, steams past Deadman's Island in Los Angeles Harbor. She was launched in 1904.

since California had become a state in 1850, the state charter held the authority to grant the Los Angeles Harbor District the right to own and develop the harbor's shoreline, tidelands, and submerged lands, of which the shoreline of thirty-three-acre Mormon Island was a part.

The harbor district in the suit laid claim to thirteen acres of Mormon Island water frontage, holding that the land in question was tidal and submerged land on February 10, 1882, when William Banning was granted the island by letters of patent. The Banning estate and the Pacific Coast Borax Company, purchaser of part of the disputed land, claimed title under those letters of patent. Historically, the Banning family claim reverted back to 1857 when Phineas, with his partner B.D. Wilson, bought 640 acres, which included the small island and much of the mainland.

Banning's heirs failed to persuade the political/legal hierarchy that they had a valid claim to Mormon Island and that they should remain as freeholders of the island. However, the Borax company's claim was validated because they continued to pursue their defense, while the Bannings compromised too soon. In the end, pursuant to a U.S. Supreme Court ruling, it was deemed unfair to take Borax Company land without just compensation. Thus the Borax company remained, and still does remain, the only private freeholder in the harbor. The Bannings compromised by giving a quitclaim deed to the port and obtaining a long-term lease. The Bannings relinquished the Mormon Island leasehold property in 1947.

By 1923, when construction of the Borax refinery and wharves was well under way, Mormon Island had ceased to be an island. Dredging of a deepwater channel for ships carrying Borax products had deposited tons of mud and sand in the Wilmington Lagoon. The island had become part of the mainland (Borax Company history compiled by Thomas M. Cramer, superintendent of the Wilmington Borax refinery, June 1962).

Except for the WTC, Phineas Banning's remarkable harbor legacy has ebbed with the tide into near obscurity. There was a bright vision of the future harbor in 1857 when a young Phineas poled his small scow through the sloughs and channels between the mainland and Rattlesnake Island. In this watery domain of salt marsh grasses, shorebirds, cockles, and clams, Phineas envisioned the development of a first-class harbor. He lost no time in directing the dredging of a channel for lighters from Deadman's Island, well to the south near the mouth of San Pedro Bay, to his landing at the head of the bay adjacent to Mormon Island. During late September of 1858, passengers and freight were brought ashore for the first time at Banning's New San Pedro, which was later renamed Wilmington.

Captain William Banning, left, and William Muller, shipbuilder.

A vestigial reminder today of the glory years of shipbuilding on Mormon Island are the buildings of the Wilmington Marine Service, performing repairs on boats up to 100 feet, at 801 South Fries Avenue, which runs into the present Mormon Island. This yard is on the site of the old shipyard where William Muller spent a half century of his vastly productive life.

37   Puppets, Tacos, and Magic

> *Let's judge a man not by his tools but toys,*
> *And count him happy when his work employs*
> *The Playthings that his secret hour enjoys.*
> GELETT BURGESS

When the big steamers arrived at the Steamer Pier in Avalon, nearly everyone in town crowded the area of Crescent and Metropole Avenues to greet the passengers walking off the pier beneath a gated, awning-covered exit. The new arrivals were serenaded by a mariachi band and sometimes interviewed by Gary Breckner, broadcasting over KHJ radio, Los Angeles, the Don Lee Broadcasting System. The latter was part of the Columbia Broadcasting Pacific Coast System, which carried dance music nationwide from the Casino Ballroom. During those halcyon days popular music flowed over valley and bay, played on Deagan Westminster chimes housed in a small white structure on the western hill above town, near author Zane Grey's home. Through a window near the foot of the pier one could watch a musician, usually Barney D. Halstead, fingering a console connected to the hilltop chimes.

During the 1950s the console, in two octaves, was moved up to the building housing the chimes. And although the chimes automatically strike the time, many fortunate people still hear them played manually by Jani Eisenhut, daughter of Donna Eisenhut, the Avalon librarian. Jani plays on Easter Sunday, during the Christmas season, and whenever she is moved to fill the air with music. Her father, Dale Eisenhut, was the resident electrical engineer at the Casino and a longtime building superintendent. He installed the console in its aerie and maintained the mechanism until his death in 1980. The chimes, built by the Deagan Company of Chicago, were given to the city in 1925 by Ada Wrigley, wife of William Wrigley Jr.

Combine the auditory romance of chimes wafting over Avalon with the visual romance of El Encanto, the wonderful early California plaza at the junction of Crescent and Marilla Avenues, and I am filled with nostalgia. Here, in my early teens, I discovered the triple delights of puppet theater, magic tricks, and tacos. The Nikabob Puppeteers were performing with their marionettes, delightful little figures on strings, in a 125-seat theater located on the south side of a large, low rectangular building housing a variety of shops that formed the perimeter of the open-air plaza.

In the early 1920s a circular structure, designed to resemble a top hat, housed the short-lived Band Box Theatre, featuring popular variety acts such as singers, magicians, and dancers. The enterprise was abandoned about a year after it started, and the building served as a Chinese restaurant. Later it was purchased by D.M. Renton at a bank sale, Renton afterward transferring title to the Santa Catalina Island Company (SCICO). El Encanto was then constructed, incorporating the circular building into its entrance. Designed and developed by Renton as a shopping and entertainment center with a Hispanic theme, El Encanto had its grand opening August 12 and 13, 1933.

The puppet theater's initial performances were given during the festive grand opening. The theater is believed to be the first in the United States specifically designed and built for marionettes, according to Jay Marshall of Chicago, puppeteer and magic historian. The Nikabob Puppeteers, originally Bob Jones, his brother, Bill, and Nick Nelson were all of college age. They had pooled their meager resources and constructed the stage as well as their puppet thespians. A simple handshake with Renton sealed their contract to play the summer season at El Encanto.

The young men arrived in Avalon July 1, prepared to open July 4, only to learn to their dismay that the theater interior required at least ten more days of work to complete. They had six dollars between them, hardly enough to cover their expenses in the interim. They were reduced to eating day-old bread and peanut butter until Jones learned that money could be made diving for coins.

"We will meet all incoming boats," Jones told his friends. "There are only three guys out there that offer competition. Try to be subtle about crowding those fellows as they surface dive, and I'll be making the catch from below. We'll only go after the

Puppeteer Bob Jones manipulates marionette in front of El Encanto's Puppet Theatre in Avalon during the late 1930s. This was the first little theater in the nation built specifically for puppet shows.

large coins; the larger the coin, the larger the pattern it makes after it hits the water. Duck your head and check them out. The water is crystal clear and you can see for at least sixty feet." The young men met all incoming boats and they prospered. Not only did they eat well, but they had more than fifty dollars in their cash box to carry them until El Encanto opened.

"Clever — rollicking — whimsical — crammed full of fun and originality — that is the Catalina Revue… of the Nikabob Puppeteers at El Encanto, worth in itself a trip to the island to see. Certainly no one should leave Catalina without first seeing one's self as others see us in the puppet show," enthused Alma Overholt in the *Catalina Islander,* July 12, 1934. The revue, as described by Overholt, had seventy-five marionettes with musical accompaniment produced by electrical transcription, a large, long-playing disc recording. The show's story was a sightseeing tour of the island. A steamer arrived at the dock; puppet stevedores in flat-crowned yellow Spanish hats, blue jeans, and red sashes made the ship fast. There were welcoming troubadours, musicians, porters, and a sightseeing bus ready to meet incoming visitors. The revue included submarine gardens with Barnacle Bill, an Octopus Quartet, a whale, Mama and Papa Swordfish, and a mermaid, each a cleverly crafted marionette.

When the Nikabobs disbanded, the theater was never again used for puppets, but Bob Jones continued his career as a puppeteer, playing Grauman's Chinese Theater in Hollywood and night clubs until late 1937 when he joined the Walt Disney studio as a cameraman. In early 1938, Jones, Joe Grant, and Jack Miller started the Character Model Department at the studio. *Snow White* was finished in production, and *Pinocchio* was still in the story department. A multitude of characters had to be designed in addition to tools, toys, cuckoo clocks, and furnishings for Geppetto's workshop. A dozen artists worked on designing the puppet Pinocchio over an eighteen-month period.

Jose A. Riojas was the majordomo of El Encanto Spanish patio restaurant in Avalon and taught card tricks to the author. Riojas's daughter, Dora, as a Wrigley flower girl, met steamers during the late 1930s.

"I concentrated on the design of his joints and his puppet control," Jones told me in 1989 when I talked with him in Fullerton, where he retired after a later career as an aircraft engineer. The full-length animated Disney cartoon of the puppet whose nose becomes longer when he tells a lie and returns to normal when he tells the truth was released December 18, 1939.

The Nikabob Puppeteers' revue captured the colorful ambience of Catalina when Philip K. Wrigley assumed further development of the island after the death of his father, William Jr., in 1932. "His vision transformed what was still more or less a fishing village, basking in the sun, into a midwesterner's dream of olden, golden California," Overholt wrote. To this end, P.K. Wrigley had mature olive and palm trees barged across the channel and planted along the beachfront and the streets of Avalon. A low, curving serpentine wall with built-in settees inset with handcrafted Catalina tiles was erected along the bayfront, and sand was barged in to cover the pebblestone beach. With the cooperation of Avalon business people, the town was given a facelift of new building fronts and small, artistic signs, symbolic of each store's business.

For several summers until the puppet theater went dark in 1937, I was a charmed partaker of El Encanto's delights, particularly those offered by Jose the Magician. Jose Riojas, El Encanto's majordomo, had a small, open-fronted shop selling curios and baby cacti in tiny Mexican clay pots and colorful hand-dipped candles. Jose attracted customers by performing magic with playing cards. I was entranced. In exchange for sweeping out his shop daily, Jose patiently taught me some fundamental sleight-of-hand with playing cards, admonishing me to go home and practice diligently, then return the next day for corrections in handling the cards. One day he gave me a dog-eared copy of a magic catalogue from Thayer's Studio of Magic, Los Angeles, published by Floyd G. Thayer, an expert wood turner. Along with master mechanic Carl Owen and his staff, Thayer created conjuring apparatus for such famous magicians as Harry Kellar, Harry Houdini, Harry Blackstone, and Howard Thurston, as well as actor-magicians such as Harold Lloyd, Chester Morris, and Orson Welles. With this catalogue, the fascinating world of theatrical conjuring opened for me. It is a passion that has endured for my entire life.

And then there were the tacos. I nearly overlooked the tacos. My magical mentor's wife, Elijia, cooked the tortillas and the taco filling over a brazier in another El Encanto space in a corner of the courtyard. An older Mexican woman shaped the tortillas by hand. Jose the magician, a great kidder, used to tell customers in all seriousness that the tortilla maker was "Pancho Villa's mother." This anecdote was related to me by one of the Riojas daughters, my age and still living on the island. She has the magnificent name of Emelda Carmen Cecilia Sara Riojas Poindexter. Another Riojas daughter, Dora, a few years older, was one of the lovely flower girls who greeted the steamers. She wore a Spanish costume and passed out flowers to the passengers. In season there were sprigs of toyon and island flowers and sometimes, only paper flowers. Dora was hired by the SCICo, greeting the steamers for several years.

Malcolm Renton reminisced to me one day about Dora's beauty and one of Jose's feats of magic — the mysterious rising of a silver half-dollar on the palm of the magician's hand. Jose showed me how to do it, and taught me to perform The Card Under the Foot, in which an indifferent card magically changes to a selected card beneath a spectator's foot. That was long ago when I was a skinny, red-headed adolescent, and I set about foisting that classical feat on anyone handy, whether they evinced any interest in conjuring or not. Such is the curse of aspiring young magicians. I still do the trick today, but somebody has to urge me to perform it.

Jose alternated his magic with a demonstration of a little, wooden, jointed cat on a board. By inserting two fingers in rings attached to strings beneath the board, he made the cat move in comical ways. He must have sold hundreds of those cats. The well of my memory still echoes with the sound of Jose demonstrating those amusing little creatures: "Thees ees eet. Thees ees the wan. El Gato, the cat. See heem jump!" Alas, Jose Riojas died in 1943. How I yearn to tell him how much he enriched my life with magic.

The Riojas family, which included another daughter, Gloria, held sway in El Encanto, where they lived upstairs, from its opening until the outbreak of World War II. The war struck the death knell to Avalon's most colorful and romantic era.

38   The Casino

I found my love in Avalon beside the bay.
I left my love in Avalon and sail'd away.
I dream of her in Avalon from dusk to dawn,
And so I think I'll travel on to Avalon.

"Avalon," a foxtrot (1920). Music by Vincent Rose;
Lyrics by Al Jolson and B.G. DeSilva

My breast swells with nostalgia at the sight of the Casino. In the 1930s and early 1940s, the walkway leading to it was planked with boards that rumbled beneath the feet of pedestrians far into the evening. This promenade, named Casino Way, had, for about five years in the 1930s, nearly a hundred illuminated wooden arches over it, each like a giant croquet wicket, extending from near El Encanto, past the Tuna and yacht clubs, to the front of the Casino — an enchanting crescent-shaped board-walk. At night its thousands of electric bulbs cast an intricate shimmering web of light across the bay.

At its Casino end there was music, the sweet music of the big-name dance bands that played in the Casino's great ballroom on the upper floor, a vast space with a capacity of 3,000 dancers. Among the bands were those led by Jan Garber, Ben Bernie, Kay Kayser, Freddie Martin, Benny Goodman, Bob Crosby, Buddy Rogers, and Ray Noble, broadcasting from Avalon over coast-to-coast radio. Naturally "Avalon" and "Red Sails in the Sunset" were favorite Casino melodies. Back home in Long Beach, after idyllic summer weeks on the island, I would listen entranced to the romantic music of Jan Garber, one of my favorite bands, over radio station KHJ. To this day, whenever I hear "Avalon," my eyes mist over with fond memories.

Entwined in this memory is the romantic arched promenade of Casino Way. The reverberation of strolling feet on the cross-planked walkway was silenced forever on December 8, 1943, when a violent southeaster swept into Avalon Bay. Vessels were driven ashore to join the wreckage of the boardwalk. Utilitarian poured con-crete, sans arches, replaced the old promenade.

Construction of the Casino, under the direction of D.M. Renton, was started in February 1928, and completed on May 29, 1929. More than sixty subcontractors were employed to execute the Casino's design by architects Walter Webber and Sumner A. Spaulding of Los Angeles. Of Mediterranean architecture with Moor-ish Alhambra influences, the Casino is famous for the art deco murals in the Avalon Theater below the dance hall and on the exterior of the building. These were con-ceived by John Gabriel Beckman, who worked on a number of theaters, including Grauman's Chinese Theater, and later became an art director for Columbia Stu-dios. Beckman's hand-picked team of artists included young Emil Kosa Jr., who

The Casino, completed in 1929, is pictured here before 1967 when the Casino Point mole (breakwater) was built.

went on to become a leading painter in the California watercolor school, a group that included Millard Sheets, Rex Brandt, Phil Dike, and Dong Kingman. The sequence of painted motifs includes exotic birds and flowers, a Spanish ship, hooded friars, leaping goats, and Indians astride charging horses. For the statistically minded, there are 500 square feet of 22-karat gold leaf and 60,000 four-inch squares of silver leaf in the building's decoration. There are also 105,000 roof tiles, produced on the island at Pebbly Beach.

The Avalon Theatre, with 1,184 seats, was designed for the projection of sound movies before its construction, even though there weren't many around. Motion picture tycoons of the period, such as Cecil B. de Mille, Joe Schenk, Louis B. Mayer, and Sam Goldwyn, traveled across the channel on their yachts to preview their new "talkies," as those born in the silent picture era used to call them.

The Douglas Fairbanks Sr. film *The Iron Mask* was originally scheduled to be screened the day the Casino opened, but was not shown due to technical difficulties with the new sound system. The first sound film, with sound on the film and not on a separate record, to play in the theater was *Rio Rita* in late February of 1930. Starring John Boles and Bebe Daniels, this musical, produced by RKO Productions, was released September 15, 1929. Leonard H. Clark, the theater's first organist who accompanied silent films, gave a special concert before the film (Moore 1979).

A Casino fact sheet, given to those taking the excellent guided tours of the Casino, states, "One of only four crafted by the Page Company in Lima, Ohio, the theatre organ is a full-scale pipe organ. There are 16 ranks of pipes, with 73 to 85 pipes per rank, in ceiling lofts on either side of the proscenium arch, and [they] are covered with grillwork. The pipes are made of lead, tin, zinc and wood and were manufactured in Germany. The largest pipe measures 16 feet, while the shortest is ¼ inch in length. The organ console has a four-manual keydesk with a bank of three curved stop rails and a complete range of sound effects." Organ concerts are presented periodically in the theater.

The Casino also houses on its ground floor the Catalina Art Association's Art Gallery and the Catalina Island Museum. The latter's former curator, Patricia Anne Moore, and her staff helped us solve a great many historical puzzles in the preparation of this book.

COURTESY SHERMAN LIBRARY

The Casino is built on the site of Sugar Loaf Rock, a natural monolith that once formed the western headland of Avalon Bay. Sugar Loaf originally stood apart on the point from the rest of the headland, although it was connected to it by a low, rocky arm. Sugar Loaf was a popular early tourist attraction; at one time a steep stairway went up its side to the top. Around 1900, a tunnel was blasted through the headland behind the rock to give better access to Descanso Bay, then called Banning Cove. The tunnel collapsed in 1906, altering the outline of the ridge and creating two peaks, Little Sugar Loaf and Big Sugar Loaf. The collapsed tunnel was transformed into a road leading to Descanso Bay where, in 1895, Captain Hancock Banning had built a house in the canyon landscaped by his brother, J.B. Banning. The Banning home remained in that location until 1918 when it was moved to the side of the canyon to make room for the luxurious new Hotel St. Catherine. The former Banning home was later used to house hotel employees.

Precarious ladder leading to top of Sugar Loaf Rock, depicted here in photograph circa 1890, was blasted away for site of the Casino in 1928.

Plans to build the Hotel St. Catherine were started by the Banning family after the disastrous fire of 1915 destroyed the Hotel Metropole along with many other buildings in Avalon. In 1918, Hancock and William Banning supervised construction of the first section of the hotel which, according to Hancock Banning Jr., had two sets of plumbing: one for salt water and one for fresh water. "All the sanitary stuff was salt water and the wash basins and showers and things were fresh water. That's how we had to hoard water over there." After William Wrigley Jr. purchased the island, the original St. Catherine Hotel was enlarged and improvements were made throughout the building.

A promotional brochure from 1929 heralds the "New Catalina Island Casino... Two Million Dollar Palace of Pleasure for Your Enjoyment" and invites visitors to "Dance Free in the magnificent ballroom... The Casino contains a mammoth motion picture theatre... Here first-run talking pictures are shown. Admission: 50 cents general; 65 cents reserved seats."

The same pamphlet advertises the Hotel St. Catherine: "All outside rooms, also bungalows in connection. St. Catherine orchestra furnishes music for luncheon and dinner... E.H. Bernegger, manager." The room rate for two persons per day, without bath, was $12.00 to $15.00; with bath, $14.00 to $22.00. Rates were on the American Plan, meals included. Meal rates separately were breakfast and luncheon, $1.25 each, and dinner, $2.00.

In Avalon, there was the "Largest One Floor Hotel in the World — 1250 Rooms. These popular 'Bungalettes' form a vast, one-floor hotel." This referred to the town's small bungalow accommodations, Island Villa and Villa Park. The summer rate for one or two persons was two dollars and fifty cents per night, seventeen dollars and fifty cents per week.

The St. Catherine was closed to the public during World War II and suf-fered considerable damage during use as a U.S. Merchant Marine training center for cooks. Although it was restored after the war by Philip Wrigley, it was finally razed in 1965. Clear evidence of the hotel site can be seen on a stroll from the Casino along the walk skirting the bay. Remnants of an old pier that afforded access by sea for yachtsmen are also visible. The entire hillside, known as the "second Sugar Loaf" was removed by the Banning Company in 1917 in preparation for the construction of a new hotel to replace the destroyed Metropole. The plan was abandoned in favor of the Descanso Canyon site where the Hotel St. Catherine was built by the Bannings.

In 1920, William Wrigley Jr. selected the leveled Sugar Loaf site for a dance pavil-ion, known as Sugarloaf Casino. This early casino, according to Patricia Moore, was an octagonal, steel-framed structure with two wings for concessions. Completed in 1920, it could accommodate 250 dancing couples, which soon proved inadequate. Sugarloaf Casino was dismantled by Wrigley in February 1928, and its girders reassembled in Avalon Canyon to form a gigantic bird cage, 90 feet high and 115 feet

Captain Hancock Banning's house, built in 1895, overlooked Descanso Bay. The home remained in that location until 1918 when it was moved to the side of the canyon to make way for construction of the luxurious Hotel St. Catherine, razed in 1965.

Hotel St. Catherine, razed in 1965, dominates Descanso Bay, immediately west of Casino Point.

in diameter. This huge aviary became the centerpiece of the world-famous Catalina Bird Park. The aviary housed a variety of exotic birds and waterfowl from around the world including Russian goldfinches, macaws, Siamese pheasants, Australian pigeons the size of turkeys, herons, pilated jays, cockatoos, and California crested quail. But the most memorable to me were the talking mynah birds. They whistled and talked in shrill, penetrating tones, saying such things as "Hello, Joe," "You're a smart guy," and "How about a dance tonight?"

The original keeper of the birds was E.H. Lewis, said to have been descended from generations of British gamekeepers and to have been a bird breeder on English estates since childhood. "In him," said a 1931 promotional piece on the Bird Park, "Mr. Wrigley found a man to carry out his ideals ... a bird sanctuary without a rival in all the world."

In 1939, Samuel Butler, a Los Angeles building contractor who first came to Avalon in 1922 to construct cottages at the behest of D.M. Renton, returned to the island to work at the Bird Park training birds.

"I had some wonderful birds," Butler said in an oral history for the Powell Library, UCLA. "They had one bird over there that was a magpie. I taught her to do many, many things. For instance, she could carry on a conversation with you just as you and I are doing at the present time."

The magpie's name was Maggie. Butler tells of a woman who went up to talk to Maggie. The bird eyed her, then declared, "You are lousy."

The woman denied this. "Well," Maggie replied, "examine yourself."

On another occasion, a Catholic priest attempted to engage Maggie in conversation, Butler recalled. Maggie remained mute. As the priest departed, but within earshot, Maggie said, "You go to hell!"

Butler later asked Maggie why she didn't talk to the priest. Here is the ensuing conversation as reported by Butler:

"She [Maggie] looks up at me and she says, 'You know why.'

"And I says, 'Well, why?'

"'Well, I don't like him,' she says."

Butler recalled that there were about twenty mynah birds at the park. "Those mynah birds are intelligent," he said.

Butler claimed to have built many of the buildings on Crescent Avenue. In fact, Avalon was dotted with little buildings — 1,400 of them — that he had built for Wrigley, "Or Renton, rather — Renton was in charge of everything, everything was Renton, then for Wrigley," he said

But back to Sugar Loaf and its demise in 1928 when it was flattened for the construction of the Casino. Not everybody in town was delighted by the destruction of the ancient rock or the construction of the Casino. Ruben V. Vaughan, an Avalon resident for forty years and possibly the most literate of the Pleasure Pier boatmen, wrote, in his *Doc's Catalina Diary*: "The great Sugar Loaf was blasted into the sea and with it went the tide pools where so many people had spent hours watching the sea anemones and crabs and all the beautiful things God has given us for our pleasure. In its place is a pile of cement."

Pieces of Sugar Loaf have created a large, underwater reef of ridges and pinnacles off Casino Point, forming a habitat for marine life. Here, enclosed by planks chained between diver-flagged buoys to keep out boaters, is California's first underwater municipal park. On a typical summer Saturday as many as 300 skin and scuba divers test its depths to take photos, hone their diving skills, or just plain gawk at undersea life, which by law may not be destroyed or removed from the park. Boundaries of the aquatic preserve were laid out in 1962 by Carl Koehler, then owner of Avalon's only dive shop. He considered the park the island's most accessible diving area.

39 An Inland Walk

Wild white Sage, abloom.
Lavender blossoms, two-lipped.
Gray-green velvet leaves,
Essence of the hills,
Pungent, fragrant.

ANN CLOUD REYNOLDS,
Mountain Trails of Catalina (1948)

Our roving about Avalon, both historically and physically, eventually leads us away from the shore through the town toward the head of Avalon Valley. Initially we pause at Crescent Avenue, the main business street that borders the bay, and recall with amusement Ernest Windle's story of Billy Bruin, proprietor of a so-called "hardware store" located where the Tuna Club was later built. "Billy's Place" was in existence before George Shatto purchased the property in 1887, Billy's "hardware" consisting of tin cups, cuspidors, a couple of wine barrels, a brass rail, and a few bottles of hard liquor. After Shatto, who objected to alcoholic beverages on the island, closed down Billy Bruin's operation on land, Bruin bought a small barge on the mainland, had it towed across the channel, anchored it in Avalon Bay, and continued his "hardware" business in the harbor. Bruin lived in Avalon for a number of years, dying in a Los Angeles hospital in 1910 when in his eighties.

Bruin was one of the colorful characters of Catalina, representing an early period when Avalon was known as Timms' Landing, a casual collection of tents, shacks, and small businesses dependent primarily on fishing and the island's mild weather, which made it a favorite summer place for those who enjoyed the out-of-doors. When George Shatto bought the island in 1887, two years after Phineas Banning's death, he envisioned it not as just a place for casual tent living but as a place that might attract affluent tourists, immediately building the Hotel Metropole and a pier for landing visitors.

Phineas Banning's sons, upon acquiring the island in 1889, parlayed their father's monopoly on cross-channel transportation into greater recreational amenities at Avalon. Having organized the Santa Catalina Island Company (SCICo), the Bannings promoted Avalon as a resort and "Fisherman's Paradise." People from the mainland purchased lots and built summer homes; others leased small lots from the Banning Company for twenty-five dollars a year, using the property for small buildings and tents that were removed after the family vacation was over.

After William Wrigley Jr. purchased the island in 1919, he allowed lessees to buy the ground under their cottages at a nominal price, took over the steamer business, started mining activities near White's Landing, and developed a dependable water

Circa 1890, the Hotel Metropole dominates Avalon's waterfront at center, while the Banning-built dance pavilion can be seen at far right. Tents abounded in Avalon.

supply for the island by drilling wells and building storage reservoirs. Avalon was on its way to becoming a year-round resort and vacation destination for people from all over the country. Most of Avalon's ambience began, however, when Philip K. Wrigley took over the island's management in 1932 and brought in Otis Shepard, director of art and advertising for the Wrigley chewing gum company in Chicago, to develop an "Early California" theme for the downtown area. Most of the travel posters, pamphlets, and newspaper and magazine advertising extolling the island originated with Shepard. Simple, bold, clean, and colorful illustrations combined with a minimum of text made forceful statements that molded the public's image of a unique, romantic place to visit.

Shepard's output, much of it devoted to Catalina, spanned thirty-nine years, although he spent only four of those years at Avalon. During the period he worked in Avalon with P.K. Wrigley, Shepard designed the serpentine wall, the fountain on Crescent Avenue, and many of the grace notes that distinguish the community. Shepard also conceived of a plan to use Catalina tile seconds to decorate the sea wall and planter boxes. Olive and palm trees were barged across the channel and installed in the giant planters. Shepard's wife, Dorothy, also a talented artist, contributed to the unique charm of Avalon by executing murals in the Marine Bar of the Casino and designing new interiors for the Hotel St. Catherine and the SS *Avalon*. Both Shepards worked on designing early California costumes for SCICO personnel.

A new sign program for Avalon was developed at the behest of Philip Wrigley. Shepard encouraged the shopkeepers to do away with neon signs and helped develop wooden signs that were crafted with band saws by local artisans. Shepard inspired and approved such hand-wrought signs as a cut-out camera for the photo shop, a wooden cornucopia for the grocery, and a white swan for the Swan Hotel.

"Unfortunately, few [of those signs] remain today, although Avalon, perhaps in tribute to Shep, still bans the use of neon signs," said Donna Harrison, retired planning assistant for the SCICO. "In four years, building on concepts which were present when he arrived, Otis Shepard transformed Avalon into one of the most romantic destinations in the world ... and all the while the beautiful white steamers were departing to the strains of 'I left my love in Avalon.'"

COURTESY REBECCA STANTON

The Avalon Shell Store on Crescent Avenue polished moonstones that tourists would gather from Moonstone Beach next to White's Landing. Today Moonstone Cove is the site of Newport Harbor Yacht Club's island facility and bereft of moonstones.

While pausing at the intersection of Crescent and Metropole Avenues where the Hotel Metropole once stood, we could envision the dismay and fright of the populace at 3:30 A.M. Monday, November 29, 1915, when nearly half the town, an area of about a half mile square, was destroyed by fire. Consumed by flames were the Tuna Club and Bath House by the side of the bay, the Hotel Metropole, hotels Bayview, Park, Rose, Grandview, Catalina, Pacific, Central, Miramar, and Sea View, as well as the sumptuous Pilgrim Club, where high stakes gambling had taken place since 1902. All cottages in the blocks between Whittley Avenue and the waterfront were leveled by flames. The fire area encompassed everything inside the west side of Viendelou Avenue, across the canyon to Whittley and over to East Whittley to the junction of Crescent and Metropole Avenues. West Crescent and the hillside above it also bore the brunt. The famous aquarium in front of the Metropole was spared the flames, but severe water damage necessitated its later razing.

Herbert A. Wegmann, who was twelve years old at the time of the conflagration, recalled to me in early 1993 that some of the old fire hoses, hardened by age, sprang leaks. Hose carts hauled by hand added to the difficulties of fire fighting. It required at least six hours, Wegmann said, to control the flames. When the SS *Hermosa II* docked at the Steamer Pier later that day, those aboard were greeted by the shock-

The 1915 fire destroyed nearly half of Avalon.

ing sight of smoldering devastation, although the pier was unscathed.

Fortunately for tourism, the fire did not happen during the summer. Otherwise many holidays would have been canceled. Prior to the fire, Avalon was often referred to as the "Rag City" because so many of its residents lived in tents or tent cottages during the summer. After the fire, the Bannings and the city of Avalon, incorporated only two years earlier, were faced with serious financial problems.

Above Crescent Avenue on a bluff below the Wrigley mansion broods the handsome Victorian Holly Hill House, built almost single-handedly over a three-year period by Peter Gano, an accomplished engineer and craftsman, who helped fashion the island's first freshwater system. Originally called "Lookout Cottage," it was completed in March 1890. A block and tackle and a faithful retired circus horse named Mercury helped Gano haul materials up from the beach. From what was a Greek amphitheater below the Gano house there once climbed a scenic railway or funicular to Buena Vista Park on the hill's summit, near where the Wrigley mansion was later built. Another car descended the hill to Lovers Cove. The Incline Railway, as it was called, was built under the supervision of Hancock Banning in 1908 and operated until 1915. One ascending cable car counterbalanced a descending car. The remains were removed in 1920.

On the hill to the west is the former home of popular author Zane Grey, now a hotel. It was patterned after a Hopi Indian dwelling, according to Loren Grey, Zane's son. Goat's milk was used in the cement to strengthen the structure, a Hopi Indian construction technique. Western movie star Tom Mix built a house nearby. Near the Grey pueblo hotel and the bell tower was a small white house occupied for many years by the late Alma Overholt, Catalina publicist and historian. The house was built in 1902 as the Pacific Wireless Telephone and Telegraph Company's first commercial wireless station communicating between the island and the mainland.

The Incline Railway, Avalon, Catalina Island, Cal.

BUENA VISTA PARK

This postcard depicts the Incline Railway as it approaches Buena Vista Park, then descends to Lovers' Cove on the east side of Avalon. Hancock Banning had it built in 1904; it was abandoned in 1915.

We walk past close-set homes on the small lots laid out by George Shatto and C.A. Sumner, his agent, when Avalon was a "paper city," simply a developer's dream. Shatto's decision to create small lots was based upon his belief that the future of Avalon would be as a summer resort. Tents and small, inexpensively built cottages were to be placed on lots he initially sold for $100 to $2,000 apiece.

We examined the original September 28, 1888, subdivision map with its small lots in the archives of the Sherman Library in Corona del Mar, with the assistance of Dr. William O. Hendricks, library director/historian. A nineteenth-century surveyor's transit sealed the town's fate as the closely packed municipality of about 3,000 population it is today.

We pass a large plaza where sight-seeing buses rendezvous. Until the late 1930s the area contained the Island Villa bungalettes, lodgings with board floors, that were double-roofed for ventilation. The bungalettes had electricity, daily maid service, and were furnished, according to a 1929 brochure, with a rug, double bed, dresser, and chairs. "When three occupy a villa, a single bed is placed therein for the third person," the brochure noted.

An earlier Island Villa, built when the Banning Company owned the island, was advertised as "a delightfully arranged collection of canvas cottages, conducted along the lines of an European plan hotel, [providing] excellent accommodations for those preferring tent life without housekeeping." Like the later Island Villa, the tents had electricity and maid service. One could rent a tent there, furnished with bed, chairs, washstand, and bureau, for $.75 a day for one person, $1.25 for two. Weekly rates were $5.00 a week for one person, $8.00 a week for two.

Also available through the Banning Company in those long-ago days were accommodations in Canvas City, furnished tents in various sizes "rented with or without kitchen equipment." These too were electrically lighted, had "high walls, smooth-board floors and [were] nicely and completely furnished" including clean linen. Prices for two people ranged from six dollars a week for a ten- by twelve-foot tent to twelve dollars a week for a sixteen-by-twenty-four-foot tent. Kitchen tents with utensils were available at additional cost.

We walk to 346 Catalina Street to see "Singing Waters," the picturesque home of Gene (Geneva) Stratton Porter, author of *A Girl of the Limberlost, Freckles,* and other sentimental romances. The author, who had rented various properties, just finished having her home built when she was killed in an automobile accident in 1924. It is now the home of the Catalina Bible Church.

Avalon had a tent city along Clarissa Avenue in the early 1900s.

Among the oldest Protestant churches in southern California still occupying its original site is the Congregational Church at Metropole and Beacon Street. Built in 1889, the lovely sanctuary of carefully carpentered wood is still intact. Charles S. Uzzell and George Morris were the original pastors of this first Avalon Church.

Up Falls Canyon Road, in the southwest part of town, is the Avalon Municipal Hospital. Built in 1960, this twelve-bed hospital played host to me briefly on April 15, 1993, after I shattered my femur during a clumsy attempt to leap from the *Herald Bird* onto a float at the end of Isthmus pier. We had come to get fuel after yet another island circumnavigation. Baywatch Isthmus took me aboard, met Baywatch Avalon stern-to-stern at Goat Harbor, and transferred this pain-wracked, cursing author/mariner from boat to boat. The Baywatch vessels are Los Angeles County Lifeguard rescue boats, manned by paramedics. Baywatch Avalon took me to Avalon, and a city ambulance transported me to the hospital, where I was X-rayed and sent flying across the channel in a helicopter to Long Beach Memorial Hospital. There I was mended by an orthopedic surgeon, Dr. Francis J. Thornton. The lessons of this incident are twofold: the island is prepared to take care of its injured and sick, and when one is seventy-plus years old, leaping from boat to float is not prudent.

Continuing up the canyon we pass equestrian stables and the nine-hole golf course of the Catalina Country Club which began as a three-hole course in 1893 during the Banning Brothers' island ownership. A year later it was expanded into a

Catalina Bird Park in Avalon housed exotic birds.

nine-hole course, still later into an eighteen-hole course, and again became a nine-hole course after World War II. The original small course gave way to the island's Chicago Cubs Baseball Park in 1921 when William Wrigley Jr. arranged to bring the team to the island for spring training. A viewing structure was built. The Cubs continued to train here until 1951 under such famous managers as Rogers Hornsby, the "Rajah"; Joe McCarthy, Gabby Hartnett, and Charlie Grimm.

Nearby is the seven-and-one-half-acre site of the world-renowned Bird Park or Catalina Aviary, closed since 1966. The aviary is abandoned, and most of the cages have been removed, but once this was a noisy place where exotic birds from all over the world were on display. They could be seen flying in the "world's largest bird cage," an octagonal cage constructed with steel girders from Wrigley's Sugarloaf Casino, dismantled in 1928.

Up this canyon once lived John Brinkley, a native of Kent, England, who came to the island in 1887. He grew figs, and raised squabs and other poultry, making a living by feeding Avalon residents and tourists. Reclusive by nature, he was known as "Chicken John," one of the town's characters. When electric service was established he eschewed it, preferring his old coal oil lamp.

Now we approach the Wrigley Memorial and Botanical Garden, which honors the memory of this visionary developer of Catalina and his wife, Ada. The memorial is an imposing structure built as nearly as possible from native Catalina materials: aggregate quarried and crushed on the island, blue flagstone rock from Little

Harbor, red roof tiles and glazed tiles made in the Catalina tile plant from Catalina clay. The nearly thirty-eight-acre garden pays tribute to Ada Wrigley, who originally conceived of a cactus and succulent garden here and supervised Pasadena horticulturist Albert Conrad who planted it. She was responsible for many of the extensive plantings that grace the island.

At the garden we learn of the rare island endemic, Catalina mahogany, its botanical name being *Cercocarpus traskiae.* Interestingly, this species was discovered by Blanche Luella Trask of Avalon around the turn of the last century during her many hikes about the island. Holder said of this early botanist, author, and poet that she "knows the heart of the island better than anyone." Another endangered endemic is the shaggy-barked Catalina ironwood or *Lyonothamnus floribundus asplenufolius.* Reforestation with its nearly microscopic seeds is a problem as the seeds seem to germinate with difficulty.

Catalina endemics that are thriving are the wild tomato, the poisonous purple blackberry, Catalina manzanita, St. Catherine's lace, Catalina bedstraw, and the Catalina cherry. In all there are approximately 100 species of native plants found only on the California islands. Of the Catalina cherry or Island islay, known by the botanical names of *Prunus integrifolia* or *Prunus lyonii,* landscape architect Ralph D. Cornell remarked in his *Conspicuous California Plants,* first published in 1938, that it "used to form one of the fresh fruit foods of the Indians and is sometimes preserved whole by the Catalinians," adding that "it has a pleasant, slightly wild-cherry taste but also suffers by nature of the fact that it is mostly seed and skin with a very meager supply of pulp between."

Riders assemble in front of Avalon's Hotel Metropole in the early 1900s. The hotel was destroyed by fire in 1915.

Terrence Martin, in his *Santa Catalina, an Island Adventure,* observed that "much of the plant life of Catalina Island is special, rare, and of biological importance... Although many types that grow on Catalina are also found on the other Channel Islands, eight exist only on Catalina itself. More than ten per cent of Catalina's native flora is rare, having not been recently observed or collected. If this resource were not protected it would lose its beauty, a glimpse of the past, and a chance to understand how ecosystems and evolutionary processes operate."

Any mariner or island visitor who enjoys poking into the island's coves and admiring the vegetation on the cliffs and mountains will profit from a visit to these botanical gardens. It will generate a greater understanding of the island's priceless heritage.

40 The Conservancy

Oh, give me a home where the buffalo roam.
DR. BREWSTER HIGLEY,
Home on the Range (1873)

As Marjie and I walked, surrounded by these reminders of past times and the vestments of nature, we paid tribute to the Wrigley family for their enlightened decision to establish the Santa Catalina Island Conservancy. It was initiated as a means to preserve and enhance for future generations an environmental and ecological quality that is rapidly being destroyed on the mainland and was beginning to diminish on the island. Originated by Philip K. Wrigley, the Santa Catalina Island Conservancy was established by the Wrigley family in 1972 as a nonprofit operating foundation dedicated to the preservation and protection of open space, wild lands, and nature preserve areas on the island, in perpetuity.

In 1974, an easement agreement was signed with Los Angeles County, giving the county the right to share the use of 41,000 acres of the island's interior and much of its coastline for park, conservation, and recreation uses for a period of fifty years. The following year, in 1975, Mr. and Mrs. Philip K. Wrigley and Philip's sister, Mrs. Dorothy Wrigley Offield, through the Santa Catalina Island Company (SCICo), deeded 42,139 acres and other assets to the conservancy. With this gift, the conservation and preservation of about 86 percent of the island's seventy-six square miles were assured.

The conservancy's legal mandate is to preserve and protect the island's native plants and animals, its biological communities, and its geological and geographical formations of educational interest. Equally important, it is charged with managing Catalina's open space lands and seeing that they are used solely for the enjoyment of scenic beauty and for controlled public recreational purposes. The conservancy provides ranger service to assist visitors, and owns and operates the popular Airport-in-the-Sky.

Assisted in part by the Los Angeles County Department of Parks and Recreation, the conservancy is also responsible for maintaining the entire preserve area and its roads. Its substantial financial burden is helped by private contributions and membership support groups such as the Marineros, the Caballeros, and Catalina Divers. Revegetation, including rare island oak seedlings and native bunch grasses, and general erosion control are under supervision of the conservancy's Native Plant Nursery at Middle Ranch in the island's interior. At this writing, Janet N. Takara supervises the Native Plant Horticulture Department, along with planning and executing native plant projects on various parts of the island, aimed at restoring the island's natural ecosystem.

The Santa Catalina Island Conservancy is administered by a board of directors elected annually by benefactor life members. The first president of the conservancy was Allen Douglas Propst.

The Conservancy's wildlife management program involves stabilizing the number of bison or buffalo and the removal — as nearly as possible — of the wild pigs and feral goats to protect the ecosystem. Bison arrived on the island in 1924 when a small herd was brought from the mainland to serve as "extras" in a western motion picture. At this point, historical confusion rides in. It has been commonly believed that the movie was *The Vanishing American*, based on a novel by Zane Grey, starring Richard Dix and released October 15, 1925. Nevertheless, research by Patricia Moore, former director of the Catalina Island museum, who viewed the film, revealed there were no bison in it. This was corroborated by Loren Grey, Zane Grey's son, who believes the island-made film was his father's *The Thundering Herd*. These films, he said, were two of about 112 made from his father's western books; *Vanishing American* was filmed in Arizona on a Hopi Indian reservation.

The origin of the island bison can be partly attributed to Iron Eyes Cody, a Cree/Cherokee Indian film actor, and his father, Long Plume Cody. "My father and I had five buffalo not doing anything," Iron Eyes told us in early 1993 when he was eighty-eight. "So we shipped them over to the island for the movie." Unfortunately, he wasn't sure of the movie's title, but he remembered that additional bison from Colorado were also brought in for the western. When the filming was over the animals proved difficult to round up so they were left behind to forage and mate on their own.

Ensuing years brought more bison to the island. Another small herd from Colorado was added in the 1930s, a herd of fifteen from Wyoming in 1969, and a herd of seven from Montana in 1971. In peak years, the island herd reaches 500 bison, even with selective management. To maintain a herd of about 100 to 150 buffalo while still protecting the island from overgrazing, excess generations are corralled and shipped to the mainland where they augment surviving herds in several western states. Some also go to commercial packers, who prize them for their low-fat meat.

Truly, the island is a home where the buffalo roam freely. And roam they do, virtually unfenced, magnificently humped, horned bulls with awesome heads, and smaller females with calves, competing sometimes for space with backpackers and hikers on trails, in camps, and on the roads. Unless one wishes to risk life and limb, it is prudent to step aside when meeting a bison of any size. Furthermore, to position oneself between mother and calf is to invite disaster and possible injury. In 1995, the conservancy issued 10,017 permits to hikers.

Public campsites are located at Blackjack, Parson's Landing, Little Fisherman's Cove, Goat Harbor, Avalon Valley, and Little Harbor. It was at Little Harbor, a stop on an inland bus ride from the Isthmus, that we saw a group of campers sitting and standing on picnic tables. Their campsite had been taken over by a large herd of grazing bison. A massive bull sauntered across the road, halted, and stared passively, demanding right of way and stopping our bus for five minutes before he moved on. The big ruminants can be seen almost anywhere, on beaches, hillsides, and watering holes, much to the delight and awe of land travelers and yachtsmen.

Descendants of early pigs gone wild were here in the early 1800s, introduced by mariners such as Captains John Hudson and William Shaler, but their numbers were small. It was not until the 1930s that a major introduction of wild pigs was made innocently by the SCICO as game for hunters and the incidental benefit that the pigs ate rattlesnakes. It was an action the company learned to regret because the pigs, their population grown immeasurably, have proved to be the most environ-

mentally destructive of all the island's alien animals, including wild goats. A planned program of hunting and trapping the pigs, with the ultimate goal of entirely eliminating them from the island, has been undertaken. Goat hunting, with bow and arrow, was planned to keep a balance between animals and plants on the finite rangeland of the island. It was inadequate. Elimination of the feral goat herds by systematic slaughter seems to be the only ecologically sound procedure.

The tiny gray fox, which is a Channel Islands' endemic; the island deer mouse, the saw-whet owl, the Beechy ground squirrel and the ornate shrew, the bald eagle and the peregrine falcon are responding well to management, their numbers increasing gradually through husbanding by the conservancy. This strong

Catalina Island bison still graze on Conservancy land.

tilt toward sane habitat enhancement is, in effect, a reverse time frame. Imagine free-ranging native buffalo foraging on native bunch grass that once carpeted the great plains of the old west. It is happening on this island off one of the most populous mainland shores in the nation.

And speaking of mainland population, there was in 1993 a total of 143,200 boat registrations in the combined counties of San Diego, Los Angeles, and Orange. Of these, a total of 29,900 were large enough to require slips. The barrier of the San Pedro Channel discourages the bulk of recreational boaters from mooring or anchoring in Catalina coves. Only during summer weekends and national holidays such as Independence, Labor, and Memorial Days does one find hull-to-hull boats on the island's 1,150 moorings. Anchorages during these long holidays are a little less popular, but we have seen enough boats in Little Harbor, anchored fore and aft, that one could imagine stepping from boat to boat.

During these peak holidays, dragged anchors, ineptly set, are a primary source of cursing and fending off drifting vessels. A stiffening of wind can keep a well-anchored yachtsman busy far into the night warding off unexpected and unwelcome visitors. We know. We've experienced it.

41 Cross-Channel Communications

Were it left to me to decide whether we should have a government without newspapers, or newspapers without a government, I should not hesitate a moment to prefer the latter.   THOMAS JEFFERSON (1787)

It has been suggested that the island's first Marconi wireless telegraphy station was set up at White's Point on Catalina Island in 1902. This is a case of mistaken geography. The telegraph facility was established on August 2, 1902, on White Point — so named because of the color of the rock — on the mainland west of Point Fermin in San Pedro. Its sister facility was above Sugar Loaf on the hill west of Avalon. Between these points Morse code signals coursed through the air twenty-five miles across the San Pedro Channel, a miracle in those days! A year later the Bannings established a telephone line linking Avalon to the Isthmus via Middle Ranch and Little Harbor.

When Lee de Forest, the father of radio, perfected his first three-electrode vacuum tube, the Audion, in 1907, he made possible the transmission of voice and music without wires. The island's first commercial radio telephone system was established at Pebbly Beach in the spring of 1919 by the Pacific Telephone and Telegraph Company. A sister station was located in San Pedro. This system continued until 1923 when two submarine cables to the mainland, the first cables ever to be manufactured in the United States, were laid.

A romantic legend that de Forest experimented with his Audion tube in Avalon's little house on the hill should be laid to rest. There is no evidence that de Forest experimented there. Nowhere in his definitive and extensive autobiography, *Father of Radio,* does de Forest mention Avalon or Catalina. He did, however, become a resident of Los Angeles in 1930, living there until his death at age eighty-eight in 1961. His early experiments on the Audion tube in California were in 1906 at the Palo Alto laboratory of the Federal Telegraph Company.

An earlier story of cross-channel communication involves carrier pigeons. On July 19, 1894, brothers Otto J. and Oswald F. Zahn brought carrier pigeons to Catalina and launched a unique airmail service between Avalon and Los Angeles. The young men, then twenty-four and twenty years of age, had made arrangements with Hancock Banning to build an office and pigeon loft on the wharf at Avalon. Antwerp carrier pigeons were being trained to fly from their loft on Bunker Hill, Los Angeles, to the loft on the island and back, thus providing two-way service. Furthermore, the young men had a contract with the *Los Angeles Times* to fly a daily "budget" of news from Avalon to Los Angeles during the three-month summer social season enjoyed at the Hotel Metropole and other hostelries in town.

Otto Zahn's arrival on the island, duly noted in the *Times* of July 12, 1894, "injected an unwonted measure of excitement into Avalon's sun-drenched serenity," noted Irvin Ashkenazy, writing in the October 1968 issue of *Westways* magazine.

"The Metropole's management had spread word of the forthcoming 'air-mail' service – America's first! Guests sauntered down the waterfront and watched curiously as Otto staggered up the wharf, laden with wicker baskets of fluttering pigeons. Some of Catalina's more colorful characters, permanent residents such as 'Mexican Joe' Presiado and 'Portuguese Jack' Williams, lent a hand installing him in his new headquarters at the head of the wharf." Even Catalina's hermit, "Chicken John" Brinkley, who made a living in the poultry business, was there, observing Otto's birds' adjustment to their home away from home.

After a few false starts with some insufficiently trained pigeons, the Santa Catalina Island Homing Pigeon Service became a success. Handbills advertised two regularly scheduled flights a day to carry messages "from Catalina Island to the outside world." Messages, on special, small onionskin forms, were folded lengthwise into half-inch-wide strips, wrapped about the carriers' legs, and tied. Messages on a 10:00 A.M. flight cost one dollar apiece. Those sent on the 2:30 P.M. flight were included with the *Los Angeles Times* news "budget" (on larger onionskin) and cost fifty cents cents apiece. The carrier pigeons' speed in flight averaged about thirty miles an hour. The brothers' loft champion, Orlando, a broad-shouldered, blue-gray five-year-old, raced across forty-eight miles in fifty minutes!

The pigeon express operated until 1898 with only two failures to make delivery, and those during the first year. However, the pigeon service was uncertain. Hawks were a source of danger to the pigeons as were human hunters. And some of the birds died from overexhaustion. After four years the pigeon express business became burdensome. The Zahns, joined by younger brother, Lorenzo, had to bicycle all over Los Angeles delivering local messages, Western Union out-of-city messages, and the *Times* news budgets. Eventually they sold the business to G.H. Humphreys, a pigeon fancier. Humphreys carried it on until wireless telegraphy was established.

The advent of wireless telegraphy heralded a first in journalism for the *Los Angeles Times:* "The only daily newspaper in the world publishing sure-enough dispatches transmitted by wireless telegraph had its birth yesterday morning in Avalon, Santa Catalina Island," read the account in the *Times* of March 26, 1903. "The event is a unique one in the history of journalism and marks the beginning of an epoch in the dissemination of news in isolated places."

The *Times' Catalina Wireless* was published and printed on a twelve-by-eighteen Gordon platen press in a small house in Avalon. The first issue consisted of four eight-by-eleven-inch pages carrying short news briefs, mostly from Los Angeles and vicinity. Some of the first day's flashes in the *Wireless:* "Rain causes worst tie up of street car lines in history of city; Robber murderer believed captured in San Bernardino; Beast assaults insane woman near arcade, [and] Midnight ride with mysterious woman cost C.E. Hayes his life." The paper also reported that the Glenmore Hotel (in Avalon) was progressing, "the framework being up to the third story. The fourth story will be a roof-garden and sun-parlor wherein warm weather guests may have unlimited fresh air and view..."

General Harrison Gray Otis, the *Times'* founder, noting that Catalina Island was quickly becoming one of southern California's top tourist attractions, and S.J. Mathes, *Wireless* editor, had decided that a morning newspaper would interest island residents and tourists who otherwise had to wait until later in the day for copies of the *Times* sent over by steamer.

News events printed in the *Wireless* were necessarily terse, but they covered what was salient in Los Angeles, on the Pacific slope, in the East, and in other countries. The foreign news (mostly from Europe) was sent by cable under the Atlantic, by Western Union across the continent to Los Angeles, from the *Times* office to White Point, San Pedro, and thence by Pacific Wireless to Avalon. The *Wireless* appears to have had a life span of only one season on the island.

The *Catalina Jew Fish* was an earlier, somewhat jocular, attempt at island journalism with a staff (on paper) of nineteen editors including C.F. Holder, submarine editor; W.H. Kennedy, floating bus editor; Dan McFarland, yachting editor; Baron Rogniat, society editor; Hancock Banning, musical editor; Frank Polley, libel editor; C.A. Sumner, hotel editor; Colonel J.J. Ayers, fish editor; Charles Bell, sporting editor; H.Z. Osborne, literary editor; C. McCandless, photo editor; W. Beach, fighting editor; Willis N. Masters, goat editor; Dr. J.M. Radebaugh, medical editor; Frank W. Conant, dramatic editor; John W. Vandervoort, astronomical editor; Captain Charles F. Remington, matrimonial editor; Mexican Joe, interpreter, and Terra Cotta John, reporter, all well known at the time. The four-page paper cost ten cents a copy and was started in 1888 by C.A. Sumner as part of a campaign to promote interest in the island.

Other newspapers that followed the *Wireless* included the *Catalina Daily Mirror,* Ernest Windle and George Channing, editors, published for four months during

Pacific Wireless Station, Santa Catalina Island, Cal.

This postcard, mailed in 1909, shows the Pacific Wireless Station that transmitted from Avalon across the channel to White's Point on the mainland.

the summer of 1907; the *Catalina Wireless,* not to be confused with the earlier *Wireless,* Willis M. Lefavor, editor and publisher, 1912 to 1915, and the *Catalina Islander,* 1914 to date under various publishers. The *Islander* began with Ernest Windle, owner, and George E. Esterling, editor, but was later owned and edited by Windle who by then had resigned from the Santa Catalina Island Company (SCICO).

"Judge" Windle, as he was called, was a respected and beloved island resident, serving for fifty-two years as justice of the peace in Avalon. Born in 1878 in Lancashire County, England, Windle arrived in Avalon in 1906 after surviving a serious

COURTESY JOHN WINDLE

injury to his legs while working as an auditor-accountant in San Pedro for the Bannings' Wilmington Transportation Company. A load of lumber tumbled from a railroad car, pinning and crushing his legs beneath it and at the same time killing two men. The accident happened about 1903 on a company dock at the foot of Fifth Street in San Pedro.

Windle was hospitalized for nearly two years from his injuries. Ever after he walked on crutches, but could ride a bicycle. After his recovery the Bannings employed Windle at the SCICO as an auditor-accountant on the island. He also managed the Aquarium in Avalon, located across from the Hotel Metropole. The aquarium, which was dismantled after the 1915 fire, had heavy glass panels framed with island steatite or soapstone to prevent saltwater corrosion.

Drawing on his newspaper, personal, and business contacts, Judge Windle became the island's first historian, writing and publishing his *Windle's History of Catalina Island (and Guide)* in 1931 and a second edition in 1940 on the press of the *Catalina Islander* newspaper. He died March 16, 1968, according to his son, John W. Windle, who was the SCICO's superintendent of transportation.

Ernest Windle, former owner, publisher, and editor of the *Catalina Islander* newspaper. He was one of the island's first major historians.

For a period beginning in 1952, the *Islander* experienced financial difficulties. Philip Knight Wrigley, through the SCICO, purchased the paper to assure the continuance of a viable newspaper for the community. From then until 1975, Philip K. Wrigley leased the newspaper's operation to Windle, Dorothy Beach, Jean Johnson, and Margaret and Gene Haney, in that order. The latter took over in 1955.

Donald Root Haney, son of the Haneys, took over the editing and publishing for the next thirty-five years, purchasing the *Islander* in 1975 with money loaned him by Wrigley. Haney said Philip had no interest in running a newspaper and was satisfied that the publication was in good hands. On August 1, 1990, Haney sold the *Islander* to West Coast Community Newspapers of Carlsbad, California, and retired to Kernville. The former publisher was Sherri Walker. The *Islander* changed ownership in November 2001. Daniel Verdugo of Community Media Corporation of Orange

County is one of the owners. A rival weekly newspaper, the *Avalon Bay News,* was founded August 9, 1990, with Barbara Crow as its editor and publisher. Island history is featured. Today, neither newspaper is printed on the island.

Beginning on June 1, 1952, this island had its own commercial radio station — KBIG — that boomed its signal into the mainland, despite the fact it had but 10,000 watts of power. Its transmitter's elevation at Renton Pass near the Airport-in-the-Sky, plus sea conductivity, more than doubled its effective power. KBIG, 740 kilocycles, was an AM station. Its studio was located on Whittley Avenue in Avalon. Music, news, weather, and fishing activities were featured during its daylight-only operation. The station was founded by John Poole, a broadcaster with interests then in several other California stations.

When KBIG went on the air, with the theme of "music you like and just enough news," its disc jockey was Carl Bailey, a six-foot-nine-inch beanpole of charm who was billed as Mr. Big of K-BIG, the world's tallest disc jockey. "I don't know how he did it, but somehow he looked a lot taller than he was — and everybody loved him, especially the children," reminisced John Poole during an interview with us in the late summer of 1993. He said that Bailey conducted interviews aboard the SS *Catalina* for several years until about 1965. A remote hookup from the ship connected the Bailey interviews to the station. A bronze plaque commemorating Carl Bailey, sponsored by his friends and admirers, is on a palm tree on Crescent Avenue across from one of Avalon's oldest restaurants, the Busy Bee.

KBIG had an auxiliary studio on Sunset Boulevard in Hollywood, communicating by microwave to the island. There were serious broadcasting problems in the early years, among which were temporary failures of the island's electric generating plant, shutting the station off the air. Poole decided to provide his own power. Diesel-powered generators were installed at the transmitter site, fed by a 2,000-gallon diesel fuel tank. This system was used until the Southern California Edison Company began supplying the island's power requirements in 1962. During the Poole ownership of KBIG, an FM frequency was added with the station letters of KBRT.

KBIG and KBRT were sold by Poole in 1969 to Bonneville International Corporation of Salt Lake City, Utah. Bonneville spun off KBRT, now AM, selling it in 1980 to Crawford Broadcasting Company of Flowertown, Pennsylvania, a conglomerate of religious broadcasting stations. The Catalina transmitter was part of the transaction, today serving KBRT's studio in Costa Mesa near John Wayne Airport. KBRT operates under Kiertron Broadcasting, Inc., a California subsidiary of Crawford Broadcasting. Bonneville continues to operate KBIG FM, with its transmitter on Mount Wilson near Los Angeles. It features popular music.

Thus is solved another island puzzle — the confusion over the historic, continuously operating radio transmitter on the island's Renton Pass for more than forty years.

The microwave system on Dakin Peak (that name again) was the world's first commercial high-frequency microwave radiophone system. Originally a secret device developed during World War II, the microwave system was installed at Pebbly Beach in May of 1946 by Bell Telephone. Later it was moved to Dakin Peak, permitting communication with San Clemente Island, seaward of Catalina, as well as the mainland. San Clemente was then, as it is now, under jurisdiction of the U.S. Navy and is used as an underwater demolition training station and missile firing range.

42   Absolutely No Hand Lines!

The gods do not deduct from man's
allotted span the hours spent in fishing.
Babylonian proverb, often quoted by Herbert C.
Hoover, thirty-first president of the United States

We cast off our mooring lines and slip carefully out of congested Avalon Bay, leaving astern the Catalina Island Yacht Club and the Tuna Club, a pair of venerable landmarks dear to the hearts of the many who sail and fish in these waters. One must be careful not to confuse the Catalina Island Yacht Club (CIYC) with the similarly named Catalina Yacht Club. The latter was organized by Hancock Banning in 1893 at the Isthmus and disbanded in 1914. The CIYC was organized in 1924 by a group that included ardent yachtsman and saltwater angler James W. Jump who, with Art Sanger, decided the island needed an official yacht club for boating enthusiasts. Jump approached David M. Renton and obtained a lease for the pilings already in place at the present CIYC location for one dollar a year.

The pilings, somehow spared during the 1915 fire, were originally set down in 1903 by the seagoing residents of Avalon who had organized the Sophia Boat Club. The facility was essentially a dinghy landing for club members, many of whom were professional boatmen. Before the fire the landing was used by J.E. (Pard) Matthewson as a boatyard where the early glass-bottom rowboats were built.

Jump canvassed the Jonathan Club of Los Angeles for founding members and secured thirty yachtsmen who paid the $100 initiation fee and dues, plus $400 each on a 6 percent promissory note to be paid as soon as possible. The money was used to build the clubhouse. Of the original founding group, eighteen were also members of the Tuna Club who felt there should be a social club in Avalon in addition to their fishing club. The first organizational meeting for the Catalina Island Yacht Club was held March 7, 1924. Except for the war years of 1942 to 1945, when the U.S. Merchant Marine used the club as a school, the facility has functioned as a social and yachting club in good standing with the Southern California Yachting Association and the Southern California Cruising Association.

When the club was returned to its members in 1945, after the merchant marine had made additions to the building, including the present quarter-deck out over the

The moorings of Avalon in 1935 are depicted with the Tuna Club (left), Yacht Club (right), and Bell Tower on the hill.

water, it became a victim of the Federal Tidelands Act. The tideland upon which the club had been built was deeded to the city of Avalon by the federal government, and the club was forced to negotiate with the city to obtain a lease for the use of the club.

The founding year of 1924 was a busy one for James Jump. That year he became the yacht club's first commodore, was elected president of the nearby Tuna Club, and — as a final fillip — caught a 117¾-pound bluefin tuna, a record among Tuna Club members for the year.

The Tuna Club was founded in 1898 by Dr. Charles Frederick Holder, popular science writer and enthusiastic fresh- and saltwater fisherman, who had moved from the East Coast to Pasadena in 1885. When Holder learned about the wonderful game fish to be found in Catalina waters including the bluefin tuna or, as it was then called, the "leaping tuna," nothing could keep him away from the island. The son of Dr. Joseph B. Holder, first curator of the American Museum of Natural History in New York, Holder first visited Avalon in 1886 when it was called Timms' Landing or Dakin Cove. There he observed men and boys standing on the beach catching yellowtail with heavy cod hand lines. As fast as the fishermen could cast, they had strikes. Holder returned to the mainland intent on purchasing Santa Catalina, which at the time was largely a sheep ranch owned by the James Lick estate of San Francisco. Holder believed that "any island so near a prospective great city like Los Angeles, where thirty-pound fishes like yellowtail could be caught so readily was better than a gold mine."

Holder, however, was not destined to own the island. His "gold mine" was his pen. For many years he devoted himself almost entirely to literature and lecturing, carving out a career that made him one of the best-known popular science and angling writers in the country. After investigating Catalina and the other Channel Islands, Holder's prolific pen told the world about them in various publications and several books including *Life in the Open, Big Game Fishes of the U.S., The Log of the Sea Angler, The Adventures of Torqua,* and *The Channel Islands of California.* The things Holder found at Catalina both amazed and horrified him. He was amazed at the size and great numbers of the island's fishes, and the magnitude of the sport boggled his mind. At the same time he was horrified to find that men were taking the fish on heavy hand lines, "almost rope," he said, yet calling it a "sport." Holder set out to remedy what he considered a deplorable situation. Based upon his experience with salmon, he worked out tackle he thought would be sufficiently strong to cope with the mighty fish of the channel's waters, yet give the quarry a better than even break.

In the meantime, Holder continued to visit the island and to fish enthusiastically with rod and reel, usually with the aid of Jose Felice Presiado or "Mexican Joe," a professional boatman often hired to row him "from one end of the island to the other, a 30-mile pull." By 1895 Holder and several sea-angler friends had formed an informal group called the Ananias Club (after an early Christian struck dead for lying) that congregated at the Hotel Metropole in Avalon to exchange information on bait, rods, reels, and various lines used for catching the "gamy fish." E.F. Hurlbut was president; the lyre (a stringed instrument of the harp class used by ancient Greeks) was used for lapel buttons and as the club insignia.

Presumably the men were swapping fish stories on June 1, 1898, when Holder successfully took a large bluefin tuna — a 183-pounder — with rod and reel from a twenty-foot open launch, powered alternately by a ten-horsepower inboard gasoline engine and a pair of oars. His boatman was an Englishman, Jim Gardner. Holder took his historic tuna on a twenty-one-strand line, a vom Hofe reel with leather thumb brake, and a sixteen-ounce wooden rod tip under six feet in length. He was relieved and satisfied that the big fish towed the boat around many times, stern first, without breaking the line, with Gardner working the oars.

The *Pasadena Daily News* of June 2, 1898, waxed eloquent about Dr. Holder's feat, reporting that he had "eclipsed all previous achievements in the line of angling for the big thoroughbreds of the deep.... For three hours and forty-five minutes, he played the big fellow with pertinacious skill and at last conquered and landed him.... The tuna... measured 45 inches in circumference and was six feet in length.... The fight was a glorious one but at its conclusion Dr. Holder felt completely exhausted."

On the day that the Tuna Club came into semiofficial existence, June 15, 1898, the newspaper was still exulting over the bluefin capture. "If anyone doubts that Dr. Holder caught a fish of 183 lbs., there is a photograph in the News office."

It should be pointed out that although Dr. Holder was the first angler to catch a truly large tuna on rod and reel, another Pasadenan, Colonel C.P. Morehouse, brought to gaff a smaller tuna in 1896, using rod, reel, and tarpon line. Holder himself remarked in *An Isle of Summer,* published in 1895: "I did not take the first tuna, but I caught the first large one," adding that Colonel Morehouse landed the first tuna on rod and reel.

During that founding year, 1898, guests at Avalon's Hotel Metropole were humming "When You Were Sweet Sixteen," a popular new song, and a continent away Captain Joshua Slocum arrived at Newport, Rhode Island, ending a three-year voyage around the world alone in his yacht, *Spray.* But attention at the Metropole was provincially centered on organizing the Tuna Club. According to Holder, there were two reasons for the club's name: first, that it provided a simple, neat, euphonic title and second, that its inauguration closely followed Holder's bringing in the first very large tuna on rod and reel.

The Tuna Club's first clubhouse was simply a desk in the Metropole. Dr. Holder called together five men who founded the club "to prevent the slaughter of game fish with hand-lines, to elevate the standard of sport on the Pacific Coast, either in fresh or salt water, and to protect game fish in every way, and to secure proper legislation affecting the fisheries of all kinds, the protection of sardines and other food fish during the spawning season, and in every legitimate way to set an example of the highest possible sportsmanship."

The founders, who drew up the original constitution in July 1898, were Dr. H.K. Macomber of Pasadena, Clifford R. Scudder of St. Louis, Fitch Dewey of Detroit, Edward L. Doran of Los Angeles, and W.J. Landers of San Francisco. The constitution stated that the club was "formed and composed of gentlemen and ladies" who through skill and perseverance on rod and reel with a twenty-four-thread (or less) line had taken a tuna of at least 100 pounds. Hand-line fishing was to be discouraged as "unsportsmanlike and against the public interest."

Sometime over the years, "ladies" were dropped from the bylaws, possibly because

The first large tuna taken with rod and reel was landed in Catalina waters in 1898 by Dr. Charles F. Holder who surveys his 183-pound prize; boatman Jim Gardner holds the gaff.

only two of them ever became members. That is not to say that the ladies didn't fish, however. One outstanding fisherwoman was Mrs. Keith Spaulding, a diminutive woman who, in 1921, caught a 426-pound broadbill, the largest broadbill brought in that summer. In total her catches of broadbill and tuna would have entitled her to five "buttons," the small lapel insignia awarded members for catching the largest game fish. An earlier female angler, Mrs. E.N. Dickerson, brought to gaff a 216-pound bluefin tuna in 1901. Except for Colonel C.P. Morehouse, who will be referred to in the following chapter, no man brought in a tuna of this size until the 1940s. As one club member wryly commented, "When a woman angler is good, she is too damned good." Nearly a century later the club, with a membership of nearly

15151. Catalina Island Tuna Club, Avalon, Catalina Island.

The Tuna Club in 1930 is captured on a postcard before the porch was widened across the entire building.

200, has no female members but does award six "ladies' trophies" to wives, daughters, and granddaughters of members.

The Tuna Club also continues its conservation efforts. Working with other conservation-oriented organizations, its members convinced the California state legislature to exclude gill netting within three miles of the offshore islands and mainland coasts. A gill net is a flat net suspended vertically in the water with various mesh sizes designed to ensnare certain fish, such as, say, albacore, by its gills as it attempts to swim through. Smaller fishes may pass through without harm. Unfortunately, many fish and mammals, regardless of mesh size, become mortally entangled in the nets, which can be a mile or more in length.

In 1899 Holder proudly told assembled Tuna Club members: "A year ago boats left Avalon Bay with from four to ten heavy hand lines, and tunas and yellowtail and sea bass were slaughtered by the ton and thrown away. Today, by your example, not a boatman of Santa Catalina will permit a hand line in his boat. All use rods and reels and the lines specified by the club and the result is that few fish are wasted, the catch is reduced two-thirds and the sport is enhanced. . . . Not only this, but the fame of the Tuna Club has gone around the civilized world, and its example . . . has been adopted in every land where the phrase, 'He fishes like a gentleman,' has any significance."

By July 6, 1908, the Tuna Club had a proper clubhouse set on pilings in the bay at its present location. The Banning Company had given the club the use of one of its best waterfront locations on Avalon Bay for the purpose of erecting a clubhouse; plans were drawn up in 1907 and building operations commenced in April 1908. Total cost of the building was $8,000. The official opening was marked by a reception in the new clubhouse, attended by distinguished anglers from across the nation including Gifford Pinchot, father of the national park system; James R. Garfield, then secretary of the interior; Dr. David Starr Jordan, famed ichthyologist and president of Stanford University, and U.S. Senator Frank Flint.

There was no insurance on the new club building and little money in the treasury when the 1915 Avalon conflagration destroyed it. However, monetary obstacles were quickly overcome by the club's loyal and generous membership; phoenix-like, the present clubhouse rose six months later. The new structure was opened to members and their friends on June 1, 1916, in time for most of the fishing season. On the lower floor, then as now, were the office, card room, large locker rooms, library, and spacious clubroom, the walls decorated with mounted trophy fishes accented by exhibits of tackle and showcases with trophies. On the second floor were fourteen bedrooms.

There must be noted a small, dark room on the first floor called the "Bait Box," a place held sacred by the old guard. It was and is a tiny bar where spirituous liquors were dispensed, and tales of great fishes, taken and lost, traded. Here Sir Winston Churchill, the great English statesman, drank his inevitable scotch and soda. Churchill had come to the island by plane, almost immediately went fishing in Monte Foster's *Sunbeam II,* and about ninety minutes later returned with a marlin. He left the next day but was made an honorary member of the Tuna Club.

In the Bait Box, William Wrigley Jr., having had a bluefin tuna on his line for forty-five minutes before losing it, attempted to illustrate the fish's great size by extending his arms to either side, then gave up. "No, you couldn't measure that tuna that way," he is quoted as saying. "You would have to start at the corner of the block and pace off the distance." Here, over the years, a distinguished cadre of dedicated anglers gathered. To name a few there were Jimmy Jump, Robert C. Mankowski, Zane Grey, George C. Thomas III, moviemakers Mack Sennett, Cecil B. and William C. de Mille, Hal E. Roach, William Farnum, Charles Chaplin, Jack Coogan, and Stan Laurel (of Laurel and Hardy fame); President Herbert Hoover, General

Harry Kellar (right), America's premier magician and dean of American Magicians, poses with 226-pound marlin swordfish he caught off Catalina September 9, 1918, qualifying him for membership in Catalina's Tuna Club. Captain S. Warren holds the gaff. Photograph was taken at the end of the Pleasure Pier.

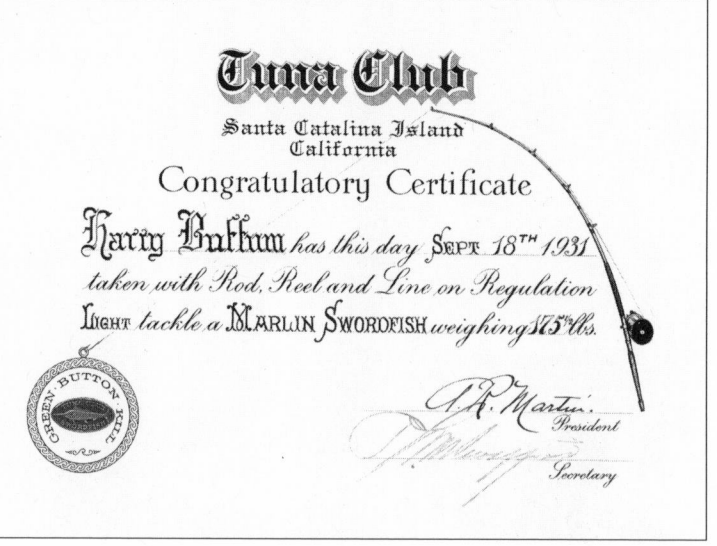

This Tuna Club document certifies that Harry Buffum took a 175½-pound marlin swordfish on regulation light tackle September 18, 1931.

The author's father, Harry Buffum, fights a marlin swordfish off Catalina Island in 1931.

Caught on light tackle off the east end of Catalina, September 18, 1931, by Harry Buffum, this 175½-pound marlin swordfish took two hours, thirty-five minutes to land. On the left is the charter boatman, Captain Harry Warner.

George S. Patton Jr., Charles S. Jones, Gifford Pinchot and, not least, for he looms brightly in my memory, the late Watts L. Richmond. It was Richmond of the Botany Woolen Mill who would growl a greeting that struck a youthful me as uproariously funny: "Hello, Bud. You got any sand or grit in your belly button?"

For a short period, America's premier magician, Harry Kellar, was a club member, qualifying for active membership on September 9, 1918, when he took a 226-pound marlin on regulation heavy tackle. My father, Harry Buffum, took a 213-pound marlin on heavy tackle on October 6, 1930, off the island's east end, earning the club's gold button and active membership. I was on the boat. Except for the excitement of the capture, my memory of it is foggy. I was nine years old and seasick, a malady I've blessedly outgrown.

No account of the clubhouse is complete without mention of its late beloved manager, Percy West, a gracious and tactful man who was invariably attired in a business suit and flat-crowned straw hat. West served the club for thirty-one years, from 1917 until his death in 1948. How clearly, as a youngster in the late 1920s and '30s, accompanying my father on his fishing quests, do I remember the kindness bestowed on me by West and by Emmett Bar, the club's Filipino houseboy. For one thing, Emmett shamelessly flattered me by his enthusiastic reception of a couple of card tricks I'd learned from Jose Riojas. "Do it again," Emmett would urge, but I always begged off. My mentor, Jose, taught me never to repeat a trick during a performance because an audience might catch on as to how it was done. There is no magic without mystery.

West and Emmett permitted me to use the big, handsome brass telescope that was mounted on a polished wood tripod at the bay side of the club's main hallway. Many an hour was spent peering through this great glass, searching out incoming boats to see if they were flying one of the club flags that proclaimed a catch of marlin, broadbill, or tuna. At other times I'd spy on yachts in the bay, hoping to catch sight of such celebrities as Stan Laurel or Charlie Chaplin. I idolized people who made me laugh. I still do.

During that period the great sport fisherman, George C. Thomas III, provided me and others with a chuckle. Thomas was particularly fond of Catalina sand dabs, those succulent little bottom fish that live at a depth of 200 to 300 feet in commu-

PHOTOGRAPH FROM *HISTORY OF THE TUNA CLUB*, 1948

The late beloved Percy West, manager-host of the Tuna Club for twenty-nine years until his death in 1947, was appointed to his position in 1918. A memoriam said that West was "the embodiment of gracious kindliness, tactful courtesy and complete selflessness," and that "he had a boundless capacity for honest friendship." The straw boater was almost constantly his headgear.

nities called "holes" by anglers. Thomas had a flag with the image of a sand dab on it. Whenever he caught "a mess" of these culinary delights, he flew this flag in the place of honor usually reserved for one of the larger fish flags. It was amusing because sand dab fishing has to be the least sporty kind of angling. You simply unreel into the depths a great length of fish line with a leader on the end outfitted with half a dozen or more baited hooks and a heavy lead sinker. If you are over the hole – its location traditionally and zealously kept secret from other fishermen – the sand dabs begin nibbling at the bait, usually small pieces of squid. You wait patiently until you think a good catch of them has built up, then you reel in. There is not much fight in them. If your line becomes too heavy or active, chances are you have caught a small sand shark or some fish other than a sand dab.

Comedian Stanley Laurel (center), of Laurel and Hardy cinema fame, strikes a friendly pose in late 1930s with Joe Deeble (left) and Richard Buffum, boyhood pals. Tuna Club manager Percy West peers over Laurel's shoulder.

Sand dabs are curious appearing flat fish. I am told that they begin their lives with their eyes placed properly, that is, one on either side of the head. Soon a bizarre thing happens, caused by constantly lying on the same side on sandy bottoms. The downside eye moves around to the upside, to lie beside the other eye. When cleaning sand dabs, I cut off their heads. To serve a whole cooked sand dab on a plate with that pair of eyes staring up at you like some weird Virgil Partch cartoon character is disconcerting, I think. At any rate, the delicate, sweet flavor of freshly caught sand dabs fried in butter or olive oil is unsurpassed.

We hardly ever visit the island without motoring out on a windless dawn to drift fish over one of our favorite sand dab holes. The hush of early morning, the stillness of it, is important. Sand dabs stop biting when the breeze ruffles the sea. A boat drifts too fast for their sedentary habits. Morning stillness has another important aspect: simply being on the water at this time of day, barely drifting with the engine turned off and the solemn bulk of the island towering above the placid sea, can be a sublime, even reverential experience. If there are clouds above the easterly horizon, and there frequently are, the rising sun pierces them with golden shafts of light to the sea. Then you expect to see a god descend.

43   Glory Years

When the fish is first hooked if he fights deeply and slowly, work him as hard and fast as you can. The slower he works the faster you should work. The faster he works the easier you must take him. When he is slow never give him an inch of line unless your refusal to let him have it would break it.

ERNEST HEMINGWAY, in *American Big Game Fishing*

During the Tuna Club's formative period, selection of presidents and vice presidents was based upon the weight of the tuna they had taken. The angler who caught the heaviest fish became president; vice presidential positions were determined in order of decreasing poundage from first to eighth vice president. By virtue of his 183-pounder, C.F. Holder was the first president. The position of "correspondence secretary" was awarded the member who had caught the largest number of fish, the first being Edward Doran, who caught eighteen tuna in 1898. The treasurer's post, initially held by Clifford Scudder, went to the angler who had the longest fight before bringing in his fish.

Holder wrote to every angler friend he could think of, inviting them to visit Catalina and take part in the newly found sport. By the end of July 1898, the club had twenty-four members who had taken a tuna of 100 pounds or more on rod and reel with a line no stronger than twenty-four-thread, these being the requirements of membership. Several years later membership had grown into the hundreds.

Sometime during the early 1900s (the date is unclear, since club records were destroyed in the 1915 fire), this quixotic method of "electing" club officers was abandoned in favor of choosing them by vote of the membership. As a practical matter, even an experienced angler did not catch a record tuna every month, or even every year.

Holder remained president of the fledgling club until 1899 when Colonel C.P. Morehouse of Pasadena became its second president after catching a record 251-pound bluefin tuna. It was captured with early official tackle, consisting of (according to club rules adopted in 1898) a wood rod not shorter than six feet nine inches overall, including the butt. The tip was at least five feet in length and weighed no more than sixteen ounces. The line was twenty-four-thread linen with a maximum breaking strength when dry not to exceed sixty-six pounds. Such linen line was known as Cuttyhunk, having originated in Cuttyhunk, Massachusetts. The reel was the old-style "knuckle-buster," with a rigid handle and no built-in mechanical drag.

Colonel Morehouse's great tuna established a rod and reel record that stood for eighty-four years until October 4, 1983, when a Newport Beach angler, Jim Slater, took a 363½-pound bluefin on rod and reel and eighty-pound test Dacron line at Osborne Bank, some six nautical miles south of Santa Barbara Island. Slater's

The glory days! This five-ton catch of albacore was taken during a half-day of fishing with rod and reel off Catalina in 1902. The fish then were considered inedible owing to bloody flesh (the flesh turns white upon cooking), so they were fed to the sea lions and sharks.

record still stands at this writing. The capture was a memorable one, coming at a time when bluefin tuna were scarce in these waters. News of his catch electrified the angling fraternity.

The Tuna Club remains a fortress of tradition. Its underlying philosophy of conservation and its regulations (aimed at giving a fighting fish a sporting chance at freedom) have not changed substantially in more than a century. For example, old-fashioned twisted linen lines that must be dried by winding them on big open spools after use, lest they mildew and rot, continue to be accepted and used. The club retains a bank of these line dryers in a locker room. Official breaking strength of these lines, which range from six to twenty-four-thread, is from sixteen to sixty-six pounds. Fish caught with these lines still qualify anglers for a class of membership.

Monofilament line has been partially accepted. This type of fishing line is barred by club regulations while trolling for big game fish because it stretches, giving the angler an added advantage over the fish. However, monofilament line up to twenty-pound test was authorized, beginning in 1967, for use with a rod and reel. Albacore, yellowtail, white sea bass, and dolphin (the fish, not the mammal) may be caught on monofilament. Another modern innovation, braided Dacron lines of various breaking strengths, is now recognized for use. Fiberglass fishing rods, instead of wood or split bamboo, are acceptable as long as they meet strict weight requirements. Technological change in tackle has been adopted cautiously, while traditional tackle is still respected. Personally I find this comforting because it recognizes an historical continuum. Such a virtue is all too often disregarded by our contemporary culture, to its detriment.

The universally favored Tuna Club rod was split bamboo until shortly after World War II. The rod goes back as far as I can remember, and even farther back to

Avalon taxidermist C.B. Parker, in his Avalon studio in 1912, displays the large variety of fish of the period.

Dr. Holder's time. It was generally made of Tonkin cane, originally from the northern part of Vietnam and used also for ski poles. Expertly tapered lengths of this cane, pie-shaped in cross sections, were joined with glue and wrapped snugly together with bands of silk thread. Guides for the fishing line — small, graduated in size, footed hoops of German silver, with agate interiors — were attached to the rod by more tightly wound silk thread around the guides' bottom projections. The finished rod was then highly varnished, and was a beautiful thing to behold. A turned wood butt, usually of lignum vitae and fitted with a metal reel seat, was connected to the rod with ferrule and socket, thus completing the outfit (interview with John Doughty, J.D.'s Big Game Tackle, Balboa Island).

Until the late 1930s, split bamboo fishing rods for big saltwater game fish, along with reels, lines, and other necessary paraphernalia, were priced beyond the financial reach of the average angler. This is not to say that serviceable big game fish rods at fairly modest prices were not beginning to be manufactured by tackle companies such as Bristol of the Horton Manufacturing Company, South Bend, and Montague. Fiberglass rod manufacturing started in 1948, first using solid glass bonded with resins, then hollow tubular glass construction.

Nonetheless, the truly fine cane rods that I have described were the result of a hands-on craft practiced by a few talented individuals. This was an era when the

word tuna was almost synonymous nationwide with Catalina waters (*The Salt Water Sportsman* magazine, June 8, 1939). I recall one fine rod maker I visited with my father in the mid-1930s, whose dusty workshop was in an old barn on the outskirts of Los Angeles. His name was Roy Shaver, and he was a Tuna Club member and its historian at the time. His primary source of income came from the *Los Angeles Times,* where he worked as a copy editor. The New York Hardware and Trading Company in downtown Los Angeles also offered fine custom-made rods created by their craftsmen, along with reels, reel repairs, and other fishing appurtenances. It was a favorite gathering place for Los Angeles Tuna Club members, according to Paul Albrecht of Long Beach, a collector of antique rods.

In Holder's time, a variety of woods were used to make big game rods: noibwood, greenheart, ironwood, and lancewood. Today these old rods are prized collector's items, along with the old single-action direct-drive reels with rigid handles and a leather thumb brake. Also collectible are later, more mechanically sophisticated reels by vom Hofe, Zwarg, Meek, Leonard, Mills, Shakespeare, and Pflueger, according to Thornton E. Ibbetson, reel collector, Long Beach. Reels made by Edward and Julius vom Hofe of New York were highly favored by Tuna Club anglers into the 1940s. The company was founded in 1867. The earlier ones were sturdy, carefully machined mechanisms of German silver, brass, and Bakelite, some with a rosewood knob on the handle.

Club member W.C. Boschen of New York City, with the help of Captain George Farnsworth, perfected the idea of using a star drag on game fishing reels. A star drag is a star-shaped device mounted next

The first broadbill sword-fish landed with rod and reel — 355 pounds — was taken by W.C. Boschen in 1913.

to the handle that permits an angler to adjust and slow the revolutions of the reel's spool by mechanical pressure, thus constraining a running fish. The early primitive thumb brake served a similar purpose. Julius vom Hofe wanted to name the improved reel after Boschen but the latter demurred, and a compromise was reached by naming the fine reel the "B-Ocean." Boschen's prowess as a broadbill swordfish and tuna angler was legendary during his lifetime. He and his captain, Farnsworth, spent weeks and months cruising the channel off Catalina, searching for broadbill fins on the sea's surface. To Boschen and his captain go the honor of landing the first broadbill (the true swordfish) on rod and reel. The year was 1913; the fish weighed 355 pounds.

No one would deny that big game fish angling from 1898 on into the 1940s was more strenuous and arduous than it is today. Slowing the rapidly diminishing line on a spool by judicious thumb pressure on the "brake" — a flap of heavy leather mounted on a cross bar set between the sides of the reel — while a big tuna charged through the water was not for the digitally weak. A tuna is capable of swimming freely at fifty-five miles an hour!

It was then the rule, rather than the exception, for the angler to have his hand bandaged after the rough treatment it received during the play for the fish. The injuries early anglers sustained, along with blistered thumbs, were caused by the old rigid-handled reels whacking them as they whirled around. The mechanics that cause a reel's spool to rotate without turning the handle were not yet in place.

A section of the Hotel Metropole porch was locally known as the "Tuna Hospital." Injured anglers reposing there impatiently waited for the opportunity to go fishing anew, even if it meant new injuries. In those early days the club had its own "surgeon," Dr. H.H. Pease, then the holder of a black sea bass record. One early angler played a fish for five hours, only to drop senseless in the boat as the fish came to gaff. Another Tuna Club member dislocated his arm during a long struggle with a mighty tuna.

This advertisement in the *Catalina Islander* newspaper, Wednesday, April 13, 1932, pictures a vom Hofe reel with star drag inward of the handle. Interestingly, the old leather thumb brake was retained.

44 Fly a Kite

During the last few years a greater development still has taken place in the
capture of exceptionally large fish — sharks, swordfish, tuna, etc. — running
up to weights of several hundred pounds and now known under the name
of big-game fishing. This fishing was inaugurated as a separate branch of the
sport by the Tuna Club of Santa Catalina.

ENCYCLOPEDIA BRITANNICA, 1946 edition

The vast congregations of big game fishes in southern California waters are so
diminished now it is hard to believe that less than a century ago, bluefin tuna made
Catalina their year-round habitat. Avalon Bay was so full of them a person needed
but a skiff and bait to hook one. Albacore also abounded. Early photographs show
Avalon anglers proudly posing before displays of dozens of albacore, caught in a
mere few hours. Those red-fleshed (until cooked) fish, now highly prized for sushi
and sold canned as the finest tuna, were originally believed to be inedible and were
dumped off the island's coast to feed local sea lions and sharks.

Zane Grey, the popular western author whose pueblo-like former home stands
near the chimes tower, told of the summer of 1917 in his *Tales of Fishes,* published in
1919 by Harper & Brothers, New York. "Barracuda and white sea bass showed up in
great schools; the ocean appeared to be full of albacore; yellowtail began to strike all
along the island's shores, even in the bay of Avalon.... In August, bluefin tuna
surged in school after school, in vast numbers; and in September returned the marlin or roundbill swordfish, that royal-purple swashbuckler of the Pacific" appeared
in abundance. The cause, Grey said,

> was a favorable season when the sardines and anchovies came to the island in
> incalculable numbers. Acres and acres of these little bait fish drifting helplessly
> to and fro, back and forth with the tides, from Seal Rocks to the west end....
>
> Albacore feeding on the surface raise a thin, low, white line of water or mul-
> titudes of slight, broken splashes. Tuna raise a white wall, tumbling and spout-
> ing along the horizon; and it is a sight not soon to be forgotten by a fisherman.
> Near at hand a big school of feeding tuna is a thrilling spectacle. They move
> swiftly, breaking water as they smash after the little fish, and the roar can be
> heard quite a distance. The wall of white water seems full of millions of tiny,
> glinting fish, leaping frantically from the savage tuna.

It required nearly fanatic dedication and steely determination not to succumb to
bleak despair, not to mention the expenditure of ample time and money, to earn the
coveted Tuna Club buttons awarded to those who caught on rod and reel the great
game fish: broadbill, marlin, white and black sea bass, tuna, yellowtail, albacore, and

dolphin fish. William Boschen was such an angler, astounding even his fellow anglers by his dogged hunt for bluefin tuna, using the club's prescribed regulation tackle. George C. Thomas III said that Boschen lost 500 big tuna in one season "simply because the line he used would not stand the fish's first run and Tuna Club rules forbade the use of anything heavier.

"Farnsworth, who was Boschen's boatman at the time, tells me that they would lose as many as a dozen hooks a day, and they never succeeded in stopping a single fish," Thomas noted in *American Big Game Fishing*, published by the Derrydale Press. "I have seen schools of tuna at Catalina where individuals would weigh over 500 pounds apiece, and have hooked some well over the 200-pound mark with always the same result." (Because of the depth of the waters surrounding Catalina, well over 100 fathoms, sounding, hooked fishes generally got away.)

Thomas, who was firmly convinced that 800-pounders were among the fish in the great schools, said he had tried loose drags and tight ones, as well as all sorts of maneuvers with the boat, but had never landed a tuna weighing more than 163 pounds. He believed the rods and reels were adequate for the fight, but the line was too small. Perhaps, he wrote wistfully in 1935, when the big tuna return to California waters, the Tuna Club will legalize heavier line for taking them. After World War II, when reliable linen line became difficult to obtain, Thomas got his wish. Dacron braided line with an approved maximum breaking strength of eighty pounds was officially accepted by the club.

I have pondered the origin of the admonition, "Go fly a kite." I like to pretend it began with Captain Farnsworth, who flew plenty of them while angling for tuna, first a box kite, then a flat one with cross sticks. Sometime in the early 1900s, recalling his fascination with kite flying as a youth in northern California, Farnsworth hit upon the idea of trolling for bluefin tuna by flying a kite, adroitly maneuvering his

Western author Zane Grey (left), whose house was on Avalon's western ridge near the Bell Tower, poses with the 415-pound broadbill swordfish he caught in 1920; the charter boatman, Captain Sid Boerstler, holds the gaff.

fishing boat to keep the kite aloft. The kite's line was tied to the angler's fishing line just above the leader with a piece of easily broken thread so that after a strike, the kite would be freed and fall into the water, to be retrieved later. The kite was flown to leeward behind the boat but not over the wake, at an altitude of several hundred feet. With careful attention to wind direction, the kite caused a hook baited with a trussed up flying fish to skip over the surface of the sea.

"The best place to put it [the kite] is just behind the leaders of the school, for it is there that the largest fish will be found," according to Thomas, who later used

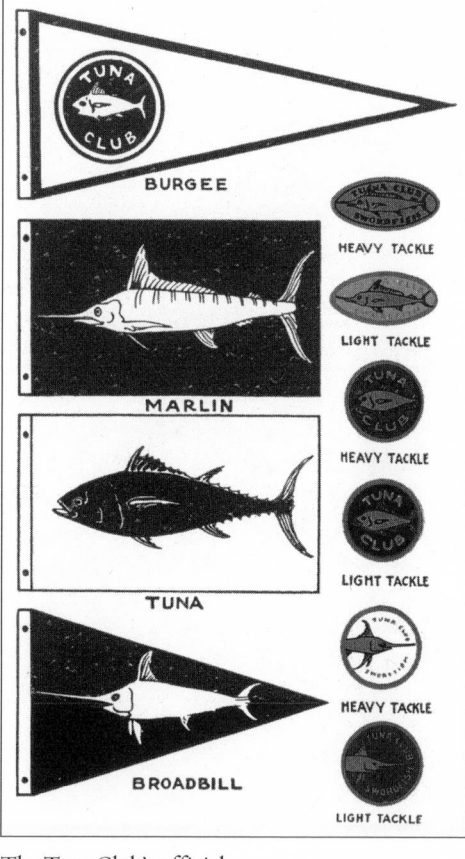

COURTESY TUNA CLUB COLLECTION

The Tuna Club's official boat flags and buttons are depicted here.

Farnsworth as the primary captain on his boat. "When properly handled, it is small wonder that tuna go wild over this amazing replica of a crippled flying fish."

Farnsworth succeeded in keeping his kite-flying technique a secret until 1911, but began to have misgivings about his success while his colleagues were having poor luck. So on July 4 of that year he cruised into Avalon Bay with a kite trolling a bait and flying an American flag. Farnsworth's kite innovation was soon adopted by other boatmen on the Pleasure Pier.

Other contrivances designed to skip bait convincingly over the sea have been tried or invented by Tuna Club members and boatmen on Catalina waters. The outrigger, a long flexible bamboo pole (today usually made of fiberglass or aluminum) was first used at Catalina around 1909. The outrigger extends over the water from the side or sides (pairs are the norm) of the vessel, with the fishing line lightly clipped to a release pin from its tip.

Before outriggers and prior to kites, anglers used sleds, a kind of small raft measuring about one by three feet, which kept the trolled bait skipping seductively over the waves. Small parachutes and even weather balloons have been tried, but the most practical was the outrigger, which required no wind, followed by the kite.

For sentimental reasons, I favor the kite. As a boy I was acquainted with Farnsworth, and my dad adored him. Farnsworth was a great man to those who fished these waters, for his piscatorial knowledge was vast.

I have in my possession a tuna kite of red Chinese silk, cut twenty-seven inches square and reinforced with heavier material at the corners and in the middle to accommodate the sticks, crossed at the center. The kite was flown from the center point. The kite was given to me by Mrs. Parker Pence who told me that she made dozens of them for her husband when he was a charter boatman on the Pleasure Pier. I've never flown the kite. I keep it as a treasured talisman to produce the magical day when legendary leaping tuna return in vast schools because of a rejuvenated marine ecosystem. Some day, perhaps, some day soon. An increasingly aware populace is gradually moving in that direction.

Marine biologists have established a definite migration pattern between Japan and Alta and Baja California for both bluefin tuna and albacore. The great bulk of bluefin are spawned off the large island of Japan and migrate into our waters only after reaching an age of about two years. Until a few years ago, the negative impact of commercial fishing on bluefin and albacore in Japanese and trans-Pacific waters was extremely heavy. Across the Pacific, hundreds of miles of small-mesh, drift gill nets, designed to catch squid, entangled quantities of everything else that swam —tuna, seals, albacore, dolphins, porpoises, swordfish, whales. Fortunately, this mindless resource depredation was halted in early 1990 through a treaty negotiated by the U.S. State Department with Japan and surrounding Asian countries.

Furthermore, concerned sportsmen, including those of the Tuna Club, the voting citizenry, and enlightened commercial interests, rallied together in 1990 to convince the California State Legislature to exclude gill netting within three miles of the offshore islands and mainland coasts. The ban became effective in 1992. Another contributing deterrent to the return of these pelagic game fish is being reversed. This was the depleted food chain. Unrestrained commercial seining before and during World War II nearly wiped out the California sardine, while anchovies were seriously diminished by the demands of the fertilizer and pet food markets.

The National Marine Fisheries Service has relieved state fish and game departments along the Pacific coast of the responsibility of regulating the commercial anchovy harvest. Reduction of anchovies for fertilizer and pet food has been banned. Regulations on the harvesting of the anchovy biomass have been imposed. Harvest quotas on sardines are being enforced by the California Department of Fish and Game. The California sardine is now making a comeback, as is the anchovy. With an adequate food supply, tuna and albacore are returning in growing numbers, although still not resembling those halcyon days of fifty years ago and more. Given certain other favorable environmental conditions such as the proper degree of water temperature and water clarity, game fish should return to these waters, again bringing pleasure and excitement to those fortunate anglers who hook them. Their eventual return will mark a cycle responding to some mysterious natural order and not to any man-made schedule.

Even so, Captain Farnsworth, a dedicated student of the habits of fishes, offered a schedule, claiming that "the big cycle of the tuna comes each 53 years." If correct, there will come a glorious day when a jubilant angler will urge his fellows: "Come on, let's go fly a kite. The bluefin have returned in big schools at long last!"

45 Hamilton Cove

As we walked out to see the cove where we were to live we stopped atop the hill to eat our lunch and looked down into the canyon at the house. It was surrounded by boats in drydock. The old ramp that used to run the seaplanes down into the water is now used to haul boats up into drydock.

EMA I. RITTER, *Life at the Old Amphibian Airport* (1970)

Despite Holder's dislike of hand lines, we keep one on board. Ours is carried on a wooden, drum-shaped holder made from dowel rods inserted between discs of pine. Simple handles extending from each side aid in reeling in the heavy line. A torpedo-shaped lead weight, located about a third of the way along the line, keeps the feather lure below the water's surface and prevents the line from fouling any vessel that passes too close to our stern. Sometimes we catch a bonito; more often nothing at all. But hope springs eternal, and putting out the hand line has become a rite of passage while we navigate the island's coast, avoiding the inshore kelp beds. If we ever got a strike from an albacore or yellowtail, we would be overcome by dis-belief and joy.

We are trolling westerly now, heading toward the White's Landing area where this circumnavigation began. We have passed Casino Point and immediately beyond, Descanso Bay, once the site of the grand Hotel St. Catherine. Soon, in less than a quarter of a mile, we come to a multimillion dollar development of villas built up from the sea on steeply graded hillsides. The red-roofed dwellings appear to be stacked on top of each other, creating a highly visible landmark rivaling the Casino when seen from the sea.

The cove at the base of this mega-condominium project retains its early name of Hamilton Beach although the natural valley has been so altered by heavy earth-moving equipment that it bears little resemblance to its original appearance. The changes began in 1970 when the Balboa Bay Club of Newport Beach announced plans to build a twenty-five-acre complex of 105 residential units with small boat storage and offshore moorings. Work on the project was halted several times, leaving half-finished structures on the stark, steeply graded hillsides. Nearly twenty-five years after it was started, with input from several developers and finan-cial institutions, the enterprise was completed by the BCE Development Company, a subsidiary of Bell Canada Enterprises, which assumed the stalled project in 1987. A total of 185 villas have been constructed on the site. Residents of the villas oper-ate small gasoline-powered carts that transport them to and from Avalon along a scenic road past Descanso Bay and the Casino. (Avalon in general is highly popu-lated with these so-called golf carts, for few automobiles and trucks are allowed on its streets). At this writing, the BCE Development Company has departed from the scene; the Santa Catalina Island Company (SCICo) continues to own the land while villa units are owned by individual purchasers.

Observant mariners passing Hamilton Cove can see a concrete ramp extending from the sea, across the narrow beach ending on what remains of the original valley floor. The ramp is a reminder of Hamilton Cove's past when the natural valley contained an amphibian seaplane airport, officially dedicated in 1931. Its terminal, designed by Malcolm Renton, incorporated both decorative and unglazed tiles produced at Pebbly Beach from high-quality natural clay materials.

The airport was operated by Wilmington-Catalina Air Line, Ltd., later Catalina Air Transport, under the umbrella of the SCICo. In the 1930s, propeller-driven, ten-passenger Douglas Dolphin amphibians took off in a welter of spray from the channel in front of the Catalina Steamship Terminal in Wilmington, soaring above Terminal Island and over the San Pedro Channel. The ocean was their landing field upon reaching the island. After splashdown they lowered their wheels and taxied up the concrete ramp to a turntable, similar to those used in railroad roundhouses. This turnaround, adjacent to the Spanish-style terminal building, was an innovation in aeronautics. The idea for it was conceived by Philip K. Wrigley, a lieutenant in the Naval Air Service in World War I, who chose the small valley for a seaplane port. A bus carried passengers over a narrow winding road to Avalon. The boat-hulled seaplanes were specially designed for the airline by aeronautical industrialist Donald Douglas Sr., a yachtsman and friend of P.K. Wrigley. Douglas frequently sailed to the island on his seventy-five-foot motor schooner *Endymion,* designed by the late Nicholas S. Potter and built of wood in 1930 at the Wilmington Boat Works.

Commercial flight to Catalina has an illustrious history of "firsts," even though it was fraught with problems: landing on the open sea, the whims of weather, loading and unloading passengers without mishap, the generally mountainous shoreline. After Philip Wrigley solved most of those problems with his unique, small Hamilton Cove amphibian port, increasing the size of the planes to make the operation profitable posed additional problems. The size element made for some bizarre solutions, but they were inventive nevertheless, and we'll approach them a little later.

The first commercial flight to the island was launched in 1919 by Sidney Chaplin, brother and business manager of the legendary silver screen comedian Charlie

COURTESY DOUG BOMBARD

Today obliterated by stacks of condominiums, Hamilton Beach was the amphibian Catalina Airport before World War II, captured in this postcard view. The bull's-eye at the top of the ramp is Philip K. Wrigley's turntable on which the planes were reversed. This landing is approximately 0.4 miles westerly of Casino Point in Avalon.

Chaplin, and his pilot, A.C. Burns. Only three passengers could be carried at one time in this light, flimsy biplane rigged with pontoons. Landing in Avalon Bay, the plane would taxi to the beach. The venture was terminated after only two months because of the high cost of operation. Burns tried again on his own in 1920 with a Curtis F flying boat and a franchise to carry star route mail. The mail amounted to two sacks a day at most. When Sears and Roebuck issued its catalogues, extra flights had to be scheduled to handle the extra weight and volume. This enterprise lasted for about one year.

The Goodyear Company attempted a short-lived flight with its pony blimp, and from 1920 to 1931, two companies, Pacific Marine Airways and Western Air Express, operated small seaplanes that ran up on Avalon beach. Again, the high cost of operation and limited passenger capacity forced the operations to close.

Sidney Chaplin and his pilot, A.C. Burns (right), launched the first commercial flight to the island in 1919 in this three-passenger biplane.

Everyone was aware that flight to Catalina was feasible because Glenn Luther Martin, age twenty-five, had proved it on the morning of May 10, 1912, a typical cool, overcast spring day in southern California. Martin made his historic flight in a black business suit, white shirt, and conservative necktie, with a compass strapped on one knee, a barometer on the other, and an inflated bicycle inner tube wrapped around his shoulders "just in case." Then, in the open cockpit of his Model 12 bi-plane fitted with pontoons, Martin took off down Newport Bay, dipping his wing to well-wishers gathered on Balboa Island. Martin headed south over the Balboa peninsula, the sound of his sixty-horsepower Hall-Scott engine fading over the sea. Thirty-seven minutes later, after averaging fifty-three and one-half miles per hour, Martin eased his plane down into Avalon Bay and taxied to the beach where he was cheered by most of the residents of Avalon, and a group of Shriners attending a convention on the island.

There was only one minor mishap to the plane, which had been nicknamed the "Copper Kettle." As it was taxiing toward the beach, one of its pontoons was punctured by a rock. A visiting yachtsman, Skip Charles, managed to make a temporary repair. On the beach, Martin had a sandwich and milk and refueled his engine from a borrowed water pitcher before taking off for his return to Balboa. Despite a loosening of the jury-rigged pontoon patch, Martin landed on Newport Bay without a problem, establishing a hydroplane record for the first recorded over-water, round-trip flight and becoming a national celebrity.

Thirty-four years later, when the technology of flight had become increasingly sophisticated and the era of large planes had made the Hamilton Cove airport obsolete, two airlines began operations to Catalina, which had been virtually without air transportation since World War II. One was United Airlines to the Airport-in-the-Sky, the other was Avalon Air Transport, headquartered at the Long Beach Municipal Airport. For three years Avalon Air also operated out of Los Angeles and Burbank Airports. At the height of the summer season the planes made as many as eighteen flights a day at the competitive price of thirteen dollars round-trip. Avalon Air also won a bid to fly the U.S. mail and flew light freight between the mainland and Avalon, including documents and small repair items. Heavy freight was transported by barge.

Recollections of Catalina's aeronautical history from 1946 to 1949 were related to us by Don R. Beaver, who served as United Airlines reservation and passenger agent and manager of the Avalon operation. Avalon Air Transport had an office in the front section of the Waikiki Bar and Hotel at the corner of Crescent and Metropole, where Beaver was in charge. Here, baggage and ticketing were handled. The baggage was taken by company personnel in handcarts to the Pleasure Pier. Passengers would board a shore boat at the pier and were ferried to a large float anchored near the mouth of Avalon Bay, where one of Avalon Air's four Grumman Goose amphibian aircraft waited to fly them across the channel.

"The operation went quite smoothly when conditions were ideal, but there were many times when the roughness of the water was such that removal of passengers was an exercise in strength and faith," Beaver said.

In 1948, the company purchased two Sikorsky S-43s, each capable of carrying twenty-eight passengers. The planes proved to be too large to dock at the float in Avalon Bay, so an enormous pontoon float with two huge ramps, one at either end, was constructed in San Pedro, towed across the channel, and anchored in Descanso Bay, west of the Casino. The plane, engines roaring, would climb up the ramp, unload and load passengers, then return to the sea down the other ramp. A small ticket office and quarters for employees were built on a portion of this huge float. Passengers were taken to and from this inventive structure by shore boat from the Pleasure Pier.

Yes, there were accidents. A particularly dramatic one was witnessed by Beaver while accompanying a departing load of passengers in a shore boat. It involved Captain Robert J. Hanley, who had amassed thousands of hours in amphibians prior to joining Avalon Air Transport and was one of the first aeronautical engineers to graduate from Massachusetts Institute of Technology (MIT). Upon splashing down, Hanley's Sikorsky S-43 struck a submerged boat's mast, which ripped a hole in the hull about eight feet in diameter. Almost immediately the plane began to sink. Hanley gave the engines full throttle and wallowed toward the old Hamilton Beach seaplane ramp. "It took every bit of power for the large [over eight tons] wounded amphibian to reach the shoreline. With wheels lowered, a great roar and smoking engines, it lumbered up the ramp with cascades of water streaming from the hole in the hull," Beaver recalled.

When the plane reached the old turntable, one wheel broke through its venerable timbers; its wing tip struck the utility shed and spun the plane around, collapsing it flat on its belly. The twenty-eight badly shaken passengers spent the night in Avalon. Nonetheless, Hanley flew the plane, its hull temporarily patched with aircraft canvas, to Long Beach Airport. She was rebuilt and continued service to the island until flights were discontinued in 1949. After that there was a hiatus on amphibian travel to the island until 1953 when another company, Catalina Air Transport, launched an astonishing operation. A floating walkway in three fifty-foot sections, with a cross float on the end, extended out into Avalon Bay from the head of the Pleasure Pier. The float and walkway, which had no railings, were constructed by an island abalone diver to accommodate a forty-six-passenger flying boat, according to Joseph E. (Jay) Guion, who flew on the big bird nicknamed "Mother Goose." She was a Sikorsky VS44A, with a wingspan of 124 feet.

Glenn L. Martin takes off from Avalon Bay in 1912 in his Model 12 biplane on the return flight to Balboa, the first recorded over-water round-trip flight.

Docking Mother Goose at the float's end entailed the use of a power launch with a rubber-padded bow. First the launch would tow the big amphibian's tail to the float, where the towline was cleated. Then it nudged in the plane's nose. Sometimes, in a strong wind, it required more than a half-dozen men hauling on dock lines, nose and tail, to bring the plane to the float. Although no passengers were lost overboard embarking or debarking along the often unsteady walkway, several baggage carts tumbled into the water, Guion said. Winter storms made docking Mother Goose impossible, so she flew only during calmer summer months.

To the relief of many yachtsmen in Avalon Bay, this harbor "airfield" was abandoned in 1959. That same year, veteran pilot Hanley founded Catalina Channel Airlines, which flew between the island's Pebbly Beach to the east of Avalon Bay, and the Long Beach Municipal Airport. An arrangement between Hanley and the SCICO resulted in the construction of a concrete ramp from the sea leading to a small terminal at Pebbly Beach. Henceforth, all amphibian flights landed there, ending with Frank Strobel's Catalina Flying Boats, established in 1984. This was essentially a freight operation using 1942 Grumman Geese. In addition, more than a half-dozen operators attempted Pebbly Beach flight service. Currently passenger service here is by Island Express helicopter.

Some prominent names in the history of Catalina aviation not previously mentioned were Dick Probert, Justin Dart, Bud Smith (United Airlines captain and mayor and city councilman of Avalon), Dick White, George White, and John Phelps, city of Avalon harbormaster, most of whom had interests in the various companies.

Ultimately, the longest-lived aeronautical ventures were those conceived and instituted by Philip Wrigley: the Hamilton Cove airport, already mentioned, and the currently operational Airport-in-the-Sky. The transition from sea to sky wasn't easy. Wrigley once pointed out: "I felt that if the dreams for the future were to be realized, we would have to have more frequent and faster transportation, and having been in aviation at its inception, I naturally looked to the airplane as the solution. "My father was, of course, of another generation and didn't believe in flying machines, but he had no objections to my trying my ideas out." Philip Wrigley took part of his profits from some earlier aviation investments to start the Wilmington-Catalina Airline in 1931, and continued to underwrite the venture "until it had been demonstrated beyond all doubt that aviation was a proven form of civilian transportation, and had a place in the development of everything in this country."

United Air Lines flew planes to the island for several years, using the Airport-in-the-Sky. A twenty-eight-passenger United DC-3 made the first commercial flight to this mountaintop airport in 1947. Three mountain peaks had been cut away and the valleys filled before World War II to provide a 3,100-foot landing strip for the proposed airport, but it had to be made untenable for enemy use during the war. When the war ended the present air terminal was built on the site. The entire airport facility was financed by the SCICo, without the aid of public funds. The airport was opened to the public in 1959 for the landing of private planes, and is still a popular destination for private pilots.

The Hamilton Beach airport was last used by U.S. Coast Guard planes during World War II. Hamilton Beach fell into disuse after the war. The increased wingspan of postwar amphibians had made it obsolete. The facility at Hamilton Beach was for a while the home of Ema and Hal Ritter of Avalon, who wrote of their idyllic experiences living there in *Life at the Old Amphibian Airport,* privately printed in 1970. The cove had also been used for a while as a boatyard operated by George Gemilere before heavy earth-moving equipment went to work, drastically reshaping the natural valley so that condominiums could perch there.

46 Torqua Discovered

And the end of all our exploring
Will be to arrive where we started
And know the place for the first time.
THOMAS STEARNS ELIOT

We motor our way opposite Gallagher's Beach, a distance of a little over a mile and a half east from Hamilton Cove. Water depth outside the kelp averages a good thirty fathoms. The few moorings at Gallagher's belong to the Inter-Varsity Christian Fellowship's Campus-by-the-Sea, a religious organization which leases from the Santa Catalina Island Company. There is fair anchorage here for three to five vessels in eighteen to twenty feet of water.

Gallagher's Beach and Gallagher's Canyon above it commemorate sheepherder Thomas J. Gallagher, said by his contemporaries to have been something of a hermit who was "very reticent concerning his own life" but was "a man of intelligence who... asked for books and magazines" (Doran 1980). Gallagher built a cabin here in the middle of the nineteenth century, and may have come to Catalina from Santa Cruz Island where a Thomas J. Gallagher was listed among the original Santa Cruz Island Company directors who were intent on developing an offshore ranch there.

At any rate, the reclusive Tom Gallagher lived on Catalina before moving to San Clemente Island where he spent thirty years in a simple home above Gallagher's (or Wilson's) Cove at the north end of that island. He is said to have been among the many evicted from Catalina by James Lick, but that didn't keep him from returning occasionally. Holder, who referred to him as one of the "characters" living on the islands in years gone by, said he saw Gallagher "sailing into Avalon Bay with his poor skiff [with a flour-sack sail], a goat, four or five hens and a dog. These he boarded out until he made up his mind to return [to San Clemente] which he did at night, rowing the skiff the thirty miles," wrote Holder.

About one-third of a mile past Gallagher's Beach is Toyon Bay with nine moorings belonging to the shore's lessee, the Catalina Island Marine Institute. A pier extending from the western side is reserved for the use of the institute. Again, there is fair anchorage in sand for about six boats in 24 to 102 feet of water. Camp Toyon, or Bannings Beach as it is named on topographical maps, is located at the foot of Swain's (Swayne's) Canyon. About a half mile up from the beach in the canyon is a thick, dark clump of trees about thirty feet tall. Their canopy of deep-green foliage is composed of finely divided fern-like leaves. These are Catalina ironwood (*Lyonothamnus floribundus asplenifolius*), an island endemic that the late Ralph Cornell, Los Angeles horticulturist, described as "a plant ancient in the genealogy of development... which seems to be clinging to the last thread of life in the dying stages of its evolution." These ancient trees are also found on Mount Black Jack and above Goat Harbor. The tree, which flowers in June, was named after botanist William S. Lyon, who explored Catalina in 1884 and 1885.

Toyon Bay derives its name from the California Christmas berry (*Photinia arbutifolia* or *Heteromeles arbutifolia*), a plant native to the chaparral belt and a favorite garden shrub. Its autumn profusion of colored berries lends a holiday air to the landscape, and for many years it was shipped from Catalina to the mainland for display and sale during the Yuletide, according to Cornell. The Spanish Californians named this plant toyon in 1848 and used the berries in the preparation of a pleasant-tasting drink, similar to cider, and a pudding. The plant is said to be the source of the name Hollywood, a misnomer because the Christmas berry is not related to the true holly. California Indians used the bright red berries as food, roasting them by tossing them in a basket with hot pebbles or wood coals. After roasting, the berries were boiled, dried, and ground into meal, much as acorns were prepared by other Indian tribes. Later, fishermen utilized toyon bark for tanning sails and nets.

Toyon's canyon bears the name Swain's Canyon on a U.S. Geological Survey topographic map. It is named for Swain Lawson, who came to live here in 1859, operating a thirty-five-foot sailboat all around the island. According to Ernest Windle, Lawson had previously owned three small ships engaged in the whaling and fishing trade near Alaska, but his boats were seized by the Russians during a controversy between Russia and the United States. After his loss, Lawson came south and established a home in one of the picturesque coves on Catalina.

The shore at Toyon has been leased by the Catalina Island Marine Institute (CIMI) since September 1979. It is a private, nonprofit corporation which offers environmental education programs to public and private organizations and educational groups. Marine science topics offered at the institute include ichthyology, invertebrates, plankton, marine algae, and oceanography, as well as snorkeling and hiking, both emphasizing island ecology. In summer, CIMI offers two sea camps, a one-week program for students eight to twelve years of age and a three-week program for young men and women twelve to seventeen.

Toyon is also known as Bannings Beach, because the Banning family used it for occasional outings after acquiring the island in 1892. From 1902 to 1910 the Whittier State School, essentially a military-type reform school, conducted a summer camp called Camp Banning here, with primitive facilities in tents. Apparently the camp served both boys and girls at various times. There were many stories about these youngsters: one year the student body formed a marching band that knew only one song, "The Stars and Stripes Forever." On their weekly trips to Avalon the band would march through town, playing the music over and over.

Subsequent camps were operated here by the YMCA and Boy Scouts of America from Los Angeles. In 1927, the Catalina Island School, a private preparatory school, was established here by Keith Vosburg, who initiated the construction of permanent buildings. The school opened in 1928 and operated until the bombing of Pearl

Harbor in 1941 forced students to move to the mainland to complete the school year. During World War II, Toyon became a high security training camp for the Office of Strategic Service, later to become the Central Intelligence Agency.

After the war, in 1946, Charlie Farrell, a former actor and founder of the Racquet Club in Palm Springs, developed a boat club at Toyon, expending nearly $1 million on improvements. Unsuccessful, the club closed in 1948. Philip K. Wrigley then backed the Catalina Guest Ranch, a dude ranch, where actress Elizabeth Taylor is said to have celebrated her sixteenth birthday. Between 1952 and 1979, various organizations leased the facilities, including a reopened Catalina Island School that was coeducational for a time. Summer programs have included a gymnastic camp, Project Ocean Search with Jean-Michael Cousteau, and John Davidson's musically oriented Singers' Summer Camp.

Immediately west of Toyon, around a high rock outcropping, lies Willow Cove, where a spring-fed creek usually trickles down a rock face in the narrow canyon about a hundred yards from a small, sandy beach. The water flows down the rock through a minute forest of mosses that streak its face. Here we found a small flow of fresh water during the height of the 1978 drought. There are no moorings at Willow Cove, but good anchorage is afforded for about four vessels in ten to forty feet, on a sandy bottom. On going ashore here some years ago in our sixteen-foot, home-built Swampscott rowing dory, *Pooh,* which the *Bird* towed to the island for several seasons, we found the chimney of a house below the spring.

The late Joseph S. Guion, who acquired a boat rental and fishing tackle business (Joe's Rent-A-Boat) on the Pleasure Pier from Pard Mathewson in 1927, told us a story about that house. He said that in 1929 he went exploring ashore here and found the house uninhabited, but all the beds made and "clean plates were in the rack, perfectly housekept." The man who built and owned the house was a free spender, Guion said, and used to throw lavish champagne parties here, bringing guests by speedboat to Willow Cove. He abandoned the house during the Great Depression and was never seen again. The house was gradually ransacked. Today in the cove there are several small buildings belonging to Toyon's lessee.

About three-quarters of a mile westerly of Willow Cove is a place marked Torqua Springs on the charts where, during the 1890s and after, residents of Avalon would row boats to fill barrels with fresh water. The only evidence of water today are seepages along the cliff face above the rocky beach, covered at high tide. In 1912, when Guion, as a youth, was working at a summer camp at nearby White's Landing, he took a skiff to Torqua Springs to obtain drinking water for the camp. At that time, a tunnel for water had been excavated into the cliff and a flume extended from the tunnel to a wooden tank on the rocky beach. From the tank, Guion said, an ordinary garden hose ran out to a mooring where there was a faucet. An enterprising seaman nicknamed Torqua Pete operated a launch, the *Torqua,* from Avalon to the spring, selling the water in Avalon at fifteen cents for five gallons.

Torqua Springs and its facilities have been covered by a landslide, possibly triggered by an earthquake in June of 1915. There was a quake of intensity 8 on the old Mercalli scale, predecessor of the Richter scale, on June 22 of that year. It was centered in the El Centro region and affected an area of nearly 100,000 square miles, according to seismographic records of the Millikan Library at the California Institute of Technology (Cal Tech), Pasadena. Another major quake that might have caused the landslide covering the spring occurred Sunday, April 21, 1918.

"According to Mexican Joe, who has been a resident of Catalina Island for the past forty years, this seismic disturbance was the severest one he has ever experienced," reported the *Islander* newspaper, adding that Hemet and San Jacinto seemed to receive the brunt of the shock.

When Torqua Springs was lost, Torqua Pete, whose proper name was Captain Peter Marelija, ran his launch to island coves such as White's Landing, carrying supplies, mail, and passengers, until his death at age seventy-three in 1932.

We passed Frog Rock, about halfway between Hamilton Cove and Gallagher's Beach, without mentioning the *Samar,* an old, four-masted, 189-foot schooner that moored off Frog Rock in the 1930s. She doubled as a fishing barge and dine-and-dance vessel featuring a four- or five-piece band. Jan Garber and his orchestra played on opening night, and for a time she had slot machines on her poop deck. In the summer she was rigged with fishing racks on her sides. The schooner was purchased by a group of islanders to lease to motion picture companies for use in epic sea dramas of the period such as *Mutiny on the Bounty* (1935), *The Hurricane* (1937), and *The Buccaneer* (1938). Islanders Al Bombard, Art LaShelle, and Joe Guion were among the partners who purchased the *Samar* and leased her.

The *Samar*'s working years under M.F. Asmussen, master, had been in trade between Australia, the Philippines, San Francisco, and San Pedro. Built in 1901 by Hay and Wright (Alexander Hay and E.B. Wright) in their northern California yard at Alameda, she was 710 tons, with a breadth of thirty-six feet, ultimately providing a sizable space for dining and dancing (Doug Bombard and National Maritime Museum, San Francisco). In the end the *Samar* was beached in Baja California and salvaged for firewood.

From Torqua Springs it is but a short run, not more than a half mile, to the White's Landing area. When rounding the easterly point of this coastal indentation, we are careful not to turn inshore too soon, for there is a small reef extending westerly. Rounding this hazard we are in Moonstone Cove, past which we motor slowly along the lines of buoys and pick a mooring off the beach of White's Landing. This vantage point affords a sweeping view up the valley, a particularly lovely place to be when the setting sun etches deep shadows on the hills and Robert Browning's "quiet-colored end of evening smiles" upon us as circumnavigators returned to our place of beginnings.

Those of you who have sailed with us in this book now know that Santa Catalina Island is far more than a microcosm in the sea, but is instead a rich, varied reflection of the macrocosm that was, and is, mainland California. Little remains but to tie up some historical loose ends, these being a rather surprising number of island owners, full and part, some afterwords, and a farewell, predicated on the pleasant assumption that you have managed to travel with us this far, and we have not lost you anchored in some cove along the way, having been lulled into lethargy by sea time, holy calm, and a current of words.

47 They Owned the Island

Broad acres are a patent of nobility; and no man but feels more of a man in the world if he have a bit of ground that he can call his own.

CHARLES DUDLEY WARNER (1870)

In the California of 1822, newly independent of Spain, any citizen, native or naturalized, could request a grant of unoccupied land from the Mexican territorial governor. Lands near the coast were excluded, as were offshore islands. The distant government, while offering little financial aid to its citizens, feared the incursion of foreigners, i.e. non-Mexicans, and was determined to keep them from landing on California shores. Even after secularization in 1833, mission lands could be leased or sold, but the islands and coast remained government property.

Everything was changed in 1838 by an order from Mexico urging the governor to grant islands to responsible Mexican citizens who might ask for them. Preference was to be given to Antonio and Carlos Carrillo of Santa Barbara, who were to have exclusive possession of an island in consideration of their services to California during the revolutionary upheavals of the day. The avowed purpose of the grants, according to H. H. Bancroft, "was not only to settle the islands, but to prevent foreigners from occupying them to the injury of commerce and fisheries."

A number of petitions for coastal lands followed. The Carrillos were given Santa Rosa Island, Andres Castillero was granted Santa Cruz Island, and there were several petitions for Catalina: Thomas Robbins applied for a grant in 1839, John Hailer and James Johnson petitioned "about the year 1839 or 1840," and the island was solicited in 1840 by Louis Vignes and J.M. Ramirez. Ostensibly, the petitioners intended to use the island for agriculture: for grazing sheep or cattle, possibly for vineyards. At the time, the applications were ignored or dismissed. It wasn't until July 4, 1846, in one of his last acts as governor of Mexican California, that Pio Pico granted the Isla de Santa Catalina to Robbins.

THOMAS M. ROBBINS

A seafarer born on Nantucket Island, Massachusetts, Thomas Meader Robbins arrived in California in 1823 as the twenty-two-year-old first officer aboard the eighty-three-ton schooner *Rover*. The ship had left Boston June 5, 1822, arriving in

Honolulu December 23, 1822. Originally owned by her captain, John Rogers Cooper, together with Massachusetts merchants Nathaniel Dorr and William Blanchard, the *Rover* was sold for $9,000 in June 1823, to Luis Arguello, acting governor of Mexican California. The "government vessel" under Cooper and Robbins purchased otter skins gathered by Aleut hunters under contract with the Russians, later trading them at a considerable profit in the Hawaiian Islands and Canton.

In 1826 the *Rover* was renamed the *San Rafael,* and at the end of the year Cooper and Robbins left the ship, probably at the Hawaiian Islands. The following year, 1827, Robbins was master of the 142-ton brig *Waverly,* owned by the government of the Hawaiian Islands. Robbins had succeeded William Goodwin Dana of Santa Barbara as master. After leaving the *Waverly* Robbins became master of the 121-ton American schooner *Guíbale,* then later, master of *El Brillante,* possibly a 100-ton Mexican schooner known to have been on the coast at the time (Bancroft, vol. 3, p. 131). In 1829 Robbins was put in command of the thirty-three-ton schooner *Santa Barbara.* She was built for Carlos Carrillo and William Goodwin Dana and constructed near Santa Barbara at a place later named "La Goleta." Salvage from the American brig *Danube,* wrecked at San Pedro, was used in her construction.

Thomas M. Robbins

Robbins took out papers to become a naturalized Mexican citizen in 1830 and converted to the Catholic religion, necessary prerequisites for his marriage, in 1834, to Encarnacion Carrillo, a daughter of Carlos Carrillo. The marriage eventually produced ten children. About the time of his marriage, Robbins opened a general store in an adobe building near the Santa Barbara waterfront which soon became a favorite rendezvous for captains and supercargoes of the ships lying in port.

"It was," recalled William Heath Davis, "a famous place for hearing stories of adventure from all parts of the world and racy bits of gossip from every part of this country. [Robbins] was generous and liked by everybody. At his table... the captains and supercargoes of vessels were always welcome."

Robbins divided his time between his "store" and the sea, continuing as master of the *Santa Barbara* until 1837 when he took the helm of the eighty-three-ton Mexican government schooner *California,* in the service of Governor Juan B. Alvarado and his associate, Mariano Vallejo. On February 11, 1839, Robbins, who had been made a Mexican naval captain on Alvarado's recommendation, applied to the governor "for the concession of the Island called Santa Catalina." Several years went by before any action was taken on Captain Robbins' petition.

Robbins also petitioned for a grant of the mainland ranch known as "Las Positas," a colloquial term for the little springs located on the one and a half square leagues Robbins requested. Las Positas, together with the adjacent La Calera Ranch later acquired from Robbins' sister-in-law, is today's elegant Hope Ranch Park near Santa Barbara. Robbins was granted Las Positas on July 1, 1846, and Pio Pico granted him Catalina Island three days later in one of his last official acts as Mexican governor. Robbins established a small ranch on the "northern" part of the island, sent over two caretakers, and had a small adobe and wood house built for them. Cattle were shipped to the island and a small garden planted, but the venture lasted only four years, possibly because of Robbins' failing health. In 1850 Robbins sold Catalina to Jose Maria Covarrubias, sold the Santa Barbara house and store to Lewis T. Burton (for whom the area was named Burton Mound), and moved his wife and family to Las Positas ranch.

The removal seems to have been occasioned by an attack of apoplexy (a stroke) that Robbins suffered: he died in 1854, after several years of paralysis, according to an article by Katherine Den Bell in the *Santa Barbara Morning Press,* October 8, 1918. Robbins left an estate valued at $16,422 including the Las Positas property, valued then at $4,000, and "a claim to the whole or part of the Island of Santa Catalina together with a note of Jose M. Covarrubias for $3,000 payable to T.M. Robbins 'deceased' whenever said Covarrubias should sell said island."

JOSE MARIA COVARRUBIAS

Although it has been alleged that Thomas Robbins conveyed the whole of Catalina Island to Jose Maria Covarrubias on August 31, 1850, for the sum of $10,000 (W.W. Robinson 1941, p. 201), Covarrubias owed $3,000 to Robbins when the latter died in 1854, and Robbins remained, according to his estate's inventory submitted to the Santa Barbara County probate court, a claimant to "the whole or part of the island." The confusion is typical of the chaos that reigned after California became part of the United States. For Californians who received land grants under the Mexican regime, it frequently took years to prove the validity of the grants, and a great deal of money to do so. Covarrubias filed his claim in February 1853; his title was confirmed by the U.S. Land Commission in 1855. There was an appeal to the U.S. District Court for the Southern District of California, which was upheld in December 1857. It was not until 1866 that the surveyor general's return was filed, the survey of the island showing 45,825.43 acres. The United States patent followed, issued in favor of Captain Robbins' successor in ownership, Jose Maria Covarrubias.

While all the litigation was transpiring, Covarrubias, the consummate politician, was not idly sitting by. A Frenchman by birth who was fluent in French, Spanish, and English, he had arrived in California in 1834 as a teacher with the Compana Cosmopolita, a colonizing expedition from Mexico led by Jose Maria Hijar and Jose Maria Padres. After 1835 he held many offices of trust, first under the Mexican regime and later under the Americans.

When Covarrubias was granted Mexican citizenship in 1837 he married Maria Carrillo, prudently aligning himself with two of the most respected families in early California: the Picos and Carrillos. Maria was a daughter of Domingo Antonio Carrillo, the grantee of Las Virgenes Ranch near Los Angeles, and Concepcion Pico Carrillo, a sister of Pio and Andres Pico. Covarrubias himself became the grantee of Castaic Rancho (today's Magic Mountain amusement park) in 1843, became secretary of the assembly, and in 1844 was elected *alcalde* (similar to mayor) of Santa Barbara. In 1845 he had the honor of becoming Governor Pio Pico's private secretary. He was sent as *comisionado* to Mexico in 1846 and that same year purchased the Santa Ines Mission, together with Joaquin Carrillo, for $7,000. The sale was invalidated the following year because it had not been by auction as required by the government and because "their acts in continuing to pay rent in 1846–7 was against the theory of a purchase... They must be regarded as renters, and must settle up and show receipts on that basis" (Bancroft, vol. 5, p. 635).

Possibly because he was frustrated by his dealings with the Mexican authorities but more probably because he was an exceedingly skillful politician, Covarrubias went on to even greater political power under American rule. When the acting governor, General Bennett Riley, called a convention in Monterey to formulate a constitution for the new state of California, one of Santa Barbara's three representatives was Jose Maria Covarrubias.

He was named, by the legislature, a brigadier general in the state militia in 1850, and in 1853 was chosen as one of the first presidential electors sent to Washington to cast California's vote for Franklin Pierce. According to newspaper reports of the period, Covarrubias spent $10,000 of the Democratic Party's money entertaining bigwigs on the trip, which was by ship, via Panama. It was reported that in New York, Tammany Hall turned out to greet the Californian, whose speech in favor of Pierce was "one of the most eloquent of the lot."

Jose Maria Covarrubias

Back home, Covarrubias was elected four times to the new state's first legislature, became a Santa Barbara County judge, and in 1857 was appointed collector for the Port of San Diego.

And Catalina Island? It seems to have been an ongoing headache for Covarrubias. He is quoted in one history as calling it "an ugly wart off the shores of San Pedro," inaccessible and unsuitable for grazing cattle. Perhaps that is why he sold the island to Albert Packard for $1,000 in October 1853, two years before his title was confirmed by the U.S. Land Commission and thirteen years before the U.S. patent was finally awarded. Or perhaps he sold it for more than that, the remainder being written off as part of the hefty legal fees owed to Packard for his work in straightening out the title.

ALBERT PACKARD

Just as Thomas Robbins and Jose Maria Covarrubias before him, Albert Packard, the third owner of Catalina Island, made his home in Santa Barbara, and seems to have had little or no actual presence on the island. Nearly a generation younger than his predecessors, Packard was a native of Rhode Island, had studied law, and is said to have practiced in Mazatlan before coming to California. Packard is known to have been in Los Angeles in 1844 as a partner of Benjamin Davis Wilson, the first mayor of Los Angeles and the person for whom Mount Wilson was named. Benjamin Wilson later became a partner of Phineas Banning.

Packard and Wilson operated a mercantile store at the corner of Main and Commercial Streets in Los Angeles while tending to other business affairs around the state. Inside their store was a large wooden tub into which residents could drop letters and pick up mail addressed to them, a crude forerunner of the later postal system.

Late in 1849 Wilson purchased the well-known Bella Union Hotel from merchant (Julian) Isaac Williams. Six months later he deeded a half interest in the hotel to his partner, Packard. It was here that the Los Angeles courts operated for a while, with the county paying rent to Packard and Wilson. That same year Packard was an agent for Thomas O. Larkin, merchant and U.S. consul in California, and the two continued to do business for several years. But Packard had his eye on the momentous changes taking place in the state. At the end of 1851 he deeded his half interest in the Bella Union back to Wilson and moved to Santa Barbara to practice law, specializing in settling land titles granted while California was part of Mexico.

Albert Packard

The matter should have been simple: by a law of 1851, claimants were required to appear before the U.S. Land Commission and support their claims with such evidence, documentation, and witnesses as they felt were necessary. When a title was confirmed, the General Land Office in Washington was to issue a patent, its boundaries based upon an official survey. Land not presented to the commission within a set time was to become public domain as was land where title was rejected by the commission. The trouble was, there could be appeals, all the way to the U.S. Supreme Court. There might be five or six trials of a single case, over several years, at ruinous cost to the landowners, who sometimes had to borrow money at rates as high as 5 percent a month to pay their legal bills. And if a landowner wanted to sell before the process was complete, he was not able to give clear title to the land.

This seems to be what happened to Catalina Island, for, although Covarrubias bought the island in 1850, his title wasn't confirmed until 1855, and the patent was not issued until 1866. "Sometimes most of [a] rancho went to pay the lawyer's fees," a paper on California land grants noted. And Albert Packard was one of the important lawyers in Santa Barbara, representing, among others, Thomas Robbins' widow and children as well as Covarrubias. His $1,000 "purchase" of Catalina Island in 1853 may have been in lieu of legal fees. Or it may have been for only a part of the island: appendix G of Doran's *The Ranch That Was Robbins'* notes that Covarrubias deeded one-quarter of the island to Packard in 1853 for $1,000, and that Packard deeded one-quarter of the island to Eugene Sullivan in June 1858, eight years before the U.S. patent was finally issued.

Packard, meanwhile, became a partner of wealthy former otter hunter Lewis T. Burton in the 42,184-acre Jesus Maria ranch where much of Vandenberg Air Force Base is located. The men did not attempt to farm the vast acreage, choosing to lease it out instead. The final patent on the Jesus Maria ranch was issued in 1871 to "Lewis T. Burton, et al."

Packard married Manuela Burke Ayres, descendant of an early Spanish settler and daughter of an Irish trader from South America who had settled in Santa Barbara in 1820. In about 1860 the Packards acquired a 200-acre property on what was then the undeveloped westside of Santa Barbara. Packard built an elegant yellow-brick mansion for his family and planted his estate with high-quality grape rootstock imported from Spain and Mexico. When the vineyards came into bearing in 1865, Packard built a winery, La Bodega, and here produced fine wines under the label "El Recodo," which were marketed in Europe. He later turned to olive culture and started California's first sericulture, or silk industry, in the attic of La Bodega.

SULLIVAN, HITCHCOCK, RAY, HAWXHURST, LICK ET AL.

A confusing and complex series of transactions took place between 1858 and 1896 during which thousands of dollars changed hands and various interests "owned" between a quarter and the whole of the island. Individuals, syndicates, and agents acting on behalf of them were involved during those decades of rapidly changing ownership. The catalyst for much of the action was the mineral wealth reportedly located near the Isthmus area. We will not attempt to untangle this financial web with its inevitable loose ends, feeling it would be a fruitless academic exercise. Instead, we will mention some of the people involved, then discuss the later owners who developed the island along the recreational lines that distinguish it today.

EUGENE L. SULLIVAN

As mentioned earlier, Albert Packard sold one-quarter of the island for $500 to Eugene L. Sullivan of San Francisco in June 1858, three months after the district court upheld Jose Maria Covarrubias's claim. Sullivan was the second husband of George Yount's younger daughter, Elizabeth Ann, and served as a state senator, collector of the port of San Francisco, and author of the bill creating Golden Gate Park. The Sullivans were married in 1850. It is entirely possible that Sullivan heard tales of the original Catalina gold discovery from his father-in-law and that he accompanied Yount on one of his three trips back to the island in search of Yount's legendary gold-outcropping. The last of these trips was made in 1854, a year of drought and business failures in northern California. It is also possible that Yount told his daughter's first husband, John Calvert Davis, about the gold, and that the two men made at least one trip to Catalina together before Davis' death in 1847.

During the 1860s, Catalina's so-called gold rush began. The first location, in what became the Small Hills Mining claim, was made in April 1863, by Martin Morse Kimberly and Daniel E. Way; on April 20, 1863, they and other miners organized the San Pedro Mining District. The boundaries of the district were somewhat indefinite and included "all the islands of Los Angeles County and the Coast Range of mountains between the northern and southern boundaries of said county."

The vast area bounded by water was a natural asset to Kimberly, a native of Guilford, Connecticut, who had arrived in San Francisco in 1851, moved to Santa Barbara in 1852, and purchased a schooner, the *Cygnet,* which he used for trading and hunting otter up and down the coast. Kimberly became a squatter on Santa Cruz Island (a situation not unlike that of Catalina, where confirmation of the owner's title dragged on for many years), then went to San Nicolas Island and raised sheep until the drought of the 1860s decimated his flock. It is not known whether Kimberly's mining venture netted him any profit, but he gave up mining shortly after his discovery on Catalina and moved back to Santa Barbara where he kept a store until 1871.

In 1872 he made a successful trading trip to the China seas and continued to hunt the increasingly scarce sea otter and seals. On a later trip to China he lost his life in a typhoon.

CHARLES M. HITCHCOCK

It was six years before another change in ownership took place, once again because of the complexity of American laws involving private land grants made by the Spanish and Mexican governments. Covarrubias's grant, originally made to Thomas Robbins in 1846, was still in the courts many years later because the Board of Land Commissioners' decision that the claim was valid was appealed to the U.S. District Court for the Southern District of California. By the time the surveyor general's report was filed, tales of gold and other valuable metals had attracted eager prospectors to the island, many of them under the impression that Catalina was owned by the U.S. Government.

In the meantime, while Covarrubias and Packard sought to obtain the final patent (which wasn't given until April 10, 1867), Sullivan sold his quarter interest on February 4, 1864, to Charles McPhail Hitchcock of San Francisco for $1,864, a profit of $1,364. Dr. Hitchcock was a former Army physician and surgeon who had been involved in several mining ventures, including the purchase of the Baraten mines in Cosala, Mexico, with Ferdinand Vassault and others (Davis, p. 165). Dr. Hitchcock and his wife, Martha Taliafero, came to San Francisco in 1851 with their eight-year-old daughter, Lillie, and moved into the newly completed Oriental Hotel, described as the "center of fashion and sociability" in newspapers of the day.

Lillie became enamored of firefighters and pursued a flamboyant lifestyle. In 1868 she married Howard Coit, a "caller" at the Mining Exchange. Dying wealthy, her lasting gifts to San Francisco were the famous Coit Tower on Telegraph Hill and a statue in nearby Columbus Square honoring the volunteer firefighters of the early city.

JAMES H. RAY

James H. Ray probably knew about Dr. Hitchcock's purchase of one-quarter of the island in February 1864, because in the closely knit social hierarchy of California, men of position communicated with each other from one end of the state to the other. News of the discovery of valuable metals on Catalina Island would have moved quickly between opposite points of the compass, traveling by sea, by horse, or by stage. At any rate, on May 14, 1864, three months after Dr. Hitchcock's purchase, Ray managed to track down Covarrubias and Packard in Santa Barbara and purchased from them the remaining three-quarters of the island.

James H. Ray acted as agent for several major investors of the period, purchasing, managing, and selling mining and other properties for them on commission while they personally remained in the background. It has been said that when Ray heard about the "discovery" of gold on Catalina, he managed to negotiate a conditional purchase of the island, borrowing the money from James Lick and mortgaging the title to put the deal over (*Society of California Pioneers Quarterly*, 1(2), 1924, p. 36).

JAMES LICK AND THE LICK TRUST

James Lick, an eccentric Pennsylvania Dutchman who had made a fortune in Lima, Peru, as a maker of fine pianos, arrived in San Francisco in January 1848 with $30,000 in gold coin obtained from the sale of his pianos and piano business. Seventeen days after Lick's arrival in San Francisco, gold was discovered at Sutter's sawmill at Coloma and the famous California gold rush was on.

Most of San Francisco soon left for the mines, but the savvy Lick began buying sand hills, lots that were under water at high tide, and other undesirable and inexpensive real estate which he was certain would rise in value. When he made a profit, Lick bought more low-priced land. He later built the San Francisco luxury hotel known as the Lick House, bought and enlarged a sawmill near San Jose, and purchased the Los Feliz Rancho in Los Angeles County. Lick also bought Catalina Island in a series of purchases between 1864 and 1867, the price in the recorded deeds totaling a little over $23,000.

James Lick had strong philanthropic leanings and thus in 1874 created a $3 million trust. The trust was given title to all his California property, with power to sell and to use the proceeds for the construction of a powerful telescope (later resulting in the Lick Observatory); his other philanthropies included an old ladies home, an orphan asylum, a library association, a society to prevent cruelty to animals, free public baths, and the building of a memorial to his mother. Lick, one of the founding members of the Society of California Pioneers, deeded the organization several valuable San Francisco lots.

James Lick

Lick apparently had no personal interest in Catalina, and by the time he purchased the final quarter of it from George W. Hawxhurst of Contra Costa County (who obtained it at a sheriff's sale and was involved in coal rather than gold), the mining boom was over and Lick was ready to dispose of the island. In 1872 he gave an option to buy the island to three leading southern Californians: John G. Downey of Los Angeles, a former governor of California (1860 to 1862); Don Juan Forster, a wealthy rancher of San Juan Capistrano; and Max von Strobel, a winemaker, adventurer, and the first mayor of Anaheim, who planned to sell the island to a syndicate of wealthy British capitalists. Strobel was sent to England to close the deal but died of natural causes in his hotel room before the sale was concluded. The option expired and the island remained the property of James Lick. During this period Lick leased parts of Catalina to sheep raisers such as Ben Weston, Frank Whittley, and some others who had large herds grazing on the island.

Lick died in 1876, and the sale of his properties, which were scattered around California, realized close to $3,000,000, with the Lick House alone going for $1,250,000. Santa Catalina Island, which had come into Lick's holdings through a mortgage, was sold for $200,000 in July 1887, according to original papers in the Mary Lea Shane Archives of the Lick Observatory at the University of California, Santa Cruz Library.

GEORGE R. SHATTO

The buyer was thirty-seven-year-old George Rufus Shatto, a midwestern speculator intent on making money during southern California's spectacular real estate boom of the mid-1880s. A native of Ohio who had owned a department store in Grand Rapids, Michigan, Shatto learned of the availability of Catalina from Charles A. Sumner, the London-born agent appointed by the Lick trustees to sell the island.

George R. Shatto

Sumner must have been a born salesman for he convinced Shatto that with a little effort and money, the barren island could be transformed from a mining and agricultural operation to a profitable and popular resort for tourists.

"Mind you, he [Shatto] had never seen the island, knew nothing of its possibilities except what I told him and had no experience in handling a seaside resort," Sumner said in a 1918 article in the *Los Angeles Times.* Sumner originally intended to form a syndicate to purchase the island for the agreed-upon price of $200,000. Terms were one-third cash, with the balance to be paid in one, two, and three years. Shatto later decided to finance the purchase himself, without using a syndicate. The sale was closed July 13, 1887, and on the following day, "Mr. Shatto and I took the trip over to Catalina on the tugboat *Falcon* [owned by the Bannings' Wilmington Transportation Company]," Sumner wrote. "The boat went over once a week, every Wednesday, and took passengers at $5 a head, returning next day."

At the end of August, Charles M. Plum, a Lick estate trustee, traveled to Los Angeles from San Francisco with the deed, abstract, and legal opinion. The money was paid, papers signed, and Shatto became the new owner of everything on the island except a pesky bit of mineral land near the Isthmus and the aforementioned Bird Rock. The island had earlier been "covered with prospectors who had filed mining claims on every conceivable bunch of croppings," Sumner explained. "After many years' litigation all the miners except one, a Frenchman named Boucher [*sic*] were ousted and their claims invalidated. For some reason or other Boucher was left and had a shanty and a tunnel near Wilson's or Johnson's harbor beyond the isthmus, so the island was offered for sale with what might be termed this encumbrance."

Anxious to survey his purchase, Shatto took another trip to the island with Sumner and, under the guidance of Frank Whittley, toured it on horseback, visiting Silver Canyon, Middle Ranch, Little Harbor, the Isthmus, and Wilson's or Johnson's harbor, spending the night in the old barracks "at least until the crawling inhabitants drove us out to finish our sleep on the beach," Sumner wrote.

Work began immediately on the "resort"; the town site was surveyed, and a wharf and hotel built. Shatto stayed on the island, supervising the workmen, while Sumner on the mainland took care of buying and shipping supplies and hiring labor, which went by tugboat twice a week. Construction was impressively fast: opening day for the town of Shatto was October 13, 1887, three months after Shatto completed purchase of the island. That eventful day, Sumner brought a group of prospective buyers to the island first by train and then by boat, fed them a free lunch in the new Hotel Metropole's dining room, and returned them to Los Angeles by evening. The next day, in his Los Angeles office, Sumner began to sell lots and contracted for the first stores and houses. And soon afterward the town of Shatto became the town of Avalon.

Business was slow in 1888, but by 1889, Sumner and Shatto were advertising and promoting the island in the leading Los Angeles newspapers. They persuaded the Bannings to use their fast, new steamer, the first *Hermosa,* for the cross-channel trip and arranged special discount fares for Saturday and Sunday round-trips. They also persuaded noted sportsman and writer Charles Frederick Holder and his wife to be guests at the Hotel Metropole for the summer and to fish and write while they vacationed there. Holder, in his inimitable style, told the world about Catalina Island, especially its fishing, and Catalina was on its way to becoming a popular tourist destination.

Sumner encouraged wealthy yachtsmen to visit in their vessels, added musicales and social activities to the Hotel Metropole's calendar, encouraged swimming (bathing, as it was then known) in the clear waters of the harbor, hired old-time resident Frank Whittley to establish a stable and organize trail rides, and started the casual dress code that has lasted for more than a century.

But there were problems. The tourist season lasted only two or three months, the Metropole wasn't large enough to house the many visitors who came during those few months, and the real estate boom ended, leaving many Avalon lots unsold. Through friends in Pasadena, Shatto, in 1889, entered into an agreement to sell the island for $400,000 to the International Mining Syndicate, a British group. They proposed to develop copper, silver, and iron ledges, shipping the low-grade ore to England on coaling vessels, which would return to San Pedro filled with English channel coal, not yet available in Los Angeles. The group planned to continue the resort development, utilizing "the excellent building stone on the island" to construct "a large hotel built after an English architectural design and intended especially for

English tourists," enthused the *Riverside Press & Horticulturist* of March 11, 1889.

The syndicate, which had paid $40,000 down on the purchase, soon discovered that mining in almost inaccessible wilderness was difficult and expensive. The investors forfeited their down payment and opted out of the deal. Shatto, meanwhile, used the down payment to build an elegant mansion on a Shatto Street hillside in Los Angeles. When he was unable to make payments on his $133,333.30 purchase price mortgage, the Lick trustees foreclosed.

"The trustees [took] the island rancho back at [the] sheriff's sale, thereby eliminating not only George R. Shatto but also the [British] Industrial Mining Syndicate, Limited, and the Santa Catalina Development Company, Limited, two corporations to whom Shatto had given an option or other interest," W.W. Robinson explained in *The Island of Santa Catalina*.

The Lick Trustees made a new sale on September 20, 1892, to William Banning, Phineas' eldest son. The price was $128,740. A year later, on May 30, 1893, Shatto lost his life in a railway accident while returning from a trip to Mojave to inspect a mine. His widow, Clara Ruth Whitney Shatto, continued to live in Los Angeles until her death in 1942.

THE BANNINGS: WILLIAM, J.B., AND HANCOCK

Although the Banning family's interest in Catalina began shortly after Phineas arrived in southern California in 1851, the family's ownership of the island came about quite unexpectedly forty years later. Phineas's sons William (born 1858), Joseph Brent (born 1861), and Hancock (born 1866) were running the Wilmington Transportation Company (WTC) and other mainland family businesses in 1889 when Charles F. Crocker sought out his friend, William Banning. Crocker was a director of the Southern Pacific Railroad, which had taken over the Los Angeles and San Pedro Railroad's Wilmington operations more than a decade earlier. Crocker explained that the English mining syndicate was pulling out of its agreement to buy the island from Shatto, Shatto's debts were growing, the real estate boom had ended, and the Lick trust was ready to sell the island (again).

COURTESY HANCOCK BANNING III

Captain William
Banning

Wouldn't the island be a perfect complement to the Bannings' WTC? Crocker asked. He was sure the Bannings could take over the island "by assuming Shatto's obligations to the [Lick] estate, plus whatever Shatto had paid for town lots and improvements in the city of Avalon," Carol Green Wilson noted in her book, *California Yankee*. Captain Banning sent his secretary, Frank Lowe, to London to query the British investors. On December 24, 1889, Lowe cabled Banning: "The island is yours." In reality it was September 1892 before the deed passed from the Lick estate to the Bannings. The consideration was $128,740. After Shatto's death in a railway accident in 1893, the Bannings paid his widow an additional $25,000 for the town lots and improvements Shatto had made in Avalon.

The Bannings expanded and improved upon Shatto's original idea for a resort: the Hotel Metropole was enlarged, family vacationing in tents was encouraged, open-air band concerts were provided, and a dance pavilion was built. The recently acquired *Hermosa I* brought increasing numbers of vacationers to Catalina, and Charles F. Holder, through his writing, attracted avid fishermen to the island from around the world.

When the brothers incorporated the Santa Catalina Island Company (SCICo) in 1894, William Banning became president, a position he held until 1919. He remained on the SCICo board until 1929. The Bannings placed title to all their Catalina Island holdings in the SCICo, and the brothers took turns managing the operations at Avalon, the Isthmus, the interior, and those involving marine activities. During their ownership of the island the Bannings improved the sanitation and water systems (*Water Lines,* first quarter 1994), planted thousands of eucalyptus (particularly at the Isthmus), added more steamer connections with the mainland, had roads built to link various parts of the island, built a scenic railway to the top of Buena Vista Park in Avalon, encouraged formation of the Tuna Club, initiated development of a steam-powered electric generation system, built a small hotel at Little Harbor and the Eagle's Nest hunting lodge, built a large aquarium in Avalon, and presided over limited development of the town of Cabrillo at the Isthmus.

In the early days the Bannings camped out at Avalon with other summer visitors, many of whom were personal friends from the mainland. Later, William and Joseph Brent built houses in town and Hancock built a home in Descanso Canyon. Joseph Brent eventually built a hunting lodge above the Isthmus, remodeled in recent years and run as a bed and breakfast.

Joseph Brent (J.B.) Banning

There were many setbacks during the Bannings' three decades of island ownership including a nine-year waterfront war in which various transportation interests competed with the WTC. The Avalon Freeholders' Improvement Association was formed in 1909 to help establish order and was given title to the new Pleasure Pier in return for the SCICo's financial subsidies for maintenance of roads and public utilities and the promotion of tourism.

Still, bitter feelings continued. In 1913, when Avalon became a city, the Bannings let it be known that the SCICo would not continue to subsidize the free band concerts, dancing, and other attractions which were provided without cost to Avalon merchants, visitors, and leaseholders.

On May 20, 1914, the *Catalina Islander* published the following letter:

> To the Honorable Board of Trustees, City of Avalon, California.
> You are hereby notified that the amount we have been paying monthly to the City of Avalon during the dull season, as a donation to help defray the city expenses, will be discontinued on June first next, until further notice.
>
> Very respectfully yours, William Banning

The paper commented:

"...the municipality of Avalon has stolen from its former [*sic*] owners, and has failed to give anything in return... The Santa Catalina Island Co. repaired, cleaned, sprinkled and lighted the streets, Freeholders' wharf and parks; furnished fire protection for the town, installed and operated the sewers, kept the town clean and sanitary; furnished free band concerts, free dancing and maintained order... The town of Avalon and practically the whole of Santa Catalina Island were maintained by the Santa Catalina Island Co. as a park for the citizens of Avalon and their guests... without cost to the people of Avalon..."

COURTESY HANCOCK BANNING III

Hancock Banning

The famous fire of 1915, which gutted over a third of the west side of Avalon, also destroyed part of the Banning family's enthusiasm for further development of the island. Nevertheless the SCICo committed $250,000 to clear away the wreckage, rebuild the bathhouse, repair the streets, and build a new tent city. In 1916 the water and power utilities were transferred to the Wilmington Transportation Company and in 1917 the SCICo began plans for a new hotel. The hotel originally was planned for an area near Sugar Loaf Rock; later plans called for its construction in Descanso Canyon and the subsequent relocation of Hancock Banning's house farther up the canyon.

The 320,000-square-foot St. Catherine Hotel opened June 29, 1918, and was, according to historian James Zordich, "the last major contribution made by the Bannings to Avalon's development." Six months later the island was sold to William Wrigley Jr.

WILLIAM WRIGLEY JR.

The contrast of sunny southern California to blustery Chicago in the wintertime proved so attractive to William Wrigley Jr., founder of the Wrigley chewing gum empire, that in 1914 he, with his wife Ada, purchased a Pasadena showplace, a three-story, twenty-two-room, 18,500-square-foot Italian Renaissance–style mansion, which today serves as headquarters of the Tournament of Roses Association. A year later the Wrigleys bought an adjacent parcel that became part of the beautiful four and one-half-acre Wrigley Gardens. But Wrigley seems to have fallen in love with southern California. In 1917 he persuaded the Chicago Cubs, of which he was a minority stockholder, to move their spring training camp from the south to Pasadena. And in 1919, according to William Zimmerman Jr., his official biographer, "a short telegram announced to the world that [Wrigley] was head of a syndicate which had bought Catalina Island."

The Catalina investment was unexpected; although the Wrigleys had heard about the island, they had never been there before Wrigley committed himself to buy into an investment syndicate that intended to purchase the SCICo stock held by the Banning family. Wrigley's initial investment in the syndicate, headed by David Blankenhorn and Robert Hunter of the Pasadena real estate firm of Blankenhorn and Hunter (which had handled the Wrigleys' purchase of their Pasadena estate), is said to have been about $1 million. Several weeks later the Wrigleys made their first trip to the island, staying in a suite at the Hotel St. Catherine. Wrigley later told a reporter that his wife, an early riser, had walked to the window and called excitedly, "I should like to live here," according to the biographer. And when Wrigley got to the window: "The sun was just coming up. I had never seen a more beautiful spot. Right then and there I determined that the island should never pass out of my hands."

The Wrigley-Blankenhorn syndicate planned to develop the island as a real estate venture, selling lots in Avalon and building a colony of thirty model bungalows to induce "the right kind of buyers to erect suitable houses of their own." Wrigley hired David M. Renton, a Pasadena building contractor who had worked on his estate, to construct the bungalows.

William Wrigley Jr.

The Bannings retained some of their stock in the SCICo; when new officers were elected in early 1919, Captain William Banning was on the board as a vice president, with David Blankenhorn elected president and Robert Hunter a vice president. It was when Wrigley began to propose one improvement after another that he ran into opposition from the other investors. Their plan, they told Wrigley, was to sell property and make money from the island, not put money into it. The two points of view were irreconcilable. Before the year ended Wrigley had bought out his partners in the syndicate and, through other stock purchases, acquired a controlling interest in the SCICo, whose assets included the WTC. By the time of his death in January 1932, Wrigley had acquired 94 percent of the outstanding SCICo stock. President of the SCICo and WTC during this period, 1920 to 1932, was Joseph H. Patrick, who had been a trusted associate of Wrigley's in Chicago.

Born September 30, 1861, William Wrigley Jr. was the eldest of nine children of William Sr. and Mary Ladley Wrigley of Philadelphia, Pennsylvania. William Sr. owned the Wrigley Manufacturing Company, makers of Wrigley's Scouring Soap, a product William Jr. began to sell on the road when he was only thirteen years old. A rebellious student in school, William Jr. soon developed the skills and instincts of a master salesman, selling to dealers in the "tall grass" towns of Pennsylvania, New York, and the New England states. He believed in promoting his products with free premiums; his key to successful advertising was "Tell 'em quick and tell 'em often."

On September 17, 1885, young William Jr. married Ada E. Foote, whom he had met on a steamboat two years earlier when she was sixteen. About six years after his marriage, having embarked on selling "Lotta" chewing gum from a supplier, the Zeno Manufacturing Company, he founded his own firm, the William Wrigley Jr. Company. He began manufacturing his own chewing gum following a merger with Zeno. In 1901 he celebrated his first decade in the gum business.

Wrigley's stewardship of Catalina Island, augmented by the highly competent skills of general manager David Malcolm Renton, created a legacy of wise environmental, recreational, and civic development. He created a fleet of cross-channel passenger vessels, its flagship the magnificent "great white steamer" SS *Catalina*. The huge Catalina terminal at the foot of Wilmington's Avalon Boulevard (formerly Phineas Banning's Canal Street, which ran alongside his early wharves) was Wrigley-directed, as was the extended steamer pier at Avalon, now razed.

Wrigley's projects included the noted Bird Park; the landmark Casino; a Pebbly Beach enterprise where furniture, pottery, and decorative tile were made; a ballpark where the Chicago Cubs trained; the bell tower above Avalon, donated by Ada Wrigley in 1925; and, of course, the Wrigley mansion. Some of these are gone now, but the city of Avalon still reflects the infusion of Wrigley capital into the SCICO with its widened paved roads, improved freshwater system, upgraded utilities, and more comfortable homes for residents. In the island's interior, the Thompson Reservoir and an eight-mile pipeline into Avalon, completed in 1925 and augmented by other dams and wells, have nearly alleviated the historic water shortage problem. (In 1962 the Southern California Edison Company assumed responsibility for providing all public utilities to Catalina Island.)

The impressive Wrigley Memorial and botanical gardens at the head of Avalon Canyon are reminders of the many benefactions bestowed upon this island community by Ada and William Wrigley Jr.

PHILIP K. WRIGLEY

In the official biography of William Wrigley Jr., the story is told that around the turn of the last century, Wrigley had a chance to sell out his chewing gum business at a good profit and decided to discuss the matter with his six-year-old son. "Phil, when you grow up, do you want to go into the chewing gum business with me?" When Philip Wrigley answered: "Yes, Dad, of course I do," Wrigley said, "That's all I wanted to know. I won't sell the business."

Wrigley's biographer noted that the subject was important to the senior Wrigley, this matter of building a business that he might hand on to his son. The same was true of Wrigley's other interests, most of which began with William Wrigley Jr., and were passed along to Philip when the time came.

Born in Chicago in 1894 when Wm. Wrigley Jr. and Company (the firm's original name) was heavily into the chewing gum business, Philip lived in several apartments and residences while growing up, each reflecting the increasing success of his father. As the senior Wrigley prospered, he sent the family away from Chicago for several weeks each summer and winter, something of a necessity there in the days before air conditioning and central heating. The favorite summer spot was Lake Geneva, Wisconsin, and later, Harbor Point, Michigan, where the family owned a cottage. In winter the family liked to go to Thomasville, Georgia, at least before they discovered southern California.

Philip Wrigley attended the Chicago Latin School, a small private school for boys, from kindergarten through his first year of high school. In early fall of 1911, Philip entered Phillips Academy at Andover, Massachusetts. He was almost 17 and nearly two years older than most of the boys in his class. His father had never hesitated to take him out of school for vacations or travel. In fact, in 1912, the senior Wrigley took Philip and his mother on a several-month world cruise. Showing proper concern for his son's education, he brought along a young law student to act as Philip's companion and tutor. Philip graduated from Phillips Academy in 1914 and was admitted to Yale, but at his father's urging, transferred his credits to Stanford University, intending to enter in the fall of 1914. Yet when he learned that the Wrigley Company planned to establish a factory in Australia, Philip asked to be entrusted with the new installation. He was only twenty, but his father consented, feeling it was a good way for the young man to learn all phases of the increasingly successful chewing gum business.

Philip Knight Wrigley

Philip returned to Chicago in 1916 and was admitted to the University of Chicago as a special student, taking only chemistry and setting up a laboratory above the garage attached to his father's house. When the United States entered World War I in the spring of 1917, Philip planned to join the cavalry but upon hearing that a naval aviation unit was being formed, he enlisted for four years in the U.S. Naval Reserve. By the end of the year the Navy flight school was moved to Pensacola and a school for aviation mechanics was established at the Great Lakes Naval Training Station near Chicago. Philip, who had already demonstrated mechanical aptitude, became superintendent of the school and was promoted to the rank of ensign. At about that time he became engaged to Helen Blanche Atwater of New York, daughter of a vice president of the Wrigley Company who was in charge of its New York office. A graduate of St. Mary's School in Garden City, New York, she was studying at Harcum School in Pennsylvania. The couple was married in March 1918, and Philip remained on active duty at Great Lakes until February 1919, when he was assigned to inactive duty.

Upon his separation from the Navy, Philip and his wife visited his parents, who were wintering in Pasadena. "Naturally my father told me about the Catalina deal, and suggested that we go over and take a look at [the island], which we did," Philip noted in a memorandum now in the SCICo archives. "We had our first sight of Santa Catalina in February of 1919 [and] we were all very much impressed . . . particularly my father . . . I think he began to visualize Catalina as it could be some day in the future with adequate transportation and water . . . with its proximity to [a rapidly growing] city, yet with the isolation that an island affords."

Philip said that although he was located primarily in Chicago because of business, he and his family "made frequent trips to Catalina in winter and summer" and that he worked closely with his father on the development plans for Catalina. Listing the major infrastructure improvements such as enlarging the steamer pier, building the

Casino, revamping hotels, and starting industries on the island to furnish local employment, he said: "Of course, all of these various things operated at a loss, but nobody was looking at the immediate picture; everyone was looking to the future."

Philip's involvement with the William Wrigley Jr. company grew steadily; nevertheless, in the early days of his father's ownership of the island, Philip personally financed the Wilmington-Catalina Airlines and worked on developing the interior of Catalina Island. After the death of his father in January 1932, Philip Wrigley was elected president of the SCICo, J.H. Patrick was made chairman, and D.M. Renton became vice president and general manager.

Despite financially lean years during World War II when Catalina was closed to tourists and its cross-channel vessels and facilities commandeered by the military, Philip managed to lavish an inherited fondness and respect upon the island. He introduced sophisticated air transportation to the island and built both the Airport-in-the-Sky and the unique amphibian airport at Hamilton Beach, now obliterated by stacks of condominiums. He made possible the University of Southern California's marine science center at the Isthmus through gifts of land and shares of stock in the SCICo. The early California ambience of Avalon was inspired by him, and the famous Arabian horse ranch at Middle Ranch was his.

By far Philip Wrigley's greatest contribution to the island was environmental: the planning and founding of the Santa Catalina Island Conservancy, embracing about 86 percent of the island. Its ecological objective was and is to conserve and restore an open wilderness, protected in perpetuity, a reminder of the way southern California used to be before the arrival of its burgeoning population. P.K. Wrigley was an environmentalist long before it became a popular ideology. Doug Bombard, president of Doug Bombard Enterprises at Two Harbors, recalled an early instance of Wrigley's environmental awareness: "I was making a proposal to lengthen the sewer outfall at Isthmus Cove and Mr. Wrigley said he didn't feel we should discharge our sewer into the ocean. [He was] very knowledgeable about sewer treatment plants that at the time I didn't know existed, and he instructed us to look into [them]. As a result of his foresight and direction, we installed our first sewer treatment plant at the Isthmus in the '60s" (*Water Lines,* SCICo, December 5, 1994).

This seemingly shy and quiet man, possessing fine technical and mechanical skills enabling him to repair nearly anything, passed away in Wisconsin in 1977. The succession of Wrigley-related administration of the SCICo continues. At this writing the president and chief executive officer of the SCICo is Paxson Offield, nephew of Philip Wrigley and son of his sister, Mrs. James (Dorothy Wrigley) Offield. Philip's only son, William Wrigley, is chairman of the board and shares his family's concern with the environmental welfare of Catalina Island and its natural ocean resources.

Afterword

This book concluded its history of Santa Catalina Island and its important relationship to southern California in late 1996. Yet, the truth is that history is a continuum in time, carrying with it, invariably, elements of change. In the interval between 1996 and 2002, a number of important changes in relation to Catalina Island have occurred. We begin with the Wilmington Transportation Company, represented by the "W" on the Santa Catalina Island Company's historic cross-channel vessels.

The stock of the venerable Wilmington Transportation Company, founded by Phineas Banning in 1877 and incorporated in 1884, was sold to a subsidiary of Foss Maritime Company on September 30, 1998, by the Santa Catalina Island Company. William Wrigley Jr. acquired the Wilmington Transportation Company (WTC) from the Banning brothers in 1919. The transaction also included the Santa Catalina Island Company (SCICo).

Foss had its roots in Tacoma, Washington, in 1889, when Foss Maritime was launched with a single rental rowboat by Thea Foss, a Norwegian immigrant, who recognized an opportunity to supplement the earnings of her carpenter husband, Andrew. Thea Foss bought, sold, and rented rowboats from the family float house. A painted sign on the roof of the float house advertised the fledgling enterprise as "Always Ready" to rent rowboats. Always Ready is incorporated in today's Foss logo. With Andrew building additional rowboats, rentals and sales burgeoned. This led to the building and operation of launches and tugboats. Today Foss Maritime, headquartered in Seattle, operates the world's largest and most powerful tractor tug, the *Lindsey Foss* — 155 feet and 8,000 horsepower — working in the Puget Sound escort service since early 1994.

Foss Maritime is the largest and most wide-ranging of the West Coast's ship assist, ocean towing, and bunker barging companies. It operates today in Long Beach, Los Angeles, and San Diego Harbors. Principal operating regions are Alaska, the Pacific Northwest, Columbia and Snake Rivers, San Francisco Bay, and, of course, southern California, according to *A Living Legend,* a company history book, produced in 1999 by Bruce Johnson Communications.

The WTC was established, primarily, to help vessels off-load supplies for the fledgling Pueblo of Los Angeles. Historically it remains the oldest, continuously operated company in Los Angeles Harbor. According to the then SCICo president, Paxson Offield, in a letter addressed to all SCICo employees announcing the WTC sale (*Water Lines,* third and fourth quarters, 1998):

> Over the years WTCo experienced numerous changes, but it always had a

"core" ship assist function. From the late 1880's to the early 1960's WTCo was also the principal provider of passenger and freight transportation services to Santa Catalina Island using, primarily, the large and ultimately inefficient steamers, SS *Catalina* and SS *Avalon*.

In the 1960's, my great uncle Philip Wrigley, made what was considered by some to be a controversial decision, and that was to have WTCo exit the business of carrying passengers and freight to Santa Catalina. He knew that what was needed was smaller, faster vessels on a more frequent time schedule. His decision created the conditions for others to step forward with innovative ideas and Catalina now benefits from perhaps the best passenger carrying services it has ever had. After leaving the passenger carrying business, WTCo returned to its roots as a first rate tug-boat company, expanding and upgrading its fleet into twin screw tug boats. In the early 1980's, in response to increased competitive pressures and in an effort to sustain profitability in the face of shrinking margins, another change was adopted when WTCo entered the bunker barge business [fuel oil carriers].

On July 1, 1999, the grande dame of Catalina's pleasure boat fleet, the *Blanche W*, was the reason for an anniversary celebration on the Pleasure Pier of the vessel's seventy-fifth year of operation. She was built, wood planked, in 1924 by William Muller in the yard on Mormon Island, Wilmington, for William Wrigley Jr. Attending the anniversary celebration was Ada Blanche Wrigley Schreiner, after whom the vessel was named. Mrs. Schreiner is William Wrigley Jr.'s granddaughter and daughter of Philip Wrigley. She had traveled from Port Orchard, Washington, for the celebration with her husband, Dr. Charles Schreiner, son Steve, and granddaughter Stephanie Rausch Schreiner. The *Blanche W* still makes trips to Seal Rocks and carries passengers on flying fish trips and sundown cruises to Two Harbors.

Doug Bombard, lessee of Two Harbors from the SCICo since 1956, has retired his Doug Bombard Enterprises; Two Harbors Enterprises, a new subsidiary, was established in early 1998. John Phelps is its general manager. Bombard now owns and operates Catalina Express with four terminals, making it the largest cross-channel passenger service to Catalina Island, with up to thirty-nine departures daily year-round. There is a terminal by the *Queen Mary*, another in downtown Long Beach, one in San Pedro, and the fourth in Dana Point. Bombard's eight vessels include a water jet trimaran, with four engines, that carries 381 passengers and travels at a speed of thirty-eight knots.

Malcolm Joseph Renton, former general manager of the SCICo, died August 1, 1997, at Lakewood Medical Center. Renton grew up on Catalina. He was the son of David M. Renton, considered the right hand of island proprietor William Wrigley Jr. After being graduated from Stanford University, Malcolm Renton became assistant to his father, the first general manager of the Island Company. At his father's retirement, Malcolm succeeded him as assistant to Wrigley.

John Windle died on March 5, 1999, at age ninety-five. Windle started work with the SCICo in 1919. From 1923 until 1950, he was superintendent of transportation. In January of 1930, the SCICo acquired the sightseeing bus business from H. Eichbaum, who had the Catalina Jaunting Car Company. Under Windle's superintendence, it became Catalina Motor Tours. Routes were extended as far as the Isthmus, and by 1941, some twenty buses and fifteen passenger sedans were in operation. Catalina Motor Tours hauled more than 880,000 passengers in 1941, coinciding with the best year ever for the big cross-channel steamers that transported more than 440,000 people. More people were hauled than the boat count because visitors took more than one bus tour (*Water Lines,* third and fourth quarters, 1999, published by the SCICo). John Windle was the son of Ernest Windle, who for fifty-two years was Avalon's justice of the peace, journalist, island historian, and author.

At its annual meeting held on April 10, 2001, the board of directors elected Ronald C. Doutt to the office of president and chief operating officer of the SCICo. Doutt assumed the position of president from Paxon H. Offield, who was reelected chairman of the board and chief executive officer. Doutt has been with SCICo since 1985 in numerous managerial capacities, including a director, chairman, chief executive officer, and treasurer of Two Harbors Enterprises. He joins only seven other individuals who have served at the helm of the corporation since 1894. They are William Banning, 1894–1919; David Blankenhorn, 1919–20; J.H. Patrick, 1920–32; Philip K. Wrigley, 1932–77; Claude Brooks, 1977–84; William Wrigley, 1984–88, and Paxson Offield, 1988–2001 (*Water Lines,* first and second quarters, 2001).

On Monday, March 8, 1999, employees of the SCICo and residents of the island were saddened to learn that William Wrigley died in Chicago from complications of pneumonia. He was sixty-six. A memorial resolution states, in part, that

> William Wrigley, following his father's and grandfather's footsteps guided the Santa Catalina Island Company with great distinction and dedication...
>
> Throughout those many years of active and unstinting devotion to the Company, William Wrigley displayed an unwavering sense of purpose and commitment to protection, preservation and enhancement of the terrestrial and marine environment of Santa Catalina Island and, during this time, he gave generously of his talents, time and personal wealth to the Santa Catalina Island Conservancy, the Wrigley Memorial Garden Foundation, the Philip K. Wrigley Marine Science Center and the Wrigley Institute for Environmental Studies. He is survived by his daughter, Alison Wrigley Rusack; his sons, Philip and William Jr.; and his sister, Ada Blanche (*Water Lines,* first and second quarters, 1999).

"John Hardy, a scuba diving pioneer and diving industry leader, who initiated the first consumer-oriented testing of diving equipment more than a decade ago and was a longtime fixture in the waters off Catalina, has died. He was sixty-two. He owned an Avalon charter diving boat and ran a light commercial operation. Hardy died on August 29, 2001, at his son's home in Carpinteria after a brief battle with cancer (*Los Angeles Times,* September 9, 2001)."

A nonprofit California corporation is attempting to salvage the ss *Catalina,* which has lain abandoned since 1985 in Ensenada Harbor. She is seriously deteriorating and listing from water in her hold. Her future is uncertain. The effort to get her into a drydock for repairs is being coordinated by the ss Catalina Preservation Association, 18242 West McDurmott, Suite J, Irvine, California 92614.

William Sanford White, whose parents were Wilbur and Gladys White, was born in Avalon and has coauthored *Santa Catalina Island, Its Magic, People, and History* with Steven Kern Tice. Published in 1997 by White Limited Editions, it is an excellent history of Avalon, its residents and visitors, particularly motion picture stars.

Four dwindling subspecies of the Channel Islands' miniature foxes are facing extinction on San Miguel, Santa Cruz, Anacapa, San Nicolas, and Santa Catalina. Some 4,800 foxes existed in 1994; in 2001, only about 300 remained. Golden eagles have devoured them. Canine distemper is killing them. Years of captive breeding may be needed to get the fox population high enough for release into the wild. Then, the species will have to be monitored. Perhaps 200 foxes remain on Catalina, 15 on San Miguel, 22 on Santa Rosa, and 50 on Santa Cruz. The fox population of San Clemente has been declining significantly. The government may increase efforts to keep stray dogs off the islands. Bald eagles, scientists believe, have long kept golden eagles away from the islands. But bald eagles, which had not hunted the fox, were nearly decimated a few decades ago by DDT exposure and hunting.

About $1.6 million in federal, state, and private grants has gone toward fox repopulating efforts since 1998, according to the National Park Service. Those funds are expected to run out by the end of 2002, and scientists say another $5 million is needed during the next decade if the docile, cat-size creatures with tufted red ears are to survive (*Los Angeles Times,* December 11, 2001).

Peter Schuler is director of ecological restoration for the Catalina Island Conservancy. The Conservancy and the Institute for Wildlife have attempted to revive the bald eagle population by incubating eggs and raising young eagles. About twelve to fifteen resident bald eagles can be found at Twin Rocks, Binnacle Rock, Seal Rocks, and the West End (*Los Angeles Times,* November 23, 2001).

Botanist Denise Knapp was overjoyed when she discovered a patch of rare rock cress growing in Catalina Island's remote and foggy Wild Boar Gully Nature Preserve. The tiny flowering plant had not been seen on the island in thirty years, but it suddenly flourished behind a fence erected two years ago to protect the area from deer and feral goats that used to browse the vegetation to oblivion.

"Now, you can almost hear plants sighing with happiness and relief," Knapp said on a hike into the 112-acre preserve where she had found the so-called Santa Cruz rock cress. She expressed her love of coming here because of its unique assemblage of rare plants, noting that the preserve is slowly returning to its natural state.

The same could be said for much of the seventy-six-square-mile island, where natural rhythms had been severely altered by nonnative animals, ranching, and farming. In one of environmentalism's emerging successes, Catalina native plants and animals are on the rebound because of experimental restoration efforts. While much attention has been placed on the removal of feral creatures such as goats and pigs from the island, equally important has been the replanting of native vegetation nurtured in greenhouses and laboratories, and the fencing off of sensitive areas, such as Wild Boar Gully.

Bibliography

Amar, Eloi. Unpublished oral history. Avalon: files of Santa Catalina Island Company, 1962.

Angle, Paul M. *Philip K. Wrigley: A Memoir of a Modest Man.* Chicago: Rand, McNally & Co., 1975.

Ashkenazy, Irvin. "Catalina's Pigeon Express." *Westways,* vol. 60, no. 10 (October 1968).

Baer, D. Richard, ed. *The Film Buff's Checklist of Motion Pictures (1912–1979).* Hollywood: Hollywood Film Archive, 1979.

Bancroft, Hubert Howe. *History of California.* Vols. 1–7, facsimile ed. Santa Barbara: Wallace Hebberd, 1966.

Bandini, Ralph. *Veiled Horizons, Stories of Big Game Fish of the Sea.* New York: Derrydale Press, Inc., 1939.

Banning Collection. Ephemera, particularly papers of the Wilmington Transportation Co. Huntington Library, San Marino, 1902.

Banning, Hancock Jr. "The Banning Family in Southern California." Oral history manuscript, Dept. of Special Collections, University Research Library, University of California Los Angeles, 1971.

Beck, Horace. *Folklore and the Sea.* Pub. for the Marine Historical Assn., Inc., Mystic Seaport. Middletown, Conn.: Wesleyan University Press, 1973.

Bell, Horace (Major). *On the Old West Coast: Being Further Reminiscences of a Ranger.* Ed. Lamer Bartlett. New York: Grosset & Dunlap, 1930.

———. *Reminiscences of a Ranger.* Santa Barbara: Wallace Hebberd, 1927.

Bell, Katherine Den. "How Las Positas Became Hope Ranch." *Santa Barbara Morning Press,* 8 October 1918.

Belloc, Hilaire. *The Cruise of the Nona.* London: Constable & Co. Ltd., 1955.

Bennett, Jenny. "His Majesty's Bark *Endeavor.*" *Maritime Life and Traditions,* spring 2002.

Beston, Henry. *The Outermost House,* 1928. In *The International Thesaurus of Quotations,* compiled by Rhoda Thomas Tripp.

Bolton, Herbert Eugene. *Spanish Explorations in the Southwest, 1542–1706.* New York: Barnes & Noble, 1976.

Boswell, Roy V. *California as an Island, Thirteen Maps, 1587–1761.* Exhibition catalog. Fullerton, Calif.: California State University, 1984.

Brittain, Kilbee. *The General Phineas Banning Residence Museum.* Wilmington, Calif.: Friends of Banning Park, 1984.

Brown, D. Mackenzie, ed. *China Trade Days in California. Selected Letters from the Thompson Papers, 1832–1863.* Berkeley and Los Angeles: University of California Press, 1947.

Busch, Briton Cooper, ed. See Phelps, William Dane.

Butler, Samuel. "Recollections, 1922–1939." Oral history for Powell Library, University of California Los Angeles, n.d.

Byrne, Henry L., ed. "The Life of James Lick." *The Society of California Pioneers Quarterly*, vol. 1, no. 2. San Francisco: Society of California Pioneers, 1924.

Camp, Charles L. "The Chronicles of George Yount." *California Historical Society Quarterly,* vol. 2, no. 1 (April 1923).

———. *George C. Yount and His Chronicles of the West.* Denver: Old West Publishing Co., 1966.

Caughey, John Walton. *California*. 2d ed. New York: Prentice Hall, 1953.

Chapman, Charles E. *A History of California: The Spanish Period*. New York: MacMillan Co., 1936.

Cleland, Robert Glass. *Cattle on a Thousand Hills*. San Marino, Calif.: Huntington Library, 1969.

———. *A History of California: The American Period*. New York: MacMillan Co., 1930.

———. *From Wilderness to Empire: A History of California*. Ed. Glenn S. Dumke. New York: Alfred A. Knopf, 1959.

Cleland, Robert Glass, and Osgood Hardy. *March of Industry*. Los Angeles: Powell Publishing Co., 1929.

Cleveland, Richard J. *A Narrative of Voyages and Commercial Enterprises*. Boston: C.H. Pierce, 1850.

Coleccion de Diarios y Relaciones para la Historia de los Viajes y Descubrimientos. Madrid: Instituo Historico de Marina, 1944. Translated for the authors by David E. Reyes.

Connett, Eugene V., ed. *American Big Game Fishing*. New York: The Derrydale Press, 1935.

Cornell, Ralph D. *Conspicuous California Plants*. Los Angeles: The Plantin Press, 1978.

Cullimore, Clarence. *Santa Barbara Adobes*. Bakersfield, Calif.: Santa Barbara Book Publishing Co., 1948.

Cunningham, Captain William H. *Log of the Courier 1826–1827–1828*. Los Angeles: Glen Dawson, 1958.

Cutter, Donald C. *California in 1792*. Norman: University of Oklahoma Press, 1990.

Daily, Marla, ed. *California's Channel Islands*. San Luis Obispo, Calif.: EZ Nature Books, 1990.

———. *Northern Channel Islands Anthology*. Santa Barbara: Santa Cruz Island Foundation, 1989.

———. *Santa Barbara Island*. Santa Barbara: Santa Cruz Island Foundation, 1993.

———. *Santa Cruz Island Anthology*. Santa Barbara: Santa Cruz Island Foundation, 1989.

Dakin, Susanna Bryant. *A Scotch Paisano in Old Los Angeles*. Berkeley: University of California Press, 1978.

Dana, Richard Henry Jr. *Two Years Before the Mast*. 2 vols. with notes by John Haskell Kemble. Los Angeles: Ward Ritchie Press, 1964.

Davis, William Heath. *Seventy-Five Years in California*. San Francisco: John Howell Books, 1967.

deForest, Lee. *Father of Radio, the Autobiography of Lee deForest*. Chicago: Wilcox & Follett, 1950.

Dickson, Samuel. *Tales of San Francisco*. Stanford: Stanford University Press, 1957.

Doran, Adelaide LeMert. *Pieces of Eight Channel Islands*. Glendale, Calif.: Arthur H. Clark, 1980, privately printed.

———. *Ranch That Was Robbins'*. Los Angeles: privately printed, revised ed., 1964.

Ellison, William Henry. *The Life and Adventures of George Nidever (1802–1883)*. Santa Barbara: McNally Loftin, 1984.

Everson, William K. *A Pictorial History of the Western Film*. New York: The Citadel Press, 1969.

Fagan, Brian M. *Cruising Guide to California's Channel Islands*. Ventura: Western Marine Enterprises Inc., 1983.

Foster, Stephen C. "A Sketch of Some of the Earliest Kentucky Pioneers of Los Angeles." *Publications of the Historical Society of Southern California* (Los Angeles), vol. 1, no. 3 (1887).

Fraser, Captain A.V. "Log Book of the U.S. Revenue Service Brig *Lawrence*, 1851." Manuscript in collection of Steven Christman, Nautical Heritage Museum (formerly in Dana Point).

Geiger, Maynard. *Franciscan Missionaries in Hispanic California, 1769–1848*. San Marino, Calif.: The Huntington Library, 1969.

Gibson, Wayne Dell. *Tomas Yorba's Santa Ana Viejo, 1769–1847*. Santa Ana, Calif.: Santa Ana College Foundation Press, 1967.

Gillingham, Robert C. *The Rancho San Pedro*. Los Angeles: Dominguez Properties, 1961.

Gleason, Duncan, and Dorothy Gleason. *Beloved Sister, the Letters of James Henry Gleason, 1841 to 1859.* Glendale, Calif.: the Arthur H. Clark Co., 1978.

———. *The Islands and Ports of California: A Guide to Coastal California.* New York: Devin-Adair Co., 1958.

Graves, Jackson A. *California Memories, 1857–1930.* Los Angeles: Times Mirror Press, 1930.

———. *My Seventy Years in California, 1857–1927.* Los Angeles: Times Mirror Press, 1928.

Grey, Zane. *Tales of Fishes.* New York: Harper & Brothers, 1919.

Griffin, George Butler, ed. and trans. *Sources on Vizcaino, Documents from the Sutro Collection.* Los Angeles: Historical Society of Southern California, 1891.

Grissim, John. "There's Something Out There." *National Fisherman,* vol. 72, no. 2. Camden, Maine: June 1991.

Guinn, J. M. "The Lost Mines of Santa Catalina." *Overland Monthly,* vol. 16 (November 1890).

Hafer, LeRoy, and Ann W. Hafer. *Old Spanish Trail, Santa Fe to Los Angeles.* Lincoln and London: University of Nebraska Press, 1993.

Hager, Anna Marie. *Winged Mail, from Avalon to Bunker Hill, 1894–1898.* Los Angeles: Dawson's Book Shop, 1985.

Hammer, Steven Hadley. "William Wrigley, Jr.'s Santa Catalina Island, 1919–1932." Master's thesis, Claremont Graduate School. Seaver Center, Natural History Museum, Los Angeles County, 1968.

Harrington, John P. *Tomol: Chumash Watercraft as Described in the Ethnographic Notes of John P. Harrington.* Edited and annotated by Travis Hudson, Janice Timbrook, and Melissa Rempe. Socorro, N. Mex.: Ballena Press/Santa Barbara Museum of Natural History Cooperative Publication, 1978.

Harrison, Captain Eddie. "Pleasure Boats." SCICo *Water Lines,* vol. 7, no. 3 (1992).

Heilner, Van Campen. *Salt Water Fishing.* Philadelphia: Penn Publishing Co., 1937.

Heizer, Robert F. *California's Oldest Historical Relic?* Berkeley: Robert H. Lowie Museum of Anthropology, University of California, 1972.

Heizer, Robert F., and M. A. Whipple. *The California Indians, A Source Book.* Berkeley: University of California Press, 1971.

Herreshoff, L. Francis. *The Compleat Cruiser: The Art, Practice and Enjoyment of Boating.* New York: Sheridan House, 1969.

Hill, Laurence L. *La Reina: Los Angeles in Three Centuries.* Los Angeles: Security Trust & Savings Bank, 1929.

Hillinger, Charles. *The California Islands.* Los Angeles: Academy Publishers, 1958.

Hiscock, Eric C. *Sou'west in Wanderer IV.* Oxford and New York: Oxford University Press, 1973.

Holder, Charles Frederick. *The Adventures of Torqua.* Boston: Little Brown & Co., 1902.

———. *Big Game at Sea.* London: Hodder & Stoughton, 1888.

———. *The Channel Islands of California.* Chicago: A.C. McClurg & Co., 1910.

———. *An Isle of Summer.* San Francisco: C. A. Murdock, 1895.

———. *Life in the Open: Sport With Rod, Gun, Horse and Hound in Southern California.* New York: G. P. Putnam's Sons, 1906.

Houston, John M. *Early Excursion Ships to Santa Catalina.* San Pedro, Calif.: San Pedro Historical Publications, 1980.

Howland, Sarah. Interview in *Annual Publication of the Historical Society of Southern California,* 1903.

Hudson, Captain John T. "Journal of the Schooner *Tamana,* from Woahoo (Sandwich Islands) to the Coast of America, 1805–1807." Handwritten journal. San Marino, Calif.: Huntington Library, n.d.

Irving, Alex. *A History of Our BYC Catalina Island Station.* Newport Beach: Balboa Yacht Club, 1986.

Johnson, Kathleen N. "History of Catalina Island Prior to 1900." Thesis for the Los Angeles County Department of Parks and Recreation and for the Catalina Island Museum, n.d.

Johnston, Bernice Eastman. *California's Gabrielino Indians.* Los Angeles: Southwest Museum, 1962.

Jordan, David Starr, and Barton W. Evermann. *American Food and Game Fishes.* New York: Doubleday, Page & Co., 1905.

Kelsey, Harry. "Did Francis Drake Really Visit California?" The *Western Historical Quarterly,* vol. 21, no. 4 (1990). Logan, Utah: the Western History Association.

———. *Juan Rodríguez Cabrillo.* San Marino, Calif.: Huntington Library, 1986.

Kemble, John Haskell. *The Cruise of the Schooner* Tamana, *1805–1807.* Worcester, Mass.: American Antiquarian Society, 1969.

———, ed. *Two Years Before the Mast.* See Dana.

Kennedy, Don H. "The American Neptune." *Quarterly Journal of Maritime History* (October 1969). Peabody Museum of Salem, Massachusetts.

Kornweibel, Theodore Jr. "The Occupation of Santa Catalina Island During the Civil War." *California History Quarterly,* vol. 46, no. 4 (1967). San Francisco: California Historical Society.

Kroeber, A. L. *Handbook of the Indians of California.* New York: Dover Publications, 1976.

Kurtz, Emil S. *Southern California Weather for Small Boats.* San Diego: National Weather Service, 1985.

Lahey, Edward C. "California's Miser Philanthropist: A Biography of James Lick." Master's thesis. Santa Cruz: Mary Lea Shane Archives of Lick Observatory, University of California Santa Cruz, 1948.

Lamont, Daniel. *The War of the Rebellion.* Washington, D.C.: Government Printing Office, 1897.

Larkin, Thomas O. *The Larkin Papers.* Vol. 3 (1845). Edited by George P. Hammond, director of the Bancroft Library. Berkeley and Los Angeles: University of California Press, 1952.

LeCouvreur, Frank. *East Prussia to the Golden Gate.* Los Angeles: Angelina Book Co., 1906.

Lever, Darcy. *Young Sea Officer's Sheet Anchor.* Reproduction of 2d London edition of 1819. New York: Edward W. Sweetman Co., 1963.

Lewis, Oscar. *Bay Window Bohemia.* New York: Doubleday & Co., 1956.

———. *Sea Routes to the Gold Fields.* New York: Alfred A. Knopf, 1949.

Lick, Rosemary. *The Generous Miser, the Story of James Lick of California.* Los Angeles: Ward Ritchie Press, 1967.

Lyman, John. *Sailing Vessels of the Pacific Coast, 1850–1905.* San Diego: Maritime Research Society, 1941. Reprinted from *Americana,* April 2, 1941.

Macrate, Arthur N. Jr. *History of the Tuna Club.* Avalon: The Tuna Club, 1948.

Martin, Terrence D. *Santa Catalina: An Island Adventure.* Las Vegas: KC Publications, 1983.

Mathes, W. Michael. *Vizcaíno and Spanish Expansion in the Pacific Ocean, 1580–1630.* San Francisco: California Historical Society, 1968.

McCawley, William. *The First Angelinos.* Banning, Calif.: Malki Museum Press/Ballena Press, 1996.

McWilliams, Carey. *Southern California Country.* New York: Duell, Sloan & Pearce, 1946.

Meadows, Don. *Place Names in Orange County.* Balboa Island: Paisano Press, 1966.

Meighan, Clement W. "California's Island Archaeology." In *A Step into the Past: Island Dwellers of Southern California,* catalog for exhibit at the Museum of Anthropology, California State University, Fullerton, 1989.

Miller, Daniel J. *The Sea Otter – Enhydra Lutris.* Marine Resources Leaflet No. 7, State of California Department of Fish and Game, 1974.

Moore, Patricia Anne. *The Casino, Avalon.* Avalon: Catalina Island Museum Society, 1979.

Morey, Shaun. *Incredible Fishing Stories.* Las Vegas: World Publications, Hodad Press, 1991.

Myers, William A. *Iron Men and Copper Wires: a Centennial History of the Southern California Edison Co.* Glendale, Calif.: Trans-Anglo Books, 1983.

Nadeau, Remi A. *City-Makers.* Garden City, N.Y.: Doubleday & Co., 1948.

Newmark, Harris. *Sixty Years in Southern California, 1853–1913.* Boston and New York: Houghton Mifflin Co., 1930.

Newmark, Marco R. Interview with Jose Felice Presiado in *Los Angeles Morning Herald,* 30 October 1903.

Ogden, Adele. *California Sea Otter Trade, 1784–1848.* Berkeley and Los Angeles: University of California Press, 1941.

Orange County Genealogical Society. *Saddleback Ancestors.* Orange, California, 1964.

Overholt, Alma. *The Catalina Story.* Edited by Jack Sargent from 1962 1st printing. Avalon: Catalina Museum Society, Inc., 1971.

Phelps, William Dane. *Alta California, 1840–1842.* Journal of Phelps, master of the *Alert,* introduced and edited by Briton Cooper Busch. Glendale, Calif.: Arthur H. Clark Co., 1983.

Phillips, Michael James. *History of Santa Barbara County.* N.p.: S.J. Clarke Publishing Co., 1927.

Pourade, Richard F. *The Silver Dons.* San Diego: Union-Tribune Publishing Co., 1963.

———. *Time of the Bells.* San Diego: Union-Tribune Publishing Co., 1962.

Probert, Alan. "Mining History, Santa Catalina Island." *Geology and Mineral Wealth of the California Transverse Ranges.* Santa Ana, Calif.: South Coast Geological Society, 1984.

Ramsey, Chris. *In All the World No Trip Like This. A Pictorial History of Catalina Island.* N.p.: privately printed, 1982.

Rathbun, Loyd, and Chuck Liddell. *The Legends of Old Ben.* N.p.: Catalina Island Museum Society, 1976.

Richie, C.F., and R. A. Hager. *The Chumash Canoe: The Structure and Hydrodynamics of a Model.* San Diego: Museum of Man, 1973.

Ritter, Ema I. *Life at the Old Amphibian Airport.* Avalon: privately printed, 1970.

Roberts, Lois J. *San Miguel Island.* Carmel, Calif.: Cal Rim Books, 1991.

Robinson, Alfred. *Life in California.* Unabridged republication of the first edition published in New York in 1846. New York: Da Capo Press, 1969.

Robinson, John W. *Southern California's First Railroad: The Los Angeles & San Pedro Railroad, 1869–1873.* Hawthorne, Calif.: Omni Publications, 1985.

Robinson, W.W. *The Island of Santa Catalina.* Los Angeles: Title Guarantee & Trust Co., 1941.

———. *Land in California.* Berkeley: University of California Press, 1948.

Rolle, Andrew F. *California: A History.* New York: Thomas Y. Crowell Co., 1967.

Rosenthal, Lee. *Catalina Tile of the Magic Isle.* Sausalito, Calif.: Wingate Press, 1992.

Ruhge, Justin M. *Drake in Central California 1579; Unravelling One of California's Great Historical Mysteries.* Goleta, Calif.: Quantum Imaging Associates, 1990.

Scammon, Charles M. *Marine Mammals of the Northwest Coast of North America and the American Whale Fishery.* Facsimile of 1874 edition. Riverside, Calif.: Manessier Publishing Co., 1969.

Schultz, Kathryn. *Muller House, 1889–1996, the Shoreline.* San Pedro, Calif.: Instant Print, San Pedro Bay Historical Society, June 1997.

Sherman, Moses H. Letters and documents of M. H. Sherman in collection of the Sherman Library, Corona del Mar, Calif., William O. Hendricks, director.

Smith, Vi. *From Jennies to Jets: The Aviation History of Orange County.* Fullerton, Calif.: Sultana Press, 1974.

Sonnichsen, C.L. *The Life and Times of an American City.* Norman, Okla.: University of Oklahoma Press, 1982.

Stackpole, Edouard A. *The Sea Hunters, the Great Age of Whaling.* New York: Bonanza Books, 1953.

Starbuck, Alexander. *History of the American Whale Fishery.* Secaucus, N.J.: Castle Books, 1989.

Sumner, C.A. "Santa Catalina Island," *Los Angeles Times Illustrated Magazine,* 12 May 1918.

Taylor, Roger C. *Elements of Seamanship.* Camden, Maine: International Marine Publishing Co., 1982.

Teller, Walter, ed. *Five Sea Captains: Their Own Accounts of Voyages Under Sail.* New York: Atheneum, 1960.

Thomas, George C. III, Ernest Hemingway, S. Kip Farrington Jr., Lynn Bogue Hunt, et al. *American Big Game Fishing.* New York: Derrydale Press, 1935.

Thompson and West. *History of Santa Barbara and Ventura Counties.* Berkeley: Howell North, 1961.

Thrower, Norman J. W. *A Buccaneer's Atlas: The South Sea Waggoner of Basil Ringrose.* Fullerton, Calif.: Patrons of California State University Library, 1982.

Thurman, Michael E. *The Naval Department of San Blas.* Glendale, Calif.: Arthur H. Clark Co., 1967.

Tompkins, Walker. *Santa Barbara History Makers.* Santa Barbara: McNally & Loflin, 1983.

———. *Santa Barbara's Royal Rancho.* Berkeley: Howell-North, 1960.

Trask, Blanche. "The Heart of Santa Catalina." The *Land of Sunshine* (Los Angeles), vol. 7, no. 4 (September 1897).

Umvert, Bob. *Catalina's Aviation History.* Robert Allen Productions, Avalon: 1992. Videocassette.

Vail, Walter L., and C.W. Gates. Original lease of rangeland from Banning Brothers, 1894. Five pages and map courtesy of Mrs. William J. Shirley, Pasadena.

Vaughan, Ruben V., with Ben S. Hunter. *Doc's Catalina Diary.* N.p.: privately printed, 1961.

Vickery, Oliver. *Harbor Heritage.* Mountain View: Morgan Press, 1979.

Walker, Edwin F. *Indians of California.* No. 10 of Southwest Museum pamphlets. Los Angeles: n.d.

Warner, Colonel J.J., Judge Benjamin Hayes, and Dr. J. P. Widney. *An Historical Sketch of Los Angeles County, California.* Reprint of the 1876 original. Los Angeles: O.W. Smith, 1936.

Wells, Bob. "Mystery (of) Japanese Submarine," *Independent Press Telegram,* Long Beach, 19 April 1959.

White, Michael. *California All the Way Back to 1828.* Dictated by White to Thomas Savage, 1877. Original MSS, on microfilm, University of California Berkeley: Bancroft Library.

Willoughby, Commander Malcolm F. *Rum War at Sea.* Washington, D.C.: Treasury Department, U.S. Coast Guard, 1964.

Wilson, Carol Green. *California Yankee.* Claremont, Calif.: Saunders Press, 1946.

Windle, Ernest. *Windle's History of Santa Catalina Island.* Avalon: Catalina Islander, 1931.

Winlund, Ed. *Chart Guide Catalina Island.* 11th ed., 1986, and 12th ed., 1987. Anaheim: Chart Guide Ltd.

Wlodarski, Robert J. *Bibliography of Catalina Island Investigations and Excavations (1850–1980).* Los Angeles: Institute of Archaeology, University of California Los Angeles, 1982.

Wood, Helen Lamont. *George Yount, the Kindly Host of Caymus Rancho.* San Francisco: Grabhorn Press, 1941.

Wrigley, Philip K. "Memorandum on the History and Development of Rancho Escondido." Typescript in Santa Catalina Co. archives, Avalon, April 16, 1952.

Wrigley-Rusack, Alison. "El Rancho Escondido: Continuing the Vision." *Catalina Explorer* (Avalon), vol. 1, no. 8 (October 1986).

Zimmerman, William Jr. *William Wrigley, Jr., The Man and His Business, 1861–1932*. Chicago: Private edition, 1935.

Vessel identification sources were helpful in various volumes of Lloyd's of London North American Yacht Registry and Registry of Shipping; Record of American and Foreign Shipping, Shipmasters' Association; and Merchant Vessels of the United States, U.S. Government Printing Office, Department of Commerce.

And finally, many important and interesting pieces of information were gleaned from the following publications: the *Branding Iron* of the Los Angeles Corral of The Westerners; *Catalina Explorer; Catalina Islander; Catalina Jewfish; Compass Rose* of the Los Angeles County Maritime Museum; the Catalina Island Museum Society newsletter; *Daily Alto California;* the *High Country* magazine; Drum Barracks Museum pamphlet; *Los Angeles Star;* the *Land of Sunshine* magazine; *Los Angeles Times; National Fisherman; Pasadena Daily News; Riverside Press and Horticulturist; Salt Water Sportsman* magazine; *Santa Ana Register; Natural History* magazine; *Scientific American; Water Lines,* a publication of the Santa Catalina Island Company; and *A Living Legend,* Foss Marine Company history, 1999, Bruce Johnson Communications.

Acknowledgments

Our gratitude to the many who read, corrected, and enhanced certain chapters with their special expertise, and whose enthusiasm kept us going during periods of frustration and discomfiture. To all of you, friends, acquaintances, and family, thank you.

We are particularly grateful to prominent Spanish-era scholars and authors W. Michael Mathes and Harry Kelsey, who spent valuable time vetting the material on early Spanish explorations. Doug, Audrey, and Randy Bombard worked on chapters pertaining to Catalina's Two Harbors and the *Miss Catalina* speedboats. Allen Douglas Probst, first president of the Santa Catalina Island Conservancy, critiqued the chapter on this important environmental program.

The chapters on the Tuna Club and big game fishing were reviewed and expanded by club historians Arthur N. Macrate Jr. and Michael Farrior, along with angling and tackle authorities Thornton E. Ibbetson, antique reel collector; Paul Albrecht, collector of antique fishing rods; and John Doughty, proprietor of JD's Big Game Tackle, Balboa Island. The chapter on Catalina's aviation history was improved by Don R. Beaver, former island manager of Avalon Air Transport.

Special thanks go to William O. Hendricks, director of the Sherman Library, Corona del Mar, and the library's helpful former secretary, Judy Buckle; to Michael Redmon, head of the Gledhill Library of the Santa Barbara Historical Society; to Roger B. Berry and William Landis of Special Collections at the UC Irvine Library, as well as Margo Allen and Lowell Herbrandson of the same library; and to Bill Kooiman, librarian at the National Maritime Museum, San Francisco, all of whom helped unearth important original material.

To the list we must add the late John Haskell Kemble, maritime historian, who put us on the trail of the unique, handwritten logbook of the schooner *Tamana* in the collection of the Huntington Library, San Marino. Huntington librarians Peter Blodgett, custodian of the *Tamana* journal, and Bill Frank, custodian of the Banning collection, assisted admirably.

Many people whose lives and historical recollections were closely linked to Catalina kindly granted interviews during the many years this work was in progress. Among them were Mrs. Jay (Sibyl) Chilton, great-granddaughter of Captain Thomas M. Robbins, the first private owner of the island, who graciously supplied the rare photographic portrait of Robbins; and Alberta Howland Lumbard, granddaughter of Captain William R. Howland, an early sheep baron and lessee of Howland's Landing. And without Mrs. Harvey (Sally) Somers, we could not have learned the story of her great-uncle, Benjamin Weston, another of the sheep barons on the island as well as the mainland.

Others linked to Catalina who rewarded us with their historical recollections were Chris Abel, Hancock Banning III, Gary Bloodsworth, Iron Eyes Cody, Bob and Lorraine Cranton, Margaret Felkey, George and Richard Geiger, Joseph S. Guion and his son, Joseph E. (Jay) Guion, Donald Root Haney, Donna Harrison, Eddie Harrison, William Muller, whose grandfather was shipbuilder William Muller, Mrs. Parker Pence, Emelda (Millie) Riojas Poindexter, John Poole, Alan Probert, Malcolm Renton, Edward T. Rinehart, Rebecca Stanton, Janet Takara, James F. Trout, Herbert A. Wegmann, William S. (Bill) White, and John W. Windle, grandson of Judge Ernest Windle.

Bill Olesen, at age ninety-two the editor of *Compass Rose* of the Los Angeles Maritime Museum in San Pedro, drew upon his remarkable memory pertaining to long-gone vessels. Hymie Singer, final owner of the SS *Catalina,* told us the story of her fate.

We cannot overlook the assistance of Richard Ogar and Jean R. Gibson Ordonez, Bancroft Library; Steven Christman, Dana Point Nautical Museum; Michael Cropper, Los Angeles Maritime Museum; Flora T. Baker, San Pedro Bay Historical Society; Pat Kelly, California Institute of Technology; William S. Myers, Southern California Edison Company; John U. Zweers, Society of American Magicians; Leonard Schiada, Connelly Pacific Company; Brenda Edwards, Los Angeles City Department of Recreation and Parks; Steve Crooke and Eddy Kono, California Department of Fish and Game; Greg G. Barjaca, vicar of St. John's Episcopal and Holy Child Philippine Independent Church, Wilmington; Sarah Temple, California Newspaper Project; Mark Ellis and Ted Faye, United States Borax and Chemical Corporation; Bob Diffill, chief executive officer of the Glendale YMCA; Jennine Pedersen, curator of collections, Catalina Island Museum Society; and Joe Ditler, San Diego Maritime Museum.

We also wish to thank the late Hale Field and his widow, Gingerlee Field McMicken, for their nautical knowledge and for putting us in touch with some of the persons we contacted. Thanks also to Jay Grier, boat builder and sailor; Lyle Hess and Nicholas Potter, boat designers; Rebecca Stanton for her wonderful early photographs; Val Detling for his early encouragement; Jim Sleeper, Orange County historian; John W. Robinson, southern California historian; Gale Schluter and Jay Marshall, puppet historians; puppeteer Bob Jones; Dana Cordrey of Dual Graphics, Inc. for leading us to cartographic material; G.D. "Grumpy" Henderson for several photo identifications; booksellers Lindy Currie and John Cannon for helping us locate some elusive material; and John (Jack) Graham, Laura Lancaster of Spaceshots, Inc., Studio City, and Fred Emmert of AirViews, Irvine, all for photographs.

Without David E. Reyes, *Los Angeles Times* journalist, we could not have deciphered an old Spanish document pertaining to the explorations of Sebastian Vizcaino. And without the *Los Angeles Times'* library and microfilm records at the paper and at the Sherman Library, a great deal of early history would have been unavailable to us. We also utilized the microfilms of the nineteenth-century *Los Angeles Star,* housed in the Anaheim Public Library.

Rudy Piltch and the archives of the Santa Catalina Island Company were gold mines of information as were Marge O'Brien of Drum Barracks Museum; Terrence Martin, former naturalist with the Catalina Island Conservancy; James Zordich and Robert Weinstein, historians; Patricia Anne Moore, Carol Kirk, and Stacey Otte of the Catalina Island Museum; Christine Shirley, Marian L. Banning, and Jan Losi of the Banning Residence Museum, Wilmington; and Dorothy Schaumberg, archivist of the Mary Lee Shane Archives of the Lick Observatory, University Library, University of California Santa Cruz.

Our appreciation also goes to Carol Bednar, librarian of California State University, Fullerton; Virgilio Biasol, O.F.M., director of the Santa Barbara Mission archive-library; Jan Timbrook, Santa Barbara Museum of Natural History; Ann Wattson, librarian, Newport Harbor Nautical Museum; Donald W. McNamee of Seaver Center, Los Angeles County Natural History Museum; Edna Marinella, librarian at Narbonne High School, Lomita; Susan Allen, Honnold Library, Claremont Colleges; Stanleigh Bry, Society of California Pioneers; Carolyn J. Strickler, *Los Angeles Times* historian; Betty A. Riekes and Alva Stevenson, oral history program, University of California Los Angeles, and Andrew Glassell VI, a descendant of Andrew Glassell Sr. who came to Los Angeles in 1867. We further thank the Sutro Library, San Francisco; Avalon Public Library; Carson Regional Library; and Newport Beach, Anaheim, and Orange County Public Libraries.

On the eastern seaboard, those who helped set our course and kept us going in the right direction included Charles Harrington, national geographer, Nautical Charting Division, Charting and Geodetic Surveys, Rockville, Maryland; Ron Grim and Jim Flatnus, Library of Congress Map Division; Robert A. Richardson, chief cartographer, National Archives and Records Administration, Washington, D.C.; and R.L. Scheina, historian, United States Coast Guard public affairs staff, Washington, D.C.

There was also useful guidance from Jacqueline Haring, Nantucket Historical Association; the New England Historical and Genealogical Society, Boston; the staffs of the Nantucket Whaling Museum, the Phillips Library of the Peabody and Essex Museum in Salem, Massachusetts, and the maritime museum at Mystic Seaport, Connecticut; and Tina McKinley, executive director of the Southern California Yachting Association.

Important contributions were made by both Sanford Smith and Alison Smith, Marjie's son and daughter. Sandy drew the island map and picked out and assembled two computers for us during the course of this work, and he and Alison taught Marjie the basics of using them. Alison also helped transcribe many chapters during the several revisions necessary over the years. In the end, the completed manuscript was carefully read for inaccuracies and omissions by Patricia Anne Moore, former curator of the Santa Catalina Island Museum.

We thank all of you for your indispensable assistance.

RICHARD AND MARJIE BUFFUM

Index

Page number references that are in italic type refer to illustration captions

The typeface used in this book is Requiem Text, from The Hoefler Type Foundry, New York City. Designed in the 1990s, the roman font was fashioned on the mid-sixteenth-century Claude Garamond model, while the italic font was inspired by the early-sixteenth-century chancery style of Vicentino degli Arrighi. The cover and title page also utilize Castellar, a twentieth-century design from John Peters. The book was copyedited by Martha Fares. It was designed by Dana Cordrey and manufactured under his supervision at Dual Graphics, Inc., Brea, California.